CONTENTS

KNOW YOUR
MEDICAL RIGHTS

BATTLE MANUALS FOR FREEDOM

KNOW YOUR MEDICAL RIGHTS
KNOW YOUR LAWFUL RIGHTS
KNOW YOUR FINANCIAL RIGHTS

A. LE ROY

UNPARAGONED

BATTLE MANUALS FOR FREEDOM

BY A. LEROY

Book 1: *Know Your Medical Rights*

Book 2: *Know Your Lawful Rights*

Book 3: *Know Your Financial Rights*

https://Geni.us/Rights

Battle Manuals for Freedom by Abdiel LeRoy

Weapons of Law and Constitutional Armour for the Battles Ahead

BATTLE MANUALS FOR FREEDOM
by A. LEROY

Book 1: Know Your Natural Rights

Book 2: Know Your Lawful Rights

Book 3: Know Your Case in Court

Book 4: Know Your Rights

KNOW YOUR LAWFUL RIGHTS

KNOW YOUR
FINANCIAL RIGHTS

BOOKS BY A. LEROY (ABDIEL LEROY)

KNOW YOUR MEDICAL RIGHTS

A. LeRoy

Battle Manuals for Freedom: Book 1

INTRODUCTION

I was brought up by my mother on the Bible, and she told me something that I've never forgotten. She said the stories in the Bible are stories about the conflict between the kings who have power and the prophets who preach righteousness, and she taught me to support the prophets and not the kings.

— TONY BENN, FORMER BRITISH
MEMBER OF PARLIAMENT, MAR. 10, 2006

I am writing this book because I have to, and because I know a confrontation is coming. No longer can I maintain the old uneasy coexistence with false authority, lamenting his folly and fraud, deploring his ignorance, and ridiculing his absurdities, but all from a safe distance. No, I am on a collision course with false authority, and I dare say you are too. We need to be prepared.

I have lived and worked on four continents, swum in

three oceans, heard innumerable foreign tongues, and observed the infinite variety of our species, but now the autocrats, bureaucrats, and technocrats, in their little, brief, and fear-fueled authority, would have us undergo invasive medical procedures, and hand over private medical information once held sacred, just to travel, to go about our lives, and even to make a living.

Time was when I could grudgingly accept mask requirements in the early days, frown at destructive lockdowns, and ignore voicemails and messages to my mobile phone from Britain's National Health Service (NHS). And I could largely dismiss the barrage of fearmongering propaganda that managed to circumvent my longstanding aversion to mainstream media. But when governments started threatening and penalizing bodily autonomy, a line was crossed.

I know in my heart that these measures are an atrocity, and my spirit rebels against them, but just having that instinct is not enough now. **WHAT ARE MY RIGHTS?!** I'm going to need more than mere disgust if I am to overrule the fearmongering autocrats who will exploit any emergency to unleash tyranny. I'm going to need constitutional armour and weapons of law, and I'm going to need them quickly. And when I have them, I will share them with those who may benefit.

Hence this book, a garment of protection for the 'COVID' era and an antidote to fear. I don't mean fear of a disease, but of the reactions—or rather overreactions —to it. Though I once entertained some background anxiety about a supposed virus, it's as nothing compared to the deep dread I've experienced about a totalitarian state emerging such as Orwell set out in *1984*.

I have also come to realize that even *that* kind of fear is being stoked by governments. At the outset, they wanted us to fear COVID, but after that got them only so far, now they want us to fear them, so that we won't make trouble.

For that type of fear, I recall the predicament of Moses' Israelites lately released from slavery in Egypt, as recounted in the Bible book of *Exodus*. Imagine their terror to realize Pharaoh's entire army was bearing down on them as they approached the Red Sea (14:10). But Moses told them not to fear, to stand firm, for they would see the Lord's deliverance. And they did, when the Red Sea drowned Pharaoh and his horde (14:28).

Therefore, no matter how bad things appear to get, the final chapter of our story sees the demise of slavery on Earth, including wage slavery, debt slavery, tax slavery, prison slavery, sex slavery, digital slavery and, of course, medical slavery, along with the deaths of tyrant politicians, bureaucrats, and corporate profiteers when, like a mighty river, Justice returns.

The 'vaccines', too, have an obvious allegory in the *Exodus* story. When Moses and his brother Aaron come to Pharaoh's court and issue their demands, Aaron demonstrates the power of God by turning his staff into a snake. Pharaoh's conjurors imitate the act, but Aaron's snake eats their snakes (7:12). Similarly, the fanged creatures of Pfizer, Moderna, AstraZeneca, and Johnson &

Johnson are no match for the lethal bite of truth-tellers, prophets, and whistleblowers today.

Also destined for destruction are the media organizations who have mouthpieced for the medical-industrial complex. I shudder to recall the *Daily Telegraph* front-page headline of July 21, 2021: "Freedom for double jabbed as UK opens to world." As if freedom can be granted or withheld at official whim, as if medical status were the qualification to receive it. No, we are born with it, and trying to take it away from us is blasphemy, no less an atrocity than the 'intercision' of Philip Pullman's novel, *The Golden Compass,* where the authorities cut children away from their 'daemon' animals, equivalent to extracting their souls.

The *Telegraph* also predicted, in a July-2021 article, "The unvaccinated will be shut out of normal life, progressively demonised, and stripped of civil rights..." And other mainstream outlets salivated at the prospect. As 2021 drew to a close, a quick glance at recent headlines showed an almost desperate eagerness to foment hatred against a vilified underclass. "The unvaccinated are putting us all at risk," squealed *The Times* of London. "I'm Furious at the Unvaccinated," howled *The New York Times.* "It is only a matter of time before we turn on the unvaccinated," thundered *The Guardian.*

Just like the cultist politicians and bureaucrats, these media mercenaries for Big Pharma know not what they say or what they do. Nor do they know or care that international statute defines persecution against an identifiable group as a Crime Against Humanity. Have all these puppets learned nothing from history and the madness of going after a targeted minority? Has it taken but a few generations to overturn what our ancestors fought and died for? Have these people lost their minds? I think they have!

We of prophetic calling have our work cut out for us, not just seeing, or warning against, future scenarios, as exemplified by Orwell, but in describing the present. That means observing the obvious and stating the obvious when populations are conditioned to overlook the obvious, to deny it to themselves and, even if they do see it, to keep quiet about it. As famed whistleblower Edward Snowden observes, "Everywhere we look, from Afghanistan to economics, from pandemic to pervasive surveillance, the obvious has been made unspeakable."[1]

And it is obvious that the medical-industrial complex, taking its playbook from the *military*-industrial complex, grooms politicians to do its bidding. It also likens the COVID response to war, reflecting the imperial and imperious mindset infecting our politics, with words like battle, beat, conquer, crush, defeat, eliminate, enemy, fight, front lines, victory, etc.

There *is* a war being waged, certainly, but of a very different kind, as encapsulated by the apostle Paul in the New Testament: "For our struggle is not against flesh and blood, but against the rulers, against the authorities, against the powers of this dark world and against the spiritual forces of evil in the heavenly realms" (*Ephesians* 6:12).

And those spiritual forces are especially murderous

towards children, recalling the ancient abomination of child sacrifice to Molech.

> "The Lord said to Moses, 'Say to the Israelites: Any Israelite or any foreigner residing in Israel who sacrifices any of his children to Molek is to be put to death. The members of the community are to stone him. I myself will set my face against him and will cut him off from his people; for by sacrificing his children to Molek, he has defiled my sanctuary and profaned my holy name. If the members of the community close their eyes when that man sacrifices one of his children to Molek and if they fail to put him to death, I myself will set my face against him and his family and will cut them off from their people, together with all who follow him in prostituting themselves to Molek.' "
>
> — *LEVITICUS* 20:1-5

Of course, fraud, corruption, and greed have always greased the wheels of government, but now we observe something far deadlier, a medical cult that demands human sacrifice, a religion of death, served by a conclave of tyrant priests in positions of false authority. The more they can kill, the higher they rise in their infernal ranks.

I wish the figureheads of our so-called 'medical-freedom movement' would see this. I wish they would realize that the pharmaceutical complex is not so much counting the dollars as it is counting the bodies.

I came to this realization when hearing renowned

liver-health specialist and author, Dr. Burt Berkson, tell Dr. Jonathan Landsman in an interview, "At many medical schools, in many university hospitals, they give an award every month to the doctor who has the most deaths on his service, and they have a party, and it's called a 'Black Crow Award'."

Is that what this is all about? Are we in the middle of a global Black Crow Award now, in which medical professionals and hospitals and so-called health ministers are competing to see who can add the most corpses to the pile of medical waste? Or have they been assigned kill quotas?

That medical-freedom leaders overlook this deeper motivation is disappointing, but many more errors, and possibly fatal ones, they make besides. Most dangerous of all is to base their opposition to medical compulsion not on the solid ground that it is eternally unlawful, but on the shifting sands of data and statistics.

For example, they argue that this disease, or that variant, is too mild to warrant medical enforcements. Meaning what? That if some more deadly disease were conjured, they'd be fine with coercion?

That is boggy ground to build on, to paraphrase Herman Melville. Of course, autocrats are always ready to unleash another emergency which they will cite as pretext for more crackdowns and despotic legislation that they falsely call 'law'.

We also hear the medical-freedom caucus arguing certain measures should not be mandated because they are unproven, unsafe, or ineffective. Or because natural immunity is a thing, or asymptomatic spread is not a thing.

Fools! There is no 'because'! No medical measure can ever be compulsory—period, end of—whatever claims are asserted for its safety or effectiveness.

And here's the stupidest slogan of all. "Where there is risk, there must be choice." Meaning what? That if some medical treatment is concocted, and safety claimed for it, then choice can be taken away?

Misguided, too, are requests for 'exemption' from medical enforcement. These buy into a fiction that government has authority to demand anything from us in the first place. It doesn't. Quite the opposite. We have authority over government, and the word "No" is, always has been, and always will be, exemption enough.

Exemption requests also desecrate medical confidentiality when your medical status is nobody else's business in the first place. It is not the government's business, not your employer's business, not a travel company's business, and not your neighbour's business. Respect confidentiality, and your medical status can never be weaponized against you.

Our resolve against medical dictatorship, therefore, can never rest on competing views about today's data and circumstances but must instead be anchored in **CONSTITUTIONALITY**. Blind to emergency by design, constitutional principles are eternal and can't be swayed by the shifting currents of perception and statistics. They don't give a fuck about conditions on the ground, and nor should they. No, these times call us to be **CONSTITUTIONAL EXTREMISTS**.

Lawyers, too, need to grasp this. They whimper about not being able to go after pharmaceutical companies, doctors, hospitals, or regulators because of 'legal immunity'. Servile creatures, I rebuke your compliance with tyrant fictions spun to enslave Mankind. The Acts and statutes you cite—and stop calling them laws—these licences to kill, are nothing more than corporate contracts that one party has drafted, one party has signed, and one party has negotiated with itself. Yet that party thinks to impose those contracts on another party, us, to codify enslavement, murder, extortion, destruction, and theft, and then to pardon itself of the crimes. As we shall see, in the coming section on Common Law, these instruments are powerless without our signature, and not worth the air they're written on.

Imagine you were a business owner seeking to procure goods from a supplier, but that supplier gets to write the contract without your review, and that contract binds you as soon as the ink is dry without your knowledge, signature, or consent. You'd tell them to get lost, wouldn't you? Yet that is precisely the bargain that governments and their corporate conspirators think to impose, and before which our conditioned cadre of cringing lawyers think to kneel. When will you stop enthroning legislation over Justice?!

One rare exception to this tendency is British human-rights lawyer, Anna de Buisseret. Interviewed in London's

Parliament Square during a Medical Freedom March of Oct. 30, 2021, she advises:

> "Learn what your fundamental, inalienable human rights are. Anyone who can access Google, you google the Universal Declaration of Human Rights, read it, read the European Convention on Human Rights, read the U.K. Human Rights Act, read the International Covenant on Social and Political and Economic Rights. Those rights are all there. It's all there in the law. The reason this is happening is because people don't know the law, so they don't know how to uphold it and assert it."

I applaud the spirit of her words, though that's an awful lot of homework for your average freedom-loving reader to do, especially if you add in the 170-page Notice of Liability, prepared by de Buisseret and her allies in Lawyers for Liberty, to serve against skin piercers and their accomplices. But I *have* done the homework and distilled into this book the key language that empowers us.

The good news is that none of this is complicated. It doesn't require a law degree, nor a thorough grounding in Latin. The beauty of these universal principles lies in their plain-English simplicity and, like the proverbial mustard seed of faith that overthrows mountains,[2] our little understanding in this arena goes a long way in vaulting the pronouncements of foolish and fearful men. A layman's expertise will do, and a layman's analysis can provide it, which is why I am as qualified as anyone else to do so here.

Brothers and sisters, it is time to release from their glass cabinets the dusty scrolls of our Rights declarations. We reclaim the keys that unleash them and, like the true prophets of old, proclaim them again to break the spells and incantations of false priests now roaming the Earth.

Our Rights, being inalienable, or unalienable if you prefer, were never granted by a gift of government nor rescinded by a denial of government. In the words of John K. Webster, creator of the documentary *Strawman*,

"GOVERNMENT IS A CREATION OF MAN, AND A CREATION OF MAN CAN NEVER BE ABOVE MAN."

So, if governments will not hear or heed the simple and time-honoured constitutional principles they are sworn to uphold, then each of us must acquire at least a little expertise in this area.

Nor will I pin my hopes on a political party or candidate to produce a regime a little less vindictive than the last. Love for our Rights straddles the old divides where antagonists are merely co-conspirators in bipartisan acts of theft. As Martin Luther wrote of the papists and anabaptists in 1531, "These foxes are tied together by the tails, even though their heads look in opposite directions. While they outwardly profess to be great enemies, inwardly they think, teach, and defend one and the same thing." Once we realize this, and expose the

unholy alliances against our core values, whether by
Democrat with Republican, Tory with Labour, or by any
other duopoly or coalition, we can be rid of this corrupt
political theatre altogether.

We are in a Declaration-of-Independence moment
when an entire *form* of government, not just a faction
within government, is destroying Life, Liberty, and the
Pursuit of Happiness. It is therefore our duty now to
abolish *this* form of government, maybe even the entire
idea of government (which means 'mind control'). We are
not fighting in a horizontal plane of 'Left' versus 'Right',
but in the vertical plane of Life over Death, Creation over
Destruction, Love over Fear.

That is a spiritual battle, the battle for which this
book is conceived. May this declaration in words
empower us to "suit the action to the word, the word to
the action"[3] as we hear and heed the rallying call from the
Captain of our souls, he whose Word "is alive and active,
and sharper than any double-edged sword"
(*Hebrews* 4:12).

Allied with that weapon is our sword of constitutional
truth. It pulses with Heaven's call for Justice, imparts
courage to those who wield it, and thirsts for the blood of
today's cabal of thieves and murderers, whether in
government, media, or any other organization. Let us
pursue them with the kind of fury that Elijah wielded in
slaughtering the false prophets of Baal on Mount Carmel
(*1 Kings* 18:40). For, as Dave Mason writes in his
masterful *Age of Prophecy* novels,[4] set in the time of Elijah,

"Those who show mercy to the cruel, bring cruelty upon the merciful."

For those of us contemplating our first run-in with would-be enforcers such as police, the task ahead may appear daunting, but here I share the vital information we will need if menaced by state or corporation, and if you have a paperback version, I hope it shall become marked up with your highlights and scribblings. Our quest may seem to present impossible odds. Well, you would have said the same of Moses and Aaron going up against Pharaoh, his court, his paymasters, slave masters, chariots, and weaponry. But he who was in the prophets was greater than he who was in Pharaoh, and he who is in us now is greater than he who is in the autocrats, bureaucrats, technocrats, and 'psychocrats' of our age. And, oh yes, the 'philanthrocrats' too!

"Hold the line, stand your ground, uphold the rule of law, step into your sovereignty," De Buisseret urges in the closing moments of her Parliament-Square interview. "The law is all there to protect you, but you're not going to get protected unless you know what it is and you uphold it."

Therefore, we look to the eternal values of Mankind— values not swayed by political convenience and expediency, nor by profiteering motives, and that have *more* currency, not less, during times of emergency, whether that emergency is real or perceived or invented. So join me in the field, my friend. These times will make prophets of us all!

PART I

OUR CORE FOUNDATION

"This Jesus of Nazareth!" he cried. "This class-conscious workingman! This union carpenter! This agitator, lawbreaker, firebrand, anarchist!"

— UPTON SINCLAIR, *THE JUNGLE*

If you feel bewildered by the flurry of government decrees issued since COVID's arrival in 2020, you are not alone. A growing chorus of dissent, though largely ostracized from mainstream media, is finding expression through independent news and analysis, and the voices are finding each other. Refreshingly, this new unity is vaulting traditional political divides, which were ever an irrelevance to our higher values of life and love.

A new and more accurate divide has formed between we who love liberty and refuse to bow before medical and financial deities, and the tyrants who order us to do so. Perhaps the most surprising development in these allegiances is that the advocates of unconstitutional enforcement include many on the so-called 'Left' who should know better, people who, until fear porn clouded their judgment, would see through mainstream-media spin and denounce corporations profiteering from crisis, call out legally sanctioned discrimination against the already disadvantaged, and rail against Big Pharma's capture of regulatory agencies.

Even the Green Party in America has aligned with Big Pharma's agenda, but its Black Caucus has not. In a statement published Dec. 13, 2021, the Caucus declares its alliance with the international Medical Freedom movement and denounces lockdowns, mandates, and passports as "the most vile, unconstitutional, immoral, unscientific, discriminatory and outright criminal policies ever enforced upon the population and go against everything the Green Party stands for under Social Justice."

BRIDGING POLITICAL DIVIDES

Allow me, then, to question any allegiance you may feel with one side or the other in any political duopoly. How many times have we poured our energies into supporting candidates who, once installed, have left us feeling disappointed at best and betrayed at worst? True voices of principle are excluded from the competition anyway, whether by manipulation within political parties, electoral fraud, or well-funded smear campaigns.

Do you really know what the terms 'left wing' or 'right wing' mean any more? Did you ever? And even if you did, is there anything to be gained in the horizontal plane of their contention? Consider the words of Colombian president, Gustavo Petro: "I no longer divide politics into left and right. I think that was a relatively logical way and a relatively realistic way to describe politics in the 20th century, but today, politics is divided between the politics of life and the politics of death."[1]

BRIDGING MEDICAL DIVIDES

Stop blaming your neighbor for the pain you are feeling... Don't be angry at a school-bus driver or a nurse or a teacher's aide. Be angry at the oligarchs. Don't let them turn us against each other, because that's what these mandates do.

— JIMMY DORE

Nor, crucially, is there a divide between vaccinated and unvaccinated. Quite the opposite. These divisions, along with various 'culture wars', are highly convenient to the pharaohs of this age who are quite happy to see us attack each other, rather than turn our collective attention towards them.

Therefore, we do not condemn the medical decision of another, much less gloat if that decision turns out to be misguided. We are all capable of making foolish, misguided, and ignorant choices, and those who suffer deserve our mercy and compassion, not condemnation. I've heard far too much "get-what-they-deserve" language on both sides and, in a chilling reminder of Death-Eater logic in the *Harry Potter* novels, reference to 'purebloods'. No, let us instead pledge to help, heal, serve, and comfort all who are afflicted, whether they made the same choice as us or not.

PART II

OUR CONSTITUTIONAL FOUNDATION

We know our Rights innately and instinctively, but they are enshrined in universal declarations to shield us from the predations of minister and monarch, bandit and bureaucrat, corporation and cult who would exploit, extort, and enslave others made in God's image if they could. These declarations, conventions, and constitutions are a sacred gift from our ancestors, from a chorus of witnesses[1] who now call on us to uphold their words, honour their legacy, and reassert our fundamental standing as sovereign men and women against the latest tide of blasphemy sweeping the Earth.

My general pattern in this book will be first to examine the bedrock principles on which our liberties rely, then to move from the universal and the eternal to international and European protections, followed by individual countries and institutions. All the emphases in the quotations are my own. First mentions of documents are in bold and linked (for those reading the electronic version of this book). Subsequent mentions are in bold and, where appropriate, in acronym form, such as **UDHR** for the ***Universal Declaration of Human Rights.***

Having lived most of my life in England and the united States, these are the nations I most readily discuss, but I am also paying closer attention to Australia and Canada now, where the totalitarian agenda is most alarmingly advanced. Later editions may go into more detail about more places, but time is of the essence, and I dare not wait another day to get this out. Still, wherever you live, the international protections apply.

And don't worry if you get lost trying to remember which declaration says what, and in what context. I've set out all the key protections in Appendix I, a handy guide to international and national Rights declarations, conventions, and codes. You will also find a link to download a PDF version for yourself.

In all, let us be motivated—and I say this as a reminder to myself too—not by fear but by love...

"Jesus replied, 'Thou shalt love the Lord thy God with all thy heart, and with all thy soul, and with all thy mind. This is the first and greatest commandment. And the second is like unto it, Thou shalt love thy neighbour as thyself.' "

— *MATTHEW* 22:37-39

This **Second Commandment** is also known as the **Golden Rule** or, as coined in the *Book of James*, **Royal Law**: "If indeed you keep the royal law according to the Scripture, 'You shall love your neighbour as yourself,' you are doing well" (*James* 2:8).

For example, is it love to impose my medical choice on another? Here, I yield the spotlight to Oscar Wilde:

> "A man is called selfish if he lives in the manner that seems to him most suitable for the full realisation of his own personality... But this is the way in which every one should live. Selfishness is not living as one wishes to live, it is asking others to live as one wishes to live. And unselfishness is letting other people's lives alone, not interfering with them. Selfishness always aims at creating around it an absolute uniformity of type. Unselfishness recognises infinite variety of type as a delightful thing, accepts it, acquiesces in it, enjoys it."

And we uphold the **First Commandment** as well—to love God—when we understand we are made in God's image (*Genesis* 1:26), that our body is a temple (*1 Corinthians* 3:16) and therefore sacred, and thus revere bodily autonomy for ourselves and others in all our representations of the divine.

But now, let's get into specifics of constitutional and Rights language. Once the **Golden Rule** is embraced, let us proceed to *Magna Carta*, our foundational

constitutional text, drafted more than eight centuries ago
as an antidote to King John, until recently the worst
tyrant in English history. Learn this key statement...

"TO NO-ONE WILL WE SELL, TO NO-ONE WILL WE REFUSE OR DELAY, RIGHT OR JUSTICE."

— *MAGNA CARTA*, ARTICLE 40

By the light of this constitutional beacon, we need
only ask of any edict, regulation, or stipulation, whether
Rights were bought or sold to obtain it. In short, follow
the money! Who paid whom to stifle our core Rights
such as free speech, protest, privacy, legal redress, or even
the Right to Life itself?

For example, what Rights were sold in 2020 when,
even before injections started to roll out, the British
government granted pre-emptive legal immunity to
pharmaceutical companies, so that no-one could sue
them for future harms?

I first became aware of this outrage to Justice in
August 2020 when the British government published a
so-called 'Consultation Document' titled *Changes to
Human Medicine Regulations to Support the Rollout of
COVID-19 Vaccines*.

That this was constructed on a foundation of lies was
obvious from the opening sentence: "COVID-19 is the
biggest threat this country has faced in peacetime
history...." Glaringly overlooking the Black Death, the

Spanish Flu, and a succession of devastating plagues in-between. The very next paragraph was, if anything, even more fraudulent: "Effective COVID-19 vaccines will be the best way to deal with the pandemic." Pure speculation!

Yet on these fraudulent foundations, the Document insisted pharmaceutical manufacturers and others in the supply chain "cannot generally be sued in the civil courts for the consequences resulting from the use of an unlicensed product."

What objective observer would fail to infer the thumb of pharmaceutical companies on the scales of Justice and to conclude that industry lobbyists were dictating government policy? Of course, this was all conducted behind closed doors, but we get an insight into Big Pharma's manipulations from a February 2001 Bureau of Investigative Journalism report titled *Held to ransom: Pfizer demands governments gamble with state assets to secure vaccine deal.* The piece reveals Pfizer demanded countries in South America "put up sovereign assets, such as embassy buildings and military bases, as a guarantee... against any civil claims citizens might file if they experienced adverse effects after being inoculated."

The report also reveals, "Pfizer has been in talks with more than 100 countries and supranational organisations, and has supply agreements with nine countries in Latin America and the Caribbean: Chile, Colombia, Costa Rica, Dominican Republic, Ecuador, Mexico, Panama, Peru, and Uruguay. The terms of those deals are unknown."

In the U.S., the legal shields for Big Pharma went up

even earlier in 2020 when health secretary Alex Azar, a former pharmaceutical executive and lobbyist, invoked the Public Readiness and Emergency Preparedness (PREP) Act. This legislation, enacted in 2005, provides legal protection to U.S. companies making or distributing medical supplies like vaccines unless there is "willful misconduct." The products of Pfizer, Moderna, AstraZeneca, and Johnson & Johnson were also exempted from the National Vaccine Compensation Program.

Again, I invoke *Magna Carta* to decry this: "To no-one will we sell, to no-one will we refuse or delay, right or justice."

Consider too, what Rights were traded when Matt Hancock, the health minister initially presiding over Britain's 'pandemic' response, was giving COVID contracts to his friends, breaking his own protocols, and planning to "deploy" a new variant of COVID and to "frighten the pants [off] everyone with the new strain." Oh, and adulterously shagging a former lobbyist he had hired into his department. Such is the level of corruption in the British establishment, and it has been replicated throughout most of the world.

So, the **Royal Law** and *Magna Carta* are good anchors of principle for our constitutional understandings. I will also refer in this book to the **UDHR**, itself inspired by *Magna Carta*, and adopted by the United Nations in 1948. Its articles, as pointed out by Anna de Buisseret in her October 2021 interview, "are enshrined in multiple Human-Rights treaties and conventions, international, European, and U.K."

In 1966, the U.N. also ratified the *International Covenant on Economic, Social and Cultural Rights* (ICESCR) which hails "the inherent dignity of the human person" in its Preamble and begins its first Article, "All peoples have the right of self-determination." (Part I, Article 1, Para. 1).

In the same year, the U.N. took up the *International Covenant on Civil and Political Rights* (ICCPR) which states in Article 3, "Everyone has the right to life, liberty, and security of person." In 1984, this Covenant was cemented with the *Siracusa Principles* to ensure its protections would apply even in times of direst emergency:

> "No state party shall, **even in time of emergency threatening the life of the nation**, derogate from the Covenant's guarantees of the right to life; freedom from torture, cruel, inhuman or degrading treatment or punishment, and **from medical or scientific experimentation** without free consent; freedom from slavery or involuntary servitude; the right not to be imprisoned for contractual debt; the right not to be convicted or sentenced to a heavier penalty by virtue of retroactive criminal legislation; the right to recognition as a person before the law; and freedom of thought, conscience and religion. **These rights are not derogable under any conditions even for the asserted purpose of preserving the life of the nation"** (Para. 58).

"Not derogable" means your Rights cannot be set aside for any reason, cannot be diluted, cannot be impaired. They are non-negotiable. "A fundamental maxim of law is that you have sovereignty over your own mind and body," says de Buisseret...

"Nobody gets to break that, not even in times of public emergency threatening the life of a nation. So the idea that a bunch of bureaucrats in 2020, 2021 get to come along and set aside our rule of law, claiming there's a public-health emergency, it's not legal, it's not lawful, it's not moral, it's not ethical."

Yes, as the *Siracusa Principles* spell out, constitutions are not plastic statements to be suspended or revoked at the whim of leaders and politicians, nor in times of emergency. On the contrary, knowing that power corrupts and will seize on any excuse to enlarge itself, they are there especially *for* times of emergency lest, reacting out of fear or panic, we find pretext to harm others. I therefore celebrate the *Principles'* use of the word 'asserted' in "the asserted purpose of preserving the life of the nation" above. The drafters knew political leaders would lie to the people about perceived dangers and claim their destructive measures were for our own good.

One such tyrant, of course, is Canadian prime minister, Justin Trudeau, who feels the unvaccinated are "taking up space." In an utter inversion of *Siracusa*, and for the first time in the nation's history, he seized so-called 'Emergency Powers' in early 2022 to persecute and terrorize truckers who opposed his Rights-crushing decrees. With the connivance of his vampiric finance minister, Chrystia Freeland, along with a supine finance industry and complicit police, he stole funds and even fuel from the movement, froze individual bank accounts of participants, and persecuted their donors and supporters. He cancelled insurance on truckers' vehicles, threatened to kidnap their children and kill their pets, dished out indiscriminate brutality at the hands of his Praetorian police force, and disappeared movement leaders who were snatched off street corners in the dark of night. Meanwhile, police in Canberra, Australia were directing radiation weapons against protestors, causing their skin to burn and blister.

Again, I say, be a **CONSTITUTIONAL EXTREMIST**! Constitutionality is the supreme authority, transcending the medical debates of the day. Even if a disease came along tomorrow to rival the Black Death and wiped out half the population, and even if there were some medical product proven 100% effective in preventing transmission and symptoms, and even if that product were completely guaranteed to be without side effects—and those, of course, are impossible ifs—any medical imposition would be a lawless atrocity, violating our sovereignty and transgressing bedrock constitutional protections as old as our species.

It is troubling to hear opponents of mandates base

their arguments on the low level, or absence of, emergency. No. Grow up in your constitutional understanding! Medical statistics are a dangerous distraction when, with awestruck wonder, we may look up and behold our true North Star of constitutionality.

CONSTITUTIONS OVERRULE LEGISLATION

The reason I talk about constitutions before addressing legislation, is that they are not the same, and often in direct opposition. Legislation, such as Acts or statutes, is typically drafted and/or applied to enforce tyranny, and then to shield the enforcers of that tyranny from any real justice.

Martin Luther King wrote in his famed *Letter From a Birmingham Jail* (1963) that "there are two types of laws: just and unjust" and that "one has a moral responsibility to disobey unjust laws. I would agree with St. Augustine that 'an unjust law is no law at all.' "

Agreed, except that King errs in calling legislation 'law'. As we shall see in the coming section on Common Law, legislative instruments are but corporate contracts written by one party who thinks to impose them unilaterally on another party, We the People, so...

STOP CALLING LEGISLATION 'LAW'!

The inherent opposition between legislation and constitutional Rights is explicitly recognized in the States in *United States Code* Title 18, Section 242, which specifies penalties for anyone who, "under color of any law, statute, ordinance, regulation, or custom, willfully subjects any person in any State, Territory, Commonwealth, Possession, or District to the deprivation of any rights, privileges, or immunities secured or protected by the Constitution or laws of the United States." If the violation results in bodily injury, the penalty can include ten years in prison. The *Code* even allows for life imprisonment or a death sentence in cases of kidnapping or sexual abuse.

History is littered with unjust legislation; indeed, it seems easier to find than just legislation. It includes Nazi Germany's legalization of forced sterilization in 1933, which followed similar measures in some American states. More recent examples of blatantly unconstitutional laws include the *U.S. Military Commissions and Detainee Treatment Act* (2006) which immunized U.S. officials, and those who gave them orders, from prosecution for torturing prisoners, a clear breach of the **Eighth Amendment**'s prohibition of "cruel and unusual punishment."

Fast forward to December 2021, when the U.K. government "is taking away our liberties on an industrial scale," to quote journalist George Monbiot in a broadcast for Double Down News. At the time, two bills were making their way through Parliament: the *Police, Crime, Sentencing and Courts Bill*, which effectively bans protest and permits police to stop and search without suspicion; and the *Nationality and Borders Bill* which, in Clause 9, assumes the power to strip people of citizenship retrospectively and without warning. As Frances Webber, vice-chair of the Institute of Race Relations, observes, "It unapologetically flouts international human-rights obligations and basic norms of fairness."

Monbiot didn't get to the *Public Health (Control of Disease) Act* which contains new tyrannical impositions in Sections 45B and 45C that weren't in the original 1984 version. These dictate that "the appropriate Minister" may impose medical examination, detention, isolation, or quarantine of persons; seize, inspect, or destroy property; impose "disinfection" of persons; prohibit the entry or exit of persons or things; and require persons to answer questions about their health.

The minister may also, "in response to a threat to public health," make regulations "imposing duties on registered medical practitioners or other persons to record and notify cases or suspected cases of infection or contamination," require that children be kept away from school, prohibit events and gatherings, and dictate how dead bodies are handled and human remains disposed. And, oh yes, the Minister may impose any other "special restriction or requirement."

So, there you have it. Our politicians, officials, and bureaucrats want to be kings, not just kings but absolute monarchs, accountable to no-one, with the power to dictate every aspect of our lives, and deaths! In these two Sections alone, we see a presumptive carte-blanche to imprison any person indefinitely, seize any property, and "disinfect" anyone they choose on any public-health pretext. None of this is permissible under international law, as I have demonstrated or will demonstrate in this book. It is totalitarian madness, and we all know it.

We are living in a time of evil legislation—lawlessness cloaked in legislation—in which the terms 'legal' and 'illegal' no longer have any meaning and are utterly irrelevant to the truth in our hearts. Parliamentary rubber stamps add not one jot of legitimacy to tyrannical statutes. As the great author Robert Graves so colourfully put it, "Parliament may vote a turd to be a rose; but a turd it still remains!"[1]

And if Acts passed by legislatures are meaningless, how much more so the pronouncements and regulations of executive branches or government officials who never bothered with the troublesome business of parliamentary oversight, deliberation, or vote? As the website Laworfiction.com observes of such edicts in the U.K., "the dressing up of unenforceable policy guidance as enforceable rule of law is an issue of serious public concern."

Therefore, in the words of Rights defender, Dolores Cahill, in an August 2021 interview with Clive de Carle,…

"We need, in each of our countries, to ensure the rule of law exists, and the politicians and the media and the medical profession are not falsely told that just because there's a guideline, you can break the law, falsely told there is indemnity to an injection, which is entirely untrue."

That's not to say I will never call on Acts, statutes, or regulations to support our cause. Though they are not law, they are occasionally beneficial or protective, and therefore lawful. You and I are not bound by them, but the corporations *are* bound to comply with their own contracts. Therefore, we may run any legislation through a Rights sieve to separate the righteous from the unrighteous and cherry-pick from their documents when it serves us to do so.

Even within its own legal framework, the U.K. government has no standing for the emergency measures it has taken. As the Oxford Constitutional Law website explains, "There is no formal constitutional procedure for declaring a national state of emergency, but the *Civil Contingencies Act* (2004) is a statutory framework functionally equivalent thereto, the 'protection of health' being an emergency category under the Act. **It was not used.**" (Para. 11)

Why wasn't it used? Presumably because it cancels emergency regulations after seven days if not approved by each House of Parliament (Section 27, Para. 1(b)) and because it requires parliamentary renewal every 30 days (Section 26, Para. 1). Having fulfilled neither of these requirements, the British government is acting illegally.

In the united States, meanwhile, there is at least a

faint glimmer of hope in recent judicial rulings checking
Joe Biden's rogue 'unitary executive'. In November 2021,
the Fifth Circuit Court of Appeals cited "grave statutory
and Constitutional issues" as it blocked a vaccine
mandate by the Occupational Safety and Health
Administration (OSHA), which "grossly exceeded
OSHA's statutory authority." A few weeks later, Louisiana
federal judge Terry A. Doughty cited this ruling in his
own preliminary injunction against Biden's national
vaccine mandate for health-care workers.

As legal texts go, Doughty's injunction is an unusually
spirited document, upholding "the liberty of individuals
to make intensely personal decisions, even when those
decisions frustrate government officials." It rebuked the
administration's "arbitrary and capricious" mandate and
presumption of executive "superpowers," and schooled
Biden in elementary constitutional principles (albeit with
errant use of the word, 'laws').

"If the separation of powers meant anything to the
Constitutional framers, it meant that the three
necessary ingredients to deprive a person of liberty or
property—the power to make rules, to enforce them,
and to judge their violations—could never fall into the
same hands. If the Executive branch is allowed to usurp
the power of the Legislative branch to make laws, two
of the three powers conferred by the Constitution
would be in the same hands.

"If human nature and history teach anything, it is
that civil liberties face grave risks when governments

proclaim indefinite states of emergency. During a pandemic such as this one, it is even more important to safeguard the separation of powers set forth in our Constitution to avoid erosion of our liberties."

If such sanity prevailed, this book would not need to exist, but what about the next 'emergency', or the one after that, when the false powers will resume their agenda of destruction and enslavement? We cannot afford to be complacent. We must keep our constitutional weapons sharp, our skills in wielding them finely honed, our verbal armour at hand.

PART III

OUR COMMON-LAW FOUNDATION

O good, my lord, no Latin....
The willing'st sin I ever yet committed
May be absolved in English.

— SHAKESPEARE, *KING HENRY VIII*

As we have seen, legislation passed by parliaments, along with decrees dictated by executive governments, can be violently at odds with constitutional and Rights protections. But legislation is overruled even more emphatically by Common Law, or 'Law of the Land', to which all are bound, whether man, woman, parliament, police, priest, or king.

In her no-nonsense book about Common Law, *Freedom Is More Than Just a Seven-Letter Word*, Veronica: of the Chapman family points out this Law of the Land "is the

only Law of the Land. And the only Law that needs to be obeyed on dry land."

As with constitutions, the beauty of Common Law rests in its common-sense simplicity, requiring us not to cause harm or loss to another and to conduct ourselves without mischief in promises and agreements. In short, **a crime is established when there is an injured party.**

"If there is no victim," explains Common-Law champion Chris Edward in a TikTok video, "if there is no-one with an affidavit or a statement against you to say you have caused them a loss, harm, or injury, where you've defrauded them or stolen something from them, if there is no human victim, there is no crime. If there is no crime, there is no fine."

"IF THERE IS NO VICTIM, THERE IS NO CRIME."

This is the reigning status in Common-Law nations, of which there are more than 40, including the U.K., along with other countries that used to be part of the British Empire, such as the united States, Canada, Australia, New Zealand, India, and Pakistan. This principle becomes especially powerful when dealing with would-be enforcers such as police.

As Anna de Buisseret explains in her Parliament Square interview, "We are a Common-Law jurisdiction in this country, and lots of countries around the world claim their jurisdiction from the U.K. And the Common-Law general principle is, '**First, do no harm.**' And what that means is that you don't get to harm anybody's person, property, liberty, etc." This phrase, which in Latin is "Primum non nocere," is supported in Common Law by "Voluntas aegroti suprema lex," de Buisseret adds, meaning, **"Over his or her mind or body, the individual is sovereign."** Our status under Common Law is akin to diplomatic immunity, or the standing of foreign embassies, according to Darren (of the family) Deojee in the *Strawman* documentary: "Jurisdiction is portable. It's not tied to land, it's tied to the party, so I can carry my jurisdiction with me, which is the whole principle of sovereignty in general."

COMMON LAW OVERRULES LEGISLATION

The powers-that-shouldn't-be can make as many laws, decrees, regulations, rules, mandates or whatever they want, if these are not in alignment with Natural law, they are simply VOID from Inception, therefore UNAPPLICABLE and INEXISTENT in reality. Their 'power' exists only in a fake system of belief.

— DOM TREMBLAY, PRESENTATION AT
FREEDOM UNDER NATURAL LAW
CONFERENCE, FEB. 12, 2022

Common Law, or that which is 'lawful', is distinct from and superior to, that which is 'legal', meaning Acts and statutes implemented by legislatures. Naturally, it also overrules dictates and regulations issued by prime ministers and presidents and all who enjoy their patronage. As U.S. Supreme-Court judge Robert Jackson wrote in 1952, "With all its defects, delays and inconveniences, men have discovered no technique for long preserving free government except that the Executive be under the law."

But public and police alike have been fooled into believing Common Law and legislation are one and the same, according to former police officer Sarah (of the family) Feeley in the *Strawman* documentary, "so that when police are policing the streets, we're enforcing policies, Acts and statutes which, when looked into, are not necessarily lawful."

Common Law sets us free from legislation as surely as "The law of the Spirit of life in Christ Jesus hath made me free from the law of sin and death" (*Romans* 8:2). At the heart of Common Law is reverence for individual sovereignty wherein you are the supreme independent authority over your own body and your own territory. A government or parliament may suggest a set of rules and obligations to us, but under Common Law, it is up to each of us whether we accept it on an individual basis as a mutually agreed contract.

LEGISLATION ONLY BINDS US IF WE CONSENT TO IT WITH OUR SIGNATURE!

This concept is beautifully expressed in *Strawman*, as I quoted earlier...

"Parliament has no say in Common Law and is bound by it. So they create Acts of Parliament, and in the U.S.,

Acts of Congress. **Because government is a creation of man, and a creation of man can never be above man, they need your consent before they have the force of law.**"

Or, as Jacquie Phoenix of Practical Lawful Dissent International puts it, **"We the people created government; they are the fiction... A fiction can never gain authority over its creator.**"

Similarly, a building cannot have authority over its builder nor, for that matter, can a parliament building or any other 'Rathaus' of Europe have authority over the people. "A Builder can make a house. A house cannot make a Builder," explains Veronica in her book. "The Builder is 'above' the house. A Human Being can make a Law. The Law cannot make a Human Being. The Human Being is 'above' the Law."

But, she writes, "a very long time ago, the Countries, the Nations, were reorganized into CORPORATIONS, for the convenience of the Global Elite." Parliament, too, is a corporation, and its statutes are merely the 'legislated rules', or company policy, of the parent corporation. **As we never signed up to join this corporation, its legislated rules don't apply to us!**

This is where we part company with the state's attempt to enroll us as a corporate employee when it issued us with a Birth Certificate. This conjured a fictional 'citizen', also a corporate entity, and regarded us as human livestock in a tax farm. The Birth Certificate inducted us into a control system that regards Rights as privileges and claims ownership of our property through registration, deeming us mere users or 'keepers' of that property.

According to Common-Law advocate @joegcards in a TikTok broadcast, the Birth Certificate is not just a ploy to steal our Common-Law Birthright by enrolling us and enslaving us in a fraudulent system of 'Admiralty Law', but a traded stock. "You've been sold on the stock exchange," he asserts. "I can tell you what price you're trading at. When you find that out and know this, that money is actually yours."

Under Admiralty 'Law'—also known as Maritime 'Law', Fleet 'Law', Commerce 'Law', or 'Law' Merchant— we are deemed dead, 'lost at sea', meaning "they can plunder and pillage your ship, and take whatever gold you earn," says @joegcards. 'Earn' is a homonym of 'urn', he continues, a means to scatter our ashes, and 'earning' happens during the working week. By the weekend, we are 'weakened' and depleted.

And the telling homonyms don't stop there. We enter this world through a birth canal, but the Commerce system regards us as a ship given a 'berth'. Also, as riverbanks direct a river's current, institutional 'banks' direct the flow of currency.

The Admiralty system, you will observe, addresses correspondence to us with our name in all caps, as it would be engraved on a tombstone. This is deliberate. "Bills are addressed to a legal fiction, not a living man," says @joegcards. "I don't live on the sea, I live on the land. Maritime Law on land is treason, just like Acts and statutes." He concludes, "There are a lot of secrets in the British empire. We need to bring it down."

Another reason the state's Birth Certificate is fraudulent, and therefore void, is because it was done without the Full Disclosure that a Contract requires. Therefore, according to Veronica, "Bingo! You are free, because you say you are free!" We are delivered from the fictional legal entity of a citizen, and citizen 'ship', and from being a permanent debtor in a system of debts, fines, and taxes.

Veronica continues,

"After all, what is the Law, anyway? How does it come about? 'Consensus facit legem.' **Consent makes the Law**. The consent of the overwhelming majority, whose one primary desire is to live their lives in peace. In peaceful coexistence with everyone else. Free to do whatever it is they choose to do, provided they do not adversely affect anyone else. Free to travel at will. Free to express opinions. Free to exchange. And so on. Freedom from imposed fictions & illusions. Freedom from tyranny. Freedom from the domination of the many by the few.

"And those Common Sense desires were codified in Common Law, as a protection of it. And this was done many centuries ago. It formed the basis of the Magna Carta, the US Constitution, and so on. It actually forms the basis of every Constitution ever written. (Any Constitution worth its salt, that is.)...

"If you don't wear the Legal Fiction Person mask then you are not a Member of THE UNITED KINGDOM CORPORATION, and its rules don't apply to you. Its Company Policy has no force of law upon you. You can just walk away."

The same goes for other nation-corporations, including the 'United States', which "means a Federal corporation," as confirmed in *United States Code* Title 28 Section 3002. Realizing this empowers our refusals. As de Buisseret advises,...

"It's as simple as saying 'no'. We are governed by consent. So **if you don't consent to these measures, they cannot force you to.** They might claim that they can, but a lot of the cases that have gone to court have been dropped because they're illegal. It's all just a threat, a coercion, a way to make you comply."

For example, do you consent to being stopped and searched without reasonable grounds, as the new U.K. policing Bill presumes? No, neither do I. They may call it 'legal', but under Common Law, it is unlawful if conducted without Consent and makes a criminal of any police officer attempting to enforce it.

As Jacquie Phoenix explains, Acts and statutes can only *add* protection to the people, not remove it. The British monarch is supposed to deny Royal Assent to any legislation that causes harm, loss, or fraud to the people or that disrupts our peace. And even when Assent is given, under Article 61 of *Magna Carta*, the legislation should still go before a jury of the people for approval. Does *Magna Carta* still apply today? Absolutely! As Phoenix points out, "*Magna Carta* is a forever-binding document. That's clearly stated in Articles 1, 61, and 63." Article 1 states...

> "TO ALL FREE MEN OF OUR KINGDOM we have also granted, for us and our heirs **for ever**, all the liberties written out below, and desire to be observed in good faith by our heirs **in perpetuity**."

I will honour the call of my ancestors, how about you? In Article 61, *Magna Carta* again states its provisions "shall be enjoyed in their entirety, **with lasting strength, for ever**." It closes with Article 63,

> "that men in our kingdom shall have and keep all these liberties, rights, and concessions, well and peaceably **in their fullness and entirety** for them and their heirs, of us and our heirs, in all things and all places **for ever**. Both we and the barons have sworn that all this shall be observed in good faith and without deceit."

Thus, *Magna Carta* was thoroughly future-proofed to be not only permanent but intact, so that no future administration could pick and choose what it would honour and what it would not.

Bear in mind too, that this is the very same *Magna Carta* that then Queen Elizabeth II celebrated and described as "enduring" during eighth-centenary celebrations at Runnymede on June 15, 2015. Also present for the occasion was then prime minister David Cameron who asserted, "It is our duty to safeguard the legacy, the idea, the momentous achievement of those barons."

Well, neither he nor his successors nor predecessors have done so. And nor has the queen. Britain's **Coronation Oath** asks, "Will you to the utmost of your power maintain the Laws of God and the true profession of the Gospel?" This is a binding contract between the Crown and the people of the nation. But the queen gave automatic Assent to Acts of Parliament that are crimes under Common Law, without even reading them, and the people's juries have been ignored for centuries.

As a result, in Phoenix's words,

"The criminals are just doing whatever they want, and the current regulations and things that we see today, they're all crimes against us, they're Common-Law crimes. They're causing us harm, they're causing us loss, they're breaching our peace. The fact that they've got us all listed as 'dead, lost at sea' is fraud against the people. So the government is currently committing all four Common-Law crimes against the people every single day before we've even had our morning cup of coffee."

So how do the most recent government actions over COVID appear in this context? "This is the largest corporate takeover of Humanity," Phoenix says, "which is all high treason."

And how do the pharmaceutical companies play into this treason? Article 61 also states:

> "We will not seek to procure from anyone, either by our own efforts or those of a third party, anything by which any part of these concessions or liberties might be revoked or diminished. Should such a thing be procured, it shall be null and void, and we will at no time make use of it, either ourselves or through a third party."

Well, Pfizer, AstraZeneca, and Moderna are third parties, aren't they? And hasn't a thing been procured from them that diminishes liberties? When will those things be rightly ruled "null and void"?

Caught courts

What about our so-called 'Judiciary' today? *Magna Carta* gives everyone the Right to Trial-by-Jury under Common Law, but courts without juries are 'de facto', according to Veronica, they are private companies, and we are "under no obligation whatsoever to accept any services any Company may have on offer." De-facto courts also expect us to stand in the 'dock' which, according to @joegcards, is an echo of Admiralty code by regarding us as a ship brought into dry dock on land.

Judges in these courts base their rulings on statutes

alone, and these statutes, as we have seen, have no authority over sovereign men and women. As Veronica observes, "it is impossible to adjudicate between Fictions (Persons/Corporations) and Reality (Humans). It is only possible to adjudicate between Fictions OR between Humans."

De-facto courts will sometimes stage a 'jury trial' but, as British Common-Law advocate, JP, points out in a newsletter, this is counterfeit. True trial-by-jury "reflects the truly ancient system of peer review of the evidence presented to support a claim; presumes innocence in the absence of a unanimous verdict; and IS the judge of both guilt and the justice of the Law cited in the claim."

But a 'jury trial', on the other hand,

"is a deliberate deceit, intended to sound like the above but framed entirely within the legal (not lawful) system of statute. The jury is not chosen from the defendant's peers; unanimity is never required; the 'judge' in the 'court' directs the jury; the jury will (generally) not consider the justice of the statute cited in the claim.

"Our constitution (yes, we have one) requires the former. Our legal system offers the latter. **The legal system tends to despotism**—judge, jury and executioner in one (legal) person—just as was overcome 808 years ago in the Great Charter."

Though I am a relative newcomer to Common-Law principles and what they mean for us, I have come to understand that, far from cowering before despotic politicians and wondering what new restriction or regulation they're going to hit us with next, we should be prosecuting them instead and, with the help of constables and military true to their oaths, seizing back our Birthright and our courts!

COMMON-LAW POLICING

The distinction between Common Law and 'lawful', versus legislation and 'legal', is especially important when it comes to police officers. Consider the *Oath for the Office of Constable* in the U.K. (included in Schedule 4 of the *Police Act* (1996), which applies to every police officer in England and Wales, irrespective of rank, as well as to British Transport and Ministry of Defence police...

"I do solemnly and sincerely declare and affirm that I will well and truly serve the Queen in the office of constable, with fairness, integrity, diligence and impartiality, **upholding fundamental human rights** and according equal respect to all people; and that I will, to the best of my power, cause the peace to be kept and preserved and prevent all offences against people and property; and that while I continue to hold the said office I will to the best of my skill and knowledge discharge all the duties thereof faithfully according to law."

And what does that final word, 'law', mean here? Not government legislation but Rights. As spelled out in the U.K. College of Policing **Code of Ethics**, **"You must uphold the law regarding human rights."** Each officer also pledges under the Code to "give and carry out lawful orders only."

These statements are also rooted in **Magna Carta**: "We will appoint as justices, constables, sheriffs, or bailiffs only such as know the law of the realm and mean to observe it well" (Article 45). As is evident from countless videos online, people wearing police costumes these days spectacularly fail the *Magna-Carta* test. They neither know the Law nor observe it well. I, as the author of this book, and you as its reader, already know the Law far better than they. We are the true inheritors of Law and, if need be, its enforcers.

Remember, too, that police are a creation of Man, and that Man always has authority over his creation. In any interaction with police, therefore, *I* am the law, I have authority over them, and I am the one issuing *them* with 'lawful orders'. If I see cops behaving unlawfully or desecrating their oath, then, so help me God, I will arrest *them*!

Other jurisdictions using the phrase 'human rights' in police oaths are Scotland, Northern Ireland, and the Irish Garda. Northern Ireland's also includes "upholding the Constitution" and forbids membership of any secret society, while the Irish Garda's requires "equal respect to all individuals and their traditions and beliefs."

Canadian police swear in their **Oath**, "I will uphold the Constitution of Canada... and discharge my other duties as Police Constable, faithfully, impartially and according to law." The **Royal Canadian Mounted Police Act** (**RCMP Act**) also requires members "to respect the rights of all persons" and "to act at all times in a courteous, respectful and honourable manner" (Section 37). These declarations alone rebuke the brutal crackdown Canadian truckers endured in February 2022 at the hands and hooves of Ottawa police.

The Canadian police **Code of Conduct** also declares officers shall not "infringe or deny a person's rights or freedoms under the **Canadian Charter**," make any unlawful detention or arrest, "treat any person in a manner that is abusive or unprofessional," or "conduct themselves in a manner that undermines, or is likely to undermine, public trust in policing."[1] Well, the scars and bruises on the faces and bodies of peaceful dissenters in Ottawa tell a different story!

The oaths of Australian and New Zealand officers are disappointingly weak by comparison with the others cited. Though, in both cases, they must pledge to keep the peace and act "according to law," so help them God, neither mentions 'rights' or 'constitution'.

When Sir Robert Peel founded the British police force in 1829, officers were issued with nine Principles of Policing that detailed the meaning of 'Policing by Consent' and the idea that police are to regard themselves, and be regarded, as **citizens in uniform**. The Principles state "**that the police are the public and that the public are the police,** the police being only members of the public who are paid to give full-time attention to duties which are incumbent on every citizen in the interests of community welfare and existence."

The Principles also require officers "to use only the minimum degree of physical force which is necessary," "to refrain from even seeming to usurp the powers of the judiciary," and to make "ready offering of individual sacrifice in protecting and preserving life." There is no mention that police forces were ever intended as revenue-collection agencies which, as corporations, they have now become.

According to the Wiltshire Police Federation website, the Oath is sworn "to ensure the separation of power and **the political independence of the Office of Constable.**" Officers "**are not agents of the police force, police authority or government. Each police officer has personal liability for their actions or inactions.**"

Let me repeat this, for it is not commonly understood, least of all by constables themselves...

POLICE OFFICERS ARE NOT, NOR EVER WERE, AGENTS OF GOVERNMENT

Let every officer, at every level, take this to heart when political figures summon them to enforce legislation or rulings that are either unconstitutional, or unlawful under Common Law. As the Nuremberg trials of 1945-1949 remind us, "I was just following orders" will never wash when Justice returns to the land.

This lesson is embraced by former Arizona sheriff, Richard Mack. "We have too many Nuremberg officers still in America and Canada, all across the world, that think we're just supposed to follow orders," he told Freedom Travel Alliance in a December 2021 interview. "We have no responsibility to obey unjust laws. Just the opposite... We will not enforce unjust laws. We will not be part of injustice. We will defend people's rights."

His mission, along with the Constitutional Sheriffs and Peace Officers Association (CSPOA), is to train 'peace officers' across the world to uphold Rights and their oaths of office, irrespective of legislation, and to protect the People against criminality by police, politicians, or judges.

The term 'peace officer' is also used in Canada's *RCMP Act* (1985) where "Every officer is a peace officer in every part of Canada." But the role may have its best chance in the united States because the post of Sheriff is filled by local election and not by political appointment.

Therefore, far from enforcing politicians' and bureaucrats' decrees without regard for constitutional protections, the job of police officers is to do the exact opposite: to protect us from those decrees.

"Acting as Peace Officers is what they are paid to do. I have no problem with that, and welcome it," writes Veronica. "Acting as Company Police Enforcement Officers (Policymen), enforcing the Law-of-Waters on dry land, and not realising it, and making absolutely no attempt to realise it, is where they have no authority, no jurisdiction, and are behaving in a grossly negligent manner. That's where the problem arises for me."

Also, as de Buisseret points out in her Parliament-Square interview, officers have a Common-Law duty "to act to prevent harm. Omitting to act is as guilty as acting to cause harm."

Look up the oath sworn by police officers where you live. Look for language that mentions Common Law, Rights, constitutions, impartiality, without fear or favour, etc. Treasure these words, assert them, and share them, especially with those who have forgotten what they have sworn. To that end, you will find a letter in Appendix V for distribution to police officers at every level of command, which you can adapt for your particular location.

PART IV

OUR MEDICAL FOUNDATION

For being a shot in the arm, people sure are bending over and taking it in the ass.

— SHAWSHA NEWCOMB,
YOUTUBE COMMENT

We've all heard of the **Hippocratic Oath**, summarized as, "Do no harm." And that alone should demolish all the coercive medical measures and discrimination now being enacted by governments. The Oath also says, as set out in *Encyclopaedia Britannica,*

"I will follow that system of regimen which, according to my ability and judgment, I consider for the benefit of my patients, and abstain from whatever is deleterious and mischievous. **I will**

give no deadly medicine to any one if asked, nor suggest any such counsel."

Are we clear? Also, as Dr Suneel Dhand points out in his popular online videos, a key element of medical ethics is individualised treatment, never 'one-size-fits-all'. But, as he laments, we have entered an age of medical absolutism in which assertion of individual sovereignty is considered heresy.

Therefore, as great swathes of the medical establishment appear to have forgotten their core values —following an oath hypocritical rather than Hippocratic —we will now revisit, revive, and reassert the medical Rights that have stood us in good stead in the millennia since Hippocrates.

MEDICAL EXPERIMENTATION

Front and centre, of course, is the *Nuremberg Code* (1947) pertaining to "medical experiments on human beings" and written to ensure these "conform to the ethics of the medical profession generally."

In the words of renowned cardiologist and epidemiologist, Dr. Peter McCullough, in a jaw-dropping interview with the DarkHorse podcast of Dec. 7, 2021, "Nuremberg Code says, under no conditions should anyone receive any pressure, coercion, or threat of reprisal for having something injected into their body as we apply it to vaccines in the setting of research—and that's what actually happened in Nazi Germany with the Nazi research program." Para. 1 of the *Code* begins,

"The voluntary consent of the human subject is absolutely essential. This means that the person involved should have legal capacity to give consent;

should be so situated as to be able to exercise free power of choice, **without the intervention of any element of force, fraud, deceit, duress, overreaching, or other ulterior form of constraint or coercion**; and should have sufficient knowledge and comprehension of the elements of the subject matter involved as to enable him to make an understanding and enlightened decision."

No coercion? Then why was injection initially made a condition of employment for NHS staff—though, in the end, the government was forced to back down—and why were doctors like Kate Goodman, as she reports in a January 2022 interview, put under "extreme pressure from hospital management,... bullied and harassed" to get a COVID shot?

Listen to the irony in NHS Trust director Andy Beeby's response to her plight: "We are supporting our staff, giving people every opportunity to discuss concerns, and supporting them to make informed decisions."

That clueless bureaucrats can destroy the lives of others with such hollow and dishonest pleasantries, is one of the most frightening aspects of our society now.

The *Code*'s ten paragraphs also stipulate a medical experiment must be "based on the results of animal experimentation" and "a knowledge of the natural history of the disease." It should be "conducted only by scientifically qualified persons," "**protect the experimental subject against even remote possibilities of injury, disability or death**," and be terminated as soon as any of these outcomes appears likely.

Even a perfunctory analysis will confirm that none of these requirements has been fulfilled for the products rushed to market by Pfizer, Moderna, AstraZeneca, and Johnson & Johnson in response to COVID. In the words of McCullough, "Our vaccine program would have been shut down in January [2021] for excess mortality... People aren't willing to sacrifice their lives for this, and that's what they're being asked for."

It amounts to "a giant abdication of medical ethics, of pharmacovigilance, and regulatory principles. And it's extraordinarily dangerous. I think historians will write about this for years to come. How did America go off the rails?"

You can find violations of **Nuremberg** in official government papers, such as the British government's aforementioned excuse for a 'Consultation Document' about the rollout of injections, originally published Aug. 28, 2020. Apart from issuing pre-emptive legal immunity for pharmaceutical companies and all in the supply chain, it paved the way for "unlicensed products," "vaccine promotion," and "expansion of the workforce eligible to administer vaccinations," such as NHS-contracted providers and the armed forces.

Suspiciously, the original text of this Consultation Document has been altered since its first appearance, a chilling reminder of Orwell's 'Memory Hole' of *1984*, where inconvenient history is cut from news archives and replaced with a narrative more aligned with the Party's fictions. Even so, the most recent iteration begins with its original falsehoods: that COVID "is the biggest threat this country has faced in peacetime history," and that vaccines "will be the best way to deal with the pandemic."

Nuremberg is also cited by British doctor Lucie Wilk in her searing Nov. 15, 2021 article, *Why have we doctors been silent?*, which denounces the British medical establishment's complicity in vaccine imperialism, especially when these products were still in experimental stages. "Despite our training to look at scientific literature and data with a critical eye," she writes, "the silence from the medical community in the UK has been deafening. Yet we are the ones who should be shouting all of this from the rooftops. This is a duty of care and an oath we have forgotten."

Our protective medical codes do not stop with *Nuremberg*. In 1964, the World Medical Association issued the *Declaration of Helsinki – Ethical Principles for Medical Research Involving Human Subjects*. It is worth reading all 37 of its paragraphs, but I pick out a couple for their particular relevance today. Para. 9 states, "It is the duty of physicians who are involved in medical research to protect the life, health, dignity, integrity, **right to self-determination, privacy, and confidentiality of personal information of research subjects.**" And Para. 15 adds, "Appropriate compensation and treatment for subjects who are harmed as a result of participating in research must be ensured."

It is not hard to find tragic examples where *Nuremberg* and *Helsinki* have been desecrated. At a U.S. Senate hearing on vaccine injuries conducted by Senator Ron Johnson on Nov. 2, 2021, Stephanie de Garay described how her daughter Maddie, aged 12 at the time, was paralyzed from the waist down after participating in Pfizer's vaccine trials for adolescents at Cincinnati Children's Hospital.

About 18 hours after receiving her second Pfizer dose on Jan. 20, 2021, Maddie developed severe nerve pain, a feeling like electric shocks going down her neck and spine, excruciating abdominal pain, and severe chest pain that felt like her heart was being pulled out. Her vaccine arm swelled up and became numb. Her fingers and toes turned white, and were ice cold to the touch. The pain in her toes was so extreme that she had to walk on her heels.

Over the following months, Maddie's condition worsened, including food regurgitation and vomiting, until she was unable to swallow any food or liquids, and had to resort to a feeding tube. The pain throughout her body persisted, especially in her abdomen, which became distended. She experienced fainting spells which developed into seizures, sometimes ten a day.

Prior to injection, Maddie had never menstruated, but on Feb. 5, 2021, she started to discharge brown fluid, which came out in chunks over the following month. Painful cysts developed on her vagina and then her head. Erratic blood pressure and heart rate were also among the symptoms, along with tinnitus, vision problems, headaches, dizziness, and memory loss. Finally, she lost feeling from the waist down, which led to paralysis and incontinence.

Nuremberg states, "During the course of the experiment the scientist in charge must be prepared to terminate the experiment at any stage, if he has probable cause to believe, in the exercise of the good faith, superior skill and careful judgment required of him, that a continuation of the experiment is likely to result in injury, disability, or death to the experimental subject" (Para. 10).

But Dr. Robert Frenck, who headed Maddie's trial at Cincinnati Children's Hospital, did not terminate the experiment. In his lead-authored article about the trial, published in *The New England Journal of Medicine* (*NEJM*) in May 2021, we learn that it ran until Mar. 13, 2021 (p.2), almost two months after Maddie got her second Pfizer shot.

Worse yet, Frenck asserted in the article that Pfizer's vaccine "had a favorable safety and side-effect profile... there were no vaccine-related serious adverse events and few overall severe adverse events" (p.1). Then he added yet more insult to Maddie's injuries when, in a May 17, 2021 phone call with her parents, he said Pfizer would not cover the staggering medical bills the family had run up at Cincinnati Children's in coping with the results of Maddie's second dose. "The doctors that have seen her so far have not found something where they thought it was research related," he said, meaning his team deemed Maddie's injuries unattributable to the clinical trial.

Maddie's debilitation was recorded in trial data as "abdominal pain," though even this was a criminal understatement as she would scream in agony from that one symptom alone. Stephanie filed a report on Maddie's behalf with the Vaccine Adverse Event Reporting System (VAERS), a database jointly managed by the FDA and the CDC, but "Neither Pfizer, the FDA, or the CDC has ever talked to us or attempted to," she told Senator Johnson's hearing. "We have never heard anything from them."

Preschool teacher Brianne ('Bri') Dressen also spoke at the hearing, along with several more men and women whose tears alone testified to Big Pharma's wanton devastation of life and even the will to live. Bri suffered devastating neurological damage after receiving her first dose in AstraZeneca's clinical trial in 2020, forcing her early withdrawal before a second dose could be given. "The heads of the NIH, FDA, and CDC have known first-hand about my case and thousands of others," she reported. "We have literally asked and we have begged repeatedly for them to acknowledge these reactions. They declined." Nor were any regulators present at the hearing. Like the vaccine manufacturers and mainstream news outlets, they ignored invitations to attend.

AstraZeneca was operating from the same playbook in the U.K., where its clinical trial was suspended in September 2020 after it produced "severe neurological symptoms consistent with transverse myelitis, or inflammation of the spinal cord," a development revealed not by press release but in a CEO call with investors. The same condition later paralyzed Doug Cameron, another witness at the hearing, who got the Johnson & Johnson shot in April 2021.

So how did the U.K. regulator respond when the AstraZeneca trial went awry? Britain's Medicines for Human Use (Clinical Trials) Regulations of 2004 are supposed to ensure 'good clinical practice', and the licensing authority is empowered to shut down any trial that fails to, but this one was resumed again within days of the suspension. I can only imagine how the parties involved justified to themselves this circumvention of medical protocol and, let's face it, common sense!

MEDICAL TREATMENT

And now we reach the crux of this book, the overthrow of vaccine mandates which, as family physician Dr Charles Hoffe points out, "are slavery" because the government "are claiming ownership over your body." He was forced out of his job in British Columbia, Canada after defending medical sovereignty for himself and his patients.

As we have seen, *Nuremberg* and *Helsinki* apply to experimental medicine. Does that mean post-experimental medical treatments would be any less subject to patient consent? Hell, no!

At a foundational level, the **UDHA** recognizes our "security of person" (Article 3), while "the right of self-determination" is enshrined in the *ICESCR* (Article 1).

The constitutions of individual nations affirm these Rights. In the united States of America, the **Fourth Amendment** protects "The right of the people to be secure in their persons...." Similarly, the *Canadian Bill of*

Rights (1960) lists among fundamental freedoms the Right of the individual to "security of the person" (Part I, Section 1(a)).

But perhaps our strongest sanctuary of all is the *Universal Declaration on Bioethics and Human Rights* (2005) (*UDBHR*) which states, "**any preventive, diagnostic and therapeutic medical intervention is only to be carried out with the prior, free and informed consent of the person concerned,** based on adequate information" (Article 6).

If you print out only one Rights document of the many listed in this book, I recommend this one. The *UDBHR* may be the most powerful key in these times, for it means no-one can be coerced or compelled to wear a mask or receive an injection ("preventive") or to take a medical test ("diagnostic") without their consent. In short,...

UNDER INTERNATIONAL LAW, NO-ONE MAY DEMAND WE WEAR A MASK, GET A TEST, OR BE INJECTED WITHOUT CONSENT.

Australia, where government agents raided the offices of doctors who issued vaccine exemptions, merits particular attention. The **Australian Constitution** forbids government provision of medical and dental services with "any form of **civil conscription**" (Section 51.23A).

Europeans have targeted protection with *Resolution 2361*, passed by the Parliamentary Assembly of the

Council of Europe on Jan. 27, 2021, which resolves that member states and the European Union "Ensure that citizens are informed that the vaccination is **NOT mandatory** and that no one is politically, socially, or otherwise pressured to get themselves vaccinated if they do not wish to do so" (Paragraph 7.3.1).

The following paragraph resolves that these nations "Ensure that no one is discriminated against for not having been vaccinated due to possible health risks **or not wanting to be vaccinated**" (Paragraph 7.3.2).

But in these lawless times, European leaders are paying no heed. Among the most glaring violations is Austria where, in November 2021, Chancellor Alexander Schallenberg announced vaccination would be a legal requirement from Feb. 1, 2022.

Then, in December 2021, Greek prime minister Kyriakos Mitsotakis announced, "vaccination is henceforth compulsory" for Greeks over the age of 60, and any who refused would pay monthly fines. This from the birthplace of democracy? From the land that Spartans defended at Thermopylae, and Athenians shielded with their navy at Salamis?

The U.K., which is one of 47 member states in the Council of Europe (with or without 'Brexit'), has additional medical safeguards of its own, including the one good thing to be added in the latest revisions to the aforementioned *Public Health (Control of Disease) Act.* Section 45E states (as of Nov. 7, 2021), "Regulations under section 45B or 45C **may not include provision requiring a person to undergo medical treatment.**

'Medical treatment' includes vaccination and other prophylactic treatment."

What are sections 45B and 45C? These are the tyrannical edicts already examined and despised above, where the 'appropriate Minister' may play the role of unaccountable king. Nevertheless, when it comes to vaccines, as British charity Liberty point out, the Act "specifically prevents ministers from creating new rules which would make vaccines mandatory."

Even so, the new sections of the Act presume a minister may impose medical examination and "disinfection" of persons. This contradicts the NHS' own *Constitution* which states, "You have the right to accept or refuse treatment that is offered to you, and not to be given any physical examination or treatment unless you have given valid consent." The NHS website also states,

> "Consent to treatment means a person must give permission before they receive **any type of medical treatment, test, or examination.** This must be done on the basis of an explanation by a clinician. Consent from a patient is needed regardless of the procedure, whether it's a physical examination, organ donation or something else. **The principle of consent is an important part of medical ethics and international human rights law.**"

And that consent, the NHS specifies, must be "voluntary," a factor conspicuously absent from the U.K. rollout of COVID injections, which many people took under duress so they could continue to feed themselves or their families, to travel, or see relatives. As de Buisseret notes, "They didn't give their consent freely. There were coerced, they were threatened, they were intimidated, they were sanctioned, they were guilt-tripped."

Uninformed consent

As we have seen, the **UDBHR** requires not just consent for any medical intervention but *informed* consent. Any potential recipient of any treatment, test, or examination must be informed of risks and alternative treatments. As the U.K. Medical Freedom Alliance points out, "you should be presented with arguments for and against each of the options."

The bar is so high for this that even a patient's signature is insufficient to affirm they were informed, as the U.K.-based Medical Protection Society explains on its website: "If there is any dispute over whether valid consent was obtained, the key issue will not be whether the patient signed a form or not, but whether they were given all the information they needed to make a considered decision."

But injectees in the U.K. and elsewhere never had the benefit of a second opinion. Deeming us too stupid to weigh our own choices, the medical establishment strove to shield us from any grain of doubt that their new and experimental serums were the only viable option. Injectors across the nation neglected to tell recipients they would be participating in a medical experiment and clinical trial, that animals had died from prior experiments with similar products, or that trial subjects had experienced anaphylactic shock, inflammation of the spinal cord, paralysis, and Bell's palsy, which causes half of a person's face to droop. All of these symptoms had appeared before the public rollout had begun!

Nor were patients informed of alternative treatments. On the contrary, alternatives were aggressively censored and suppressed. As Robert F. Kennedy Jr., author of *The Real Anthony Fauci,* points out in a December 2021 interview with political comedian Jimmy Dore, emergency-use authorization of vaccines is prohibited under U.S. legislation "if there is an existing medication that has been approved for *any* purpose that shows it's effective against the target illness." Therefore, **any official acknowledgement of alternative COVID treatments would have caused the entire vaccine program to collapse.**

All this has been orchestrated in a climate of manufactured fear that shuts down rational analysis and thought. As de Buisseret comments, "Not a single person in the U.K. is able to give their informed consent due to the military-grade psychological warfare that's being conducted on them, let alone children. Now, what that means is that no consent that's been obtained is lawful or legal."

This makes U.K. vaccinators criminally liable under Sections 20 and 47 of the *Offences Against the Person Act* (1861), carrying prison sentences up to seven years and two years, respectively. "The moment you pierce someone's skin," says de Buisseret, "that's a wound. You've just conducted a live human experiment on someone by wounding them, and anything that happens to them will therefore be your personal civil and criminal liability."

The only conclusion to be drawn amid the bewildering impositions of this age is that entire echelons of our government, civil service, and legislature, along with the medical, corporate, and security establishments, are criminally liable en masse for a barrage of physical and psychological assaults on their own populations.

They would do better to echo what South African president Cyril Ramaphosa said on Feb. 1, 2021 as his nation received its first doses:

"Nobody will be forced to take this vaccine. I want to repeat. Nobody will be forced to take this vaccine. Nobody will be forbidden from travelling to wherever they want to travel to, including from enrolling at school or from taking part in any public activity if they have not been vaccinated. Nobody will be given this vaccine against their will."

Or Japan's Ministry of Health, which says on its website, "No vaccination will be given without consent. Please do not force anyone in your workplace or those around you to be vaccinated, and do not discriminate against those who have not been vaccinated."

I find it baffling how any political actor would assert

bodily autonomy and the 'Right to Choose' when it comes to abortion, but deny it when it comes to injections. And why they would mandate the involuntary insertion of pricks when, in another context, this is rape, or *persuade* insertion of pricks through fear and manipulation when, in another context, this is grooming? Even as I write this, I can hear the anger and denouncements my questions will provoke, but if they have this effect on you, why not try to answer them honestly?

Children

> *You shall not give any of your children to devote them by fire to Molech, and so profane the name of your God.*
>
> — *LEVITICUS* 18:21

Prohibitions against medical enforcement are especially compelling, and the Crimes Against Humanity especially grievous, when it comes to the child who, as recognized in the U.N. *Convention on the Rights of the Child* (1989) (*UNCRC*), "needs special safeguards and care, including appropriate legal protection, before as well as after birth." And in Britain, the *Serious Crime Act* (2015) specifies that the offence of child cruelty "covers **cruelty which causes psychological suffering or injury as well as physical harm.**"

But, far from protecting children, governments and

Big Pharma raced to pierce their vulnerable bodies with experimental serums. In May 2021, the FDA extended Emergency-Use Authorization (EUA) for Pfizer's injection down to 12-year-olds, then to five-year-olds in October 2021. In supporting the latter, Dr Eric Rubin, a member of the FDA's advisory committee, and editor-in-chief at the *New England Journal of Medicine*, infamously said, "We're never going to learn about how safe the vaccine is unless we start giving it. That's just the way it goes."

If real-world results were truly the benchmark for Rubin to evaluate vaccine safety, he could have found clear and overwhelming evidence of harm long ago, not just by extrapolating the death and destruction already doled out to older age groups, but by looking at the devastation already inflicted on the youngest recipients who had been prematurely injected before the authorizations reached their age group.

In May 2021, the FDA formally received Pfizer's Biological Product File, including its clinical-trial data, as the company applied for official licensure, or 'approval', of its serum, instead of mere 'authorization'. Pfizer achieved this status on Aug. 23, 2021.

Comprising hundreds of thousands of pages later wrested from the FDA through intense legal action and then released to the public, the file includes an explosive document titled *Cumulative Analysis of Post-Authorization Adverse Event Reports of PF-07302048 (BNT162B2) Received Through 28-Feb-21*.

This *Cumulative Analysis* document tallies adverse-event reports Pfizer received from 63 countries between December 2020, when regulators began issuing their authorizations, and the close of February 2021. No child was supposed to receive a Pfizer shot during that reporting period, but Pfizer knew of 34 children, aged between two months and nine years, who did. Twenty-nine of them were in the U.K.

Of the 34 children, 24 experienced at least one serious adverse event (p.13). One was "a 7-year-old female subject who received the vaccine and had stroke (unknown outcome); no follow-up is possible for clarification" (p.25). Yet Pfizer's paper concludes, "No new significant safety information was identified based on a review of these cases compared with the non-paediatric population" (p.13).

Should we be comforted by this language, telling us the outcomes for children were no worse than the outcomes for adults? Not when the document counted 1,223 post-injection deaths among all age groups (p.7). These numbers, shocking as they are, represent but a sample of the total because, as the document notes, "Reports are submitted voluntarily, and the magnitude of underreporting is unknown" (p.5).

Childhood harms and deaths were also showing up early in the vastly underreported VAERS. A targeted search of the database finds more than 100 cases of serious injury in under-15s by Apr. 30, 2021...

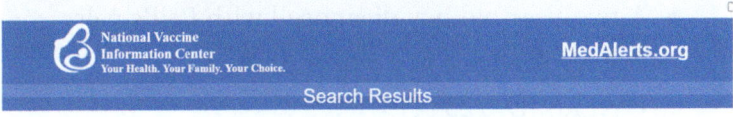

National Vaccine
Information Center
Your Health. Your Family. Your Choice.

MedAlerts.org

Search Results

From the 8/11/2023 release of VAERS data:

Found 117 cases where Age is under-15 and Vaccine is COVID19 and Serious and Vaccination Date on/before '2021-04-30'

Government Disclaimer on use of this data

Table

Age	Count	Percent
< 6 Months	17	14.53%
6-11 Months	5	4.27%
1-2 Years	12	10.26%
3-5 Years	8	6.84%
6-17 Years	75	64.1%
TOTAL	117	100%

They include...

- A one-month-old girl diagnosed with Guillain-Barré syndrome, meaning her immune system was attacking her own nervous system and destroying the myelin sheath coating nerves. She lost sensation in her hands and feet and had breathing difficulties after a Pfizer shot (VAERS ID: 1067714).
- A two-month-old boy who went into cardiac arrest the same day he received a Pfizer dose. "No follow-up attempts possible. No further information expected" (VAERS ID: 1015467).
- A four-month-old boy diagnosed with myocarditis, where the heart muscle becomes inflamed and thereby weakened, 18 days after he was Pfizer-jabbed (VAERS ID: 1113390).
- A one-year-old boy who went into convulsions and seizure two days after a Moderna shot, and died (VAERS ID: 1261766).

- A two-year-old boy diagnosed with Bell's palsy one week after a first Pfizer dose (VAERS ID: 1234413).

- A two-year-old girl who died four days after a second Pfizer dose "during Pfizer's COVID-19 vaccine experiments on children" (VAERS ID: 1297169).

- A three-year-old girl who went into spasms about five hours after Pfizer (VAERS ID: 984229).

- A three-year-old child (gender unknown) who started having hallucinations three days after Moderna, with "uncontrolled thoughts of being stalked raped hearing voices." For some reason, the child was given a second dose of Moderna, after which the psychosis escalated (VAERS ID: 1294861).

- A six-year-old boy who went into anaphylactic shock five minutes after Pfizer. "The patient was hospitalized and condition was considered life-threatening" (VAERS ID: 999492).

- A six-year-old boy who developed vertigo and an "alarming" loss of balance after Moderna (VAERS ID: 1314766).

- A seven-year-old girl who went into a confused state with decreased mobility after she got a Pfizer shot. "The overall decline of the patient on an unspecified date since the first dose has been rapid and distressing to watch. The reporter has no doubt it was connected to the vaccine. She has just got the second vaccine today. The reporter will be monitoring the patient's reaction very closely. The events were reported as serious, disability... The patient had not recovered from the events. No follow-up attempts are possible" (VAERS ID: 1050594).

But the FDA didn't let any of these outcomes interfere with its reckless race to the cradle. By November 2021, Moderna was being trialed in six-month-old babies. Finally, the FDA extended EUAs for both Pfizer and Moderna shots down to six-month-olds on June 17, 2022.

At the following press conference, Dr. Peter Marks, director of the FDA's Center for Biologics Evaluation and Research (CBER), asserted that the 'vaccines' were "safe and effective for use in our nation's youngest children." Note that he said this more than a year after the FDA received Pfizer's devastating *Cumulative Analysis* report and more than a year after all the VAERS cases I listed above.

Reading from a teleprompter, he continued, "The FDA was acutely aware of the trust bestowed on it by the American people." Parents, caregivers, and health-care providers could "trust that both of these vaccines have been authorized with science and safety at the forefront of our minds."

Pfizer would have gone even younger if it could, as I discovered in another paper in the Biological Product File titled *License Action Recommendation Documents*. There, an entry for July 20, 2021 shows Pfizer was in talks with the FDA about "another study to enroll infants <6 months of age" (p.10).

20-JUL-2021   Y   Telecon. Information Request - Clinical IR for a revised pediatric plan to include study C4591007 for subject 6 months to 11 years of age and proposal of another study to enroll infants <6 months of age. (NAIK, RAMACHANDRA)

What kind of informed consent is that?! It is child sacrifice. It is the idolatrous worship of Molech. It is an abomination in the eyes of God and Man. It is service to a cult, a cult blind to facts, reason, and truth, blind to Rights, and deaf to the Spirit's call in our hearts.

As Robert F. Kennedy, Jr. explained in another December 2021 interview, pharmaceutical companies *need* to inject children to prolong legal immunity.

"The Emergency-Use Authorization vaccines have liability protection under the PREP Act and under the CARES Act. So as long as you take an emergency use, you can't sue them. Once they get approved, now you can sue them unless they can get it recommended for children, because **all vaccines that are officially recommended for children get liability protection, even if an adult gets that vaccine.** That's why they're going after kids. They know this is going to kill and injure a huge number of children, but they need to do it for the liability protection."

Meanwhile, in September 2021, the U.K.'s then prime minister Boris Johnson, and then health secretary Sajid

Javid, overruled the government's own Joint Committee for Vaccination and Immunisation (JCVI) after it refused to recommend jabs for healthy 12- to 15-year-olds. This reversal violates the "Obligation on the Secretary of State to ensure implementation of JCVI recommendations," set out in Britain's *Health Protection (Vaccination) Regulations* (2009).

As the *ICCPR* declares, "The family is the natural and fundamental group unit of society and is entitled to protection by society and the State" (Article 23). But, in their rush to roll out red-carpet treatment for Big Pharma, governments are even setting aside parental consent, allowing children to get injected behind their parents' backs. GB News host, Neil Oliver, said of these developments in August 2021,

"I say this is worse than madness, that it is wickedly wrong. Over and above the safety or not, the efficacy or not, of experimental injections rolled out under the terms of Emergency Use Authorization and for which we have no long-term data, I am scared to the pit of my stomach by any government that seeks to come between parent and child...

"Governments, if they know what's good for them, stay the hell away from law-abiding parents and their kids. Down through history, one totalitarian regime after another, one ideology after another, has identified the family as the fundamental building block of society and thereby the most stubborn stumbling block on the road to establishing their brave new worlds. Those ideologies and regimes that seek total control over the lives of populations, always seek to undermine the family. 'Give me the child until he's seven,' as the saying goes, 'and I will show you the man.' As I say, I call that madness, wickedness, and I say that it scares me the most."

MEDICAL TESTING

I am writing this book primarily as a response to vaccine mandates, which do great violence to medical Rights. For me, as for millions of others who went along with masking requirements for a grudging while, vaccines are the last straw, the line that must not be crossed. But what of compulsory testing which, as we have seen, is included in revisions to the U.K. *Public Health Act*, whereby a minister may impose medical examination, detention, isolation, and quarantine?

Again, the **UDBHR** is our rock as it enforces prior, free, and informed consent for "diagnostic" interventions too. In short, there is to be **NO TESTING WITHOUT CONSENT**. The NHS' own definition of Consent says, "a person must give permission before they receive any type of medical treatment, **test, or examination.**" Therefore, as Lawyers for Liberty counsel, consent to diagnostic intervention "must be freely given without pressure or undue influence."

These findings also mean any employer who enforces COVID testing as a condition of employment or "strongly recommends" it, is behaving coercively and in violation of Consent.

MEDICAL CONFIDENTIALITY

There will be, in the next generation or so, a pharmacological method of making people love their servitude, and producing dictatorship without tears, so to speak, producing a kind of painless concentration camp for entire societies, so that people will in fact have their liberties taken away from them, but will rather enjoy it, because they will be distracted from any desire to rebel by propaganda or brainwashing, or brainwashing enhanced by pharmacological methods. And this seems to be the final revolution.

— ALDOUS HUXLEY

Close cousin to Informed Consent is Medical Confidentiality.

IF THIS ONE PRINCIPLE WERE RESPECTED, THEN ANY COERCION OR DISCRIMINATION

BASED ON MEDICAL STATUS WOULD BE
IMPOSSIBLE.

The Right to Medical Confidentiality is rooted in the
Right to Privacy. The **UDHR** states, "No one shall be
subjected to arbitrary interference with his **privacy,**
family, home or correspondence" (Article 12).
This is echoed in Article 8 of the **European Convention
on Human Rights** (ECHR), where "Everyone has the right
to respect for his private and family life, his home and his
correspondence," and in national constitutions such as
the **Canadian Charter** with "the right to be secure against
unreasonable search or seizure" (Section 8). Similarly, in
the united States of America, the **Fourth Amendment** of
the **Bill of Rights** states,

> "The right of the people to be secure in their persons,
> houses, papers, and effects, against unreasonable
> searches and seizures, shall not be violated, and no
> Warrants shall issue, but upon probable cause,
> supported by Oath or affirmation, and particularly
> describing the place to be searched, and the persons or
> things to be seized."

This means your medical status, including of course
your immunization status and any documentation
pertaining to your medical status, is nobody else's
business. It is not the government's business, it is not
your employer's business, it is not a travel company's
business, and it is not your neighbour's business. Nor is

it Google's business as it harvests your Internet searches about medical conditions to sell your data to the highest bidder. If anyone demands to know your medical status, they have to go to court and get a Warrant. No statute or regulation can sidestep this.

So we have a ready instrument if facing unlawful demands in the united States to disclose vaccination status. Even if you are a visitor or immigrant, demand a Warrant, for the Fourth Amendment applies to "the people," and people come in various nationalities.

And what do the medical codes themselves have to say about confidentiality? A physician's pledge to keep our information confidential has been central to the practice of medicine from the beginning, including the **Hippocratic Oath** excerpted before, which states,

> "Whatever I see or hear in the life of men which ought not to be spoken of abroad, whether in connection with my professional practice or not, **I will not divulge**, as reckoning that all such should be kept secret."

"I WILL NOT DIVULGE."

Helsinki also embodies **"privacy, and confidentiality of personal information of research subjects"** (Para. 9).

And again, the *UDBHR* also proves a tower of strength: **"The privacy of the persons concerned and the confidentiality of their personal information should be respected"** (Article 9). That means information collected by healthcare professionals is never to be divulged to politicians, bureaucrats, corporations, employers, travel companies, police, army, or anyone else.

In the U.K., the **NHS** *Code of Practice* (2003) states that, as established in case precedent and professional codes of conduct, "**A duty of confidence** arises when one person discloses information to another (e.g. patient to clinician)," and that practitioners must ensure the public "give their consent for the disclosure and use of their personal information."

This applies even to sharing information between healthcare professionals.

> "Sometimes, if patients choose to **prohibit information being disclosed to other health professionals** involved in providing care, it might mean that the care that can be provided is limited and, in extremely rare circumstances, that it is not possible to offer certain treatment options."

So, if physicians may not share confidential patient information even among themselves without the patient's consent, then certainly no-one in Government nor any enforcer has any business demanding it.

Again, all this demolishes the pretensions of the revised U.K. *Public Health Act*, which assumes a minister may require persons "to provide information or answer questions (including information of questions relating to their health)." No, he most certainly may not!

Therefore, let us all be sovereign in this. Nowadays, I

won't answer even casual enquiries about my medical status or medical history, but reply that I'm upholding medical confidentiality. For one thing, there is far too much riding on it, and people seem to have forgotten that personal medical information is sacred. I suggest you remind them!

MEDICAL DISCRIMINATION

All animals are equal, but some animals are more equal than others.

— GEORGE ORWELL, *ANIMAL FARM*

Given that our medical information is sacrosanct and confidential, medical discrimination on the basis of it should be impossible. I shouldn't even have to write this section. How can you discriminate against people on the basis of medical status when you don't even know what that status is?

But as we see, the tyrants are acquiring and sharing data that doesn't belong to them and using it to impose apartheid systems, scapegoating the unvaccinated, and fomenting hatred against sovereign people as spreaders of disease, a claim easily refuted when uncorrupted science is allowed to do its job. Some doctors and hospitals are even unlawfully withholding medical treatment for unrelated issues, based on a person's standing according to the COVID dictatorship.

And though all this demonization of the unvaccinated is itself demonic, illogical, and unscientific, it is grooming the gullible to go along with any atrocity against their brethren, whether by state or mob, in the name of staying 'safe'.

I often envisage the architects of this villainy as greedy, bloated frogs lording it over an evaporating puddle of tadpoles while sucking the water out, lest their kin should survive to enjoy the same benefits. Then persuading the tadpoles that their woes are the fault of another group of tadpoles, inciting them to blame and turn against each other, rather than attribute their suffering to the self-exalted amphibious overlords. I have written a short fable based on this idea, *The Parable of the Frogs*, which you can find at my Substack account, poetseye.substack.com.

But international Rights declarations are on the side of the tadpoles. As the **UDHA** declares, "Everyone is entitled to all the rights and freedoms set forth in this Declaration, without distinction of any kind, such as race, colour, sex, language, religion, political or other **opinion**, national or social origin, property, birth or **other status**" (Article 2). And "All are entitled to equal protection against any discrimination" (Article 7).

This "other status" language also appears in **ICESCR**

(Part II, Article 2, Para. 2) and in **UNCRC** (Article 2) applying to children, whether that status is the child's or its parents.

These protections are further bolstered by the **Rome Statute** of the International Criminal Court (1998), which includes **"persecution against any identifiable group"** in its list of 'Crimes against humanity' (Article 7).

Yet that is exactly what French president Emmanuel Macron did in January 2022 when he said he would reduce the minority of the unvaccinated "by pissing them off even more" and "by limiting, as much as possible, their access to activities in social life."

Similar happened in Israel, as pointed out by Professor Ehud Qimron, head of Microbiology and Immunology at Tel Aviv University. In a January 2022 open letter to the Israel Ministry of Health, he wrote,

> "You branded, without any scientific basis, people who chose not to get vaccinated as enemies of the public and as spreaders of disease. You promote, in an unprecedented way, a draconian policy of discrimination, denial of rights and selection of people, including children, for their medical choice. A selection that lacks any epidemiological justification."

Europeans, including British people, are also guarded by **ECHR**, which in Article 14 prohibits discrimination "on any ground, such as sex, race, colour, language, religion, political or **other opinion**, national or social origin, association with a national minority, property, birth or **other status**."

Furthermore, the European Court of Human Rights, which ultimately adjudicates *ECHR*, confirms in its published *Guidance* on Article 14 that it applies to "discrimination based on disability, **medical conditions** or genetic features" (Para. 164).

The key distillation for our purposes is:

NONE MAY DISCRIMINATE AGAINST US BASED ON MEDICAL STATUS!

And that status, of course, includes whether or not we are vaccinated. The *Guidance* goes on to say...

"As regards discrimination against people with infectious diseases, the Court has considered that a distinction made on account of an individual's health status, including such conditions as HIV infection, should also be covered – either as a disability or a form thereof – by the term 'other status' in the text of Article 14 of the Convention" (Para. 171).

Among its case studies, the *Guidance* cites I.B. v. Greece, 2013, in which the Court determined a violation had occurred with "dismissal from work of an employee suffering from HIV infection" (Para. 208).

British people are also protected by this because the U.K. *Human Rights Act* (1998) (HRA) adopts *ECHR*, and 'Brexit' has not changed that. As the Oxford

Constitutional Law website explains, the Act "gives direct domestic effect to the UK's obligations under the European Convention on Human Rights (ECHR). **Any public executive action, including statutory instruments, that violate Convention rights is unlawful...** There was no decision to derogate from the ECHR, or any other international convention" (Paras. 9 and 10).

Even on a stand-alone basis, the *HRA* enshrines Rights and freedoms "without discrimination on any ground such as sex, race, colour, language, religion, political or other opinion, national or social origin, association with a national minority, property, birth or **other status** (Article 14).

Also, the U.K. *Equality Act* (2010) specifically protects us from discrimination by public bodies and service providers such as police. Its 'protected characteristics' include religion and belief.

British police must also comply with the *Public Sector Equality Duty* (2011) (PSED), requiring them in all decisions and policies to "eliminate discrimination, harassment, victimisation and any other conduct that is prohibited by or under the Equality Act 2010." But more than that, police officers must "**take a proactive approach to opposing discrimination,**" as asserted in the U.K. College of Policing's aforementioned *Code of Ethics*.

Continental drift

So how well are European politicians doing when it comes to medical discrimination? Abysmally! By the time of writing, Austria had ordered a national lockdown that applied only to unvaccinated people; Germany required its citizens to show COVID passes in workplaces and on buses and trains, and Macron had told French citizens, "Vaccinate yourself so that you can lead a normal life... Being free in a nation like France entails being responsible and showing solidarity."

Sickening that he or any other political figure should regard vaccine compliance as a ticket to 'freedom', forgetting that freedom is inalienable, not something to be bestowed or withheld at government whim.

In the U.K., Boris Johnson was similarly mafioso when, on Nov. 16, 2021, he told the nation that getting a third jab "will make life easier for you in all sorts of ways." Jaw-dropping stuff from the land that gave us *Magna Carta*!

Worse still, at the time of writing, his government was planning further abominations with a so-called Consultation Document calling to replace the *HRA* with a 'Bill of Rights' that would "restore a proper balance between the rights of individuals, personal responsibility and the wider public interest."

It's not hard to see the end-game here: medical coercion as individuals are forced to take "personal responsibility" in the name of "the wider public interest."

This is not reform, as the U.K.'s so-called 'Ministry of Justice' claims, but constitutional rape.

It is also a chilling echo of the eighth principle—"Balance personal rights with social duties"—of the infamous Georgia Guidestones.[1] Completed in 1980, this monument in Elbert County, GA, called for world government and was inscribed with ten principles, beginning with, "Maintain humanity under 500,000,000 in perpetual balance with nature," a thinly veiled call for genocide.

The British government claims in its 'Consultation' that it "remains committed to the European Convention on Human Rights," but then argues in the same document that "the meaning of a right in the Bill of Rights is not necessarily the same as the meaning of a corresponding right in the European Convention on Human Rights." In short, the government gets to decide what words mean, however much we or the dictionary may beg to differ. You can see the letter I sent in rebuke to the government in Appendix VI.

Meanwhile, in collusion with Secretary of State for Justice, Dominic Raab, and Attorney General, Suella Braverman, Johnson sought an *Interpretation Bill* that would allow government ministers to overrule decisions of judges. So we see, the British government has gone full rogue.

Therefore, Messrs. Schallenberg, Mitsotakis, Macron, Johnson, and others of your ilk, we put you on notice: No matter what you enforce in your own countries, you are criminals by international definition and easily proven to be so. By persecuting a group of people based on medical status, you have committed a Crime Against Humanity under Article 7 of the *Rome Statute*, you have openly violated Articles 2 and 7 of the **UDHR**, Article 2 of the **ICESCR**, and Article 14 of the **ECHR**, and you have desecrated the Rights of the child set out in Article 2 of the **UNCRC**.

MEDICAL INCARCERATION

The vilest deeds, like poison weeds,
Bloom well in prison air.
It is only what is good in Man
That wastes and withers there.
Pale Anguish keeps the heavy gate,
And the Warder is Despair.

— OSCAR WILDE, *THE BALLAD OF*
READING GAOL

Confinement based on medical pretext began in the early days of COVID with national lockdowns, travel restrictions, and border closures throughout the world. Anxiety, loneliness, and despair set in among the imprisoned and isolated populations, while small businesses, education, and the performing arts collapsed.

No benefits were ever proven from such measures, but the costs were obvious and devastating, including surging levels of addiction, domestic abuse, suicide and, ironically, ill health from other causes left undiagnosed and untreated.

But, as if to reinforce insanity's definition as the repetition of old patterns in search of new results, authorities not only pressed on with such destructive measures but intensified them, compressing our room for movement (and for many, the room for thought) into smaller and smaller spaces. In the U.K., authorities imposed medical testing at every port, mandated filthy quarantine hotels for healthy travellers (at our own expense), and mounted all manner of bureaucratic hurdles that impeded or prevented travel abroad.

The medical discrimination was quite explicit, even on the U.K. government website which stated, "There are different rules for people who are fully vaccinated [or] not fully vaccinated." Boom, right there, blatantly flouting prohibitions against medical discrimination in the *ECHR* and Britain's own *HRA*.

Canada, with its isolation facility in Battleford, Saskatchewan, went even further under Theresa Tam, the nation's chief 'health' officer. In a 2010 documentary titled *Outbreak: Anatomy of a Plague*, she treacherously set out the tyrannical measures she seeks:

"If there are people who are non-compliant, there are definitely laws and public-health powers that can quarantine people in mandatory settings. It's potential you could track people, put bracelets on their arms, have police and other setups to ensure quarantine is undertaken. It is better to be pre-emptive and precautionary and take the heat of people thinking you might be over-reactionary, get ahead of the curve, and then think about whether you've overreacted later..."

Australia, meanwhile, with its network of COVID detention camps, border closures, and extreme police violence, has been perhaps the most zealous tyrant of all.

We have had the air sucked out of our lives. We are being suffocated, slowly, while false authority presumes to hand out tokens that will restore a little air if only we relinquish our Rights to Privacy, Travel, and bodily autonomy. It's a devilish bargain to strike, a tyrant's kiss from the likes of Boris Johnson who, shortly after the convenient emergence of the 'Omicron' variant—or rather, scariant—in December 2021, told the British population, "Get Boosted Now to protect our NHS, our freedoms and our way of life."

Easy for politicians to throw around words like "freedom" while doing exactly the opposite, demanding that we relinquish our Birthright in return for a bowl of imperial stew.[1] The bowl is poisoned, obviously, but 'old yer nose, shut yer eyes, and eat yer gruel!

Worse is planned, however, as governments build enormous internment camps in front of our noses. Private prison corporations must be salivating at the prospect of containing the medically uncooperative in Britain where, to this day, as a recent *File on 4* episode reveals, mental-health patients are imprisoned, ambushed and held down, stripped naked, and forcibly injected. The seeds of tyranny were sown in Britain long ago, and bad King John is back on the throne.

We don't have to look far to hold unlawful such measures of medical incarceration. *Magna Carta* states in Article 39,

"No free man shall be seized or imprisoned, or stripped of his rights or possessions, or outlawed or exiled, or in any way destroyed, nor will we proceed with force against him, or send others to do so, except by the lawful judgment of his peers or by the law of the land [Common Law]."

This means, as Rights advocate Andrea Tokaji points out, in a November 2021 interview with FamilyVoice Australia, **"quarantine measures can only be applied on an individual basis by a court of law."**

Magna Carta's principle is also embodied in the **Fifth Amendment**, where none shall be "deprived of life, liberty, or property, without due process of law," and in the *Canadian Bill of Rights* (1960), which lists among fundamental freedoms "the right of the individual to life, liberty, security of the person and enjoyment of property, and the right not to be deprived thereof except by due process of law" (Part I, Section 1(a)). Nor shall legislation "authorize or effect the arbitrary detention, imprisonment or exile of any person" (Part I, Section 2(a)).

And what of property seizures in the name of public health where, as we have seen with revisions to Britain's *Public Health Act*, the government feels entitled to "seize, inspect, or destroy property"? In addition to the government's Common-Law obligations, *Magna Carta* is very clear on this in at least two articles, first in Article 39 just quoted, where none may be stripped of possessions except by the lawful judgment of his peers, and then again in Article 52: "If anyone has been dispossessed or removed by us, without the legal judgment of his peers, from his lands, castles, franchises, or from his right, we will immediately restore them to him." And again I cite the **Fifth Amendment** where "No person shall... be deprived of life, liberty, or **property**, without due process of law."

Travel Rights

> *No port is free, no place,*
> *That guard and most unusual vigilance*
> *Does not attend my taking.*

>   — SHAKESPEARE, *KING LEAR*, II.III.

As Veronica notes, "Common Law provides the uninhibited Right to Travel. Actually across National

Boundaries **without the need for any kind of Passport, as it happens.**"

Here, we call on *Magna Carta* again, which recognizes our Right "to **leave and return to our kingdom unharmed and without fear**" (Article 42). As the Missouri Bar website observes, the U.S. Supreme Court cited this in a 1958 case, Kent v. Dulles, "to demonstrate the ancient roots of the right to travel freely."

And this Right echoes in the *Act of Union* (1707) between England and Scotland, which states in Section IV...

"That all the Subjects of the United Kingdom of Great Britain shall from and after the Union have full Freedom and Intercourse of Trade and Navigation to and from any port or place within the said United Kingdom and the Dominions and Plantations thereunto belonging. And that there be a Communication of all other Rights Privileges and Advantages which do or may belong to the Subjects of either Kingdom..."

Then we can cite Articles 13 through 15 of the **UDHR** where everyone has freedom of movement both within a state or to leave any country and return to it. Everyone also has freedom to seek and enjoy political asylum, and to change one's nationality, and none may be arbitrarily deprived of nationality.

Similarly, the *Canadian Charter* states, under the heading 'Mobility Rights',...

"(1) Every citizen of Canada has the right to enter, remain in and leave Canada. (2) Every citizen of Canada and every person who has the status of a permanent resident of Canada has the right (a) to move to and take up residence in any province; and (b) to pursue the gaining of a livelihood in any province" (Section 6).

Community Rights

We peoples of the so-called democracies of the West now find ourselves being bossed about by politicians and bureaucrats who, though they are our servants and employees, consider themselves our masters. With a barrage of 'mandates', they are treating our inalienable Rights—or *un*alienable Rights if you prefer—as if they were alienable. Other than the attacks on bodily autonomy/medical sovereignty already discussed, governments have tried to withhold other key Rights, including access to education, entertainment, assembly, and protest.

Here's a brief look at what international statute has to say in some of these areas. The *ICESCR* upholds "the right of everyone to education" (Article 13, Para. 1) and to "take part in cultural life" (Article 15, Para. 1), while the *ICCPR* recognizes "right of peaceful assembly" (Article 21) and "the right to freedom of association with others" (Article 22, Para. 1).

These are mirrored famously in America's **First Amendment**: "Congress shall make no law respecting an establishment of religion, or prohibiting the free exercise thereof; or abridging the freedom of speech, or of the press; or the right of the people peaceably to assemble, and to petition the Government for a redress of grievances." In Britain, the **HRA** states, "Everyone has the right to freedom of peaceful assembly and to freedom of association with others" (Article 11 (1)).

PART V

THE ERA OF FALSE
PROPHETS

The masses have never thirsted after truth. They turn aside from evidence that is not to their taste, preferring to deify error, if error seduce them. Whoever can supply them with illusions is easily their master; whoever attempts to destroy their illusions is always their victim.

— GUSTAVE LE BON: *THE CROWD: A STUDY OF THE POPULAR MIND*

If you have paid close attention to the 'Warp Speed' development, approval, and rollout of COVID 'vaccines', the widespread breach of scientific and medical protocols along the way, and the rush to puncture compliant or coerced bodies over every reasonable objection; if you have gasped at the orders issued by politicians, or marvelled at the coordinated messaging of governments, corporations, media, and social media, you may be wondering what dark intelligence is behind all of this. Is this just the love of money being the root of all evil, corrupting common sense and conscience? Or is there some other unseen force at work, manipulating the motivations and actions of manipulatable men and women?

Here, I will turn again to Scripture for more understanding. It really doesn't matter whether you buy into the whole Christian narrative about a fallen angel named Satan who rebelled against the Holy One, was thrown into Tartarus with his fellow conspirators, and has literally been Hell-bent on destroying God's image in Mankind ever since. None of that matters for our purposes, though you have to admit it's a great story, especially when seen through the lens of John Milton's great epic poem, *Paradise Lost*.

What *does* matter, though, is that through the character of Satan, whether regarded as an individual demon or as a metaphor for evil (in much the same way as our mythologies conjure dragons), the Bible instructs us in the stratagems now being used against us. When we understand them, we are better prepared to resist and to win our **inevitable victory** "against the authorities, against the powers of this dark world, and against the spiritual forces of evil in the heavenly realms" (*Ephesians* 6:12).

How can I be so sure this victory is inevitable? Well, I could readily draw on generalized Biblical lore, such as "Love casts out fear" (*1 John* 4:18) or "Love is stronger than death" (*Song of Solomon* 8:6). I could observe the physics of light dispelling darkness, or I could cite the Lord's words to Moses' successor, Joshua, as he prepared to attack the Amorites at Gibeon: "Do not be afraid of them; I have given them into your hand. Not one of them will be able to withstand you" (*Joshua* 10:8).

Then I could recall how the Holy One sowed confusion among the oppressors at Babel and overthrew man's arrogance (*Genesis* 11:1-9) and, crowning all, Christ's ultimate victory where, "having disarmed the powers and authorities, he made a public spectacle of them, triumphing over them by the cross" (*Colossians* 2:15).

But when it comes to the COVID story, I can be more specific by returning to the *Exodus* scene in Pharaoh's court where Aaron turns his staff into a snake. Pharaoh's sorcerers imitate the act, but Aaron's snake eats their snakes (7:10-12). Similarly, today's prophets of God are devouring the sharp-fanged creatures spawned by Pfizer and its ilk today.

What follows in the *Exodus* account? A period of struggle as the prophet brothers bring Pharaoh's kingdom to its knees. Finally, Pharaoh agrees to their demands, but then mounts a last-ditch military effort to restore the old order, culminating in his death and the demise of his army, in the Red Sea.

THAT'S HOW OUR COVID STORY ENDS TOO: WITH THE DEATHS OF PHARAOHS,

ALONG WITH THEIR EMPIRES OF SLAVERY AND MILITARISM.

Keep this ending in mind. It will sustain you when the going gets tough. The pharaohs are racing to their destruction. Deep down they know it, and they are filled with totalitarian fury because their time is short.[1]

The specific manner of their end remains to be seen. If the medical priesthood are lucky, theirs will be a quick death at the hands of mob violence as befell the false prophets of Baal after Elijah defeated them on Mount Carmel (*1 Kings 18*:40). If unlucky, they will hear their Crimes Against Humanity read out for all the world to hear before sentence is delivered.

I shudder at the prospect of seeing the perpetrators strung up and hung like butchers' carcasses, or strapped down and punctured to death with their own serums. I can't bear the idea of doing this to someone whose body was also made in the image of God, but I must admit my merciful impulses are overruled in this case. I quote again the wise words of Dave Mason, in his *Age of Prophecy* novels set in the time of Elijah. "Those who show mercy to the cruel, bring cruelty upon the merciful."

And I recall the ruthlessness Joshua instilled among his captains after they routed the five kings of the Amorites at Gibeon.

"When they had brought these kings to Joshua, he summoned all the men of Israel and said to the army commanders who had come with him, 'Come here and put your feet on the necks of these kings.' So they came forward and placed their feet on their necks. Joshua said to them, 'Do not be afraid; do not be discouraged. Be strong and courageous. This is what the Lord will do to all the enemies you are going to fight.' Then Joshua put the kings to death and exposed their bodies on five poles, and they were left hanging on the poles until evening. At sunset Joshua gave the order and they took them down from the poles and threw them into the cave where they had been hiding. At the mouth of the cave they placed large rocks, which are there to this day."

— *JOSHUA* 10:24-27

In the meantime, like Joshua, who commanded the sun to stand still over Gibeon, we will pray. How magnified are our efforts when, in faith performed and service to the Lord, we mortals reap an immortal reward. "So the sun stood still in the middle of the sky and delayed going down about a whole day. And there was never a day like it before or since, that **the Lord hearkened unto the voice of a man**" (*Joshua* 10:13-14).

THE FATHER OF LIES

Because the regime is captive to its own lies, it must falsify
everything. It falsifies the past. It falsifies the present, and it
falsifies the future. It falsifies statistics.

— VÁCLAV HAVEL, *THE POWER OF THE*
POWERLESS

So what are we up against in the spiritual realms? We can
learn much from Satan's opening scene in the New
Testament, when he comes to test Jesus in the
wilderness. Just as he invites Jesus to jump off the
highest pinnacle of the temple (*Matthew* 4:5-7), we are
invited to sacrifice our bodies to the sharpest needle, and
just as he offers Jesus the kingdoms of the world "if you
will bow down and worship me" (*Matthew* 4:8-9), we are
promised access to the world's benefits if we will
prostrate ourselves before its medical idols.

Then, as the New Testament unfolds, more patterns emerge in Satan's schemes: he is the **Father of Lies** (*John* 8:44), **Prince of the Air** (*Ephesians* 2:2), and **Accuser of the Righteous** (*Revelation* 12:10). He **masquerades as an angel of light,** and his servants masquerade as servants of righteousness (2 *Corinthians* 11:14-15), and he manipulates through **fear, greed,** and **idolatry.**

It would be impossible for one author to document the scale of deception practised on us since 'COVID' showed up in 2020, but here's a thumbnail sketch: It begins with the production of respiratory distress in residents of Wuhan, China, followed by similar symptoms showing up in other parts of the world. A devastating fear campaign ensues, with governments, media, and social-media companies concocting dread of an airborne disease. The pharmaceutical companies cash in, mounting sham vaccine trials in which they falsify data and hide the devastating injuries inflicted on trial participants. Following public rollout, they continue to conceal the ensuing mutilation and deaths, often laundering them as COVID deaths. All this is aided and abetted by captured regulatory agencies and medical journals.

Did COVID suddenly turn Big Pharma bad? No, merely made it even worse. As Russell Brand notes in a March 2021 commentary, "The transnational global megacompanies that are creating the vaccine for COVID also created the drug that led to an opioid epidemic." Front and centre in this sordid history is Johnson & Johnson which, according to an August 2019 ruling by Oklahoma judge, Thad Balkman, "lied about the science."

Exaggerating threat

> *And therein we find, neglected by us, the simplest, most accessible key to our liberation: a personal, non-participation in lies! Even if all is covered by lies, even if all is under their rule, let us resist in the smallest way.* **Let their rule hold not through me.**
>
> — ALEXANDER SOLZHENITSYN, *LIVE NOT BY LIES*

So how has the COVID threat been exaggerated all along? Let me count some of the ways. One dirty trick is to attribute *any* ailment, hospital admission, or death to COVID.

Here are some representative comments on a YouTube video, posted in December 2021, that illustrate the point:

> "I know three people who died of cancer and one person who died in a motorcycle crash, and they put Covid on their death certificates!!! Wake up, people."

> "I suffered a bilateral pulmonary embolism in April. The hospital put down it was Covid-related despite me not having any Covid in my system. Had to fight tooth and nail to get it removed from my records. Disgusting abuse of the reporting systems."

"My uncle, 90 with heart problems, died at home in March 2020, no test or symptoms, was put down as Covid death, not a heart attack. My cousin fought to have it taken off, threat of court action made doctor change death certificate."

We have also seen establishment statisticians counting admissions and deaths "with" COVID as admissions and deaths "of" or "from" COVID. Then, of course, politicians and media seize on the falsehoods to foment the fear. Sneaky stuff, isn't it?

Hiding injection injuries

You belong to your father, the devil, and you want to carry out your father's desires. He was a murderer from the beginning, not holding to the truth, for there is no truth in him. When he lies, he speaks his native language, for he is a liar and the father of lies.

— *JOHN* 8:44

And while overstating COVID damage, the authorities are desperately concealing injection damage. It began in the trials where, as we have seen, the Pfizer-induced paralysis of 12-year-old Maddie de Garay was logged as abdominal pain, and the AstraZeneca-induced devastation of Brianne Dressen was entirely omitted from results because she didn't make it to the second dose.

Meanwhile, Brook Jackson was fired from her position as a regional director of Pfizer's phase III trial in Texas on the very day she complained to the FDA about poor laboratory management, data integrity issues, and patient-safety concerns including forged signatures on informed-consent forms.

But Pfizer had been cooking the books long before COVID showed up, and its litany of medical malpractice includes kickbacks to doctors who over-prescribe.

The concealment over COVID shots continues. As Albert Benavides and others have shown, VAERS is riddled with deception, delay, and outright deletion of inconvenient truth, and fails by design. The U.S. military has also falsified vaccine-injury data for its own personnel. In Israel, meanwhile, "You have not set up an effective system for reporting side effects from the vaccines," writes Professor Qimron in his letter to the nation's Ministry of Health, cited above,

> "and reports on side effects have even been deleted from your Facebook page. Doctors avoid linking side effects to the vaccine, lest you persecute them as you did with some of their colleagues. You have ignored many reports of changes in menstrual intensity and menstrual cycle times. You hid data that allows for objective and proper research (for example, you removed the data on passengers at Ben Gurion Airport). Instead, you chose to publish non-objective articles together with senior Pfizer executives on the effectiveness and safety of vaccines."

Here's more evidence from a tweet I came across on Dec. 27, 2021, one of many like it:

> "My wife had reaction and doctor and nurses in a+e said yes it was a reaction to the jab. When she saw a report a few weeks later it said dehydration."

Another tweet of the same day shows that injection deaths are being laundered as COVID deaths:

> "Just been informed by my daughter that scumbags at the hospital are trying to class her 'fully vaccinated' dad's death as a covid one because he tested positive for it after getting blood clots from the jabs. This is how the bastards are hiding jab deaths and inflating covid ones."

The murderous powers are even offering bribes to grieving relatives to falsify death records, as attested by Ernest Ramirez, another witness at Senator Ron Johnson's hearing. Ernest's only son, 16-year-old Ernesto, died from myocarditis after Pfizer's shot inflamed his heart to more than double its normal size. Interviewed by Stew Peters, Ernest recounted how the U.S. Federal Emergency Management Agency (FEMA) called and offered him money if he would remove 'enlarged heart' as the cause of death on his son's death certificate and replace it with "COVID." Ernest told FEMA he would not falsify documents for financial gain.

As encapsulated by Peters, "FEMA called you and asked you to lie about how your son died to perpetuate a narrative, a lie, that will kill more kids." Meanwhile, Texas-based doctor, Ivan G. Melendez, who has made television appearances promoting COVID shots for children, denied Ernesto had been injected at his hospital. As Ernest told Peters,

"THESE DOCTORS ARE IN ON IT... THEY'RE ATTACKING OUR CHILDREN."

I marvel at the ingenuity of official falsehoods. Australian doctor, Peter Johnson, reports that "vaccine murders" in his country are being counted as deaths of the unvaccinated "because they define them as unvaccinated until 14 days after the jab." The same sleight of hand is at work in the Canadian province of Alberta, as reported by independent media analyst, Joel Smalley.

The medical-industrial complex must try to keep these tactics going as injection injuries mount, attributing them to the next variant of COVID, or even to another disease. Kieran Morrissey, an engineer who has worked for more than two decades at a teaching hospital in Dublin, warns the next pandemic of fear may hinge on a hitherto rare disease called 'Marburg', which presents with symptoms similar to COVID-injection injuries. Institutions aligned with Microsoft cofounder and pandemic-profiteering billionaire, Bill Gates, have already prepared for Marburg, Morrissey reports, with test kits, media scare stories falsely claiming asymptomatic spread, and a new round of emergency-use 'RiVax' shots based on the ricin toxin.

Yet another concealment strategy is the invention of a new diagnosis to mask vaccine harm. Called Post Pandemic Stress Disorder (PPSD), it could "result in a 4.5% rise in cardiovascular cases nationally," according to a British *Evening Standard article* of Dec. 14, 2021, "with those aged between 30 to 45 most at-risk." How convenient!

Amid all the mendacity, the world's power brokers can't even keep their story straight, including of course White House chief medical adviser and self-appointed high priest of 'Science', Anthony Fauci. For example, he said in August 2020 that the public "have the right to refuse a vaccine," but then called for them to be mandated for schoolteachers a year later.

The medical journals have also lined up with the vaccine establishment, as Dr Marcia Angell observes in her article, *The Faux Faith of Modern Science…*

"It is simply no longer possible to believe much of the clinical research that is published or to rely on the judgment of trusted physicians or authoritative medical guidelines. I take no pleasure in this conclusion, which I reached slowly and reluctantly over my two decades as an editor of the *New England Journal of Medicine.*"

Pfizer's Abortion Jab

How dreadful it will be in those days for pregnant women and nursing mothers.

— *MATTHEW* 24:19

James A. Thorp MD is among the fiercest critics of medical tyranny, especially against pregnant women in his own field of obstetrics and gynaecology. Having reviewed the VAERS data, he reported in a December 2021 interview,

> "There are more fetal deaths, fetal miscarriages, and fetal malformations that have been reported to VAERS in just six or eight months than all the other vaccinations in pregnancy in the last 32 years... And the childhood diseases I've seen, children of vaccinated moms that will be completely destroyed for their entire life. They have completely wiped out immune systems. They have chronic inflammatory diseases and autoimmune diseases, lifelong diseases."

Contrast that with an NHS press release, issued around the same time on Dec. 4, 2021, urging pregnant women to get jabbed. Among nine uses of the word 'safe' to describe the injections, it quotes then vaccines minister Maggie Throup saying, "The COVID-19 vaccines are safe and effective for pregnant women and I urge everyone to get their vaccines as soon as they can to secure this significant protection."

By then, U.K. authorities had known for at least nine months that Pfizer's jab was obliterating pregnancies. We know this because Britain was the second-largest source of pregnancy data gathered in Pfizer's *Cumulative Analysis* document that tallied worldwide adverse events from its COVID injection by the end of February 2021.[1]

In this early reporting period, Pfizer recorded 270 cases where women received the jab during pregnancy. Of 27 known outcomes, including one set of twins, 26 resulted in "spontaneous abortion," and one resulted in "premature birth with neonatal death." There was but one survivor, listed as "normal outcome," among the 28 potential babies (p.12).[2]

Furthermore, if babies do somehow survive these 'transplacental' harms from their injected mothers, they are not safe from the 'transmammary harms' of tainted breast milk. The earliest VAERS reports include...

- A five-month-old boy who died after his mother got a second Pfizer dose on March 17, 2021. The next day, he "developed a rash and within 24 hours was inconsolable, refusing to eat, and developed a fever. Patient brought baby to local ER where assessments were performed, blood analysis revealed elevated liver enzymes. Infant was hospitalized but continued to decline and passed away. Diagnosis of TTP. No known allergies. No new exposures aside from the

mother's vaccination the previous day"
(VAERS ID: 1166062).

- A 16-month-old girl who developed jaundice one day after her mother received the Johnson & Johnson shot on Mar. 10, 2021 (VAERS ID: 1099241).

- A one-year-old boy who went into intense febrile seizures on Feb. 19, 2021 after "vaccine exposure via breast milk." His mother had received a first Pfizer dose four days earlier (VAERS ID: 1161763).

- A six-week-old boy who died on July 17, 2021 "from clots in his severely inflamed arteries," as reported to VAERS by his 36-year-old mother. "I had been breastfeeding my 6 week old baby at the time that I received the first Pfizer vaccine... I am curious if the spike protein could have gone through the breast milk and caused an inflammatory response in my child" (VAERS ID: 1532154).

What motive shall we attribute to Big Pharma's ruthless campaign of violence against children? According to investigative reporter, Lara Logan, the assault is as much spiritual as physical. "For them, the younger you are, the closer you are to God, the more pain they can inflict on God," she explained in a June 2022 interview with Vigilant Fox. "So the more you can make a baby or a small child suffer, the greater your victory over God. And that is the only consideration for them."

From this perspective, Pfizer is not just a corrupt corporation counting the dollars but a rapacious priesthood counting the bodies. The younger its sacrificial victims, the greater its prestige before medical deities. What else can explain its industrial slaughter of children, not just in the cradle, but in the womb and even at the breast?

PRINCE OF THE AIR(WAVES)

I don't think I'll tune in anymore,
I don't believe in Radio 4,
It never will be the same to me...
What will I use my radio for?
I don't believe in Radio 4,
And certainly not in Radio 3.

— JAY FOREMAN, LYRICS TO SONG,
RADIO 4

How have media sources performed in sorting fact from fiction? Treacherously, diabolically, serving their corporate masters with propaganda disguised as news. And yes, I'm looking at you, Reuters, where I used to be a journalist back when you had a soul, and at you, British Broadcasting Corporation, with your manicured production line of fear, or as some aptly call you, the British Bullshit Corporation or Body Bag Corporation.[1]

Pfizer has proven especially adept at coordinating media messaging, as demonstrated by a montage of its news sponsorship that did the rounds on social media in October 2021. Meanwhile, Bill Gates has been working a more subtle version of the Pfizer playbook, giving hundreds of millions of dollars to news organizations around the world—including *The Guardian*, *Financial Times*, *Daily Telegraph*, *The Lancet*, and yes, the BBC, among a long list revealed by *MintPress*.

As Robert F. Kennedy Jr. told Jimmy Dore in their December 2021 interview, news sources "are being paid to promote pharmaceutical products, and they're doing that through direct promotion but mostly through indirect promotion by drumming up fear, by drumming up fear of infectious disease, and then telling us the only solution is vaccines."

ACCUSER OF THE RIGHTEOUS

Every genocide—whether it's Rwanda, the Holocaust—begins with 'we versus them'. So Hitler used the Jews, and later other people, as scapegoats for all that was wrong in Germany.

— SUSAN BENEDICT, *THE KILLING NURSES OF THE THIRD REICH*, 2017

With Big Pharma so embedded in Big Media, it is hardly surprising that no counternarrative is permitted, that information, perspectives, and opinions outside the official fiction are systematically silenced, and that the messengers who bring them are persecuted, prosecuted, stifled, smeared, and starved. You are likely well aware how social-media posts and even entire accounts are shut down if they don't conform. Big-Tech companies such as YouTube, Facebook, and Facebook's Instagram app are deeply saturated with government messaging, even daubing it onto individual posts, while alternative views are dispatched to oblivion with skewed search results and various bans, blocks, and deletions.

The censorship is partly enforced by Big Tech's ill-qualified and ill-informed cohort of so-called 'fact checkers', themselves financed by Big Pharma, who rig the debate, but even more insidiously by invisible 'bots' and secret equations, or 'algorithms', running in the background.

I have been on the receiving end of such censorship myself, with 'shadow-bans', strikes, and even the deletion of an entire TikTok account. Amazon.com has repeatedly blocked me from advertising some of my books on its platform, while the Canadian book retailer Kobo has outright deleted three of my books from its store altogether, including this one, on the grounds they contain 'Inappropriate content'. Meanwhile, book-promotion sites I have worked with for years are refusing to host this very book, and I am even censored from mentioning the censorship in author groups on Facebook.

Meanwhile, Internet search engines are reporting to law enforcement keywords used in searches, a blatant attack on the **First** and **Fourth Amendments** of the *Constitution*.

Such actions accord with a World Economic Forum article of April 2021 that complains "how friends fell down the wrong YouTube hole and came out speaking another language." Similarly, in a June 2021 paper, the U.N. Office of Counter-Terrorism called for 'deplatforming' "in preventing the spread of harmful narratives" and for on-line search results to be steered towards "positive, de-radicalizing content." It explicitly targets COVID 'disinformation' (intentional), 'misinformation' (unintentional), and 'mal-information' (true, but deemed harmful) that might "undermine trust in the government." Similarly, TikTok's Community Guidelines outlaw 'misinformation' that causes "the undermining of public trust in civic institutions and processes such as governments, elections, and scientific bodies."

That the medical-industrial complex feels entitled to manipulate media is obvious from an October 2020 email exchange, obtained by the American Institute for Economic Research, in which U.S. NIH director, Francis Collins, is reacting to the *Great Barrington Declaration* (GBD), a statement led by public-health scientists that warns of "the damaging physical and mental health impacts of the prevailing COVID-19 policies."

Collins tells NIAID director Fauci, "There needs to be a quick and devastating published take down of its premises. I don't see anything like that online yet. Is it underway?" In the subsequent email chain, Fauci sends back a piece from *Wired* magazine that he says "debunks this theory" and another from *The Nation*, and Collins sends Fauci a link to a *Washington Post* article opposing the *GBD*, in which Collins is quoted.

They're trying awfully hard to keep a lid on things, aren't they? As news analyst Kim Iversen observes in a December 2021 broadcast, "It was once encouraged to get a second opinion when it came to our medical care, but now, you need to go with the state-sanctioned advice, and anything other than that is a dangerous conspiracy theory."

Among the doctors and scientists standing strong against official mendacity and mandates is Dr Thorp, who described in his interview how American medical boards threatened to decertify inconvenient practitioners who speak out, meaning, "We're under a gag order." This includes the American Board of Obstetrics and Gynecology (ABOG) which in September 2021 warned members of "disciplinary actions, including suspension or revocation of their medical license" for any who provide "misinformation about the COVID-19 vaccine."

Not one to be cowered, Thorp responded,

"You threatened me, and you threatened every other Ob/Gyn doctor—all 22,000 in the United States of America—and you have indirectly forced this vaccination on pregnant women, and there is zero safety data... You need to retract that. You need to specifically state that the vaccination should not be used in pregnancy."

The inevitable result when health-care systems are taken over by government and corporate messaging, and doctors and nurses can no longer fulfil their role as patient advocates, is a total collapse in public trust. "We've lost all of our credibility," said Thorp, "because you can't give honest, informed consent when a nurse or physician have a gag order on."

Another group targeted with censorship, smearing, and character assassination are, tragically, the injection-injured, whose cries for acknowledgement and help are not only unheard and unheeded but often met with cruelty and derision. "Vaccine-injured people are mocked; their lives have been completely destroyed," Thorp added.

> "The cartel, including the health care, the physicians, the hospitals, the three-letter agencies, the mainstream media, mock them, deride them, kick them out of the ERs, tell them they're fraudulent, take away their platforms, don't even let them tell their stories. They're banned from social media, they're banned from everything... You deride them, you mock them, you take away their voice, you throw them under the bus, and you've destroyed their lives, and you don't even give them a platform to tell their stories."

But the censorship doesn't stop there. Another class of voices that must be silenced are whistleblowers inside Big Pharma. *The Intercept* reports that Pfizer, AstraZeneca, and other large pharmaceutical corporations are trying to "block legislation that would make it easier for whistleblowers to hold companies liable for corporate fraud."

Where does all this lead? If dissenting voices are completely driven out from medicine, media, and other core institutions, there will be no more room for compassion and empathy, much less truth, and we'll be left with a hard core of compliant executioners willing to repeat the atrocities perpetrated by doctors and nurses during the Nazi era.

So let us return to our foundation of inalienable Rights. As Article 19 of the **UDHR** sets out, "Everyone has the right to freedom of opinion and expression; this right includes freedom to hold opinions without interference and to seek, receive and impart information and ideas through any media and regardless of frontiers." Freedom of Speech is also, of course, the key Right of America's **First Amendment**.

A REIGN OF FEAR

And when men are afraid, they feel safer if they can make others afraid as well—afraid of them.

— DAVE MASON, *THE LAMP OF DARKNESS*

"The perceived level of personal threat needs to be increased among those who are complacent, using hard-hitting emotional messaging." This was the advice the British government procured from its Scientific Pandemic Influenza Group on Behaviour (SPI-B) in March 2020.

Pile on the fear they did, and to devastating effect, creating a 'trauma bond' between citizen and state. Remember how fear stripped supermarket shelves in the early days of collective madness? It narrowed the field of vision to a base imperative for survival, then the fearful could be conditioned to scapegoat Rights defenders as murderers and, on the pretext of safety, to accept, welcome, and even call for tyrannical measures against them. So much for "love your neighbour as yourself." As Dr Dhand warns in a December 2021 broadcast, "Human beings are capable of all kinds of madness once they have been infected with fear."

And what happens when awareness spreads among the vaccinated that they may have been mutilated? Some will reach across the vaccine divide to find kinship and healing with the unvaccinated, realizing that both groups have a common enemy in the 'frog' oligarchs, but others will lash out in anger at the easiest target, the nearest unjabbed person, and find some temporary relief if others can be forced into the same sinking boat.

It won't be rational, but what is rational when fear and anger reign? Still, under international medical codes, none should know the medical status of another in the first place!

Fear, rather than hate, is perhaps the most fitting antonym for love in these times. Fear shuts down thought, stifles the spirit of enquiry, and divides people who would otherwise have no quarrel. As Laura Dodsworth notes in *A State of Fear: How the UK government weaponised fear during the Covid-19 pandemic*, "We were the most frightened population in the world" after COVID's purported arrival in 2020. She attributes this to the British government's relentless campaign, informed by behavioural scientists on the payroll, and with the connivance of media and especially the BBC, to intensify the sense of threat among the population.

These behavioural scientists are using 'nudge' tactics,

according to Dodsworth, meaning the use of psychological drivers beneath surface awareness to "change your thinking and behaviour without you even being aware of it." Britain, she reports, is a pioneer in nudge theory and has operated a 'Nudge Unit', officially known as The Behavioural Insights Team (BIT), since 2010.

> "Britain is so good at behavioural insights that we export it all over the world. The Nudge Unit is now a profit-making 'social purpose limited company' with offices in London, Manchester, Paris, New York, Singapore, Sydney, Wellington, and Toronto. It has run more than 750 projects, and in 2019 alone worked in 31 countries."

Isn't it remarkable that the cities listed happen to be in the nations spearheading COVID authoritarianism?! It seems that our great British ingenuity that cracked the Enigma Code during the Second World War has now been weaponized against the home population to crack the psyche and break the will. What a tragedy that the British boffin has become an operative in Satan's workshop!

What's more, this boffin is marching in lockstep with, rather than opposing, counterparts at Germany's Ministry of the Interior who are doing the same or even worse. Dodsworth quotes a *Welt am Sonntag* article showing German scientists sought to create a 'shock effect' on their population to lay the groundwork for 'measures of a preventive and repressive nature.' "The German government, and the scientists it employed, collaborated to bring images of people choking to death at home, and to inflict fear and guilt on children, in order to make the population follow rules for an epidemic which had been deliberately exaggerated."

And Satan's workshop continues to recruit. "In the autumn of 2020," Dodsworth observes, "I notice 10 new behavioural science roles advertised in the NHS and Public Health England." The Nudge Unit even attempted to recruit her too. At least ten government departments now deploy behavioural insights teams, she writes, including one at the Home Office that "attempts to covertly engineer the thoughts of people."

And all this for a purported disease called 'COVID', which Public Health England downgraded from a 'High consequence infectious disease (HCID)' on Mar. 19, 2020 (yes 2020, not 2021), where it had briefly sat alongside Ebola.

Is it not the job of statesmen to see a bigger picture than the hired nerds of any field? If they did not, then John F. Kennedy might have been persuaded to "fry" Cuba with nuclear weapons in 1962, as advised by his Air Force Chief of Staff, Curtis LeMay, during the Cuban missile crisis. Enlightened leaders would dismiss the dystopian dreams of behavioural scientists—dismiss them from government altogether—in favour of common sense and a long-term view.

But not this lot. The British government, armed with a compliant BBC, have pursued the fear narrative with a maniacal zeal that even chief Nazi propagandist Joseph

Goebbels would admire. When one disease 'variant' has exhausted its shock value, the government conjures another, such as 'Omicron'. It exhibits all the ferocity of a common cold but as, in BBC parlance, it "ripped through" the population, Boris Johnson raised the 'Covid Alert level' to its second highest level of '4' and warned the nation in a Dec. 12, 2021 speech, "Do not make the mistake of thinking Omicron can't hurt you; can't make you and your loved ones seriously ill."

All to persuade citizens to take a third dose of Big Pharma's serum:

> "A wave of Omicron through a population that was not boosted would risk a level of hospitalisation that could overwhelm our NHS and lead sadly to very many deaths. So we must act now. Today we are launching the Omicron Emergency Boost, a national mission unlike anything we have done before in the vaccination programme to Get Boosted Now."

I counted the number of times Johnson said "booster", "boostered", or "boost" in this short speech— 18! It's one of those words that sounds weirder, the more you say it. The speech might make for a fun drinking game, but it's no basis for public-health policy.

As Dodsworth saw and foresaw in *A State of Fear*, "A government could keep new variant bait and switch policies going for as long as there are viruses. That's forever, by the way."

But politicians will end up blowing on dying coals as

fear fatigue sets in. The public are getting ever more weary of the propaganda and tune it out as more and more people realize we've witnessed a well orchestrated fiction, its methodology akin to the light shows of different colours used to depict varying levels of terrorism threat. It's a smoke-and-mirrors magic show engineered to keep the population on edge and primed to accept even more Government interference and control in their lives. Yet the measures imposed on the basis of this fiction are very real and injurious, destroying lives, livelihoods, and the very fabric of society.

And what about the trauma inflicted on children? I quoted Britain's **Serious Crime Act** before. Let's take another look now, for its definition of cruelty against children includes "**psychological suffering or injury as well as physical harm.**" Has any child in the U.K. been left psychologically unharmed by the government's blitz of fear, shaming, lies, and threats?

Has any adult for that matter? Quite apart from all the physical violations of the *Hippocratic Oath* now underway, what about the psychological ones? Are they not Crimes Against Humanity too? Article 6 of the *Rome Statute* says they are! Acts "causing serious bodily **or mental harm** to members of the group" are listed there as a form of 'Genocide'.

As Dodsworth writes, "the government weaponised our fear against us." Yes, we have been psychologically tortured.

Furthermore, when Government and Media incite us to turn against each other, isn't that also a Crime Against

Humanity? Remember the headlines I quoted in the Introduction? "The unvaccinated are putting us all at risk." "I'm Furious at the Unvaccinated." "It is only a matter of time before we turn on the unvaccinated." As Article 25 of the **Rome Statute** points out, anyone who "publicly incites others to commit genocide" is also criminally liable.

Why hasn't there been more resistance from Parliament? I find it hard to fathom. And why has Britain's so-called Opposition, the Labour Party, completely rolled over? What bribes or threats are in play? What secret-society oaths? And what blackmailing material—or 'kompromat'—is ready to be unleashed against any who dares call out the murderous agenda of autocrats?

But let us also read between the lines of Johnson's Omicron scare speech to see where the threat *really* lies. "We will also assist this emergency operation," he said, "by deploying 42 military planning teams across every region... and training thousands more volunteer vaccinators." This is where things get really chilling for those who see through the façade. With thousands more hastily assembled skin-piercers roaming the land with military support, yet clueless about **Nuremberg, Helsinki,** or the **UDBHR**, Britain is cooking up a kind of tyranny we've never seen before.

THE LOVE OF MONEY

Though I travel to the ends of the earth, I find the same accursed system -- I find that all the fair and noble impulses of humanity, the dreams of poets and the agonies of martyrs, are shackled and bound in the service of organized and predatory Greed!

— UPTON SINCLAIR, *THE JUNGLE* (1906)

The lubrication for all the demonic tactics we have seen is, of course, the love of money. And there is an awful lot of it at stake. The People's Vaccine Alliance reports profits from COVID injections spawned nine new billionaires and that the pharmaceutical enterprises took $34 billion in profits—profits, not revenue—in 2021.

We need look no further than Anthony Fauci to see the financial ties linking corporations, governments, bureaucrats, politicians, and media in unholy alliance. As Robert F. Kennedy Jr. told Jimmy Dore, Fauci "walks those drugs through the FDA approval process which he completely controls from the bottom up, and then he gets them approved, and then in many cases he himself profits." In the case of Moderna, "His agency owns half of that vaccine, and they stand to make billions of dollars."

Financial ties also quickly snuffed out altruistic impulse when the Bill & Melinda Gates Foundation persuaded Britain's Oxford University, a major beneficiary, to change its vaccine distribution model from an open-licence, royalty-free platform available for any manufacturer, to an exclusive license controlled by AstraZeneca. Gates, who has a long history of collaboration with Fauci, is also a leading funder of the World Health Organization through his foundation.

The medical-industrial complex has also been helping itself liberally to the public purses of our nations, including Canada, where the government refuses to account for CA$240 billion it dispensed in COVID-19 aid, though we do know some of it went to bribing media outlets.

In America, meanwhile, public money is used to incentivize hospital deaths. In a January 2022 interview, Truth for Health Foundation president, Elizabeth Vliet MD, explains that the U.S. government is running "a bounty on people's lives" by paying hospitals per positive COVID test, per patient put on a ventilator, and for each death attributed to COVID.

Rights attorney, Leigh Dundas, calls this a 'murder-for-hire scheme'. Speaking at a January 2022 conference, she said of Fauci, "You are the new Josef Mengele, and we are living through another genocide or holocaust, and the hospitals have become the new ovens of Auschwitz."

What other financial ties do we see? Too many to mention, but a representative sample includes White House adviser Anita Dunn, whose consulting firm represents Pfizer; Biden's domestic policy adviser, Susan Rice, who holds up to $5 million in Johnson & Johnson; and White House science adviser Eric Lander, who has up to a million dollars in shares of Pfizer partner, BioNTech. Many in Biden's inner circle also have links to consulting firm Albright Stonebridge Group, which has represented Pfizer.

As former professional mountain-bike champion Kyle Warner came to realize, after Pfizer's product "broke my heart literally and figuratively" and put a stop to his career, "There is a party in this situation that's making tens of billions of dollars from this situation. They're operating with immunity, they're also responsible for a lot of the scientific data and clinical trials being pushed through, and they also sponsor a lot of the mainstream-media narrative."

Are things any better in the U.K.? The Medicines and Healthcare products Regulatory Agency (MHRA) also receives funding from Gates, and the new BBC chairman, Richard Sharp, has donated over £400,000 to the ruling Conservative Party. Also, as *The Guardian* reported (drawing on the little integrity it had left), drug companies are secretly lining the pockets of British members of Parliament.

Following the money in all this reveals a similar

mechanism for COVID profiteering as that described by Julian Assange in 2011 for the West's invasion and decades-long occupation of Afghanistan. There, the aim was to wash money out of national tax bases and into the hands of the military-industrial complex. Now, it's the *medical*-industrial complex that's rejoicing!

I close this section by saying I could never understand the ignorant faith so many people, including many of my friends, put in Big Pharma's products. Had they taken even a cursory look at the fraud and corruption at the root, they would surely have inferred corrupt products would be the fruit.

THE RISE AND FALL OF IDOLATRY

The state takes the place of God,... and State slavery is a form of worship.

— CARL JUNG, *THE UNDISCOVERED SELF*

By now, you are aware that the COVID response has awakened monsters among us, that we are witnessing a phenomenon far beyond the commonplace fraud, corruption, and greed that have always greased the wheels of Government. There is something utterly demonic at work here. A cult has taken control in this time of revived idolatry, a cult of service to false gods and medical deities who demand our obedience, our sacrifice, our perpetual tithes and enslavement, while offering us nothing but poison in return, all to achieve some ghastly final solution.

In the words of astrologer Sarah Varcas,...

"The new religion of Covid, which tolerates no debate, no question, no doubt, has spread its reign of terror across the globe whilst those who struggle to preserve the most basic human rights and retain some semblance of a life worth living – an independent livelihood, the right to make personal health choices free of state and societal coercion, a nurturing social network of real-life human connection – they are vilified and silenced. Independent, nuanced thought is now a crime in a world where propaganda rules, and facts are sacrificed on the altar of mob-rule and the tyranny of fear."[1]

Big Pharma has done all this in the name of 'Science' but, as Dr Dhand points out in his December 2021 broadcast, "When you're no longer allowed to ask reasonable, proper questions, you're no longer in the realm of science, you're in the realm of something akin to religious extremism."

It conjures the nightmare image of Fauci and Gates officiating at some unholy communion where supplicants are called forth to the altar, bend the knee, and drink from a poisoned chalice while, from twisted pipes, discordant sounds swell from an infernal organ.

The sacrificial child is brought forth, masked and muted, trembling, his eyes wide with fear. Deaf to his muffled screams, they force him onto the altar while his proud parents, honoured guests of the assembly, look on with stoic resolution.

Perhaps there is a hint of a tear in the mother's eye, a twitch of the father's lip, but when the boy's eyes appeal to theirs, he sees no light in them. He struggles, squeals, and writhes, but the cheers of the crowd drown out his cries. Fauci's cardinals hold him down. Lifting the sacred needle, the high priest proclaims:

"To the one who gave us Pfizer and Moderna, to the bringer of the miracle cure, the saviour of humanity, and to the one who sent his servants Johnson & Johnson and AstraZeneca, receive thou this offering that we, thy devoted and worshipful acolytes, may receive great abundance."

And as the cold steel pierces the tender flesh of the child, there is great jubilation among the assembly.

For, in these evil days, children are being lined up as sacrificial lambs, Molech is ascendant, and now, instead of provoking the outrage that followed his child rapes in the Catholic Church, he is winning applause for his predations.

An evil soul producing holy witness
Is like a villain with a smiling cheek,
A goodly apple rotten at the heart :
O, what a godly outside falsehood hath.

— SHAKESPEARE, *THE MERCHANT OF VENICE*, I.III

For Molech, too, masquerades as an angel of light, while his accomplice Pfizer is "playing Messiah," to quote WION broadcast host Palki Sharma in a Feb. 24, 2021 broadcast. Meanwhile, Satan's servants, themselves masquerading as servants of righteousness (2 *Corinthians* 11:15), are drunk on their new-found power. They presume, for example, to tell nurses if they may receive 'religious exemptions' from medical mandates when "No" is, was, and always will be, exemption enough.

They are, of course, oblivious to Article 18 of the *ICCPR*: "No one shall be subject to coercion which would impair his freedom to have or to adopt a religion or belief of his choice" (Para. 2). As set out in Appendix IV of this book, a letter intended for 'religious-exemption' hearings, no individual or committee gets to play God and say who will ascend to Heaven or who descend (*Romans* 10:6-7). That kind of presumption is about as Satanic as it gets!

> You said in your heart,
> "I will ascend to the heavens;
> I will raise my throne
> Above the stars of God;
> I will sit enthroned on the mount of assembly,
> On the utmost heights of Mount Zaphon.
> I will ascend above the tops of the clouds;
> I will make myself like the Most High."
> But you are brought down to the realm of the dead,
> To the depths of the pit.
>
> — *ISAIAH* 14:13-15

But the favoured ones, the virtue signallers, the self-righteous who masquerade (and mask-erade) as servants of righteousness, bring their servile sacrifices to the state altar. To paraphrase Christ's tirade against the pharisees in *Matthew* 23, they are a brood of vipers, venomous in their denouncements, and poised to strike at any heretic. They strain out gnats in the lives of others but swallow the camel of genocide themselves, and though exalted in their own eyes and in the eyes of the totalitarian state, they are but whitewashed tombs, clad with worldly respectability but filled with the bones of the dead and everything unclean.

"In the totalitarian religion," explains Academy of Ideas in a January 2022 essay, "there are the chosen people, and there are the sinners. The chosen ones... are the pious who follow the state's commands with unquestioning obedience. The sinners are the non-believers, the heretics who stand in the way of the so-called greater good and prevent the forward march of history."

Thus, every voice of moderation is driven from the unholy orders until only the extremists are left. For example, in August 2021, Dr Marion Gruber resigned in protest as director of the FDA's Office of Vaccines Research and Review because the Biden administration rolled out booster shots before officials had a chance to review them. Her deputy, Dr Philip Krause, also resigned.

"The social transformation that unfolds under totalitarianism is built upon, and sustained by delusions," the Academy of Ideas observes in another essay, "for only deluded men and women regress to the child-like status of obedient and submissive subjects and hand over complete control of their lives to politicians and bureaucrats. Only a deluded ruling class will believe that they possess the knowledge, wisdom, and acumen to completely control society in a top-down manner, and only when under the spell of delusions would anyone believe that a society composed of power-hungry rulers on the one hand, and a psychologically regressed population on the other, will lead to anything other than mass suffering and social ruin."

Are these the end-times foreseen in *Revelation* 18:23? "By thy sorceries were all nations deceived" is the *King James Version*. "By your magic spell, all the nations were led astray" is the *New International Version*.

In the original Greek, the sentence is "ὅτι ἐν τῇ φαρμακείᾳ σου ἐπλανήθησαν πάντα τὰ ἔθνη," in which the word used for 'sorceries' or 'magic spell' is 'φαρμακεια', 'pharmakeia'. Ring any bells? As explained more fully in the Non Toxic Home blog, the term means 'potion', 'poison', 'medicine', 'drug', or 'spell'.

Well then, since we are in a spiritual battle, let us draw inspiration from the Old-Testament prophets who railed against the idolatry of political leaders... and killed them! Yes, Moses killed Pharaoh and his army, and Elijah killed Ahab and Jezebel and their son Ahaziah, and oh yes, 450 false prophets and a hundred men at arms. Not with the weapons of the world, but by the Word of God.

Elijah's victory over the establishment priests is one

of the crowning moments of Bible history and, like the snake battle in Pharaoh's court, offers compelling prophecy as to how the COVID story will play out. He challenges the corrupt priesthood to a contest on Mount Carmel. They are to build an altar and call on their god Baal to send down fire upon it. Then Elijah will build an altar of his own and call on the Lord to send down fire. "The god who sends down fire, is god" (*1 Kings* 18:24).

Elijah's opponents fail in their call to Baal, though they cut their own flesh to ribbons in the attempt, but Elijah spectacularly succeeds, after which he orders the people to seize his opponents and let none escape. A massacre ensues, filling the Kishon Valley with blood.

Clearly, the people of Israel were seething with rage for all they and their kin had suffered from this cult, and the mob justice they delivered was swift and merciless.

Imagine, then, the fury that will be unleashed when Justice befalls this current crop of miscreants who, worse than cutting their *own* flesh, sought to cut *ours*, and that of our children, and to profit from it, who imposed locked-down misery and incarceration on the people while they partied in high places. What revenge will be exacted for the elderly parents who died alone in care homes, for the lives lost to addiction and suicide, the ruined livelihoods, murdered businesses, and shattered dreams?

And what price shall be demanded for loved ones injured, crippled, or killed by injection, for children sacrificed, athletes maimed, musicians silenced, and a generation traumatised for life? And all to make the obscenely rich even richer and their middle-class functionaries a little more comfortable, while the public purse was looted to fill the coffers of ministers' friends.

WITH SO MUCH BLOOD CRYING OUT FROM THE GROUND, WHAT COURT COULD DISPENSE JUSTICE FOR ALL OF THAT?!

THE NEPHILIM DESCENDANTS

Truth is stranger than fiction, it is said. And, as Shakespeare reminds us, "There are more things in Heaven and Earth, Horatio/ Than are dreamt of in your philosophy" (*Hamlet*, I.v). Therefore, until the hidden is made known (*Luke* 8:17) and prophecies cease (*1 Corinthians* 13:9-10), permit me to talk of things unseen as well as seen.

The first recorded attempt to defile our genetic inheritance is described in *Genesis* 6:4: "The sons of God went to the daughters of men and had children by them. They were the heroes of old, men of renown."

With words like 'hero' and 'renown', it makes this hybrid race — part angel and part human, and known as the 'Nephilim' — sound somehow noble and virtuous, but what if the passage were instead rendered, "Rebellious angels raped women, and their resultant offspring grew up to be murderous bandits, men of ill repute."

Going by the excellent analysis of author Ryan Pitterson, in his 'Beginning and End' podcast series on the Nephilim, the latter seems more accurate. For Satan knew, as decreed in *Genesis* 3:15, that a descendant of the woman would arise to destroy him, and therefore initiated this defilement of the daughters of Eve as a "large scale, widespread assault on human DNA, to make humanity something other than image-bearers of God and by doing this, potentially corrupting the lineage that would lead to the Messiah."

Though these Nephilim were wiped out by the Flood, a trace may have persisted through the wife of Noah's son, Ham. This mutant race were a "wicked demon brood," in the words of third-century theologian, Tertullian (c. 155-240 AD), whose "great business is the ruin of mankind."

Could this demon-infused bloodline explain the resurgence of the psychopath in our age, someone who can kill without remorse, someone who shares not our natural instinct to love others as we love ourselves? When we witness people behaving with unspeakable cruelty, we may say, "They have a screw loose," but could that loose screw be the genetic disposition of a Nephilim descendant?

If Satan's idea was to corrupt God's image in Mankind by hybridizing our race, and the Flood set him back, wouldn't he try again? It's a question worth considering in light of Pfizer CEO Albert Bourla's boast, in a November 2021 interview, that mRNA injections—the technology used in COVID 'vaccines'—are a doorway to 'gene editing'. What mythical beast would he have in mind?

PART VI

A NEW EARTH

A more unequal match can hardly be.
Christian must fight an angel, but you see
The valiant man by handling sword and shield
Doth make him, though a dragon, quit the field.

— JOHN BUNYAN, *THE PILGRIM'S*
PROGRESS

The bewildering pace of authoritarianism in recent years has put us on the back foot, scrambling to make sense of it all. That seems part of the plan, to knock us out before we realize what hit us, a cynical replay of the 'Shock and Awe' strategy the U.S. military rained down on the people of Iraq in 2003.

But what happens when the autocrats have played their last hand? There will be a great and mighty reckoning that not only overthrows them but the system that spawned them. Each member of the oppressors' network, at every level of command, will find nowhere to hide. There will be no place of refuge from a people ready to assert their Birthright and to abolish forms of Government that were destructive of the Life, Liberty, and Pursuit of Happiness championed in the *Declaration of Independence*.

A similar outcome is foreseen in **Magna Carta** where, in Article 61, if the governing power "offend in any respect against any man" and redress is not given within 40 days, we may "assail" it "in every way possible, with the support of the whole community of the land" and seize any of its lands, buildings, or property (Article 61).

Will it involve violence, which I understand in the narrow sense of conventional violence to people? I have no moral argument to offer here, only a practical one, that the state is better funded and equipped than we are. If we are playing to our strengths, it's not our best option. We also have Christ's admonition that those who live by the sword will die by the sword (*Luke* 22:36). However, if police forces and military are true to their oaths, defend fundamental Rights, and defy dictatorship, some righteous violence may unfold.

In any case, prophets have greater forces at our disposal than mere weaponry. Moses wielded plague and wiped out an army, Elijah killed the entire house of Ahab and all the false prophets of Baal, slew Queen Jezebel with a prophet's decree, and called down fire from the sky to destroy two detachments of soldiers (2 *Kings* 1:9-12).

His successor, Elisha, blinded enemy soldiers, unleashed panic among a besieging army, and thwarted every ambush attempted by invaders, all without lifting a sword (2 *Kings* 6-7).

> "The man of God sent word to the king of Israel: 'Beware of passing that place, because the Arameans are going down there.' So the king of Israel checked on the place indicated by the man of God. Time and again Elisha warned the king, so that he was on his guard in such places. This enraged the king of Aram. He summoned his officers and demanded of them, 'Tell me! Which of us is on the side of the king of Israel?' 'None of us, my lord the king,' said one of his officers, 'but Elisha, the prophet who is in Israel, tells the king of Israel the very words you speak in your bedroom.' "
>
> — *2 KINGS* 6:9-12

For other parallels to our story's conclusion, see *Exodus* 7:12, 14:28, *1 Kings* 18:40, 22:37-38, *2 Kings 1*, 9:32-33, and *Esther* 7:9-10.

Then, instead of us trembling before governments, they shall tremble before us, wondering what horror shall befall them if they cross the elect and trigger our prophets' curses. Quoting from my epic poem, *Elijah*,...

For what can armour, helmet, sword, or shield
In that arena do where prophets wield
Their power, and works of angels are unsealed?
This is a battle of another field.

But I am not defining property damage as violence. If any property or infrastructure serves the tyrants and corporate aggressors, or funnels the flow of corrupt funds or serums, then it is fair game. Its destruction and sabotage are holy and righteous acts, akin to Christ's zeal when he overturned corrupt tables in his father's house (*Mark* 11:15-16).

THE TIME OF TRUE PROPHETS

And when he has tried me, I shall come forth as gold.

—*JOB* 23:10

Of course, the oppressors will not hesitate to wield violence themselves, for violence is their native language. They even paint their response to COVID in the language of war, though an alleged virus can be no more injured by their weaponry than water stabbed with a knife, nor visible to their surveillance than a fart in the wind.

In H.G. Wells' novel, *The War of the Worlds*, it is a pathogen that saves the people of Earth from alien invaders who sought to wipe them out or enslave them. (Excuse the plot spoiler if you didn't know.) Well, we have had our sovereignty invaded too, and by creatures who in their behaviour and demeanour are no longer recognizable as our own species, aliens who would alienate us from the inalienable.

But it won't work. I guarantee you. In the end, it won't work. Their end shall be what their deeds deserve. Moreover, we have unseen allies fighting alongside us.

> "When the servant of the man of God got up and went out early the next morning, an army with horses and chariots had surrounded the city. 'Oh no, my lord! What shall we do?' the servant asked. 'Don't be afraid,' the prophet answered. 'Those who are with us are more than those who are with them.' And Elisha prayed, 'Open his eyes, Lord, so that he may see.' Then the Lord opened the servant's eyes, and he looked and saw the hills full of horses and chariots of fire all around Elisha. As the enemy came down toward him, Elisha prayed to the Lord, 'Strike this army with blindness.' So he struck them with blindness, as Elisha had asked."
>
> — 2 KINGS 6:15-18

Therefore, as fear is assuaged when barriers of perception are removed, let us pray to receive that sight with which Elisha and his servant were gifted.

Our revolution will also move in prophetic prayer, wielding intercessory 'keys' in Heaven that open and close things on Earth. "Truly, I say to you, whatever you bind on Earth shall be bound in Heaven, and whatever you loose on Earth shall be loosed in Heaven" (*Matthew* 16:19).

So take your stand before the throne of the Most High and claim the keys that shut down the toxic flows of funds and serums, that unlock the bank vaults of tyrants and spill their contents to the poor and hungry. Murderous weapons we destroy, broken bodies we mend, rulers seated on high we topple from their already tilting thrones.

As exemplified in the lives of Moses and Elijah, we call down Heaven's intervention in the overthrow of leaders and their functionaries. Moses did according to the word of God in his dealings with Pharaoh, but the Lord also did according to the word of Moses (*Exodus* 8:13,31). As Dave Mason reminds us, in his aforementioned *Age of Prophecy* novels, "What the righteous decree, the Holy One carries out."

And that status of righteousness is not because we've had a good life or done the right things. It is a gift conferred on us from above. Listen to the testimony of John Bunyan:

"But one day, as I was passing in the field, and that too with some dashes of conscience, fearing lest all was not right, suddenly this sentence fell upon my soul, Thy righteousness is in Heaven; and methought withal, I saw, with the eyes of my soul, Jesus Christ at God's right hand; there, I say, is my righteousness; so that wherever I was, or whatever I was a-doing, God could not say of me, he lacks my righteousness, for that was just before him. I also saw, moreover, that it was not my good frame of heart that made my righteousness better, nor yet my bad frame of heart that made my righteousness worse; for my righteousness was Jesus Christ himself, the same yesterday, and today, and for ever (*Hebrews* 13:8)."[1]

Bunyan understood that, as a member of the body of Christ, he was "flesh of his flesh, and bone of his bone" and that, "if he and I were one, then his righteousness was mine, his merits mine, his victory also mine." Bunyan could imagine God saying, "Behold! My son is by me, and upon him I look, and will deal with thee according as I am pleased with him."

Yes, God will deal with me and you according as he is pleased with Christ. Therefore, doubt not your worthiness to carry the divine flame, to be the Lord's messenger of holy Rights declarations. You are clothed in him, and all his merits are yours! And if you ever *do* doubt your fitness for the task, lean on *his* immortal worthiness instead.

Nor do not worry when oil- and stock-markets appear eternally bullish, when billionaires make a killing literally and metaphorically, and the deities of 'pharmakeia' glean extortionate and extortioned profits, nor that the forces of authoritarianism appear to be winning. These are but temporary trends. Moses didn't bring down Pharaoh overnight; it took a sustained campaign in which Egypt cajoled and threatened, relented and reversed, bargained and broke its promises. We know how earthly power works.

But the autocrats' ball is over, the writing's on the wall, their downfall is inevitable. We are not fighting this battle alone, equipped only with a mortal's instruments of hand and voice, though these are powerful in themselves, but with decrees of divine enforcement!

CASTING OUT FEAR

We don't do fear as followers of the Lord Jesus.

— MARK GORING, CANADIAN
CATHOLIC PRIEST

Stories need villains. Our modern myths testify to this. Who would Harry Potter be without Voldemort; Batman without Joker; or Luke Skywalker without Darth Vader? Now, with so many villains at large, we have a target-rich training ground for honing our tyrant-slaying skills. These include the utterance of Rights declarations, knowing that when we do so, we invoke the Creator's authority...

He does as he pleases
With the powers of Heaven

And the peoples of the Earth.
No one can hold back his hand
Or say to him: 'What have you done?'

— *DANIEL* 4:35

Most in the magical community of Harry Potter's world would not speak the name, Voldemort, instead referring to him as "he who must not be named." Some realities seem too horrific to face, which was my experience in hearing British funeral director John O'Looney, a man who works at the coal-face of life and death, bear witness both to the genocide already unleashed by the British government—with the NHS as its accomplice—and to even worse planned.

It's terrifying stuff, worse than any horror film I have seen or Hollywood could imagine, not for solo viewing perhaps, and certainly not before bedtime. It put me in a fever of fear, but it also made me more aware of the devil's schemes (2 *Corinthians* 2:11) and, after the fever passed, more immune to another onslaught.

O'Looney says in the interview, "I'm not frightened of dying. I'm frightened of living like this." Well, I *am* frightened of dying, but would still choose death over a life enslaved. If we are facing a genocidal cult—and it appears that we are—then we are all targeted already. Better to be targeted for expressing our views than anonymously crushed under the wheels of an imperial juggernaut.

With Christians the world over, I yearn for Jesus' return now more than ever. May it be soon, O Lord, for your people are sore distressed. I feel overmatched by an enemy who is relentless and seems unstoppable. I am even tempted in moments of weakness to ascribe to this enemy the omniscience and omnipotence that are only yours!

Yet I remind myself and the Reader that he who is in us is greater than he who is in them (*1 John* 4:4). I have never been keen on "us and them" language before but it fits now, and it has nothing to do with medical status. The 'us' are we who always wanted to be left alone to get on with our lives, and the 'they' are those who want to imprison us, enslave us, torture us, rape, maim, mutilate, and murder us, and even tear out our hearts. 'THEY' are "The Hierarchy Exploiting You" (I forget who coined this acronym.) We therefore claim in Heaven, that they are bestowed on Earth, the protections of *Psalm* 91, not just from "the pestilence that stalks in the darkness" but also from "the arrow that flies by day."

What antidotes are there to fear? One is to realize that fear fantasies are not prophecies. How many of us have taken flights and imagined the plane falling from the sky, or swum in the sea and imagined a shark attack? I gather too from a friend more experienced in this, that the kind of fear fever I went through is something of a rite of passage in this arena.

I also contextualize fear with the help of Shakespeare's famed lines in *As You Like It*...

All the world's a stage
And all the men and women merely players.
They have their exits and their entrances…

Consider the actor playing Hamlet. His character enters in Act I and exits after Hamlet's death in Act V, but the actor himself does not die. His simultaneous offstage life is untouched by the Danish court and its deadly politics.

In the same way, we actors, clothed in mortal skin to play a role on the world's stage, have a greater life and existence off-world, outliving our exit and preceding our entrance. This greater life is untouched by the make-believe, the theatre of this world. What's more, we have a direct line to the Playwright who made this stage, and we may call on him to write new scenes, summon new allies, shine new lights, and even to change the plot. Quoting again from my epic poem, *Elijah*,…

How false our fears may be, whether in thought
Or dream, and do they not often precede,
As in this case, fulfilment of hopes sought?
Fears tempt us to inaction, to concede,
Or test if we are resolute in deed
To see through phantom menaces, transcend
Illusory distractions, reach our end.

There's a physical metaphor we can invoke too, called The Unbendable Arm Exercise, which I learned from soul teacher, Darren Eden: Make a fist and crook your arm, with elbow by your side, so that your forearm is parallel to the floor, knuckles facing downward. Ask a friend to try and push your fist up to your shoulder, and try to resist them. Now do the same again, but instead of trying to resist them, pick a point on the wall and imagine a beam of light going from your fist to that point. Your arm becomes unbendable!

What does this mean in an era of dictatorship? That when we gaze upon the object of our love—love of constitution, love of God's image in Man, reverence for our ancestors who loved us so much that they wrote these declarations to protect us—then the fears that seek to bend us are rendered powerless.

I recall the wise words of the late Vladimir Zelenko MD, the much maligned doctor who was among the first to see through, and call out, the 'COVID' deceptions...

"Each human-being is being given a choice right now. The choice is: 'Do I give into the fear or not?' And you have to have a mechanism in place to deal with the fear. Otherwise, it overtakes you. So for some people it's faith. For me, it's faith. So if I ever find myself in a fear state, I realize that **anxiety can only live in the psychological space where God is absent.** So if I fill the void with the consciousness of the divine, and that suppresses my anxiety, what I've done is taken that potentially negative event and I've used it as a motivation for spiritual growth. And that's one choice. The other is, you get into the fear and it causes you to go down the slippery slope of psychological co-dependence on human beings and on vaccines and on the whims of man. And it's obvious to me which will have a better outcome."

I remember, too, that the devil must flee from us when we resist him (*James* 4:7)—now, that's a statement we may call 'Law'—and that we have authority to overcome all the power of the enemy (*Luke* 10:19).

Above all, love casts out fear, and love is stronger than death. We love our inalienable Rights, and we love the immortal documents on which they are written. Even if we walk through the Valley of the Shadow of Death, the Lord is obliged by his own promises to uphold us as we uphold this love.

"If you follow your conscience, that stops the devil in his tracks, because he doesn't know how to handle it," attests former Salt Lake City police officer, Eric Moutsos, in a December 2021 interview on the Sheriff Mack Show. "He doesn't have authority over you when you follow your God-given conscience. *God* has authority over you when you follow what's inside of your heart."

And if Satan has no authority over us, much less do his lackeys. When we stand in the authority of Christ and say, "I do not consent," we wield an otherworldly power against Satan and his operatives. As the *Strawman* documentary reminds us, "They always need your consent, and this is where your power really lies. With knowledge always comes power—the power not to fear, the power to take a stand against anyone or any corporation that threatens you, the power to say No."

Moutsos acknowledges this is the 'narrow path'
(*Matthew* 7:14)...

"You need to follow your conscience because that is the
light of Christ inside of you, that is the Word of God
inside of you. And if you do that, it's going to be hard.
God never says it's going to be easy. That road, when
you follow your conscience, that's going to be a lonely
road. But that's the whole test, that's the whole reason
why we're here on Earth."

Though our faith is under assault like never before,...

"God will have your back. He's bound. That's a gift. He
wants to bless us. He wants to show us, he wants to
prove that he's the one in charge. Right now is the test.
We've grown up reading all of these scriptures our
whole lives. Now it's test time. Who are you going to
turn to? What god are you going to look to when the
going gets tough?"

The Satanic forces could not have pressed their agenda
this far unless the Almighty had extended their room for
manoeuvre. Though they always sought to effect a
genocide, they were kept in abeyance until the appointed
time. Perhaps the timing of that time had something to
do with our readiness to face it. I dare say none of us *feels*
ready, but perhaps our life experiences thus far have
prepared us. Then, if the Holy One has temporarily
shifted the barriers in Satan's favour, then that same Lord

of Hosts is Lord of Barriers and can mount them protectively around us.

Bear in mind, too, that the authorities are deathly afraid of us! And with far better reason.

Thrice is he armed that hath his quarrel just,
And he but naked, though locked up in steel,
Whose conscience with injustice is corrupted.

— SHAKESPEARE, *HENRY VI, PART II*

Their acts of censorship alone show how desperate they are to hide from the light, and how fearful. They are weak, they are cowards, cowering in the dark until the inevitable day when Justice finds them. No amount of riches or apparent security, nor all the sunshine of an island beach, could dispel the cold fear in their hearts, and nor will their torment end with their deaths.

Finally, on the subject of fear, I recall my favourite scene in Homer's *The Odyssey*, when Odysseus, the great warrior-strategist and hero of the Trojan War, is back at last in his Greek homeland of Ithaca. In Book 22, he and his son Telemachus, aided by Odysseus' swineherd and his cattle foreman, are pitted in a fight to the death against scores of men who, during his absence, had plundered his house, bedded his maids, and made a bid for his wife, Penelope.

When Odysseus runs out of arrows during the fight and sees that one of his enemies has managed to find some weapons, the "master of battle... felt his knees go slack,/ his heart sank." But, taking up spears, and with divine help, the four slay every remaining suitor.

Brothers and Sisters, the pulse may quicken, palms sweat, and knees tremble when the odds seem insurmountable but, like Odysseus who wins back his home, his Birthright, and his wife, we shall win back our Rights that await the hero's return to reclaim them.

PART VII

OUR BRUSH WITH FALSE AUTHORITY

The welfare of the people in particular has always been the alibi of tyrants... but in truth, the very ones who make use of such alibis know they are lies; they leave to their intellectuals on duty the chore of believing in them and of proving that religion, patriotism, and justice need for their survival the sacrifice of freedom.

— ALBERT CAMUS, SPEECH DELIVERED DEC. 7, 1955, AT A BANQUET IN HONOUR OF EDUARDO SANTOS, POLITICIAN AND EDITOR OF *EL TIEMPO*, WHO HAD BEEN DRIVEN OUT OF COLOMBIA BY THE DICTATORSHIP.

You may find the following alarming, but it gets better...

You wake up one morning to find the lights don't come on. Oh dear, a power cut. You'll have to boil water on the gas ring this morning. You go to the sink to fill a pot with water, but when you turn the tap on, only a trickle comes out, and then nothing. One flush of the toilet, and then no more. What the hell is going on?

You turn on your phone, there's some battery left. Find out what's happening. No phone signal. Alarmed, you look outside. Your neighbours are starting to gather on the street, trying in vain to get their dogs to stop barking, asking each other if they know anything, if anyone received a notice from the council. None did. At this point, a few are getting in their cars and driving off or walking hurriedly away with packed suitcases.

It is not long before a mechanical vibration fills the air. You look up. There are military helicopters overhead. The ground starts to shake. Armoured vehicles are driving along the street, accompanied by police cars with flashing lights. You and your neighbours rush back inside and lock the doors. But it is too late.

Your friends tried to warn you totalitarianism was coming, tried to warn you the government's COVID response was a ruse designed to kill and destroy, but you didn't listen. Those people were conspiracy theorists, covidiots, good for a laugh but not much else. No, you trusted the BBC, you sat glued to the television day after day to be bombarded with nightmarish scenarios about a new disease or a new variant. You heeded the messages to your mobile phone from the NHS telling you what to do with your body, you even clicked on those NHS messages pasted onto social media everywhere.

But there's no time to think about all that now. Masked men in black fatigues, armed with machine guns, are swarming over your street, going from house to house, rounding up anyone who can't or won't show their papers or QR code. The detained are taken to concentration camps to be enslaved, harvested for their pristine internal organs, forcibly injected, or otherwise disappeared. The circle has closed and, like thrashing fish scooped up in a net, the population is doomed.

Same are raped and kept as sex slaves. Some choose suicide over captivity or starvation. Meanwhile, the choicest land, houses, and vehicles now vacated are rewarded to the autocrats and their favourites, to complicit military and police personnel, and to compliant citizens, much as King William took the lands of the conquered English and parcelled them out among the Norman nobility in the 11th century.

Until that day, they had taken away your freedoms with your tacit consent, telling you it was for your own good and for the health of the nation. You dutifully wore your mask in shops and on public transport, shelled out for a barrage of meaningless tests, paid the exorbitant prices to stay in their shitty quarantine hotels, answered the summons to get shot, and let them compel your children to receive the life-altering toxin too. Was it all an elaborate con? Yes, but now it's too late to put the evil genie back in his bottle.

For you had conditioned the government to learn it

could get away with all this, that you were docile and willing to be pushed around, that it could strip your rights with impunity, that it could literally get away with murder. They did all this while lying to you, scaring you, and turning your island nation into a prison which you could only leave and enter with a special pass issued by the warden. But now, they don't need to pretend any more, the trap has sprung, and overnight you have been enslaved.

What am I doing here? Am I Fiver in *Watership Down* warning that the warren is about to be annihilated? Am I a Cassandra trying to tell fellow Brits that the vaccines are a Trojan horse? How long before an increasingly desperate British government pulls the trigger on such a totalitarian plan?

I have written this scenario not as a prophecy but as a warning if the government's sprint to totalitarianism is not checked—totalitarianism on a level and genocidal scale never seen before. I write it too as a call to mutiny in our armed forces, that if weaponry is to be used, to turn it on the autocrats and their operatives, not on the population you are supposed to serve and protect. And if there is prophecy in what I have described, may it be self-negating, not self-fulfilling. Nor, when I say 'you', do I mean the Reader of this book, but as a literary device to take you to the scene as one might watch a movie.

But understand this, that we are in the fight of our lives, a fight for the soul of Mankind, a fight which, like

Moses and the Israelites of old, **WE WILL WIN**. As I write this, a surge of joy affirms that yes, this is prophecy! The evil powers won't win this. Though they seem to be winning now, their downfall is written. Keep that in mind, follow it like the star that led the three kings to Jesus. That star is shining in the heavens, and they cannot pull it down, shift its position in the sky, or tell it to stop shining!

Here's what we do in the meantime...

ASSERTING AND UPHOLDING
OUR RIGHTS

Disobedience is the true foundation of liberty. The obedient must be slaves.

— HENRY DAVID THOREAU,
CIVIL DISOBEDIENCE

So now for the rubber-meets-the-road moment where we suit action to word, and word to action. "Hold the line, stand your ground, uphold the rule of law, step into your sovereignty. The law is all there to protect you, but you're not going to get protected unless you know what it is and you uphold it," to repeat Anna de Buisseret's conclusion to her Parliament-Square interview.

By now, we're well versed in what the True Law is, but what do we do, say, or write when we face the agents and structures of legal lawlessness? Of course, there will be an element of improvisation in any situation, but I here endeavour to assemble best practices so we may be as thoroughly prepared and defended as possible.

And take our stand as *early* as possible! From bitter experience, I have learned it is always best to be sovereign at the outset of any encounter. It's so much more time-consuming, expensive, and exhausting to recover a situation afterwards. As the saying goes, "An ounce of prevention is better than a pound of cure."

Dolores Cahill is exemplary in this regard, especially when it comes to asserting Travel Rights. In her August 2021 interview with Clive de Carle, she explains how to deal with people "dressed up" as airport security, police, army, or judge if they are trying to obstruct her. It's worth listening to the whole interview, but here's a summary of the main actions she takes...

1. If dealing with several individuals, ask, "Which one of you is taking the responsibility for doing this?"

2. Ask that person, including any judge, if they are acting under their Oath. They have to answer yes. Tell them you accept their Oath.
   Remember that the British Constable's Oath binds police to "upholding fundamental human rights" and "the law of the land" (not Admiralty code or corporate policy), so **once they answer yes, they can only uphold Common Law, and are not entitled to enforce acts and statutes.**

3. Find out their name.

4. Tell them the Rule of Law applies to you, which means you have the inalienable Rights of Freedom of Travel, Freedom of Speech, and bodily integrity.

5. Tell them any attempt to interfere with your freedom, or to infringe on your inalienable Right to Travel, is regarded under the Law as kidnapping or unlawful detention and carries a long prison sentence. "So if you're in the airport and they say they want to quarantine you, you say, 'No, I do not consent. Do not touch me. And then you tell them, 'I am free to go.' "

6. Inform them that if they touch you, it's assault, punishable by a prison term. "No-one can touch your body without your consent."

7. Inform them that if you are taken to prison, you will bring proceedings against them for unlawful detention and ensure they are personally and individually charged.

8. Understand, and tell them if necessary, that there is no indemnity or protection from individual liability in their role as police officer or judge.

Cahill has also interceded over the phone for detainees taken to a police station. It makes sense for each of us to prepare a hotline for ourselves, and the U.K. group Lawyers for Liberty (lawyersforliberty.uk) offers referral to 'freedom-friendly' law firms. I have also listed them in the Resources section (Appendix VIII) at the back of this book.

When it comes to international travel, imposition of tests, quarantines, and medical disclosures is deeply unlawful, and we are irrevocably empowered to refuse consent. "They know that what they're doing is criminal and unlawful," says Cahill, "infringing, forcing someone to have a PCR test when they don't consent, implying that it's mandatory quarantine at the airport when actually they are trying to entrap people and coerce them and deceive them into entering a contract which is not explicit and is misrepresented."

She continues, "What is being presented to us now, is that there is a health problem, but really that is masking a rule-of-law issue..." Anyone attempting to cause us harm, loss, or injury, whether a president or prime minister or someone dressed as police or judge or army, anyone who misrepresents the law or unlawfully detains another (kidnapping), has committed a criminal act, says Cahill. They are responsible in their private and personal capacity, and "can be sued and put in prison for the harm they do. There is no indemnity." Boris Johnson, she points out, is guilty of treason.

We can also learn from the stand taken by British life coach and fitness trainer, Harry Thomas, when landing in the U.K. from Brazil. Refusing to be quarantined, he was threatened with fines, unlawfully arrested by British police, and held for five hours in a cell. But, as he relates in a video testimony, by sticking to his inalienable Rights, he was released without quarantine or fine. "I am now a free man, no quarantine, no £2000 10-day hotel prison service, all charges dropped, and now I will be going after the individuals that harassed me and the officers that went against their oath."

He explains "how we are tricked and feared into decisions that we do not want to make" and too often give up our Rights when pressured into it, but "we must stick up for our truths and Rights and always keep our power." Here's the key takeaway from his testimony:

"BY LAW, THEY CAN NOT ENFORCE ANY RULES AND RESTRICTIONS ON TO US, UNLESS WE AGREE TO THEM."

Therefore, whenever any costumed one seeks to impose a rule, you can ask for Proof that you have consented to it which, of course, they can never supply.

INTERACTING WITH POLICE

It's helpful to know the standards expected of police officers according to the U.K. College of Policing's *Code of Ethics*. There, each officer pledges, "I will act with self-control and tolerance," **"Respect the rights of all individuals,"** "Give and carry out lawful orders only," "Treat information with respect, and access or disclose it only in the proper course of my duties," and will not "abuse my position." Also, and this is especially important in the current environment, each officer promises to "Report, challenge or take action against the conduct of colleagues which has fallen below the standards of professional behaviour."

We also have *Magna Carta* to lean on, where "We will appoint as justices, constables, sheriffs, or bailiffs only such as know the law of the realm and mean to observe it well" (Article 45). Nor may any official "place a man on trial upon his own unsupported statement without producing credible witnesses to the truth of it" (Article 38).

Here's some more practical advice I gleaned from the documentary, *Strawman*...

1. Avoid entering into a verbal contract with the police, such as saying "yes" if they ask, "Do you understand?" What they really mean is, "Do you stand under me?" You do not! Use phrases like "I do not understand" and "I do not consent."

2. Avoid giving your name or date of birth. This means they can't do their paperwork. Ask, "Am I obliged to give you my details?" They have to answer no. If they say you do have to, they're lying and going against their Oath.

3. If helpful, read aloud the following, from Section 26 of the **Criminal Justice and Courts Act** (2015), where: any constable who "exercises the powers and privileges of a constable improperly," or to the detriment of another person, is liable on conviction to **imprisonment for up to 14 years and a fine.**

4. You don't have to engage in conversation with police. If they detain you without reasonable grounds, they're in breach of their Oath.

5. Ask, "Am I detained?" or "Am I free to go?"

6. If you are arrested, the custody officer at the police station must explain your Rights which

include: telling someone where you are, and getting free legal advice.

In one of his TikTok videos, Chris Edward advises those who live in Britain, America, Canada, Australia, New Zealand, or any other Common-Law jurisdiction:

"If someone asks you a question, whether it's a policeman, someone in a court room or a council, you can simply say, 'I would like to remain silent.' If they continuously pressure you, say, 'Do I have the right to remain silent?' They will say, 'Yes, of course you do.'

"And then remain silent. Do not say your name, and do not sign anything... If you do not speak your name, you are not entering yourself into their jurisdiction, and thus you are completely free... You do not have to answer questions. You do not have to sign anything."

Protests

The U.K.-based group, Liberty, have additional suggestions if you attend protests...

1. Leave your phone at home, and only bring an old phone with essential numbers on it. Make sure it is locked with a passcode and switch off any facial and fingerprint unlocking technology. You may wish to bring a portable phone charger if you have one.

2. Bring a notepad and pen to keep notes of any issues and to record the shoulder numbers of police officers.

3. Write important phone numbers on your arm. Include an emergency contact, a friend or family member, a solicitor with specialist knowledge about protests, and the Protest Support line operated by Green & Black Cross (07946 541 511), a project run by volunteers to help with legal matters arising from protest and actions.

4. Bring earplugs, a washcloth, and first-aid supplies.

5. Look out for Legal Observers wearing high-vis jackets. They are independent volunteers who monitor police, gather evidence of arrests, and counter any intimidation or unlawful behaviour protesters might face. They may be able to provide support. They will also have phone numbers of specialist solicitors.

Filming the police

If police become hostile, it is a good idea to film them. They're not allowed to prevent you. The U.K. Metropolitan Police's own website states, "Members of the public and the media do not need a permit to film or photograph in public places and police have no power to stop them filming or photographing incidents or police personnel."

This principle is even more firmly stated in a 2010 letter from Chief Constable Andrew Trotter, sent to all police stations, which reminds officers "citizen journalism is a feature of modern life…" and that…

> "There are no powers prohibiting the taking of photographs, film or digital images in a public place. Therefore members of the public and press should not be prevented from doing so… Once an image has been recorded, the police have no power to delete or confiscate it without a court order."

In the united States, the Right to film cops is founded on the **First Amendment**'s Freedom of the Press, that whatever our eyes can see in public, our camera can record.

Searches

If an officer intends to search you, they can only do so with objectively "reasonable suspicion" under the *Police and Criminal Evidence Act* (*PACE*) (1984), and must clearly state the reason and what they're looking for. The required set of procedures are encompassed by the mnemonic, GOWISELY…

- Grounds—a clear explanation of the reasons for the officer's search, i.e., why he finds you suspicious.
- Object—what the officer will be looking for.

- Warrant—a warrant card to be produced if the officer is not in uniform.
- Identity—the officer must state their name and collar number.
- Station—the officer must identify the station at which they're based.
- Entitlement—the officer must inform you of your entitlement to a copy of the stop/search record.
- Legal—the officer must specify the legislation under which they're searching you.
- You—the Officer must clearly explain to you that you are being detained for the purpose of a search.

"If a police officer insists on searching you, do not resist," counsels the *Strawman* documentary. "Tell the officer you do not agree with the search and are being searched under duress." If the police do not follow the requirements of **PACE**, the search is unlawful, and an assault charge can be filed against the officer or officers.

If the officer is looking for drugs, then the **Drugs Act** (2005) determines, "**A drug offence search shall not be carried out unless the appropriate consent has been given in writing**" (Para. 3, subsection 3a).

INTERACTING WITH YOUR EMPLOYER

Monsters exist, but they are too few in number to be truly dangerous. More dangerous are the common men, the functionaries ready to believe and to act without asking questions.

— PRIMO LEVI

When governments are checked from imposing direct medical mandates, they can usually get servile employers to do their dirty work for them. By imposing treatment or testing as a condition of employment, these companies are effectively changing work contracts retrospectively and unilaterally. Then, like citizens of ancient Rome who had offended an emperor, the employee must choose either to take poison or to fall on the sword of financial ruin.

The **UDHR** states, "Everyone has the right to work"

(Article 23). This is expanded in the **ICESCR** where "In no case may a people be deprived of its own means of subsistence" (Part I, Article 1, Para. 2). Furthermore, the work must be freely chosen (Part III, Article 6, Para. 1) and come with "just and favourable conditions" (Part III, Article 7).

Employees are now being confronted with, to say the least, hostile work environments, and some, when already facing financial insecurity, are having to pay lawyers to uphold Justice against their oppressive taskmasters. There are some important steps you can take before it comes to that, though. The most obvious is to write a letter to your employer demanding respect for the contract of employment between you, which says nothing about vaccination or medical testing.

As Anna de Buisseret explains in another interview, "An employment contract is a contract between two people, equal parties to the contract. One party doesn't get to unilaterally impose a change in the contractual terms. You have to consent to it."

So a letter to your employer could say, "You cannot change my contract of employment without my agreement, and if you seek to do so, I will have Rights under constructive or unfair dismissal law."

You could also demand to know the medical status of all other employees, including all cases of AIDS, hepatitis, flu, measles, and mumps, and insist other employees are sectioned off if they have any illness that could spread, including the common cold. Conclude with "I would like to reach a satisfactory conclusion between us, but if that's not possible, I will have no choice but to raise this matter as an official grievance, and take legal action as may be necessary."

Another step de Buisseret recommends is to demand the employer give you an individual risk assessment under Regulation 3 of *The Management of Health and Safety at Work Regulations* (1999). This places a legal statutory duty on the employer to provide an individual risk assessment conducted by a qualified occupational-health physician. That assessment will include examination of the psychological harm of being in a coercive and hostile work environment.

The next stage would be to bring a grievance, and if the grievance is not upheld, to appeal it. "If the appeal is not upheld, don't resign. Consider the contract to be breached and bring a claim for constructive dismissal and breach of contract," de Buisseret advises.

In the specific case of healthcare practitioners seeking religious exemptions, refer to the letter in Appendix IV.

INTERACTING WITH YOUR CHILD'S SCHOOL

If there is anything more heinous than getting employers to coerce people to be injected, it is using schools to coerce children! If that is what you're facing, Lawyers for Liberty has prepared a template letter for parents at lawyersforliberty.uk/schooljabs. You can also opt to join the group's Whistleblowers' Register, meaning you have established a record of when you contacted the group about this matter.

MASKS

If you read Laura Dodsworth's book, *A State of Fear,* you will realize that masking requirements in shops or public transport were never about protecting health but were the imposition of behavioural scientists who "like masks because they convey a message of 'solidarity'... entirely unrelated to the scientific evidence regarding transmission."

But face masks are a medical intervention and require informed consent. "If a medical intervention (i.e., mask wearing or testing) is mandated," explain Lawyers for Liberty on their website, "or if an individual is coerced or manipulated into providing consent to that medical intervention, it would be in direct violation of the principle of Informed Consent and would be a breach of that person's legal rights."

Not wearing a mask is one small act of resistance we

can all practise, knowing Law is on our side. According to Lawyers for Liberty, "you don't need to produce evidence of your reason for not wearing a mask. You can simply say, 'I am exempt.' If the other party does not respect this, they are guilty of discrimination and can be sued in court."

This is not really a principled stand, though, is it? Exempt from what? Why ascribe to the state any authority to make an unlawful demand in the first place? The same fraudulent bargain is struck when individuals get fake vaccination certificates or test results to satisfy official demands.

As we have seen, the **UDBHR** states, "Any **preventive**, diagnostic and therapeutic medical intervention is only to be carried out with the **prior, free and informed consent** of the person concerned, based on adequate information." Masks are posing as a preventive intervention and, as such, require Informed Consent. Furthermore, we are not required to comply with an Act or statute to which we have not consented, nor any decree issued by politician or bureaucrat.

It is more powerful and truthful to say instead, "I am not required to." The medical aggressors will have no answer for that because there is none. If they ask you for evidence of this, you can point out that they have just attempted to breach your Medical Confidentiality. This stance applies equally if you encounter intrusive healthcare professionals. As we have seen, under the **NHS** *Code*, they're not allowed to share our medical information even among *themselves* without our written permission, much less with Government, police, border agents, or venues.

You can also ask them to show you the law that says you have to wear a mask. In the highly unlikely event they produce anything, ask them to show you where you signed it. Without your signature, it's not worth the air it's written on.

JUDICIAL REVIEW IN BRITAIN

Whenever a U.K. public authority has acted unlawfully or with bias or procedural unfairness, you can complete claim form 'N461' to mount a legal challenge in the form of a Judicial Review. You'll need to do so within three months of the decision, action, or inaction you want to challenge, or six weeks for planning decisions. Or, if the authority has acted contrary to the *HRA*, complete claim form 'N1' and file it at the relevant court building.

FINES

With regard to fines, the English *Bill of Rights* (1689) remains in statute, and says, "That all Grants and Promises of Fines and Forfeitures of particular persons before Conviction are illegall and void." This builds on *Magna Carta*...

> "No free man shall be seized or imprisoned, or stripped of his rights or possessions, or outlawed or exiled, or in any way destroyed, nor will we proceed with force against him, or send others to do so, except by the lawful judgment of his peers or by the law of the land [Common Law]" (Article 39).

In short, no-one may fine you or take any of your property without presenting evidence and obtaining a conviction in a court with trial-by-jury. Nor may they tax you, but that's another book.

My investigations suggest that the most effective strategy to adopt when false authorities or, more accurately, corporations disguised as authorities, make demands or impose levies, is to reply with 'conditional acceptance' or 'conditional offer', meaning we will agree to a demand only on condition that the enforcer or debt collector supply certain Proofs.

For example, as the demand is addressed to the ALL-CAPS legal fiction 'PERSON', I can ask for Proof of the implicit claim that I am that 'PERSON' and not a Living Man. I can ask for Proof of their claim that the levy was the result of a lawful investigation unmarred by prejudice. I can ask for clarification on the meaning of a word. I can ask for verification of the debt asserted and for an Invoice with a human signature on it. I can ask for Proof of the obligation to pay. I can ask for the lawful, two-party Contract that put us in a commercial relationship in the first place, and so on.

As they cannot supply these Proofs, I demolish their pretensions. If, after that, they persist with further collection efforts, then I can start levying financial penalties against them for each infringement. As @thequeenoffreedom explains in a TikTok video,...

"They cannot provide a contract, because there isn't one. I have done this with my credit card. I've done this with my council tax, my water, gas, and electric. And you will treat them all exactly the same. So you will ask each and every one of them, 'First of all provide the contract.' "

She continues, "Remember the only law: cause no harm, cause no loss. By not paying unlawful bills and fines, you are not causing anyone any loss. The only loss there would be to the company, which is a corporation, and a corporation cannot be a victim."

Although these corporations don't deserve our attention, respect, or even the time of day, it is deemed dishonour if we fail to respond at all when a contract is offered. We remain in honour by giving a response, and as we do not outright refuse the demand, the corporate courts have no controversy in which they can get involved.

"All men are born equal, and so nobody has the right to command you, made demands of you, or force you to do anything," writes David E. Robinson in the powerful little book, *Meet Your Strawman*. "The most that anyone can do is make you an offer to perform. Even though they may say that is is an 'Order', or a 'Demand', or a 'Summons', it is in reality an offer which you are free to accept or not as you so choose."

Generally speaking, we want to bring our contracts, transactions, and communications into the 'Private', and that includes creating or joining private member associations. That too, is another book.

PART VIII

OUR OVERTHROW OF FALSE AUTHORITY

The soul is a spark, but sparks do not shine in the bright light of day. As darkness deepens, the soul reveals its hidden light.

— DAVE MASON, *THE LAMP OF DARKNESS*

As we uphold our Rights, let us applaud those who have already struck a fierce constitutional blow on our behalf, such as Anna de Buisseret and the Lawyers for Liberty team, who are serving their 170-page Notice of Liability on skin-piercers.

"What we're doing is identifying people who are breaking the law," says de Buisseret, "and we're serving them with a Notice of Liability which says to the individual, 'You personally are causing harm. You are in breach personally of not only the Common Law but of international treaties, the European Conventions, U.K. domestic law.' "

And she knows by instinct what our Bible prophecies attest:

"Anyone who thinks they're not going to be blamed, they're not going to be held accountable, does not know their history. What happened after the last war, people's courts were formed in all jurisdictions. People knew who the perpetrators were, knew who the complicit people were, in their local communities. They found them, they took them from their homes, they put them in court, they judged them, and they handed down the sentence."

THE NEW NAZI HUNTERS

The Spirit's wind will sweep the land,
Its reach from shore to shore,
The Earth will shake with thunderous sound,
Then hear my lions roar.

Turn upward your eyes to gaze upon
Heaven's open door.
I come for you, my ready bride,
And parted never more.

Look up, look up, my faithful ones.
Nigh is your reward.

— RAPTURE RESCUE, YOUTUBE
VIDEO, APR. 21, 2021

When Justice returns, prosecutors will invoke several articles of international Rights declarations, including the *Nuremberg Code*. The *Rome Statute* of the ICC will also play a prominent role. We have already looked at *Rome* Article 7, which lists Crimes against Humanity. These include "**persecution against any identifiable group**," apartheid, and "Imprisonment or other severe deprivation of physical liberty."

Rome Article 6, applying to Genocide, will also come into play. In addition to killing members of a group, the definition includes serious bodily or **mental harm**, inflicting "**conditions of life calculated to bring about its physical destruction**," and "measures intended to prevent births."

Rome Article 8, on War Crimes, should also keep prosecutors busy. Here, the definition includes biological experiments, subjecting persons "to physical mutilation or to medical or scientific experiments of any kind," and using poisonous "liquids, materials or devices."

Are we clear? Anna de Buisseret is fiercely joined in this cause by fellow Rights campaigner and former nurse, Kate Shemirani, who has put the autocrats on notice. "You are going to stand trial while there's breath in my body," she said in an August 2021 interview with Charlie Ward, "and I pray that I live long enough to see it because I myself personally, for every child in this country, and every vulnerable child and adult, I will be the new Nazi hunter. I'm not going to stop."

Of course, the mainstream media have done their best to smear Shemirani. Wikipedia describes her as "a British conspiracy theorist, anti-vaxxer, and former nurse who lost her licence to practise in 2020 for misconduct. She is best known for promoting conspiracy theories about COVID-19, vaccinations and 5G technology."

Well, they would say that, wouldn't they? They've said similar about de Buisseret, Dolores Cahill, and many more outspoken heroes of this age. Haven't the censors run out of fingers to plug the dike by now?

Courageous forces are aligning to prosecute the criminal pharma cabal. In December 2021, the International Criminal Court accepted a Crimes-Against-Humanity filing (Reference OTP-CR-473/21) against Boris Johnson and his coterie, along with Bill Gates, Anthony Fauci, pharmaceutical executives, and others in the medical-industrial complex, for violations of *Nuremberg* and of Articles 6, 7, and 8 of *Rome*.

Later that month, Dr Sam White, solicitors Lois Bayliss and Philip Hyland, and retired police constable Mark Sexton filed a criminal complaint at Hammersmith Police Station, London (Crime Number 6029679/21) citing...

> misfeasance in public office, misconduct in public office, conspiracy to commit grievous bodily harm, conspiracy to administer a poisonous and noxious substance to cause serious harm and death, gross negligence, manslaughter, corporate manslaughter, corruption, fraud, blackmail, murder, conspiracy to commit murder, terrorism, genocide, torture, crimes against humanity, false imprisonment, multiple breaches of our human

rights, war crimes, multiple breaches of the *Nuremberg Code* (1947), and multiple breaches of the *Human Rights Act* (1998).

A treason charge is also likely to follow. The Criminal Complaint reads...

"In accordance with Section 3 of the Criminal Law Act (1967), we now call on you to assist us in the closure of all vaccine centres within your jurisdiction. The Criminal Law Act (1967) Section 3 states, '**A person may use such force as is reasonable in the circumstances in the prevention of crime**, or in effecting or assisting in the lawful arrest of offenders or suspected offenders or of persons unlawfully at large.' These gene therapy drugs are the murder weapon. This is the weapon that the U.K. government is using to hurt, maim, and kill millions of people in the U.K.

"The evidence must be seized by the police as part of this investigation. It is incumbent on you to do that without fail in all police jurisdictions around the U.K. The Criminal Law Act (1967) gives any man or woman the authority and the power to prevent crime. We also have authority to use force as is reasonable, necessary, and proportionate in order to prevent that crime from happening.

"You may be resistant to this. However, there is now a live criminal investigation in place. You have a duty to protect the people. You are public servants who we pay with public taxes and public money. You work for us. If crime, injury, serious harm, and death is being committed, it is incumbent on your office of Constable on Oath which you swore to protect us the people from said harm.

"If you are in attendance, it is your duty to gather evidence and seize the weapon which, in this case, are the vaccine vials. These vaccine vials should then be taken into protective custody and detained in your property evidence stores to be independently forensically tested as a matter of urgency.

"This is a fact in law. The law is the same, whether you are a police constable in uniform or whether you are a citizen, a man or woman that is sovereign. The police have a duty. That duty is to respond and act accordingly. If the police fail to do their job, they are committing an offence of misconduct in public office and perverting the course of justice. If they know offenders are responsible for these crimes and they do anything to assist those offenders or prevent those crimes from being detected, or deliberately frustrate the criminal investigation, they are also guilty of an offence of assisting a known offender.

"May I remind you that you work for the people, you do not work for the government. It is the government ministers, the civil servants, and the media bosses who are committing these disgusting and heinous atrocities against millions of people throughout the United Kingdom.

"It is ridiculous to expect us to address members of Parliament. They are the very people committing these crimes. We do not speak to the offenders. That is the job of the police, and these people must be arrested. So we now demand that you assist us in forcing all vaccine centres within your jurisdiction to cease and desist with immediate effect."

Following this declaration, plaintiff Mark Sexton clarifies in a January 2022 video that we are all entitled under the *Criminal Law Act*, Section 3, to intervene against crime ourselves. He also invokes *PACE* (the aforementioned *Police and Criminal Evidence Act* of 1984), Section 24A, by which a person other than a constable may arrest without a warrant anyone who is in the act of committing, or has committed, an indictable offence, including injury to any other person, if "it is not reasonably practicable for a constable to make it instead."

Thus, when it comes to injection centres, we are required first to remind any police present that it is their duty to shut the centre down and to seize vials for evidence. If they do not act, then we are empowered under Section 24A of *PACE* to shut them down ourselves and to carry out arrests. "The police know this," Sexton adds. "They use Section 24. Their laws are our laws. Their powers are our powers. But we employ them to carry out these laws and powers with consent."

CONCLUSION

We will not be driven by fear into an age of unreason, if we dig deep in our history and our doctrine, and remember that we are not descended from fearful men – not from men who feared to write, to speak, to associate, and to defend causes that were, for the moment, unpopular.

— EDWARD R. MURROW, 1954

As Shakespeare said of Love, "It is the star to every wandering bark." So are Rights declarations to us, enduring stars of guidance untouched by the storms playing out beneath. Listen, for example, to these opening words of the **UDHR**...

"The Universal Declaration promises to all the economic, social, political, cultural and civic rights that underpin a life free from want and fear. They are not a reward for good behaviour. They are not country-specific, or particular to a certain era or social group. They are the inalienable entitlements of all people, at all times, and in all places."

Words this majestic must have been written in love, and God is love. This charter, and others like it, give us the words to rebuke the propaganda and lies if we will but assert them. Their power overthrows the diktats of men, proud men, dressed in their little brief authority, most ignorant of what they're most assured.[1]

Bravely we set forth, and whenever our vessel nears a shore, we look with the eyes of discernment to know whether it offers true sanctuary or sings a siren song promising security at the cost of our souls.

Now, you may say our charters and constitutions are mere collections of words, and what good are words against such murderous hatred now unleashed upon the world? I answer, what are the orders of politicians but words? And what are Acts of Parliament or Congress but words? And when words are empty, as Homer reminds us in his epic about a sea voyage, they are evil.[2]

We are in a fight to the death, whether we like it or not, and our enemy is like a prowling lion, ever hunting for someone to devour (*1 Peter* 5:8). His malice shocks us. We gasp at his brazen lies, shudder at his cowardly tactics, and seethe as he tortures, maims, and kills for pleasure, but we have authority to overcome *all* of his power (*Luke* 10:19).

We wanted to be left in peace to enjoy our lives and

pursue our happiness, but now that we see Hatred pursuing our destruction, we are stirred with the spirit of battle. As Shakespeare's King Henry V says on the eve of Agincourt (IV.i),...

We would not seek a battle as we are,
Nor, as we are, we say we will not shun it.

Henry then isolates himself to pray...

O God of battles, steel my soldiers' hearts.
Possess them not with fear. Take from them now
The sense of reckoning, lest the opposed numbers
Pluck their hearts from them.

The next day, he and his army, though tired and depleted, achieve a stunning victory over "The confident and overlusty French."

Do not overestimate our foe now. At heart, he is weak and deathly afraid, while his craven agents know not what they do or what they say or what they think and, in their haste for satisfaction, are making fatal errors along the way. Their very logic is rooted in fear, the truth is not in them, and their protestations of care and service are but clanging cymbals that can never drown out the divine whisper in our hearts. Their ultimate end, I say again, echoes that of Pharaoh and his cohorts drowned in the Red Sea. In the words of author and broadcaster, Mike Adams, "The demonic anti-human forces that currently control Big Tech, Big Media, Big Pharma, and Big

Government, they will be dismantled and defeated and ultimately destroyed by God."[3]

Until then, I marvel at the resolve, courage, dedication, and resourcefulness of allies who have emerged in these dark times, image bearers of the divine, brothers and sisters afire with the Spirit that overturns tables in our temples defiled. Most defiled of all in these times is the body itself, the last frontier of resource extraction, a goldmine to be drilled and plundered by corporate opportunists until, used up and depleted, it is discarded as medical waste. Yes, into this holy place they have brought many abominations that cause desolation, to echo *Matthew* 24:15.

This is also the time to be wise as serpents (*Matthew* 10:16), to probe the air as a snake would, and to sniff out deception. It is a time to know and hear the Shepherd's voice (*John* 10:16) and to heed only his true prophets (*Matthew* 7:15). I dare say that, as a seeker of truth, you have already cultivated this skill, but a handy rule of thumb is to follow the money. Who is paying the latest false prophet? Who has sponsored his statements? And do his words, or the consequence of those words, accord with or defile international Rights protections?

You have witnessed others compliantly follow into annihilation, even as they bleated a chorus of disapproval to denounce you. But you have joined a new alliance of black sheep.

Above all, it is time to step into our power. In my braver moments, I consider it a gift that we now have such obvious villains, and such demonstrable villainy, to oppose. They call forth our greatness, so that the glory of God may be revealed in us.

Here, I quote Dr Zelenko again: "I see the transformation of humanity as a whole into a much more enlightened state of consciousness where truth and goodness will reign, and ultimately the revelation of the divine."

If, on the other hand, you are part of the state's apparatus for enforcing unconstitutional orders and atrocity, beware how you treat protestors, naysayers, whistleblowers, doctors of conscience, investigative journalists, and civic-minded citizens, for whatsoever you do to them, you do to Christ (*Matthew* 25:41-46), and he will embrace you or discard you accordingly.

I'm not just talking to physical enforcers such as police, but to hospitals and medical professionals, and to financial institutions now called on to persecute dissenters. Welcome a prophet as a prophet, and receive a prophet's reward (*Matthew* 10:41), but incur a prophet's curse, and you shall find it carries a power that neither you nor your weapons nor your wealth, nor all your political or mercenary connections, can even begin to imagine, much less oppose.

Remember too, that there never was, nor ever will be, any comfort or validity in the defence, "I was just following orders." It didn't work in **Nuremberg** 1.0; it won't work in **Nuremberg** 2.0.

If you do not, then this decree is for you: You will not eat, though your plate is full; you will not sleep, though your bed is soft; you will go to your torment, despised of

God and Mankind; you will go to your doom. This is decreed in Heaven, and now effected on Earth. Amen, and so be it.

Love compels us to act and speak now lest, "as we remain silent, the destruction continues," to quote the British doctor Lucie Wilk again. And in our speaking, let us waste no words trying to persuade others that government oppression is wrong on the shaky ground that current conditions do not warrant it. Missing the point, missing the point, so dangerously and utterly missing the point! No conditions could *ever* warrant it. No emergency, not even another Black Death, could warrant it. Ever! Rights are eternal, the rulings of politicians pissing in the wind, and our constitutional cause transcends all other contested discourse. If they call you an idiot for exercising your sovereignty and declining their medicine, so what? International Law protects our Right to be an idiot!

And no, we are NOT looking to 'balance' individual Rights against some tyrannical depiction of the collective good. No, our Rights are our North, our South, our East, our West, our working week and our Sunday rest, to paraphrase Auden. We are not going to compromise them or bargain them away. Life is simply not worth living without them. What is the point of deferring death at all costs only to preserve a life so joyless and locked down that it is not worth living? I say again, and for the third time in this book, we are **CONSTITUTIONAL EXTREMISTS!**

Nor is there any point in arguing with the tyrants

themselves, trying to persuade them to be a little less unkind to us. Nor, when they feel cornered and start talking about concessions, shall we pay them any more heed than Odysseus paid Penelope's suitors who wanted to negotiate just before he slaughtered them.

Seared of conscience, the puppet tyrants don't care in the least what is reasonable, fair, or just, and will remain determined, for as long as they think they can get away with it, to impose top-down destruction on the lives they have sworn to protect. There is but one recourse left to us now...

MASS COORDINATED SABOTAGE OF THE AGENDA; DESTRUCTION OF VACCINE AND SURVEILLANCE INFRASTRUCTURE; DISOBEDIENCE TO MEDICAL MANDATES AND DECREES; ARREST AND PROSECUTION OF ALL IN THE 'VACCINE' SUPPLY CHAIN, INCLUDING MEDIA PROPAGANDISTS.

(AND arrest of all in the 5G supply chain too, though that's another book.) As Kate Shemirani reminds us, "We can only be abused if we allow ourselves to be." What if thousands of us descended on the new internment camps and reduced them to rubble? What if we tore down the shelves of vile vials? What if everyone told to show their medical status refused, knowing that the very demand was an abomination? What a mighty impulse of joy would the world receive!

Medical confidentiality is at the core of everything

we've looked at. If all upheld this one principle, then none of the horrors predicated upon its breach could follow. I mean, how can people hate others who made a different medical choice, as mainstream media so eagerly call on them to do, if they don't know whom to hate?

Again, I appeal for unity between 'vaxxed' and 'unvaxxed'. We have a common enemy who regards all of us as disposable—as tadpoles, to return to my *Parable of the Frogs*. The sooner we all realize this, the quicker sanity returns.

To help with that, here's a thought experiment for any reader who has been injected. Imagine that the false powers declare one day that oops, turns out that *you* are in the group showing higher levels of infection and transmission. *You* are now among the outcasts, barred from society, and denied hospital treatment, so that the newly exalted 'purebloods' can take your place. Or worse, imagine *you* are in the group to be exterminated in concentration camps.

You would regard this as a totalitarian violation of your Rights, wouldn't you? Then, under the **Royal Law** of loving others as yourself, why would you think it OK to do this to today's nominated group of outcasts?

The so-called leaders don't love you, never have, never will. You may be a favoured child of the patriarchs today, a convenient tool to be used against those who resist, but tomorrow, when you have served your purpose, off you go to the hells you assigned to others. Would you not rather stand up for the Rights of all now so that your future, and that of your children, can be safeguarded too?

I also call for unity between police or army personnel of conscience and civilians. The choice for appointed enforcers is stark: fealty to life, to your public oath, and to eternal values; or obedience to orders and secret oaths, to a living death, and everlasting torment. Which is it?

Every warrior's boot used in battle
and every garment rolled in blood
will be destined for burning,
will be fuel for the fire.

— *ISAIAH* 9:5

As I just said to cheerleaders of Government, do you think your political and corporate masters care one jot about you? What will they do to you and your children and your loved ones, once you have outlived your usefulness? Send you off with a nice pension so that you can say of yourself, as Aleksandr Solzhenitsyn would say of you, "I am cattle, I am a coward. I seek only warmth and to eat my fill."?[4] Is it a company house you're after, or a company car? Don't kid yourself. You too were a useful tadpole for a while, ready to oppress and kill other tadpoles, but the frogs will never allow you to become one of them, or to share in their bounty.

As Sarah (of the family) Feeley says in the *Strawman* documentary,…

"People need to get educated. People need to start waking up and realize what's going on around them.

Generally, people only tend to give a damn what's happening when it's actually on their doorstep and it's happening to them. But we can't wait for that to happen, we need to realize that we're all one and the same. We all need to look out for each other and protect each other because we've got a system now that's been built up around us, we've got a corporate web of an empire that's completely taken over every aspect of our lives."

In his essay, *The Power of the Powerless*, Czech dissident and playwright turned statesman Václav Havel documents the kind of transformational change that comes about when we realize "not standing up for the freedom of others... meant surrendering one's own freedom." He chronicles how a young Czech rock band, The Plastic People of the Universe, by refusing to obey the totalitarian state in Czechoslovakia, sparked a movement in 1989 that brought the system down.

"For the crust presented by the life of lies is made of strange stuff. As long as it seals off hermetically the entire society, it appears to be made of stone. But the moment someone breaks through in one place, when one person cries out, 'The emperor is naked!', when a single person breaks the rules of the game, thus exposing it as a game, everything suddenly appears in another light and the whole crust seems then to be made of a tissue on the point of tearing and disintegrating uncontrollably."

A cursory glance at history shows, alas, a litany of atrocity, but there was never a time when the totalitarian assault was this, well, total in its geographic range, nor the options for flight so few. Even Florida, to which many have fled, is servant to medical tyranny. In May 2021, Governor Ron DeSantis signed state legislation, SB 2006, confirming the state's health officer may, "upon declaration of a public health emergency," order an individual...

> "to be examined, tested, vaccinated, treated, isolated, or quarantined for communicable diseases... If there is no practical method to isolate or quarantine the individual, the State Health Officer may use any means necessary to vaccinate or treat the individual. Any order of the State Health Officer given to effectuate this paragraph is immediately enforceable by a law enforcement officer."
>
> — TITLE XXIX, CHAPTER 381,
> SECTION 00315

I dare say that, should Republicans retake the Oval Office and Congress, the boot of tyranny will merely shift to the other foot. Then it will be a politically motivated Democratic Party, rather than a constitutionally principled one, denouncing medical mandates, while those who had initially fled California's COVID tyranny will flood back in, looking for sanctuary.

I agree with Anna de Buisseret's assessment that we're seeing "the biggest crimes against humanity ever committed in the history of humankind." But I am also encouraged by her message that time is on our side, that the powers-that-shouldn't-be are not only on the wrong side of the Law but on the wrong side of history, and that "We are going to get the right results."

Time will also recruit allies to the constitutional cause as more people realize governments have not only betrayed their Social Contract with us but are waging undeclared war against us. As podcast host Bret Weinstein observes, "This is a failure that has breached the walls of medicine and is now toppling the most basic elements of our societal agreement with each other."

Yet, having outdone themselves this time, the autocrats have done themselves in! They have pushed the agenda too far, got too greedy, tipped their hand, given the game away, and like the jubilant murderers who nailed Christ to the Cross and thought to get away with it, have exposed themselves to Justice resurrected. And what a glorious and healing resurrection it will be when a new kingdom is established on Earth and when, to the increase of the Holy One's merciful reign, there will be no end (*Isaiah* 9:7).

Are we in the end times of *Revelation*? Or is this a rehearsal for the end-times, as the tyrants maim and indoctrinate the next generation of psychopaths to be even worse than the last? Either way, the field of battle lies ahead. What a glorious time to be alive!

CODA

On the very day this book was to be published, I had a dream that revealed more about the power structures we are contending with. It warrants this last-minute inclusion...

I am helping to bring a patient into a hospital, but when I go in, the building is something like a church, yet it feels menacing. I go up a winding staircase and along a narrow corridor. I sense danger, and fear I will be trapped in there. I drop the patient off. I want to protect her, but fear what will happen to me if I stay. I go back down the winding staircase and make my way out quietly. As I leave the building by a side door, an old man in charge of the building exits by the main door. He shouts, "Fire her!" at a woman on his staff.

I make my way along a street. Now, I am in some kind of wheelchair and, moving slowly by the strength of my hands, I fear being caught because I can't get away from the building fast

*enough. But I have two brothers walking beside me on each side.
The one on my left turns and smiles at me. His face is all love
and benevolence. Though I can only move slowly, he will
protect me.*

Upon waking, I recall a commentary by Russell Brand
about World Economic Forum (WEF) co-founder, Klaus
Schwab, and Schwab's demand a woman on his staff be
fired for using his parking spot while he'd been away. So I
realize that Schwab, hitherto unmentioned in this book,
is presiding over today's unholy alliance of hospital with
Satanic temple. His centrality to the plot is only
confirmed by a BBC 'Reality Check' analysis that attempts
to dismiss 'conspiracy theories' about his 'Great Reset'
agenda.

With its Forum of Young Global Leaders—begun in
1992 as Global Leaders of Tomorrow—the WEF has
groomed today's crop of tyrant notables, including Justin
Trudeau of Canada, Emmanuel Macron of France, Jacinda
Ardern of New Zealand, and European Commission
president, Ursula von der Leyen. Schwab himself boasted,

"When I mention our names like Mrs. Merkel, even
Vladimir Putin and so on, they all have been Young
Global Leaders of the World Economic Forum. But what
we are very proud of now is the young generation like
Prime Minister Trudeau, the president of Argentina, and
so on, that we penetrate the cabinets. So yesterday I was
at the reception for Prime Minister Trudeau, and I know
that half of this cabinet, or even more [than] half of this

cabinet, are actually Young Global Leaders of the World Economic Forum. It's true in Argentina, and it's true in France now."

I gather that Schwab expects a Nobel Peace Prize for his services to Humanity. Well, if they can give it to the likes of Barack Obama, Aung San Suu Kyi, and Abiy Ahmed, he might just get one. His agenda, though, is anything but peaceful. Schwab's lizard sidekick at the WEF, author Yuval Noah Harari, said in an interview:

"People could look back in a hundred years and identify the coronavirus epidemic as the moment when a new regime of surveillance took over, especially surveillance under the skin which, I think, is maybe the most important development of the twenty-first century, this ability to hack human beings, to go under the skin, collect biometric data, analyze it, and understand people better than they understand themselves."

At the WEF annual Davos forum in 2020, Harari advised, "We humans should get used to the idea that we are no longer mysterious souls. We are now hackable animals."

That Harari could be so open about this dystopian agenda shows the WEF is operating in a bubble of delusion, completely untethered from reality. It seeks to desecrate the Creator's image in us, and assumes we will welcome our own enslavement under the most intrusive surveillance imaginable.

One shorthand word for all this is 'transhumanism', which expects to upgrade human beings by technology. It includes, in Schwab's own words to the Chicago Council on Global Affairs in 2019, "a fusion of our physical, digital, and biological identities."

It's a hideous idea and, in these early days of the attempt, clumsy and botched, resulting in all manner of mutilation. But that's not a problem for the 'globalists', who regard us as guineapigs. As New Zealand doctor Sam Bailey observes in a February 2022 commentary,

> "The globalists have some sick agendas they are attempting to roll out, and they want to disconnect us from spirituality in their perverted plan for humanity. Dr Harari and his Davos buddies are so unconscious that they think they are gods. To them, you are livestock that is ripe for their transhumanist experiments and eventual enslavement."

I ask myself why old men like Schwab and Fauci and Gates would be so intent on clearing the planet of us 'useless eaters' when they have so little time left to enjoy it, and must then face hellish consequences in the hereafter. There can be only one reason…

THESE MORONS ACTUALLY BELIEVE THEY HAVE FOUND SOME KEY TO IMMORTALITY THROUGH THE SACRIFICE OF OTHERS.

Here's the thing about false prophets. What comes

out of their mouth is, by definition, false prophecy, meaning that which shall NOT come to pass. When the plans of our gracious and compassionate God are to prosper us and not to harm us, to give us hope and a future, do you think an arrogant pipsqueak like Harari, with his plans for a 'digital dictatorship', could succeed? The idea is laughable!

Yet I shudder to think what ritualistic horrors are now being practised in secret temples, given that wealthy individuals routinely harvest the blood of young people in a bid to extend their own lives. In a December 2019 *MintPress* article on the booming blood market, Alan Macleod reported, "Teenager blood is in high demand in, of all places, Silicon Valley, where anti-aging technologies are the latest trend. One company, Ambrosia, charges $8,000 per treatment to aging tech executives, infusing them with the blood of the young." Among the keenest customers, according to Macleod, is PayPal co-founder Peter Thiel who, in his own words, stands against "the ideology of the inevitability of the death of every individual."

We cannot expect any check of conscience from this cult. The WEF claims, in a January 2022 article citing unnamed 'experts', that vaccine mandates are not Human-Rights violations: "Not really, say experts on actual human rights violations," the article asserts. "In fact, some point to the more fundamental right of everyone to be protected from COVID-19—particularly as variants continue to disproportionately impact the unvaccinated."

This purported Right to be protected from an ephemeral disease is an invention that our ancestors never thought to insert into their own constitutions, much less nominate as "more fundamental" than all the other Rights, based on lasting values, that have stood the test of time. As we saw near the start of this book, there is no Law more fundamental than the 'Royal Law', the Law written by the Author of Life himself, to love others as we love ourselves. That means no-one gets to impose their medical will on someone else. This should be self-evident, but we are living in an age when we must once again tear down Satanic arguments and pretensions that set themselves up against the knowledge of God (2 *Corinthians* 10:5).

And what about the word, 'mandate'? Is it any coincidence that 'mandate' is the very word Freemasons use when the head of a lodge issues instructions to members of the lodge? Was it a lodge that I saw in my dream? If governments are going for medical enforcement, why not use more commonplace terms such as 'order', 'command', 'requirement', 'regulation', or 'policy'? And why say 'mandatory' if 'required' or 'compulsory' is meant?

Secret-society coordination, I have come to realize, is the key explanation for the globally orchestrated tyranny we have seen since the COVID era. The reason doctors can routinely desecrate the *Hippocratic Oath* is because they have sworn a secret oath that usurps it and because they have participated in horrific initiation rites that have seared their consciences into silence. They wear white coats by day but black robes by night, kill with knives in the darkness but with needles in the light, and they have turned hospital beds into sacrificial altars.

Secret oaths are also the reason that politicians can flout their oaths to constitution, bureaucrats their oaths of office, and police their **Constable's Oath.** Above ground, they are organized in corporate pyramid structures, but below ground in the hidden depths, they are mirrored by an inverted pyramid whose apex descends to Satan himself. Freemasons think to rise when they progress through their 33 levels, but in reality, they are descending with each promotion deeper and deeper into the abyss.

Or think of the governments, agencies, corporations, hospitals, and institutions as a poison tree producing poison fruit. As a tree's visible structure is mirrored by its root structure underground, the root system of today's tyranny is bound with secret oaths, secret rituals, and secret pacts, and nourished with the blood of innocents. Our visible societies have become infested at every level with secret-society parasites doing the bidding of Lucifer, who is Satan masquerading as an angel of light, and of his infernal conspirators, Baal and Moloch.

Yet they shall find no chamber, dungeon, or tunnel deep enough or dark enough to hide them and their crimes from the searing light of the Holy One, whose penetrating gaze I now direct from Heaven upon them. From Heaven, we unmask and expose them, that they are unmasked and exposed on Earth, so that all shall know who they are, and what they are, and what they have done, and whom they serve.

These days, Christians waste a lot of time debating where we are in the End-Times calendar, looking for a Rapture any day now to lift us beyond the tyrant's reach. They argue too about whether this divine rescue operation occurs before or during the 'Tribulation'. I prefer to keep things simple, to know that Christ has given me authority to overcome all the power of the enemy, that he who is in me is greater than he who is in the tyrant parasites, and that when I resist the devil, he will flee from me. So it is written, and so shall it be.

Much love,
Abdiel LeRoy

APPENDIXES

APPENDIX I

A HANDY GUIDE TO CONSTITUTIONAL AND RIGHTS PROTECTIONS

Printable version at
Geni.us/HumanRights
(case sensitive)

Here are listed the most egregious categories of
government banditry in the COVID era, followed by their
constitutional antidotes. Please feel free to inform the
author   (RenewedTestament@protonmail.com)   of
additional protections you would like to see added.

Government Is Inferior to the People

International

"Because government is a creation of man, and a creation of man can never be above man, they need your consent before they have the force of law."

— *STRAWMAN* DOCUMENTARY

"We the people created government; they are the fiction. A fiction can never gain authority over its creator."

— JACQUIE PHOENIX

All Emergency Measures

International

"No state party shall, **even in time of emergency threatening the life of the nation**, derogate from the Covenant's guarantees of the right to life; freedom from torture, cruel, inhuman or degrading treatment or punishment, and **from medical or scientific experimentation** without free consent; freedom from slavery or involuntary servitude; the right not to be imprisoned for contractual debt; the right not to be convicted or sentenced to a heavier penalty by virtue of retroactive criminal legislation; the right to recognition as a person before the law; and freedom of thought, conscience and religion. **These rights are not derogable under any conditions even for the asserted purpose of preserving the life of the nation.**"

— SIRACUSA PRINCIPLES (1985),
PARA. 58, APPLYING TO UNITED NATIONS
INTERNATIONAL COVENANT ON CIVIL
AND POLITICAL RIGHTS

United Kingdom

Emergency measures must be scrutinised by Parliament within seven days of being made, and renewed every month.

— CIVIL CONTINGENCIES ACT 2004

"Upholding fundamental human rights."

— CONSTABLE'S OATH (WHICH APPLIES TO EVERY POLICE OFFICER AT EVERY RANK)

Injections in Experimental Phase or 'Emergency Use Authorization'

International

"**The voluntary consent of the human subject is absolutely essential.** This means that the person involved should have legal capacity to give consent; should be so situated as to be able to exercise free power of choice, **without the intervention of any element of force, fraud, deceit, duress, overreaching, or other ulterior form of constraint or coercion.**"

— NUREMBERG CODE, PART 1

"It is the duty of physicians who are involved in medical research to protect the life, health, dignity, integrity, **right to self-determination, privacy, and confidentiality of personal information of research subjects.**"

— HELSINKI DECLARATION, 1964,

PARA. 9

Injections at Any Time

International

"Any **preventive**, diagnostic and therapeutic medical intervention is only to be carried out with the **prior, free and informed consent** of the person concerned, based on adequate information."

— UNITED NATIONS UNIVERSAL
DECLARATION ON BIOETHICS AND
HUMAN RIGHTS (2005), ARTICLE 6

"The inherent dignity of the human person."

— UNITED NATIONS INTERNATIONAL
COVENANT ON ECONOMIC, SOCIAL AND
CULTURAL RIGHTS (1996), PREAMBLE

"All peoples have the right of self-determination."

> — UNITED NATIONS INTERNATIONAL
> COVENANT ON ECONOMIC, SOCIAL AND
> CULTURAL RIGHTS (1966), PART I,
> ARTICLE 1, PARA. 1

"Everyone has the right to life, liberty, and security of person."

> — UNITED NATIONS INTERNATIONAL
> COVENANT ON CIVIL AND POLITICAL
> RIGHTS (1966) ARTICLE 3

Europe

"**The vaccination is NOT mandatory** and that no one is politically, socially, or otherwise pressured to get themselves vaccinated if they do not wish to do so."

> — RESOLUTION 2361, PARLIAMENTARY
> ASSEMBLY OF THE COUNCIL OF EUROPE,
> PARAGRAPH 7.3.1

United Kingdom

"You have the right to accept or refuse treatment that is offered to you, and not to be given any physical examination or treatment unless you have given valid consent."

— NHS CONSTITUTION

"A person must give permission before they receive **any type of medical treatment, test, or examination.**"

— NHS WEBSITE

"Regulations... may not include provision requiring a person to undergo medical treatment. 'Medical treatment' includes vaccination and other prophylactic treatment."

— PUBLIC HEALTH (CONTROL OF DISEASE) ACT 1984, SECTION 45E

United States

"The right of the people to be secure in their persons...."

— FOURTH AMENDMENT

Australia

No **"civil conscription"** in government provision of medical and dental services.

— AUSTRALIAN CONSTITUTION,
SECTION 51.23A

Law of the Commonwealth prevails over the law of a State.

— AUSTRALIAN CONSTITUTION,
SECTION 109

Canada

Fundamental freedoms include the right to "security of the person."

— CANADIAN BILL OF RIGHTS (1960),
PART I, SECTION 1(A)

Interventions by Members of the Public
(closing injection centres and arresting skin-piercers)

United Kingdom

Any man or woman "**may use such force as is reasonable in the circumstances in the prevention of crime**, or in effecting or assisting in the lawful arrest of offenders."

— CRIMINAL LAW ACT (1967), SECTION 3

A person other than a constable may arrest without a warrant anyone who has committed, or is in the act of committing, an indictable offence, including injury to any other person, if "it is not reasonably practicable for a constable to make it instead."

— POLICE AND CRIMINAL EVIDENCE
ACT (1984), SECTION 24A

Police Conduct

United Kingdom

"Upholding fundamental human rights."

— OATH FOR THE OFFICE OF CONSTABLE
(INCLUDED IN SCHEDULE 4 OF THE
POLICE ACT 1996), WHICH APPLIES TO
EVERY POLICE OFFICER AT EVERY RANK.

"You must uphold the law regarding human rights."

— CODE OF ETHICS,
U.K. COLLEGE OF POLICING

"Give and carry out lawful orders only."

— CODE OF ETHICS,
U.K. COLLEGE OF POLICING

Any constable who "exercises the powers and privileges of a constable improperly," or to the detriment of another person, is liable on conviction to **imprisonment for up to 14 years and a fine.**

— CRIMINAL JUSTICE AND COURTS ACT
(2015), SECTION 26

Canada

"Every officer is a peace officer in every part of Canada."

— ROYAL CANADIAN MOUNTED POLICE
ACT (1985), PART I, 11.1 (1)

"Respect the rights of all persons" and "act at all times in a courteous, respectful and honourable manner."

— ROYAL CANADIAN MOUNTED POLICE
ACT (1985), SECTION 37

"I will uphold the Constitution of Canada... and discharge my other duties as Police Constable, faithfully, impartially and according to law."

— CANADIAN POLICE OATH OF OFFICE

Officers shall not "infringe or deny a person's rights or freedoms under the *Canadian Charter*," make any unlawful detention or arrest, "treat any person in a manner that is abusive or unprofessional," or "conduct themselves in a manner that undermines, or is likely to undermine, public trust in policing."

— CANADIAN POLICE CODE OF
CONDUCT

Medical Testing

International

"Any preventive, **diagnostic** and therapeutic medical intervention is only to be carried out with the **prior, free and informed consent** of the person concerned, based on adequate information."

— UNITED NATIONS UNIVERSAL DECLARATION ON BIOETHICS AND HUMAN RIGHTS (2005), ARTICLE 6

Masks

International

"Any **preventive**, diagnostic and therapeutic medical intervention is only to be carried out with the **prior, free and informed consent** of the person concerned, based on adequate information."

— UNITED NATIONS UNIVERSAL DECLARATION ON BIOETHICS AND HUMAN RIGHTS (2005), ARTICLE 6

United Kingdom

"Regulations... may not include provision requiring a person to undergo medical treatment. 'Medical treatment' includes vaccination and other **prophylactic treatment.**"

— PUBLIC HEALTH (CONTROL OF DISEASE) ACT (1984), SECTION 45E

Confidentiality and COVID 'Passports'

International

"No one shall be subjected to arbitrary interference with his privacy, family, home, or correspondence."

— UNIVERSAL DECLARATION OF HUMAN RIGHTS, ARTICLE 12

"Nadie será objeto de injerencias arbitrarias en su vida privada, su familia, su domicilio o su correspondencia."

— UNIVERSAL DECLARATION OF HUMAN RIGHTS, ARTICLE 12

"Whatever I see or hear in the life of men which ought not to be spoken of abroad, whether in connection with my professional practice or not, **I will not divulge**, as reckoning that all such should be kept secret."

— HIPPOCRATIC OATH

"The privacy of the persons concerned and the confidentiality of their personal information should be respected."

— UNITED NATIONS UNIVERSAL DECLARATION ON BIOETHICS AND HUMAN RIGHTS (2005), ARTICLE 9

"Privacy, and confidentiality of personal information of research subjects."

— HELSINKI DECLARATION, PARA. 9

United Kingdom

"A duty of confidence" and "consent for the disclosure and use of their personal information." Patients may deny sharing of personal information between healthcare professionals.

— NHS CODE OF PRACTICE (2003)

United States

"The right of the people to be secure in their persons, houses, papers, and effects, against unreasonable searches and seizures, shall not be violated, and no Warrants shall issue, but upon probable cause, supported by Oath or affirmation, and particularly describing the place to be searched, and the persons or things to be seized."

— BILL OF RIGHTS, FOURTH
AMENDMENT

Medical Discrimination

International

"Persecution against any identifiable group" listed among 'Crimes against humanity'.

— ROME STATUTE OF THE
INTERNATIONAL CRIMINAL COURT
(1998), ARTICLE 7

"Everyone is entitled to all the rights and freedoms set forth in this Declaration, **without distinction of any kind**", including opinion or other status.

— UNITED NATIONS UNIVERSAL
DECLARATION OF HUMAN RIGHTS,
ARTICLE 2

"All are entitled to equal protection against any discrimination."

— UNITED NATIONS UNIVERSAL
DECLARATION OF HUMAN RIGHTS,
ARTICLE 7

Europe

"Ensure that no one is discriminated against for not having been vaccinated due to possible health risks **or not wanting to be vaccinated.**"

— RESOLUTION 2361, PARLIAMENTARY
ASSEMBLY OF THE COUNCIL OF EUROPE,
PARAGRAPH 7.3.2

No discrimination on any ground, including "discrimination based on disability, **medical conditions** or genetic features."

> — EUROPEAN CONVENTION ON HUMAN RIGHTS, ARTICLE 14, AND EUROPEAN COURT GUIDANCE ON ARTICLE 14 (PARA. 164)

Violation when an employee is fired for having an infection.

> — GUIDANCE ON ARTICLE 14, CITING EUROPEAN COURT CASE PRECEDENT, I.B. V. GREECE, 2013 (PARA. 208)

United Kingdom

No discrimination on any ground, including "discrimination based on disability, **medical conditions** or genetic features."

> — HUMAN RIGHTS ACT (1998), WHICH INCLUDES EUROPEAN CONVENTION ON HUMAN RIGHTS (ARTICLE 14) AND EUROPEAN COURT GUIDANCE (PARA. 164)

No discrimination on any ground, including **other status.**

> — HUMAN RIGHTS ACT (1998),
> ARTICLE 14

No discrimination on the basis of religion or belief.

> — EQUALITY ACT (2010)

Police required to "eliminate discrimination, harassment, victimisation and any other conduct that is prohibited by or under the Equality Act 2010."

> — PUBLIC SECTOR EQUALITY DUTY
> (2011)

"Take **a** **proactive** **approach** to opposing **discrimination.**"

> — POLICE CODE OF ETHICS, COLLEGE OF
> POLICING

Lockdowns, Curfews, Quarantines, etc.

International

"No free man shall be seized or imprisoned, or stripped of his rights or possessions, or outlawed or exiled, or in any way destroyed, nor will we proceed with force against him, or send others to do so, except by the lawful judgment of his peers or by the law of the land [Common Law]." Therefore, **quarantine measures can only be applied on an individual basis and by trial by jury.**

— MAGNA CARTA, ARTICLE 39

"Right to freedom of association with others."

— UNITED NATIONS INTERNATIONAL COVENANT ON CIVIL AND POLITICAL RIGHTS, ARTICLE 22, PARA. 1

United States

No person shall be "deprived of life, liberty, or property, without due process of law."

— BILL OF RIGHTS, FIFTH AMENDMENT

Canada

Fundamental freedoms include "the right of the individual to life, liberty, security of the person and enjoyment of property, and the right not to be deprived thereof except by due process of law."

— CANADIAN BILL OF RIGHTS (1960),
PART I, SECTION 1(A)

Legislation shall not "authorize or effect the arbitrary detention, imprisonment or exile of any person."

— CANADIAN BILL OF RIGHTS, 1960,
PART I, SECTION 2(A)

Right to Assembly

International

"Right of peaceful assembly."

— UNITED NATIONS INTERNATIONAL
COVENANT ON CIVIL AND POLITICAL
RIGHTS, ARTICLE 21

United Kingdom

"Everyone has the right to freedom of peaceful assembly and to freedom of association with others."

— HUMAN RIGHTS ACT, ARTICLE 11

United States

"The right of the people peaceably to assemble, and to petition the Government for a redress of grievances."

— BILL OF RIGHTS, FIRST AMENDMENT

Right to Travel

International

Anyone may **"leave and return to our kingdom unharmed and without fear."**

— MAGNA CARTA, ARTICLE 42

Everyone has freedom of movement both within a state and to leave any country and return to it. Everyone has the Right to seek and enjoy political asylum, to change one's nationality, and none may be arbitrarily deprived of nationality.

> — UNITED NATIONS UNIVERSAL
> DECLARATION OF HUMAN RIGHTS,
> ARTICLES 13 THROUGH 15

United Kingdom

"That all the Subjects of the United Kingdom of Great Britain shall from and after the Union have **full Freedom and Intercourse of Trade and Navigation to and from any port or place** within the said United Kingdom."

> — UNION WITH ENGLAND ACT (1707),
> SECTION IV

United States

"The ancient roots of the right to travel freely."

> — U.S. SUPREME COURT CASE,
> KENT V. DULLES, 1958

Canada

Every citizen has the Right to enter, remain in, or leave Canada; to move to, take up residence in, and gain a livelihood in any province.

> — CANADIAN CHARTER OF RIGHTS AND
> FREEDOMS, SECTION 6

Right to Work

International

"Everyone has the right to work."

> — UNITED NATIONS UNIVERSAL
> DECLARATION OF HUMAN RIGHTS,
> ARTICLE 23

"In no case may a people be deprived of its own means of subsistence."

> — UNITED NATIONS INTERNATIONAL
> COVENANT ON ECONOMIC, SOCIAL AND
> CULTURAL RIGHTS, PART I, ARTICLE 1,
> PARA. 2

Work must be freely chosen.

— UNITED NATIONS INTERNATIONAL
COVENANT ON ECONOMIC, SOCIAL AND
CULTURAL RIGHTS, PART III, ARTICLE 6,
PARA. 1

Work must come with "just and favourable conditions."

— UNITED NATIONS INTERNATIONAL
COVENANT ON ECONOMIC, SOCIAL AND
CULTURAL RIGHTS, PART III, ARTICLE 7

Right to Education

International

"Right of everyone to education."

— UNITED NATIONS INTERNATIONAL
COVENANT ON ECONOMIC, SOCIAL AND
CULTURAL RIGHTS, ARTICLE 13, PARA. 1

Right to Cultural Life

International

Right to "take part in cultural life."

— UNITED NATIONS INTERNATIONAL
COVENANT ON ECONOMIC, SOCIAL AND
CULTURAL RIGHTS, ARTICLE 15, PARA. 1

APPENDIX II

THE 'MEDICAL-FREEDOM MOVEMENT' COULD GET US ALL KILLED!

To you leaders of the so-called 'Medical-Freedom Movement'. Whose side are you on, really? Your lazy thinking and wilful ignorance have cost untold numbers of lives. You repeat the same old strategies and tired old phrases that merely trim the weeds of medical tyranny while allowing its poisonous root to spread. Your errors could get us all killed.

Your most dangerous mistake is to base opposition to forced medicine not on the solid ground that it is eternally unlawful, but on the shifting sands of data and statistics. You say something to the effect of, "This disease, or that variant, is too mild to warrant this or that measure." Or, "You shouldn't have a mandate when there is possible risk."

You utter, utter fools! What you are saying is that you'd be absolutely fine with forced medicine if the circumstances were different, such as a more serious disease, or if a safer countermeasure were produced.

Your stupidity is breathtaking. If Rights are expendable depending on conditions on the ground, or depending on statistics that so-called experts tell you, then they're not rights at all; they're flimsy conveniences.

So fuck the 'Science', and uphold our Rights! Forced medicine is eternally unlawful yesterday, today, and forever. And no emergency, whether real or perceived or invented, removes one single medical Right or any other type of Right.

Even if there were a plague on the scale of the Black Death that wiped out half the population, and even if there were some medical intervention proven to be 100% safe and 100% effective, no-one ever, under any circumstances, would have authority to impose it.

And here's your second biggest mistake: that you never defend medical confidentiality. The *Hippocratic Oath* doesn't just say, "First, do no harm" and, "I will administer no deadly medicine," it also says, "I will not divulge." And that principle of Confidentiality is enshrined in international Rights declarations and the **Fourth Amendment** to *The Constitution of the United States of America.*

Yet you're absolutely fine with the government, or an employer, or a travel company knowing your medical status or your vaccination status. It's none of their goddamn business. No-one has to divulge their medical status, and if you're not divulging your medical status, no-one can discriminate against you or persecute you on the basis of it.

Also, if they don't know your medical status, there's no need to apply for a so-called exemption. The word "No" is exemption enough. It always has been, and always will be, exemption enough.

I'm telling you to be a **CONSTITUTIONAL EXTREMIST**. Anything less, and you're dead!

Here's your third mistake. You are forgetting to tell people that, as enshrined in the *Universal Declaration on Bioethics and Human Rights*, along with many more medical codes, we have the Right to **refuse diagnostic measures**, including tests, not just purportedly preventive measures such as masks, injections, quarantines, and lockdowns.

If you had told people that before they went into the charnel houses that hospitals have become, how many more could have been saved? Armed with this information, patients would refuse the supposed 'COVID' tests that have been channeling them into corridors of death and the hospital protocols designed to kill.

But you didn't tell them that, did you? And you're still not telling them. How many lives have been lost through your complicit silence?

Fourth mistake: Lawyers staying inside your little legislative boxes, whinging that you can't go after Big Pharma or doctors or politicians or bureaucrats because they have 'legal immunity'. Do you not realize that all the Acts and statutes that confer this supposed 'legal immunity' are nothing more than corporate contracts that only one party has agreed to and only one party has signed?!

You and I, we the People, were never consulted about these contracts, did not write these contracts, did not negotiate these contracts, didn't even read these contracts, and we certainly didn't sign these contracts. Without our signature, these corporate contracts are not worth the air they're written on. Yet you lawyers are taking them as gospel.

And why, lawyers, instead of drawing on universal and international constitutions, declarations, and conventions, are you confining yourselves within the walls of a shrinking domestic legislative box that provides cover for atrocity and injustice, while you echo the oppressors by mislabeling their tyrannical codes 'law'?

Fifth mistake. Expecting any salvation from a political party or a political candidate, such as Florida governor, Ron DeSantis, just because he throws you a few bones, while you overlook the state statutes he has signed that glaringly promote medical tyranny, including forced quarantine and forced vaccination (SB 2006 and SB 7014), or that desecrate the **First Amendment** (HB 269 and HB 741)?

Remember the duty conferred on us by the *Declaration of Independence*. It doesn't tell us to abolish a political party or a political candidate. It tells us to abolish any *form* of Government that is destructive of Life, Liberty, and the Pursuit of Happiness. And that includes a form of Government that offers a political duopoly where both sides are united in trying to destroy us.

Sixth mistake. You lean disproportionately on the Nuremberg Code, which applies to experimental medicine, while overlooking other international Rights protections and medical codes that apply to all medicine, whether experimental or not. They include the *Universal Declaration on Bioethics and Human Rights*, the *Siracusa Principles*, the **NHS** *Code of Practice,* and the **NHS** *Constitution.* Where are you going to go when the authorities, the powers-that-shouldn't-be, say, "It's no longer experimental because we've fully approved it. So Nuremberg doesn't apply any more." Where are you going to go?

Finally, you're using the enemy's definitions of words, such as what 'pandemic' means or what 'vaccine' means.

Here's an example that includes the most egregious mistakes. In January 2023, Children's Health Defense (CHD) rejoiced that the New York State Supreme Court ruled against the state's vaccine mandate for healthcare workers. So far, so good, but...

The judge didn't overturn the mandate because it was inherently unlawful, which it is; he did it because it came from an executive order and was not voted on by the legislature. Meaning what? That if the governor can't be sole tyrant, the legislature can? Does an unlawful mandate become valid if only it follows the prescribed procedure?

The court also decided that the mandate was "arbitrary and capricious" on the basis that the "vaccines" do not stop transmission of the "virus"! Meaning what? That if another medical product is conjured that they say *does* stop transmission, you'd be fine with forcing it on people?

CHD's lawyer said that if the mandate "can't stop the spread of COVID, then it's just arbitrary and irrational." Meaning what? That if a product *could* stop the spread of a disease, then forcing it suddenly *would* become rational? Is this what they taught you in law school?

Oh, and she talked about the mandate causing a staffing shortage in New York hospitals. Why are you making all these peripheral arguments that don't address the core tyranny? You are leaving the door open for future tyranny!

Afterwards, CHD president Mary Holland said, "We are thrilled by this critical win against a COVID vaccine mandate, correctly finding that any such mandate at this stage, given current knowledge, is arbitrary."

"At this stage?" "Given current knowledge"? What is she thinking? No! The mandate is arbitrary, period, end of story, eternally, in every circumstance, at every stage, and whatever the current levels of knowledge or ignorance!

Holland's statement echoes another hollow slogan we've heard in 'medical-freedom' circles. "Where there is risk, there must be choice." Again, you're conferring on medical tyrants a false authority to remove choice when they claim there is no risk.

The Children's Health Defense lawyer also complained that the mandate didn't have a religious exemption. So you'd be fine with forcing it on people who don't claim to follow a religion?

My friends. This is a hollow, hollow victory, because you didn't address the core desecrations at work. Again, I say, be a **CONSTITUTIONAL EXTREMIST**. You cannot mandate medicine of any kind, at any time, or in any circumstances.

So before you get more people killed, understand and uphold...

1. All medical coercion is outlawed eternally, whatever the circumstances.
2. Medical confidentiality is eternally sacred.
3. The word "No" is exemption enough.
4. Refuse the tests!
5. Bring Justice, regardless of Acts and statutes, and stop bending the knee to unlawful legislation.

Without all these, all you're doing is nibbling around the edges of medical tyranny but never striking at the root. And that, as I've said, could get us all killed!

Abdiel LeRoy

APPENDIX III

TO BROTHERS AND SISTERS IN 'HEALTHCARE'

Dear brother or sister in healthcare –

We, the people of the United Kingdom, are aware you may experience growing tension between the millennia-old codes of medicine we have inherited and the orders you are asked to carry out.

This tension mirrors the growing discrepancy between international Rights declarations and constitutions, versus Acts and statutes passed by parliaments or regulations decreed by politicians, officials, or institutions. There is also growing divergence between **Common Law**, by which we are all sovereign, and legislation, which is decided by politicians and other tyrants.

But the *Hippocratic Oath* leaves no doubt which applies whenever there is a discrepancy. The Oath also has close kinship with the original 'Royal Law' to love others as we love ourselves. By a small act of imagination, we may put ourselves in the shoes of someone across from us and love them as we would a brother, sister, mother, father, daughter, or son.

The fundamental Rights we all treasure are set down in long-standing declarations such as *Magna Carta* (1215) and the *Universal Declaration of Human Rights* (1948). Furthermore, as the United Nations' *Siracusa Principles* (1984) point out, Rights remain steadfast **"even in time of emergency threatening the life of the nation."**

These and many more international conventions, along with bedrock medical codes such as the *Nuremberg Code*, the **NHS** *Constitution*, and the **NHS** *Code of Practice*, ensure that a person's medical status is confidential, shared only with a chosen and trusted physician. Healthcare workers have to get a person's consent even to share such information with a colleague. Much less is medical status grounds for discrimination, persecution, or enforcement of any kind.

Furthermore, the *Universal Declaration on Bioethics and Human Rights* (2005), to which all nations and jurisdictions are bound, states that "any preventive, diagnostic and therapeutic medical intervention is only to be carried out with the prior, free and **informed consent** of the person concerned, based on adequate information." This means no-one can be coerced or compelled to wear a mask or receive an injection ("preventive") or to take a medical test ("diagnostic") without their consent. So-called leaders may not like this, but as your heart and mind will tell you, it is the Truth.

We recall that our nation once stood as a bastion of liberty when tyranny swept across continental Europe. And that, in the wake of this dark episode, the defence pleas of "I was just following orders" proved useless when Justice returned.

If you wish to avoid your own destruction, you will always choose Rights over regulations and love over fear, and if you ever witness medical coercion of any kind, you will uphold your sworn duty to fight it.

A Concerned Man or Woman.

[Download one-page PDF letter at Geni.us/Healthcare.]

APPENDIX IV

TO ARBITERS OF 'RELIGIOUS EXEMPTION'

I would not want to be in your position today. You have been charged with deciding the standing of another soul in the eyes of God, something no-one can determine for another.

The Bible says this directly: "Say not in thine heart, 'Who shall ascend into heaven?' Nor, 'Who shall descend into the deep?" (*Romans* 10:6-7).

Yet it seems you are presuming to do just that, not only making judgments that are God's to make, but threatening the livelihoods of men and women made in God's image on the basis of your own human understanding.

However, I don't need to rely on Scripture to denounce the folly and hubris of these proceedings. International Rights declarations and millennia-old medical codes will do...

The *Hippocratic Oath* does not merely say, "First, do

no harm." It also says, "I will not divulge." In other words, it upholds **Medical Confidentiality**. That means you should not even *know* the medical status of the person before you, much less make any judgment on the basis of it. Confidentiality is also the key protection of the **Fourth Amendment** of the *Bill of Rights*, our "right to be secure in our persons, houses, papers, and effects."

But the criminality of this proceeding does not stop there. Under the *Universal Declaration of Bioethics and Human Rights* (2005), "Any preventive, diagnostic and therapeutic medical intervention is only to be carried out with the prior, free and informed consent of the person concerned." Threatening to destroy a person's livelihood is not consent but naked coercion. Much less is it *informed* consent, especially when an experimental product is proposed, itself a violation of the *Nuremberg Code* (1947) and the *Helsinki Declaration* (1964).

Furthermore, under the *Rome Statute* of the International Criminal Court (1988), persecution against any identifiable group is considered a Crime Against Humanity, as is causing mental distress against a targeted group.

Therefore, consider carefully the sacrilegious basis of these proceedings, and do not presume to rule against anyone put in the contemptible position of having to request from you something that was, is, and always will be their inalienable Right, and that was never yours to withhold or bestow in the first place. As you well know, the word "NO" is, was, and ever will be exemption enough.

Perhaps you are sitting on this panel because you are deemed to have religious expertise, but no religious expertise can presume to play God. That is blasphemy.

Therefore, if you deny religious or other exemption to any nurse or other practitioner who comes before you, prosecution will proceed against you individually by name. As for the consequences for your soul at Judgment, I can only imagine.

[Download one-page PDF letter at Geni.us/Exemption.]

APPENDIX V

TO BROTHERS AND SISTERS IN POLICING

To you, brother or sister in 'law enforcement' –

We, the people of the United Kingdom, are aware you may experience growing tension between your **Oath** and the orders you are asked to carry out.

This tension mirrors the growing discrepancy between international Rights declarations and constitutions, versus acts and statutes passed by parliaments, or regulations decreed by politicians, officials, or institutions. There is also growing divergence between **Common Law**, under which we are all sovereign, and legislation, which is imposed by politicians and other tyrants.

But your **Oath** leaves no doubt you are sworn to uphold **"fundamental human rights."** These are all rooted in the original 'Royal Law' to love others as we love ourselves. By a small act of imagination, we may put ourselves in the shoes of another and love them as we would a brother, sister, mother, father, daughter or son.

The fundamental Rights we all treasure are inalienable and are set down in long-standing declarations such as *Magna Carta* (1215) and the *Universal Declaration of Human Rights* (1948). Furthermore, as the United Nations' *Siracusa Principles* (1984) point out, Rights remain steadfast **"even in time of emergency threatening the life of the nation."**

These and many more international protections, along with bedrock medical codes such as the *Nuremberg Code* and the **NHS** *Constitution*, ensure that medical status is confidential, shared only with a chosen and trusted physician. Much less is medical status grounds for discrimination, persecution, or enforcement of any kind. On the contrary, your own *Code of Ethics* from the College of Policing demands you "take **a proactive approach to opposing discrimination."**

Furthermore, the *Universal Declaration on Bioethics and Human Rights* (2005), to which all nations and jurisdictions are bound, states that "any preventive, diagnostic and therapeutic medical intervention is only to be carried out with the prior, free and **informed consent** of the person concerned, based on adequate information." This means no-one may be coerced or compelled to quarantine, wear a mask, or receive an injection ("preventive") or to take a medical test ("diagnostic") without their consent. So-called leaders may not like this, but it is the truth.

We recall that our nation once stood as a bastion of

liberty when tyranny swept across continental Europe. And that, in the wake of this dark episode, the defence plea of "I was just following orders" proved useless when Justice returned.

If you wish to avoid your own destruction, you will always choose Rights over regulations and love over fear, and if you ever witness medical coercion of any kind, you will uphold your sworn duty to fight it.

A Concerned Man or Woman.

[Download one-page PDF letter at Geni.us/Police]

APPENDIX VI

LETTER TO U.K. 'MINISTRY OF JUSTICE' REGARDING PROPOSED DESECRATION OF U.K. HUMAN RIGHTS ACT

'Ministry of Justice'
HRAReform@justice.gov.uk

To the British 'Ministry of Justice' —

When Rights protections are regarded as inconvenient by governments, it is clear a tyrannical agenda has taken hold of your hearts.

But I am here to tell you that you and your agenda will be overthrown. This is decreed in Heaven and now unassailable on Earth. We have long seen through your self-righteous façade and your hollow protestations about the good of society, knowing full well that your only intent was ever to harm and destroy.

We are also well aware that all your so-called 'Consultation Documents' are no more than a smokescreen. The intention was never to 'consult' but to confirm under a phoney veneer of consent. Well, neither I nor the British people consent, and without our consent, your decrees are not worth the air they're written on.

I realize that no argument, no matter how true, reasonable or even irrefutable, will normally dissuade you from your malicious intent. So why am I even bothering to write? Because there may be some among you who yet have a shred of decency left, and if not decency, then some shred of conscience, and if not conscience, then fear about the Crimes-Against-Humanity prosecutions that will come your way, and if not fear about prosecution, then fear of the various non-judicial acts of violence stored up for you, and if not fear of what men can do, then fear of God, which I now instill in your hearts.

Even now, the blood of murdered Mankind cries out against you, and your soul will stand naked and trembling before God and Man when Justice returns, as it inevitably will.

There is still time for you to repent of your abominations. If you do not, you shall find the empty words you have drafted will avail you nothing. You shall go to your appointed place, where there is never a moment's joy, despised of God and Mankind, you will go to your doom. This too is decreed in Heaven and now effected on Earth. As for the consequences for your soul at Judgment, I can only imagine.

[Email sent to U.K. 'Ministry of Justice',
HRAReform@justice.gov.uk.
Download one-page letter at Geni.us/JusticeLetter.]

APPENDIX VII
DECLARATION TO RIOT POLICE

Well, look at you all in your battle gear, hiding behind your shields and masks. Are you officers of the 'Law'? The Law is to love others as you love yourself.

Will you honour your oath to the people, to uphold eternal Rights? Or will you be cowards and serve the politicians, those kiddie-fuckers in Government, those criminals who are less than farts in the wind, here today, gone tomorrow?

The Nazis said they were just following orders, then they were put to death. Will you uphold your oath because you care about your soul? Or because you don't want to swing from a noose?

I am the Law, and have authority over you, and if you take one action against us, I will not hesitate to bring death to your door and to your house. And you will go to your eternal destruction, despised of God and Mankind, you will go to your doom. We are watching. God is watching. This is *your* final warning.

Amen, Amen, Amen.

[Download one-page PDF declaration at Geni.us/RiotPolice]

APPENDIX VIII
OTHER RESOURCES

Constitutional Allies

International

Family Guardian Fellowship
https://famguardian.org

Common Law Courts
https://commonlawcourt.com

InPower Movement
https://www.inpowermovement.org

United Kingdom

Big Brother Watch
Website: https://bigbrotherwatch.org.uk/campaigns/
stopvaccinepassports/
Tel.: 24h media line: 07730 439257
Email: info@bigbrotherwatch.org.uk

The White Rose
Website: https://thewhiterose.uk/downloads/

White Rabbit Trust
Website: https://www.youandyourcash.com

Peace Keepers
Website: https://peacekeepers.org.uk.org

Probity Lawful Tax Resistance
Website: https://www.probityco.com

Do Not Consent
Website: https://www.donotconsent.co.uk

Save Our Rights
Website: https://saveourrights.uk

Laworfiction.com
Email: laworfiction@gmail.com

UK Medical Freedom Alliance
Website: http://www.ukmedfreedom.org

Workers of England Union
Website: https://www.workersofengland.co.uk/
Tel.: 0161 883 2552
Email: admin@workersofengland.co.uk

pjhlaw
Website: https://pjhlaw.co.uk/coronavirus-dossiers
Tel.: 01780 757589

Resistance GB
https://www.resistancegb.org

FreeMan-On-The-Land
FMOTL.com

WhatDoTheyKnow.com
whatdotheyknow.com

United States

The Healthy American (Peggy Hall)
https://www.thehealthyamerican.org

Disabled Rights Advocates
Website: https://dradvocates.com

Vaxx Choice
Website: https://vaxxchoice.com

Truth for Health Foundation
Website: https://www.truthforhealth.org
Tel.: 520-777-7092
Fax: 520-797-2948
Email: Info@TruthForHealth.org

Millions Against Medical Mandates
https://mamm.org

Public Health and Medical Professionals for Transparency
https://phmpt.org

InPower Movement
https://www.inpowermovement.org

The Renegade Nation
https://therenegadenation.org

Universal Community Trust
https://www.universal-community-trust.org

Canada

A Warrior Calls
https://awarriorcalls.com

Stand4Thee
https://stand4thee.com

Canadian Covid Care Alliance
canadiancovidcarealliance.org

Australia

AJ Roberts Forum
Website: http://www.mrajroberts.com/community/

Travel

International

Freedom Travel Alliance
Website: https://www.freedomtravelalliance.com/
Email: hello@freedomtravelalliance.com

Injection Injuries

International

Real Not Rare
RealNotRare.com

COVID-19 Vaccine Reactions
https://covidvaccinereactions.com

React19
https://www.react19.org

My Cycle Story
An independent research study collecting data about
changes in menstrual cycles
https://mycyclestory.com

German New Medicine
Five Biological Laws that overthrow medical slavery
https://learninggnm.com/SBS/documents/five_laws.html

Cardiovascular Docu-Class
https://stopcardiovasculardisease.com

United States

My Free Doctor.com
https://myfreedoctor.com

Lawyer Referrals

United Kingdom

Lawyers for Liberty
Website: https://lawyersforliberty.uk/, Resources tab

Liberty

Website: https://www.libertyhumanrights.org.uk/advice-and-information/

Advice Line tel.: 0800 988 8177

United States

Concerned Lawyers Network

Website: https://concernedlawyersnetwork.net/resourcestemplates

Law Firms

United Kingdom

Forbes Solicitors

Website: www.forbessolicitors.co.uk

Tel.: 0800 689 3206

Education department: Lucy Harris—01254 222443

The following solicitors have offered 24/7 support in London:

Commons

Tel.: 020 3865 5403

ITN Solicitors

Tel.: 020 3909 8100

Hodge Jones Allen (HJA)
Tel.: 0844 848 0222

Bindmans
Tel.: 020 7305 5638

United States

Liberty Counsel
Website: lc.org

Legal Aid

United Kingdom

Civil Legal Advice
Tel.: 0345 345 4 345

Protest Support

United Kingdom

Green & Black Cross (GBC)

Volunteers operating a Protest Support Line for when you witness an arrest, want support, or have legal questions.
Tel. 07946 541 511
Email courtsupport@protonmail.com

Discrimination

United Kingdom

Equality Advisory Support Service (EASS)
Advice and explanation of Rights under the Equality Act.
Website: https://www.equalityadvisoryservice.com
Tel.: 0808 800 0082
Email: https://www.equalityadvisoryservice.com/app/ask

Employment

United Kingdom

The Legal Cafe
www.legalcafe.co.uk

The Federal Trust for Education and Research
+44 (0)24 7765 1102 info@fedtrust.co.uk

APPENDIX IX
REPAIRING INJECTION DAMAGE

Following are some supplements and therapies said to counter the harmful effects of COVID injections and of other toxins now proliferating. Not medical advice, obviously, but included in case helpful.

Venom/ Spike-Protein Neutralization

EDTA (ethylene diamine tetra acetic acid)
Nicotine (start with minimal dose, 2 mg tablets or patch)
N-Acetyl Cysteine (NAC, 4 x 500 mg/day)
Selenium (200 ug/day, to produce glutathione)
Melatonin
Bromelain (500 mg, twice a day)
Nattokinase (100 mg, twice a day)
Liquorice root extract
Curcumin (nano curcumin, 500 mg, twice a day)

More Spike-Protein Neutralizers

Vitamin C
Hydroxychloroquine
Hyssop
Serrapeptase
Quercetin
Resveratrol
Dandelion leaf extract
Aloe
Prunella vulgaris
Pine-needle tea
Emodin
Neem
Fennel tea
Star anise tea
St. John's wort
Comfrey leaf

Removing Graphene, Nanotech, Heavy Metals

C60 (present in shungite), including 'carbon nano-onions'
Activated charcoal
Humic acid
Clays: Bentonite, Diatomaceous
Tulsi (Ocimum Sanctum) infusion, plant grown at home
Houttuynia cordata infusion, plant grown at home

Aluminium Removal

Orthosilicic acid (OSA)

Cell Health

Alphalipoic acid
Coq10

Other Antioxidants

Astaxanthin
Vitamin D3
Zinc

Myelin Sheath Repair

Omega-3 fatty acids (3000 mg/day)
Ahiflower oil
Goat's milk

Heart Health

Dandelion root tincture

Liver Support

Milk thistle
Desmodium

Kidney Support

Horsetail (evening)
Nettle (evening)

Radiation Mitigation

Melatonin (evening)
Shungite items

Diagnostics

Serum troponin level
D-dimer level
Dark-field blood microscopy
Infrared thermography

Therapies

Intravenous Vitamic C
Hyperbaric oxygen
Ozone therapy
Infrared sauna
Baths with Epsom salts or 1 cup of regular Chlorox
Hydrogen-peroxide nebulization

KNOW YOUR LAWFUL RIGHTS

A. LeRoy

Battle Manuals for Freedom: Book 2

INTRODUCTION

The elite's goal is disturbingly straightforward: to hollow out the individual, leaving an empty shell while stripping away the soul.

— A LILY BIT, *THE EXPOSE*, MAR. 15, 2024

We were born into slavery, but until recently, most of us did not know it. With subtle treachery, banks, corporations, and governments have stolen our Birthright. Spiritual vampires, they have drained us of our time and energies, even of life itself, to enrich themselves. It took the atrocities of COVID to alert us to this, to shake us awake, and to break the spell that has been perpetrated against Mankind for centuries and even millennia.

Some were aware of the tyrants' genocidal plans even

before COVID, and for that you have my deepest respect. You did your best to warn everyone what evil was afoot, and you saved lives. Though you were censored and reviled, you stuck to your message, and then I joined you to expose how broad and deep is the conspiracy against us. In early 2022, I published *The COVID Protocols: Upholding Your Rights in Authoritarian Times,* now retitled *Know Your Medical Rights.* I thought this would be enough, but when the despotism spread from the medical arena to every other area of life, I realized COVID was just the first round in a barrage of assaults aimed at demolishing our lives, our livelihoods, and all that makes life worth living. I would need to write more books.

I agree with Dr. Rima Laibow's observation, in a March 2024 interview with Maria Zeee, that…

"There is no aspect of human life which will be allowed to continue as we know it, as we value it. And most of all, what is being destroyed is the capacity to love and to trust one another. So we are being separated from our wisdom, from our bodies, from our DNA, from our children, from our property, from our very capacity to bring food forth from the Earth. We are being separated from our ability to think, to communicate, all of it in the interest of a vast and total suppression of humanity into a slave caste that can never rise up again. To which my response is, 'No! Out! I want out of your system!'"

Yes, Dr. Rima has poetically described the breadth of tyranny now afoot, but I am astonished too by its depth.

It starts with international puppet masters, usually described as 'globalists', who take their orders from secret societies and the infernal influences that inspire them. Then, the tyranny is channeled through their network of despots installed in national governments and other corporations.

The infestation doesn't stop there, though, for regional and local governments, county councils, town councils, planning departments, and even school boards and housing associations are fully on board with the despotic agenda of enslavement and destruction, either as complicit operatives or as useful idiots.

Police forces, meanwhile, corporate henchmen and bandits for hire, are enforcing all of this. How refreshing it would be if just one stood up and said, "No sir. That's an unlawful order." What a revelation if just one upheld their Oath. Instead, we are treated to the shameful spectacle of police beating up, trampling, and irradiating protesters, menacing journalists, arresting people for praying in public, and even issuing tickets against those who feed the homeless. And that's just what they do in public. Meanwhile, they give protective escort to today's agents of doom when angry crowds come too close.

COVID also taught me a new word: democide, defined in the *Collins Dictionary* as "the killing of members of a country's civilian population as a result of its government's policy, including by direct action, indifference, and neglect." I now realize that governments of the West have been doing this for decades, but they got much more unsubtle and extreme about it with COVID, both with the murderous protocols deployed in hospitals and nursing homes, then with the coerced poison injections they called 'vaccines'. Since then, among many vectors of attack, they have gone after our food, our fuel, and funds too.

I laugh when I hear people talk about "government overreach" or when they say, "The government doesn't have your best interests at heart." OK, I suppose you could call genocide 'overreach', but strip away the varnish and you will see a regime that wants to enslave you, to extract every ounce of value it can from your life and labour then, when you've nothing left to give, to discard you as cheaply as possible and add your corpse to the growing pile of medical waste. And if that's too much of a mouthful, your government simply wants to kill you!

Nor are legislators doing much to check rogue administrations. As 'Health Ranger' Mike Adams said in a May 2024 broadcast,...

"All they do every single day in the halls of Congress is they figure out, 'How can we hurt America today? How do we harm the American people? How do we vote against the interests of the American people?' They're straight-up traitors. Every single day, they conspire of how to destroy this country from within."

And that conspiracy is entirely 'legal' in the sense that politicians, or rather their handlers, have drawn up documents that not only codify their thefts and murders but shield them from consequence with so-called 'legal immunity'. I tend to agree with Max Igan's encapsulation, in a February 2024 broadcast, that "Every single problem on Earth exists because it has been legislated to exist."

Which brings me to a central theme of this book, and that is to draw a clear distinction between 'legal' and 'lawful', for they are very different things and usually contrary. 'Legal' pertains to the legislation that men create—Acts, statutes, rules, regulations, decrees, and codes, the injustice of which corporate courts cement with their rulings. 'Lawful', by contrast, belongs only to the Creator, whom to serve is Freedom (*John* 8:36; *2 Corinthians* 3:17) and whose burden is light (*Matthew* 11:28-30), and it respects our inherent Rights and dignity. These Rights may be enshrined in constitutions but they don't depend on constitutions for their existence or applicability.

As Living Men and Women operating in the Lawful, which is our Birthright, we are wholly above the Legal. Indeed, as three-dimensional beings, we are an entire *dimension* above the Legal, which operates only in the two-dimensional realm of words on paper. Those words cannot reach up from the page, grab us by the neck, and pull us down into their flattened space, though that is what their devisers intend. No, those documents are dead to us, and we refuse to breathe life into them by consenting to them with our signatures. In the three-dimensional realm where we live and move and breathe and have our beings, Government cannot even touch us, much less dictate to us.

Yet politicians, along with enforcers and

commentators, routinely ascribe to tyrant code the false label of 'Law'. It's all fiction, all counterfeit. By True Law, or 'Common Law', those who deliberately do harm must face Justice, while the falsely accused are innocent if there is no victim.

More troubling still, the fallacy of calling rules made up by men and women 'Law' is echoed by so-called alternative voices, Freedom warriors, and 'truthers' who should know better. This one error has me "shouting at the radio" more than any other.

For example, Katherine Watt, whose work I respect, routinely makes the mistake of calling legislation 'Law', so does Sasha Latypova. I have heard James Delingpole, Catherine Austin Fitts, Peggy Hall, Greg Reese, James Roguski, Jane Ruby, Scott Schara, and Maria Zeee all err on this point. Mike Adams makes this error in almost every episode of his Health Ranger Report, and Todd Callender in almost every sentence.

I respect their research, but through this one abuse of language alone, they unwittingly confer on governments a false authority to play God in the lives of others; dictate to us what we must do with our bodies, our property, our children, and even out thoughts; and then have us bend the knee and plead for 'exemptions' that they may grant at their pleasure by a counterfeit mercy.

Lawyers, too, are generally taking government writ as gospel by confining their range of motion to the shrinking legal box of legislation. Even to call them 'lawyers' is a misnomer when, for the most part, they are not dealing in Law at all but in the muck of legislation. They are not lawyers but corporate power-brokers and negotiators cutting deals with corporate entities, wherein you and I are regarded as no more than corporations.

So, if there's only one thing you take away from this book, let it be this...

STOP CALLING LEGISLATION LAW!

This one shift in mindset will produce good fruit. You will see legislation for the toilet fodder it really is, and even 'legislation' may be too generous a term because the entities that forge it, pretend to debate it, and dutifully pass it are all corporations, that is to say, invented things, and their prolixious documents amount to nothing more than corporate policy, binding only upon themselves and their own employees. All governments, parliaments, courts, and police forces *are* corporations, and their policies, procedures, and decrees have no more authority over us than if McDonald's or Starbucks had written them.

It boils down to this: God makes Law, man makes legislation, and corporations make company policy. How dare they ascribe to men and to the institutions of men the authority to make Law? When there is already so little airtime afforded genuine voices for Freedom, we cannot afford to build on such a broken foundation.

Further, Acts and statutes are, in effect, contracts that one party draws up, one party negotiates with itself, and one party signs, and then thinks to impose on another party, us, without our signature or consent, much less our

Informed Consent. Governments and corporations may not impose any demand on you unless you have voluntarily, and with full knowledge, signed a contract that includes your agreement to the demand. Therefore, if some would-be enforcer tells you, "You have to do this. This is the law," you say, "Show me the document that says this, and show me where I signed it."

Still, I wrestled with calling this book, *Know Your Legal Rights* instead of *Know Your Lawful Rights*. Though the Lawful is as far above the Legal as the heavens are above the Earth, we may on occasion operate in the Legal, and though we are not subject to the pieces of paper written by men, we may still cite them on a Legal stage to compel enforcers to obey the contracts binding upon themselves.

If we enter the Legal, therefore, we do so as an actor puts on a costume to play a role. We do not *live* in the Legal, any more than an actor would live his entire life in the costume and lines of his character, but we may play a role in it sometimes. Imagine the hell of an actor trapped forever in the fictional time and place of his theatrical persona with no way out, even worse if he lost all memory of his prior life outside the role and forgot there was an exit. That nightmarish condition describes much of Humanity today, but not you or me. If we ever operate in the Legal, we remember that we are not *of* the Legal.

In the end, I went with *Lawful* for the title, because that is the realm of Truth, whereas Legal is the realm of fiction. Like a thieving usurper, Legal has crept into the throne room of our Sovereignty and presumes to rule as

King, but he is an impostor and must be ousted if we are to restore our Birthright in the Lawful.

This requires a shift in mindset. We have much to learn, or rather unlearn, as we dismantle the lies, programming, and conditioning that have kept us from ourselves. The walls of my own perception too must dissolve to write this book. Ironically, COVID did much of that work for me by exposing the evil, and the doers of that evil, that have long crouched in the shadows and quietly infested our institutions. As the poet Theodore Roethke wrote, "In a dark time the eye begins to see." I imagine God's hand on the dimmer switch of our awareness and gradually turning up the light.

And as that dawn returns, Government shall no longer be enthroned in the minds of men, nor shall its ideologies, stupidity, or stupid ideologies. Alas, the evildoers have been assisted in their acts of theft and destruction by a largely compliant population. People seem to have embedded in their consciousness, "I must obey Government," turning it into a religion. Even after the COVID era, with its ample demonstration that Government is a cult seeking our enslavement and death, this idea is still firmly lodged in most people.

For example, I notice when taking flights in the U.S. that I am the only one refusing the body-scan chambers that the Transport and Security Administration (TSA) puts people through, the photos taken after international arrivals, and the biometric scans even at departure gates, all of which are Fourth-Amendment violations and, in the case of the body scans, medical violations too. Seeing the compliance of others is deeply frightening to me because they will passively watch tyranny happen to others and just stand idly by, or perhaps get out their mobile phones to record it and win coveted clicks on social media. At their worst, they will turn in their neighbours, or even other family members, and report non-compliance to the authorities.

I also recently saw a New Zealand honey producer torching his hives and with them, millions of bees, because the government told him to. Before that, an Australian producer allowed government agents on to his property where they drowned his bees in petrol. It is an enraging spectacle. The bees, at least, have enough regard for their own survival to sting their attackers, but many compliant humans have no sting of their own, even when directly assailed.

In Britain, meanwhile, households keeping even a single chicken are "required" to register their bird. To anyone paying even perfunctory attention, it is obvious the government will at some point try to use this information to destroy every last vestige of independent food production by conjuring some disease scare such as 'bird flu' and culling yet more hens.

Why do people keep falling for these deceptions? I want to shake them and say, "Moron, the government is trying to destroy you and your business, and the food supply along with it!" And if the autocrats can't entirely cause starvation, they are doing their best to destroy independent farmers who might produce clean, healthy food. That way, they can force consumption of their highly processed, poison-laced megacorporation stomach fillers sold in supermarkets which, in turn, are extremely vulnerable to supply-line sabotage.

Even the very word, 'Government'—which means 'mind control'—is offensive to me now. Who do these people think they are to 'govern' anyone, let alone to tax us, especially when they operate in, and are promoted by, a system that rewards corruption, laziness, and incompetence, in a culture of failing upwards? As Christ said of the Pharisees in his day, "they bind heavy burdens and grievous to be borne, and lay them on men's shoulders, but do not lift a finger to help them" (*Matthew* 23:4).

In Jesus' day, the Pharisees were a hypocritical religious cult, whitewashed tombs full of dead men's bones as he described them, a brood of vipers who strain out gnats but swallow camels (*Matthew* 23). Similarly, today's Pharisees strain out gnats by punishing speech that offends them while swallowing camels of rape, genocide, and theft. Meanwhile, their religion demands of us extortionate tithes, offerings, sacrifices, and ritual performances as, almost every day, they issue some new decree to control us, some new fine or some new fee, and then expect us dutifully to follow and to obey, to follow and to pay.

In the process, our constitutions and Rights declarations are routinely trampled in the name of virtue-signalling slogans such as 'diversity', 'equity', 'inclusion', 'prevention', 'safety', 'security', 'sustainability', and so on. These are empty words when they come from the mouths of tyrants and, as Homer reminds us in *The Odyssey*, "Empty words are evil" (XI.544).

We must therefore reclaim our inherent authority and remember the obvious and irrefutable truth, as stated in the documentary *Strawman*, that "Government is a creation of Man, and a creation of Man can never be above Man." You and I have authority over every thing that Government is and every thing that Government creates. That's just the authority of logic, but Christians have the even more potent authority from our Lord and Saviour to "overcome all the power of the enemy" (*Luke* 10:19), and in case you haven't realized it, governments *are* the enemy.

So I try never to forget, should I face official, police officer, or judge, that I have authority over them and that I am the one giving *them* 'lawful orders', not the other way round, and that, like their father the devil, these operatives must flee when resisted (*James* 4:7). With this book, I am giving shape to that resistance, assembling not just our constitutional weapons but, for those who "put on the full armour of God" (*Ephesians* 6:13), our spiritual weapons too.

I will admit the enormity of this task feels daunting sometimes, for the subject is vaster than any one author can encompass. I do not pretend to have all the answers, and some of my analysis may yet be naive. Just untangling the history of how we got here would take several volumes, delving back even to Biblical times, but what I can do is present the conceptual frameworks to reclaim our Rights, dispel the illusions that have tried to imprison us, fortify your heart for the battles and skirmishes ahead, and introduce you to solutions and solvers.

I also want to minimize the cost and dangers of the non-compliance we must embrace if we want to get through this. Your instincts are already telling you not to comply, and you may be willing to sacrifice for the cause, but let us be smart about our non-compliance, disciplined, and prepared. Let us also be open to learning more, and honing our skills, as time passes, for these are early days in clawing back our Sovereignty.

The God Stuff

Now, having got Biblical with you a few times by now, I recall that some readers objected to my Scriptural references in *Know Your Medical Rights*. If that is you, season your skepticism a while and acknowledge that even our enemies are deeply religious and that their destructive influence cannot be otherwise explained. For example, do they lie? Then entertain the possibility that they serve the Father of Lies (*John* 8:44). Do they couch their tyranny in virtue-signalling language? Then ask if they serve he who masquerades as an angel of light (*2 Corinthians* 11:14-15). Do they persecute those who tell the truth and who try to warn others? Then consider if they worship he who accuses the righteous (*Revelation* 12:10). And, are they predatory? Then witness how they take after the devil who "prowls around like a roaring lion looking for someone to devour" (*1 Peter* 5:8).

Ask yourself, too, if the assaults against our bodies—not just from venomous injections but from poisons in our food, water, air, sea, and land—are motivated by a hatred of the Most High in whose image we are made (*Genesis* 1:26-27).

Also, do they act in concert across nations, writing the same legislation, telling the same lies, and issuing the same decrees, all at the same time? Then consider how they must be coordinating in secret, making secret oaths and secret pacts, and that secret oaths are the currency of secret societies such as Freemasonry. Have you observed officials, elected or otherwise, along with doctors, judges, and police, desecrating their public oaths, whether to the Constitution or Oath of Office, Hippocratic Oath, or Constable's Oath? Could that mean they are instead cleaving to secret oaths? Would you describe them as psychopaths, meaning they can kill, loot, steal, and destroy others, including children, without remorse? Then is it possible their consciences have been seared (*1 Timothy* 4:1-2) during initiation rites of atrocity? You and I have empathy enough to imagine ourselves in someone else's shoes if they tell us we are causing them harm, but that mechanism has been annihilated in the politicians and bureaucrats of today.

And if you are disposed to excuse the naive ranks of secret-society orders, where the higher-ups—or rather, the lower-downs of an inverted pyramid—conceal the real agenda from initiates, know that even at the First Degree of Freemasonry, they have already condemned themselves by an oath of atrocity. As reported at evangelicaltruth.com, the initiate swears to secrecy "under no less a penalty than that of having my throat cut across, my tongue torn out by its roots, and buried in the rough sands of the sea at low-water mark."

Therefore, show me a Freemason who purports to be a Christian, and I will show you a child of Hell. Christ warned us that no-one can serve two masters, for he will love one and despise the other (*Matthew* 6:24). We infer that the Hell-spawn of today are not just ignoring their public oaths but actively hating them, and that they hate the *Bill of Rights, Magna Carta,* and every other righteous text. Christ also warned that these traitors would plead their good works to him at the Judgment, to which he will reply, "Away from me. I never knew thee!" (*Matthew* 7:22-23).

Meanwhile, you may observe how governments are serving dogmas that try to turn reality upside-down, even going beyond Orwell's "War is peace. Freedom is slavery. Ignorance is strength." In their worldview, good is evil and evil good, love is hate and hate love, health is sickness and sickness health, male is female and female male, truth is lies and lies are truth. Democracy is dictatorship, food is starvation, medicine poison, and justice injustice. Child protection is child trafficking, and to serve and protect is to extort and destroy.

Also, when it comes to climate-change deceptions, hot is cold and cold is hot. If you find this last element jolting, note how the climate-change narrative has followed the same playbook as COVID: take a threat that is negligible or non-existent and inflate it into a harbinger of planetary doom. To bring about such overthrows of reason requires a constant barrage of indoctrination, censorship, propaganda, fear-mongering, and psychological torture, areas where so-called 'intelligence agencies' have long honed their dark arts.

With such intense attack in the arena of ideas, and with ideas being broadcast through the invisible medium of the air, might you infer this is a spiritual battle too? Do you sense a malevolent spiritual entity or network behind the scenes? Might you call that entity Satan or Lucifer? And if such an impostor set up a throne and called himself God or Messiah, would that not be the king of all inversions?

Still, I venture that you and I are so *over* state-sanctioned lies by now that the tyrants have given up trying to persuade us. Yet they must still convince *themselves*, if only to quell any protest from Conscience. "Uncertain way of gain," to quote Shakespeare's *Richard III*, "but I am in/ So far in blood that sin will pluck on sin./ Tear-falling pity dwells not in this eye" (IV.ii).

Meanwhile, if you harbour distrust of Christians, bear in mind that not all who *call* themselves Christians are truly members of the Body of Christ. Some are wolves in sheep's clothing or, calling on Shakespeare again, beautiful tyrants, fiends angelical, dove-feathered ravens, honorable villains, serpent hearts (*Romeo and Juliet*, III.ii). And some are false prophets, eager to share what "God told me."

Beware, too, of 'Controlled Opposition', those tasked with drawing dissidents into a 'Limited Hangout' that refuses to look at deeper and more horrid realities. Keep your wits about you, practise discernment, and sniff out the spiritual rot of these whitewashed tombs full of dead men's bones (*Matthew* 23:27).

But seek out those who genuinely *are* in Christ and who have chosen his ultimate authority over the false authority of men. We Christians may be all that is standing between you and annihilation. Have you noticed how Christian voices have taken the lead in recent years in denouncing and exposing the perpetrators? When, since the days of Moses or Joshua, has there been such a need for a fierce Christian army?

Do not resent your protectors, who are already paying a price for our faith. As Harrison Smith observed in a May 2024 interview with Maria Zeee, Christianity is under attack today because it impedes the totalitarian agenda...

"It makes it hard to control people. It makes it hard to deceive and manipulate. When the whole society is sincerely righteous and desires truth and desires justice, then you can't get away with things very easily. You have to have a whole system that's corrupt and fallen, and then it makes it easy to scam, it makes it easy to get one over. They want the dog-eat-dog world where they can screw somebody over and destroy them and suffer no consequences. So Christianity is a barrier to control, it's a barrier to oppression. **It gives you something higher than earthly authority, and that naturally pisses off the earthly authority**" (emphasis mine).

Speaking of earthly authority, I will not pin my hopes on a political solution to our woes. The *Declaration of Independence* doesn't tell us to "abolish" this or that political party or political candidate, nor does it call on us to favour one traitor, despot, pussy-grabber, or paedophile over another. No, it is our "duty" to abolish any *form* of Government that is destructive of Life, Liberty, and the Pursuit of Happiness.

Many more people are aware now that political parties oppose each other in only the most superficial ways, but when it comes to matters that really affect our lives, they are firm allies in trying to despoil us. As Mike Adams observed, in an April 2024 article,...

"The Democrats have actively destroyed this once-great nation, but the Republicans were either wholly complicit or stood by and did nothing while the arsonists set fire to the pillars of our constitutional republic. As is now obvious to anyone paying attention, we no longer have a functioning civil society in the United States of America. We have a failed government, failed election integrity, a failed justice system, a failed counterfeit currency, fake corporate media, fake war propaganda, a failed educational system, and a weaponized system of science and medicine that literally develops and deploys biological weapons against the American people."

Why do politicians act in concert against us, no matter what party they're in? Because, deep down, they're not really Democrats or Republicans, Conservatives or Labour, or whatever. These are just convenient labels for their sham political theatre. No, they serve but one party, and that is the party of Freemasonry. According to Bible scholar David Carrico, in a November 2019 episode of *Now You See TV*,…

> "If you look at the Democratic Party and the Republican Party, if you look close enough, both are Masonically controlled… These two American political parties, they are just the expression of two Masonic philosophies that both have the same ultimate goal, and that will be the New World Order."

That's why petitions and protests are useless when you're dealing with them. So too are polls when they have no compunction about rigging elections. As Max Igan observes, "There's nobody you can vote in. There's nobody you can vote out. There's no political remedy to this system."

True, Max. There is no political remedy, but other remedies are at hand. That's why I have written this book, a battle manual for warriors determined to overthrow tyrants of every stripe. One way or another, we must reclaim our Sovereignty, our freedom of action, even our freedom of thought. I do not mean a 'Great Reset' such as our enemies have conceived, but at least a Great Reckoning to restore Justice and consequence for the innumerable Crimes Against Humanity unleashed against Mankind. When, like a mighty river Justice returns, the overlords will be destroyed as surely as Pharaoh and his chariots were destroyed when they chased Moses into the Red Sea (*Exodus* 14:26-28). I trust this book shall serve as armour and weapon in the battle ahead, for battle it is, and battle it will be.

Abdiel LeRoy

CONCEPTS

1

A TYRANT-SLAYING MINDSET

Fear is the mind-killer. Fear is the little death that brings total obliteration. I will face my fear. I will permit it to pass over me and through me. And when it has gone past me, I will turn to see fear's path. Where the fear has gone, there will be nothing. Only I will remain.

— FRANK HERBERT, *DUNE*

I am in a living nightmare. Life is hell. I get at most a few hours of sleep each night, sometimes none at all, and my heart-rate refuses to calm down. At any moment, tanks will be rolling down the street, helicopters thudding above, and swarms of black-clad mercenaries going door-to-door to round us up and take us to concentration camps. The streets are narrow here, and escape routes easily cut off. We are surrounded, trapped like rabbits in a doomed warren.

That's my recollection of Christmas 2021. I was house-sitting in a suburb near Cambridge, England and close to completing my book about upholding medical rights. I was already in a state of high alert when I got there, not because of a purported virus, but because of the Orwellian walls closing in around me.

But then I watched an interview with funeral director, John O'Looney, and it put me over the edge. I could handle his account of the medical murders he had witnessed—I had heard similar from other sources—but when he talked about several huge prisons built in Britain to disappear political and medical dissidents, and about swarms of U.N. soldiers shipped into the country to take down the population, I descended into a tailspin of fear. Britain was poised to become a military dictatorship worse than the juntas that terrorized Argentina, Chile, and Uruguay in the '70s and '80s.

I wrote a scene in my book describing the horror that would unfold if the British government pulled this "totalitarian trigger." Meanwhile, I was confining my supermarket trips to late evening, when fewer people were around, to minimize the risk of being assaulted for not wearing a mask. I called my friend, JP, who at times annoyed me with the flurry of emails he sent about conspiracy findings. Yes, findings, I said, not theories.

"Fuckin' 'ell!" were the first words out of my mouth. He laughed. He had been through something similar before. Seems it's a rite of passage for those of us who pay attention and have come up to speed with the horrors in play and worse in plan.

By the grace of God, the military trigger was not pulled that Christmas, though our enemies continue to prepare for what Mike Adams calls "activation day... when the enemy occupying forces inside these countries activate and then begin attacking and sabotaging domestic infrastructure and carrying out a purge operation of the local people."

Still, the experience taught me something about handling fear, especially as I was then reading *A State of Fear* by Laura Dodsworth, where she describes how governments collude with 'behavioural scientists' to inflict terror and psychological torture on domestic populations. Later, we learned about a Dec. 13, 2020 WhatsApp exchange in which Britain's health minister at the time, Matt Hancock, wrote to an adviser, "We frighten the pants of[f] everyone with the new strain" and asked, "When do we deploy the new variant".

All the World's a Stage

Perhaps the most effective antidote at such times is to stop fearing death. John O'Looney has acknowledged on several occasions that, given the revelations he's shared, his life may be in danger, but he says he's not afraid to die. I responded in my last book by admitting that I *was* afraid to die, and of course I have read in *Revelation* about the Beast who "was given power to make war against the saints and to conquer them" (13:7), and I can't unread that.

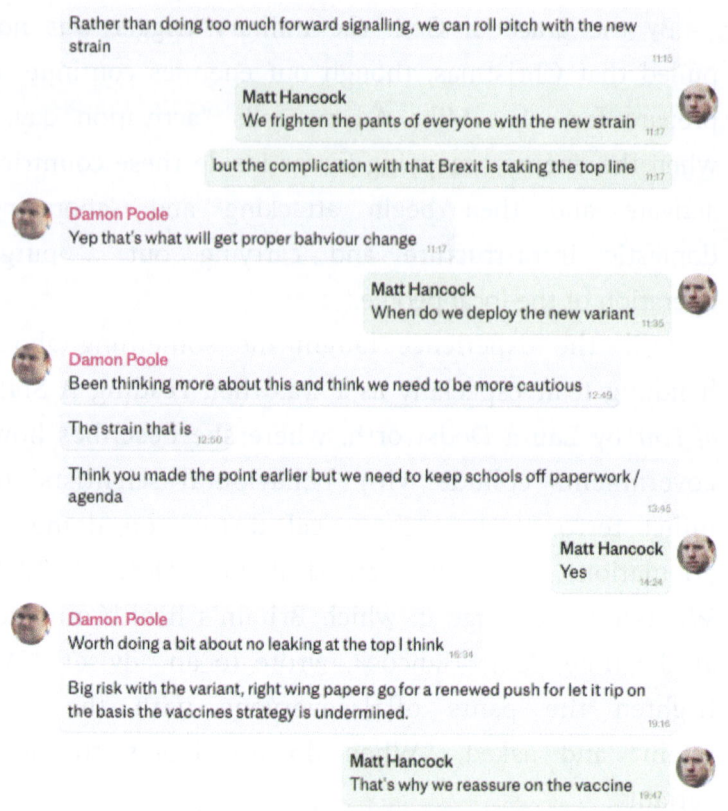

WhatsApp exchange, Dec. 13, 2020, between then U.K. health minister, Matt Hancock, and adviser, Damon Poole.

Yet the fear has largely dissipated by now. Recently, I experienced a kind of waking vision in which a warm and welcoming light was shining behind a thin hanging sheet of purple cloth. I knew instantly and instinctively that the cloth represented so-called 'death' and that the light of Christ was immediately on the other side.

I also like to expand on Shakespeare's lines in the play, *As You Like It...*

All the world's a stage
And all the men and women merely players.
They have their exits and their entrances...

In *Hamlet*, for instance, the hero dies in the closing scene, but the actor playing him lives on. What we call 'death' is merely exiting the stage and casting off one's costume, and as this world gets more evil by the day, the idea of leaving it becomes more acceptable too.

And I derive great comfort from Job's story in the Old Testament. Satan had to ask permission before he could afflict Job, and even then, the Almighty set limits to what Satan was allowed to do (*Job* 1:6-12). Though great evil is afoot again today, it is only within the parameters our Heavenly Father allows. I am learning to take what sensible precautions I can and not worry about the rest, for no-one can prepare for every eventuality.

You could argue it is dangerous to speak out in these times because you might get targeted, but I would counter we're in danger anyway, just for the faith in our hearts. Even without that faith, you may still be in danger when entire populations are targeted for destruction. So those who have faith may as well speak about it.

We who are in Christ cry out for his return. We know that he who saw Satan fall like lightning (*Luke* 10:18) could, with the flick of a finger, flatten the lordly scum opposed to us (*Luke* 11:20) and, with a word, dispatch hosts of angels to sweep our enemies from the Earth. I imagine the angels themselves are eager for the work. They strain like greyhounds in the slips, urging their

Captain to release them, but still his hand is raised to restrain them. Why? Because he wants his children on Earth to show their mettle first.

Certainly, our heavenly Father has given us a target-rich environment. His foes are everywhere, from the stages of Davos to parliament buildings to Freemason lodges and their underground theatres of horror. They're in schools, media organizations, police stations, and hospital wards. Our job is to bring them down, and we have the spiritual weapons to do so. Witness, for example, how Moses destroyed Pharaoh, Elijah took down Ahab and Jezebel, and Esther brought about the execution of Haman, all recounted in the Old Testament. Kings, soldiers, priests, and all worldly power do not stand a chance against our decrees in Heaven.

Nor, in destroying these tyrants, will I heed calls to forgive and forget, nor show them mercy, much less 'amnesty', though they may plead for it. Nor will I be persuaded to "Love your enemies." I will rebuke any purported Christian who quotes these slogans to dissuade me. Fools, you are in error because you do not know the Scriptures, and your interpretations are ungodly monstrosities.

I will also remember my authority in Christ to overcome *all* the power of the enemy (*Luke* 10:19), that I am more than conqueror (*Romans* 8:37), and that no weapon forged against me will prevail (*Isaiah* 54:17), and I will echo Caleb's call, after Moses sent him to spy out the Promised Land, to "Let us go up and take possession of the land, for we can surely do it" (*Numbers* 13:30). Of all the spies Moses sent, only he and Joshua urged they go forward, while the other spies wanted to hold back because they saw a land occupied by intimidating giants.

We don't see literal giants nowadays, and their historical presence on the Earth has been Memory-Holed from our collective awareness, but we do encounter their murderous relatives in autocrats, bureaucrats, psychocrats, and technocrats today. They clothe themselves in titles and awards, costume their enforcers in hi-vis yellow jackets, and deploy sophisticated weapons and surveillance tools against us. Cowards to the core, they are all destined for destruction.

Our victory over them begins in the mind, as it did with Joshua and Caleb, and with the truths that correct our perception for, "as a man thinketh in his heart, so is he" (*Proverbs* 23:7). What we think, therefore, is my main focus in the first part of this book. In the second part, I look more at solutions and the actions we can take, but you will need the solid foundation that I set out in the first. Our enemy, too, knows that the battle begins in the mind. As Alan of Salisbury points out, in a 2016 lecture at Birkbeck University, "They know, if they can control your mind, your body will follow."

I will show you, therefore, that all is counterfeit, all theatre, and that counterfeit governments, issuing counterfeit fiat currencies and writing counterfeit legislation masquerading as Law, are wielding counterfeit authority. It's so much easier to refuse and refute that authority when you know its agents are beneath you and that they are peddling fictional constructs.

So let us pierce through their illusions and mind-tricks, and remember who we are and who they are. As Max Igan explains in a March 2024 broadcast,...

"Government have tricked the people into believing that they are their parents, that you've got to ask permission for everything, and without the government there to protect you, things would be terrible. The government isn't protecting you, the government is breaking down the food chain, the government is working to starve most of the population and to get them completely enslaved to a government system. That's what all this stuff is about. That's what this whole climate agenda is all about... Stop believing government is your ruler. These are people who are supposed to manage infrastructure in a responsible way for us."

We must "bring the servants who think themselves as Master back into subjection," writes David E. Robinson in *The UCC Connection*. "God did not intend for us to spend our lives in statutory slavery for the benefit of a handful of secret world manipulators, even if the 'masters' grant us some token of diversions and pleasure."

Yes, God intends us to reclaim our mastery over the public servants or, as writer and performer Amy Harlib calls them, 'public serpents'. We are like that master, spoken of in parable by Christ, who returns home from a long trip and finds his household in disarray because, during his absence, his steward neglected his duties, raided the wine collection, abandoned the garden, and drove the master's car into a ditch. But now, just like that master, we take back ownership of our estate and assign that worthless servant a place with the hypocrites, where there is weeping and gnashing of teeth (*Matthew* 24:48-51; *Luke* 12:45-46). We may do this with bold, in-your-face declaration or, like Homer's Odysseus, taking back his house and kingdom in Ithaca, return in disguise and ambush the foe. Famed for his cunning and guile, Odysseus' example may instruct us as we embrace Jesus' command to be "wise as serpents" (*Matthew* 10:16).

What an intriguing simile! The serpent is commonly associated with Satan, but here, Christ is ascribing some of its qualities to us. Christian cunning and Christian calculation, then, informed by the Mind of Christ, have a critical role to play in these times, and the skills we develop now may rival even Aaron's accomplishment when, with his brother Moses, he confronted Pharaoh, threw down his staff, and it turned into a snake. Pharaoh's conjurors imitated the act, but Aaron's snake ate their snakes (*Exodus* 7:10-12).

Included in our serpent wisdom is discernment. We are not unaware of the devil's schemes (2 *Corinthians* 2:11), and that includes his resort to "legalese and double-talk and word salad," to quote social-media channel, HighImpactFlix. Our forked-tongue foes have twisted and weaponized words against us but, with the Mind of Christ, we demolish their double-speak when they use words like 'law', 'mandate', 'income', or even 'understand'. We trample their deceptive rhetoric, skewer their devious euphemisms and, when they make righteous proclamation, dismiss these clanging cymbals for the liars they are.

We are also quick to sniff out 'Controlled Opposition', those who pretend to align with us but whose real purpose is to surveil us and confine analysis to a 'Limited Hangout'. Controlled Opposition dissipates the energy and resources of resisters, hides from public view the full horrors at work, and shields from scrutiny the unseen puppet-masters who pull the strings of the visible villains.

Elections, too, even the ones that by some miracle are conducted without tampering and rigging, are a Limited Hangout and lock us into a perpetual cycle of hope and betrayal, like Sisyphus forever rolling his boulder up a mountain, only to lose it just before the summit. "It's all very well, shaking one's head and wailing that 'We just need to get the right people into power!'," writes Veronica: of the Chapman family in a May 2024 email. "Even if you ever achieved that, it WOULD NOT LAST! You cannot possibly expect 'to get the right people into power' until the End of Time. You must surely know that. 'Democracy' is NEVER going to work!"

So what will work, Veronica? "NO RULERS," she writes, "NO PARASITIC, PSYCHOPATHIC, RULING CLASS." You can read more of her insights in the book,

Freedom Is More Than Just a Seven-Letter Word, which I quote often in *Know Your Medical Rights.*

Sun Tzu's *The Art of War* can also train us for battle, according to author and man of God, Kevin Annett, who quotes this ancient work frequently in his life's mission to expose crimes of church and state against the native people of Canada, or rather, the Republic of Kanata. Also known as Eagle Strong Voice to his indigenous friends, Annett has authored many books, including *Establishing the Reign of Natural Liberty: A Common Law Training Manual* (2017) and its companion title, *Truth Teller's Shield: A Manual for Whistle Blowers & Hell Raisers* (2016). We shall hear more from him later.

Among the precepts he cites from Sun Tzu are to... establish the conditions of battle before it begins; lead the enemy rather than be led by it; act unpredictably and outside the enemy's experience; conceal your intentions and movements and then strike unexpectedly where the enemy is weak and vulnerable; and attack first, forcing the enemy to follow your lead.

You may not feel ready for the battles ahead, and neither do I, which is partly why I am writing this book. It is also why I echo the words of Shakespeare's King Henry V who, before he led a tired and depleted English army into battle against a much larger French force at Agincourt, told the French ambassador, "We would not seek a battle as we are/ Nor, as we are, we say we will not shun it" (III.vi.).

I cannot hope to map out every path and avenue ahead, but if I can keep my eyes on the author and perfecter of our faith (*Hebrews* 12:2), then I shall improvise wisely. Like the star that guided the Wise Men to the infant Jesus, he is our constant, whatever twists, turns, setbacks, diversions, or delays we experience on the way.

2

THE 'BERTH' CERTIFICATE

If they can trick us to identify as a corporation, then whatever they do to us, they're not doing to Man.

— SIMON ('SI THE SPANIARD')
GOLDBERG

In the brilliant science-fiction trilogy, *The Three Body Problem*, author Liu Cixin imagines a weapon that flattens three-dimensional space into two-dimensional space, so that planets are squashed into discs and all life on them is wiped out. I don't know whether he intended it as a metaphor, but this describes what the powers-that-shouldn't-be have done to us. We came to this Earth as living, breathing, three-dimensional beings, but then a Birth Certificate was drawn up that represented our lifetime monetary value to tyrants who would extract our property for the rest of our lives. They would do this through fines, fees, taxes, inflation, and debt, and by paying us less for our time and labour than we're worth.

The Birth Certificate was, in effect, a Bond, and it led to bond-age. What is a Bond? Suppose I make a loan to you, and you write on a piece of paper your promise to pay back in installments over time. That piece of paper is a Bond; it is worth something to me based on your promise of future payments.

Now, suppose I decide I don't want to wait for your installments. I can't demand you pay faster than you've promised, but I can go to someone else and sell the Bond to them. They receive your installments instead and I receive a lump sum.

What's that got to do with the Birth Certificate? It is treated as a Bond, and whoever holds it gets to receive your lifelong installments. Let us call that bondholder Mr. Global. He gets a piece of you for the rest of your life, or he can sell your future flow of installments to another institution and pocket a lump sum instead.

What a great deal for him! A regular slave-owner only gets to collect his slave's output as it happens, but Mr. Global can collect on your expected future output by selling it as a packaged financial instrument, or 'Security'. If you live in the united States, take a look at your 'Social Security Card'. The Bond account number is inscribed on the back in red ink.

All this runs in the background throughout our journey from womb to tomb. We are treated as debtors, though we never took out a loan, and are traded like livestock. You can even look up these trades, I gather, on a CUSIP Report, where 'CUSIP' stands for 'Committee of Uniform Security Information Procedure', a numbering system for U.S. financial instruments. As I have been separated from the Birth Certificate assigned to me, I cannot verify this, but others advise: 1/ Go to Fidelity.com, 2/ Make a free account, 3/ Go to "Get a Quote," and 4/ Enter the number of your Birth Certificate to find the CUSIP number.

We were turned into financial instruments, or 'securitized', but the picture gets even more horrifying when, according to the late Jordan Maxwell, the Birth-Certificate Bonds "are used as collateral to persuade the banks to make loans to the government." In other words, governments outspend their budgets, borrow the difference, and tell the banks they're borrowing from that the people are good for it. Our labour serves as their collateral. The loan is to be repaid by what the government plans to extract from us and future generations.

That is why I said at the outset we were born into slavery. Your mother was a slave, and when her newborn arrived, her slave-master claimed ownership of you too and compelled her to sign the Certificate to prove it. You were registered, and that which is registered is given away. Thus, our Birthright as three-dimensional beings was exchanged for a two-dimensional fiction on pieces of paper representing monetary value. In this inversion of Jesus' mission, of the Word who became flesh (*John* 1:14), through the Birth Certificate our flesh became word or rather, our flesh became number.

What is the extent of that stolen Birthright, considering that we were collectively given "dominion... over all the Earth" (*Genesis* 1:26)? According to White Rabbit Trust, if you take all the usable, arable land in the world and divide it by the population of Earth, each individual would receive an area four times the size of Twickenham rugby field. I hope this analysis dispels any notion you had that slavery was abolished. It wasn't. It just took a more subtle form that operates through deception—a deception by which governments today are little more than extractive industries mining the people for all they can get on behalf of banker puppeteers.

ALL-CAPS NAMES

So how was this deception effected? In part by assigning you a fake name in ALL CAPITALS. Look at your Birth Certificate, your driving licence, passport, bank cards, and bills. Your name has been falsified into an ALL-CAPS format. Same goes for your social security card or national insurance card or what have you. The ALL-CAPS NAME, often preceded by 'MR', 'MRS', or 'MS', is your 'STRAWMAN', 'legal person', or 'citizen', a word co-opted by the state to effect our enslavement. We have been tricked into believing we *are* that fiction and that we must, with our living, breathing, toiling bodies, pay all the taxes and levies charged against it.

As observed in a paper titled *The Curse of Co-Suretyship: Why You Are Held Accountable for the National Debt*, ALL-CAPS spelling "is the standard method for designating the name of corporations" and "falls completely outside the accepted rules of English grammar for the spelling of proper names of men and women."

In his 2016 lecture, Alan of Salisbury points out, "This is where you get the term 'capitalism' from, because your life has been monetized and capitalized as a bonded slave." ALL CAPS is also the format used on gravestones, reflecting the state's regard of you as a dead person. Once you're safely dwelling with the dead, then your estate is up for grabs.

Another advantage for tyrants in designating us corporations is to treat us as Rights-less. In the words of author and historian Anna von Reitz, writing in a blog post, "corporations can be owned as slaves."

A Cargo of Souls

Ships, too, are named in ALL CAPS, and this signals your designation as a waterborne vessel for the purposes of Commerce. Your cargo is what you're expected to produce over a lifetime, and it is traded back and forth by merchants without your knowledge or consent. We may be sailed, steered, or scuppered at their whim, or boarded and pirated by other shipowners. Thus, when *Revelation* describes the coming demise of the merchant class, it lists among their cargoes "bodies and souls of men" (18:13).

The legal structure facilitating this Commerce is variously called 'Admiralty Law', 'Maritime Law', 'Merchant Law', 'Equity Law', 'Administrative Law',

'Papal Law', 'Roman Law', 'Law of Commerce', or some other delusional name. I call it all bullshit. As we have seen, 'Law' is not attainable by the decisions and decrees of men, so I'll use other terms such as statute, code, policy, or regulations.

According to @Love.lee.777 on TikTok,...

> "When you were born, they took your name, and they created a corporation out of it and that corporation, that dead entity, has claimed your name. That dead entity is im-PERSON-ating you. You are not that entity. So whenever you're interacting in Commerce with the government, it has nothing to do with you. You are the living being standing on the land, a Child of God. They're actually interacting, taxing, criminalizing, persecuting that corporation, that corporate entity."

None of us was given any say in the matter, none of us was given Informed Consent. We were sold into slavery from the day of our birth, and the Birth Certificate was the sales receipt. Not that we or our parents received any compensation in this transaction. It came at zero cost to the purchaser. No wonder the state so readily steals children from their parents. It already thinks it owns them!

Think of Government, then, as a cuckoo bird that deposited in our nest a usurping egg from which a murderous hatchling emerged and pushed the true inheritors out of the nest. Yet the parent bird was fooled into feeding the impostor as its own.

Lethal Legalese

In order to keep their illusions in play, the parasite class exploit homonyms, meaning words that sound the same but have different meanings. For example, 'birth' is a homonym of 'berth', a mooring for a ship, and the 'dock' of a court is a homonym for a loading 'dock'. 'Currency' is close to 'current of the sea', and a 'bank' that handles currency sounds the same as a 'bank' beside a river. Also, crucially, 'YOUR NAME' (in ALL CAPS) is a homonym for 'Your Name' (in Title Caps).

Corporate fictions can only interact with other fictions, much as characters in a play interact with other characters in the same play on a stage. Therefore, from time to time, such as appearances in court, the manipulator corporations will try to flatten you again through a procedure called 'Joinder', by which they seek your contractual agreement to take responsibility for the levies imposed on your STRAWMAN.

Joinder can happen in seemingly innocent ways, such as asking you to confirm your name for the court, and I shall explore this further in a later chapter. The key deception is to conflate the real and living with the fictional and dead. You may think you're saying "My Name" (in Title Caps) but what they choose to hear is "MY NAME" (in ALL CAPS).

As we have seen, God gave Man Dominion over the Earth, so Government must identify you as something other than Man, something below Man, for if it ever acknowledged your true, three-dimensional self, it could no longer profit off you. No, you are chattel to be harvested and worked to death, all so some banking family can accumulate obscene wealth at your expense.

Nor, in their statutes, will they use the words 'man', 'woman', or 'people' to describe us. Instead, it is 'person', 'resident, 'taxpayer', 'tenant', 'occupant', 'constituent', 'consumer', 'patient', 'member of the public', and so on. And, to deny us the Right to Travel freely, they call us 'drivers', not 'travellers'. Imagine the absurdity of having to apply for a 'travelling licence', but that's what they've got us doing!

That is one of many examples where governments have converted inalienable Rights into 'privileges' and then sold us licences to exercise them. In the words of truth.to.the.rescue on Instagram,...

"150 years ago, you didn't have to ask permission from the government to go fishing, own a property, build on your property, renovate your home, use a transportation vehicle, start a business, get married, own a weapon, hunt, cut hair, sell a product, protest, grow your own food, sell that food that you grow on your own property, or even just set up a lemonade stand. And now, you virtually can't do anything without asking for the government's permission first. So if you still think you're free, you're deluding yourself. Hate to break it to you but you're a free-range human in a tax farm."

Cestui Que Vie

How did we get here? It would take several volumes, covering millennia of history, to explore all the legislation that has codified Hell on Earth, but the *Cestui Que Vie Act* of 1666, passed shortly after 'The Great Fire of London', is key. Its title in archaic French, which was the dominant language used for legal documents in England at the time, means something like, "Whoever Is Alive."

Spanning just two pages, the Act addresses what to do about the estates of missing persons "beyond the Seas or absenting themselves," and it determined that the missing person "shall be accounted as naturally dead" after seven years of absence if there is no proof that he is alive. Then his property would be handed over to a 'Reversioner', meaning the one to whom the property reverts, the one in line to receive it after his death.

This Act has been applied to us. The Birth Certificate has deemed us missing "beyond the Seas," and when we reached the age of seven, we were accounted as dead, and the banking cabal, which set itself up as Reversioner, took over our estates. As Allegedly Dave explains in a September 2024 interview with James Delingpole, "They've used this idea of everyone's dead to claim our shares of the country."

But the *Cestui Que Vie Act* also says that if the supposed dead man shall "returne againe from beyond the Seas" or prove to be alive, then he "may reenter repossesse have hold and enjoy" his property again, and recover the revenues withheld from him, with interest, from the time the Reversioner took over his property. Brothers and Sisters, we have a life-changing amount of property and back-pay due to us, and under the tyrants' own legal structure, our announcement that we are alive entitles us to repossess it.

In the meantime, according to von Reitz, our rightful inheritance is held in "a Cestui Que Vie ESTATE trust by THE DEPARTMENT OF COMMERCE which is then 'removed to Puerto Rico for safekeeping,' all without your knowledge or consent." In a June 2022 video, she explains, "They began using our assets—our gold and silver, our land, even our bodies and our labor—as assets that they could use as collateral and create credit for themselves and their operations." This involved 'personage'—that is to say, impersonation or identity theft—by inventing the fake, ALL-CAPS NAME and then making charges against it that the Title-Caps real being is expected to pay.

Seems to me the bankers are now calling in their loans from the governments who, with infernal zeal, are in turn seizing as much collateral as they can from the people to pay off their debts. Killing off the elderly is the low-hanging fruit because it liquidates the pension obligations they would otherwise have to pay.

Another Exodus

But now that we see the deceptions, freedom from the 'Beast System', 'Beast of the Sea', or 'Babylon' as some call it, has begun, and once our minds are free, our actions will follow, fulfilling the angel's command in *Revelation* to "Come out of her, my people" (18:4), where the "her" is Babylon.

Through the Birth Certificate, we were unwittingly signed up, without Informed Consent, to a Contract of enslavement but, as David E. Robinson points out in *Meet Your Strawman*, "for any contract to be valid, there has to be full and open disclosure of all of the terms of the contract, and then, unreserved acceptance by both parties, and in these cases, that has most definitely not occurred." Therefore, Brothers and Sisters, the Birth-Certificate Contract is null and void. Furthermore, we decline any secondary Contract that seeks to bind us to our mother's signature.

Our liberation from corporate Birth-Certificate bondage is sometimes called, going from 'the Public' to 'the Private'. In a 2013 document titled *Introduction to the Private*, the author writes, "The Private is living men, women, and children. The Public is Government and registered corporations called 'Persons'." Governments "profit from the people's ignorance while milking them as members of the general PUBLIC. If the people knew they are not PUBLIC but PRIVATE with PRIVATE rights superseding PUBLIC government, the people could rebel and expose the magnitude of PUBLIC wrong doings."

Some freedom advocates advise "claiming" the STRAWMAN but, as Simon ('Si the Spaniard') Goldberg of White Rabbit Trust and youandyourcash.com points out, ownership brings liability. In a June 2024 video, he explains, "The STRAWMAN is a reference to the LEGAL

PERSONALITY which is 'attached' to you at birth/BERTH. The LEGAL PERSONALITY is a collection of Rights & Duties and is the CODE by which LEGAL LAND 'sees' you… It comes with LEGAL responsibilities, LEGAL duties, LEGAL obligations, and LEGAL DEBT."

Why would you want to own this dead thing or its legal obligations? Why would you want to hug those bones? Why lug about a corpse, a corporation, or a ship? The STRAWMAN is dead to us, and if we let that false, two-dimensional self be lost, we shall find our *true*, three-dimensional self (*Matthew* 16:25).

A Christian could go further and say that the STRAWMAN was crucified with Christ (*Galatians* 2:20), so that the new, three-dimensional self could rise. "If anyone is in Christ," wrote the apostle Paul, "he is a new creation. The old has passed away, the new has come" (2 *Corinthians* 5:17).

"We were a dead man," says @Love.lee.777, "devoured by the Beast of the Sea, but now, like Jonah, we come onto dry land, a living man again." Coming out of the Admiralty/Maritime jurisdiction and being restored to the Land is like emerging from baptism, another Exodus, by which we reclaim our inheritance of Christ's kingdom. We become 'Is Real' again, she continues, an Israel of the heart, not on a map.

That is why freedom advocates talk about being a 'Free Man on the Land' and about the Law of the Land, notions that the false authorities are quick to attack and ridicule because they scare them so much. @Love.lee.777

recommends doing paperwork to express this. Claim your living status and proclaim your age of majority under Minnesota 220 law, she advises, and publish that in a newspaper for four weeks. This confirms your emancipation from being property of the U.S. government.

Others argue such steps are unnecessary because our freedom was never lost. We have never not been a Living Man or Woman. We simply need to stop cooperating with the processes by which they have been taking our freedoms and property from us. I see merit in this argument too, for the Almighty has promised "to restore the land/ and to reassign its desolate inheritances..." (*Isaiah* 49:8), and Christ's burden is light (*Matthew* 11:28-30). Why run around with letters, notices, filings, affidavits, and so on, when we are naturally above all that?

But then again, if you are in water and want to get onto land, you still need to take a few steps to get there, don't you? And you'll want to rub yourself down with a towel after you do. Also, even if it's just a placebo effect or a security blanket, I feel more empowered when facing would-be enforcers, if I've got a document or two to hand.

Let the pen be mightier than the sword, for even our enemies pay attention to words, and "The devil can cite Scripture for his purpose" (Shakespeare, *The Merchant of Venice*, I.iii.). Why else would they go to such lengths to twist them, craft tyrant codes, and churn out their vile propaganda with them? It makes their work of destroying us easier if they can first persuade us to destroy ourselves.

The passage I cited in *Revelation* continues, "Give back to her as she has given," so, with the pen of a gifted writer (*Psalms* 45:1), let us pierce our enemies with words, including the words in this book. Ultimately, the destroyers will not even have their Maritime jurisdiction left to them for, as *Genesis* records, Man was given "dominion over the fish of the sea, and over the fowl of the air, and over the cattle, and over all the earth..." That's it. Earth, air, *and* sea.

3

COMMON LAW

'Natural Law' means 'Common Sense' which means 'Common Law'.

— VERONICA: OF THE CHAPMAN FAMILY

True Law is neither complex nor burdensome. "Jesus said unto him, Thou shalt love the Lord thy God with all thy heart, and with all thy soul, and with all thy mind. This is the first and greatest commandment. And the second is like unto it, Thou shalt love thy neighbour as thyself. On these two commandments hang all the law and the prophets" (*Matthew* 22:37-40).

Do No Harm

Loving others as you love yourself is an eternal principle, and we may therefore call it Law. As Veronica points out, only that which is immutable merits the title of Law, such as the Law of Gravity or the Laws of Motion, something no man or woman can conjure, alter, or repeal.

Does not your heart yearn to restore simplicity in what we call Law? Imagine the joy that would spring forth if everyone at least made an effort to treat others as they would wish to be treated, otherwise known as the 'Royal Law' (*James* 2:8) or the 'Golden Rule'. Even hardcore atheists will see the merit in this. For example, no-one wants to be medically compelled, so no-one has the right to inflict medical compulsion on others.

Loving others as you love yourself includes, of course, doing no harm, and that is the basis of Common Law, also referred to as the 'Law of the Land'. As John Smith of commonlawcourt.com explains, in a November 2020 interview with David Icke, "Common Law relates to the basic principles of cause no harm, cause no loss, cause no injury, and ensure that you're honorable in your contractual dealings."

For those of us who don't set out to harm or cheat others, Common Law is protective. Without a victim, there is no crime; without a crime, there can be no fine or other penalty nor, for that matter, taxation. Under Common Law, we cannot be penalized just because we didn't comply with yet another illogical and absurd decree from a government agency or enforcer. As David E. Robinson points out in *Common Law Handbook*, "The State cannot be the victim." Common Law also includes the Right to Silence, Presumption of Innocence (in contrast to today's state apparatus that presumes guilt 'til proven innocent), and indifference to prior court rulings and precedents.

For tyrants, however, Common Law is a terrifying prospect because it holds them individually accountable. It does not recognize such a thing as 'legal immunity', which is a corporate fiction, nor does it allow individuals to hide behind a corporate shield. How many times have we heard a court or government agency order this or that pharmaceutical company, police department, or bank to pay a fine after it caused harm, only to see the individual perpetrators get off with a slap on the wrist and sometimes, not even that? Common Law will not tolerate such injustice, which is why the false authorities hate it so much.

In the words of Veronica, writing in an email, "... one may have every reason to say, 'I do not consent to the legislation created by the Parliament or Congress, because I have not sworn any allegiance to those organisations and that system,' but one CANNOT remove consent to the Common Law, because Common Law comes with the Universe."

Imagine the revolution Common Law shall bring about when it pierces the immunity and impunity now cloaking globalist conspirators and their puppet organizations such as the Bank for International Settlements, United Nations, World Economic Forum, and dozens of central banks. In an article titled *"Who Is THEY?"*, journalist Corey Lynn lists the forms this immunity takes:

"... all of their archives are inviolable, their property and assets are immune from search and seizure, they are exempt from every kind of tax regular people pay, including property taxes, officers and employees are exempt from legal suits, employees and their family members can travel the world without checks from customs, military and police are not allowed to enter their headquarters, and much more. Once people understand that THIS is the control framework—the structure that was created nearly 80 years ago so that they can operate outside the law and never be held accountable, it's easy to see how all of the other pieces fall into place."

Common Law is mentioned twice in the Seventh Amendment of the *Bill of Rights*, which comprises the first ten Amendments to *The Constitution of the United States of America*...

"In suits at common law, where the value in controversy shall exceed twenty dollars, the right of trial by jury shall be preserved, and no fact tried by a jury shall be otherwise reexamined in any court of the United States, than according to the rules of the common law."

If, like me, you have felt baffled, confused, and exhausted trying to get your head around the legislation, regulations, and court decisions engineered to enslave us, know that this is by design. The corporate operatives go to great lengths to conceal their tyranny in word soups and word salads that leave us none the wiser. Trying to decipher their mind-numbing code is like trying to unravel the Gordian Knot which, according to legend, thwarted all who made the attempt. Let us rather take the approach of Alexander who, we are told, put the Knot's torment to rest by cutting through it with his sword. For us, that means wielding Common Law.

4

GOVERNMENTS ARE
CORPORATIONS

The issue is not that power corrupts, it's that power attracts those who are easily corrupted.

— MAX IGAN, THECROWHOUSE,

MAR. 28, 2024

Dethroning Government and its usurpation of authority begins in the mind, and it will serve us again to quote the irrefutable logic, encapsulated in the documentary *Strawman*, that "Government is a creation of Man, and a creation of Man can never be above Man." The required adjustment to our perception is greatly assisted when we realize that governments these days are corporations whose purpose is to mine the people for all the wealth and property they can extract.

According to the *United States Code* (*USC*), a compilation of legislation organized by subject matter, the

Know Your Lawful Rights 351

term 'United States' is defined as "a Federal corporation" (Title 28, Section 3002 (15)(a)).

(15) "United States" means—

(A) a Federal corporation;

(B) an agency, department, commission, board, or other entity of the United States; or

(C) an instrumentality of the United States.

And that corporation is in the District of Columbia (DC), according to the Uniform Commercial Code (UCC), a body of legislation that governs commercial transactions (§9-307 (h)).

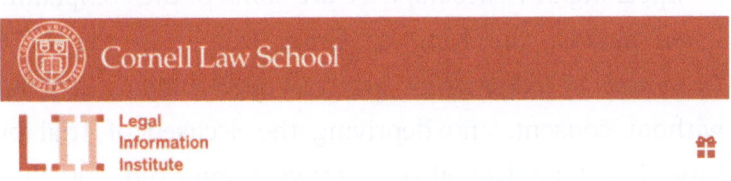

(h) [Location of United States.]

The United States is located in the District of Columbia.

The United States corporation is even more alienated from us by being foreign to the States of the Union. As described in *Corpus Juris Secundum*, an encyclopaedia of legislation, "The United States government is a foreign corporation with respect to a State" (Vol. 19,

Section 883). This statement rests in turn on a U.S. Supreme-Court ruling of 1894 in *Merriam's Estate*: "It is suggested that the United States is to be regarded as a domestic corporation, so far as the State of New York is concerned. We think this contention has no support in reason or authority."

What does all of this mean? That **the States United are under foreign occupation** from a corporation located in DC. It also means the 'J6' protestors now being tortured in DC jails are behind enemy lines, literally prisoners of war. According to Miki Klann of Bonds for the Win, "Every single police precinct, every single court, every single jailhouse, they're all working for the foreign corporation, the foreign enemy, the foreign invaders. The Redcoats are here," she told Ann Vandersteel in a 2024 interview.

Speaking of Redcoats, here are some of the complaints listed against the King of Great Britain in the 1776 *Declaration of Independence*: arbitrary government, taxation without consent, and depriving the accused of Trial by Jury. The king had also "erected a multitude of New Offices," "sent hither swarms of Officers to harass our people, and eat out their substance," and "combined with others to subject us to a jurisdiction foreign to our constitution."

Any of this sound familiar? And if you have observed with alarm the millions of migrant soldiers—described in polite circles as "men of military age"—now swarming our nations in the guise of refugees, you will sympathize with another complaint in the *Declaration* that the king was "transporting large Armies of foreign Mercenaries to compleat the works of death, desolation and tyranny."

According to Anna von Reitz, "Our diligent research of many years duration proves beyond any rational doubt that our lawful government has been usurped by 'governmental services corporations' in the business of selling us—guess what?—more governmental services. In the process they have set up a web of deceits and false legal claims designed to support and expedite their racketeering and use of armed force to make us buy and pay for more and more and more 'governmental services'."

Dig enough, and you will find that governments throughout the world are corporations. For example, the company named 'CANADA' is filed with the U.S. Securities and Exchange Commission under the organization name, International Corp Fin, and file number 033-05368.

```
COMPANY DATA:
        COMPANY CONFORMED NAME:                    CANADA
        CENTRAL INDEX KEY:                         0000230098
        STANDARD INDUSTRIAL CLASSIFICATION:        FOREIGN GOVERNMENTS [8888]
        ORGANIZATION NAME:                  International Corp Fin
        IRS NUMBER:                                000000000
        FISCAL YEAR END:                           0331

        FILING VALUES:
                FORM TYPE:              18-K/A
                SEC ACT:                1934 Act
                SEC FILE NUMBER:        033-05368
                FILM NUMBER:            24889163

        BUSINESS ADDRESS:
                STREET 1:               CANADIAN EMBASSY
                STREET 2:               501 PENNSYLVANIA AVE NW
                CITY:                   WASHINGTON
                STATE:                  DC
                ZIP:                    20001
                BUSINESS PHONE:         613-369-3646
```

Von Reitz suggests you browse online for

governments at opencorporates.com, Dun & Bradstreet, and Companies House. Here are some results I found...

Corporation: THE QUEEN'S MOST EXCELLENT MAJESTY IN RIGHT OF CANADA
Company Number: OE022586
Legal Form: Government Department

Corporation: THE QUEEN'S MOST EXCELLENT MAJESTY IN RIGHT OF NEW ZEALAND
Company Number: OE021881
Legal Form: Government Department

Corporation: THE UNITED STATES OF AMERICA
Company Number: OE015146
Legal Form: Government Department

Corporation: THE GOVERNMENT OF THE RUSSIAN FEDERATION
Company Number: OE028105
Legal Form: Federal Republic

Corporation: GOVERNMENT OF IRELAND
Company Number: OE031961
Legal Form: Non-Uk government

Corporation: THE STATE OF ISRAEL
Company Number: OE027515
Legal Form: State

Oh what a tangled web they weave! Among their crimes, von Reitz lists semantic deceit, press ganging, false claims in commerce, inland piracy, kidnapping, human trafficking, and genocide. And it's not just governments that are corporations but individual departments and agencies within them...

Corporation: THE SECRETARY OF STATE FOR
TRANSPORT
Company Number: 0745
Legal Form: UK PARLIAMENT SIS

Corporation: SECRETARY OF STATE FOR
INTERNATIONAL DEVELOPMENT
Company Number: OC305927

Corporation: THE MINISTRY OF DEFENCE OF THE
GOVERNMENT OF THE REPUBLIC OF ITALY
Company Number: OE032221
Legal Form: Government Entity

Nor is the corporatization limited to national governments; it extends to the provincial, regional, State, county, district, and local levels too. As von Reitz explains, the 'Municipal United States', doing business as THE UNITED STATES, INC., comprises "10,000 INCORPORATED Franchises operating as Municipal Oligarchies: 'STATE OF,' 'CITY OF,' 'TOWN OF,' 'TOWNSHIP OF,' 'BOROUGH OF'."

Meanwhile, in the U.K., the *Local Government Act*

(1972) states, "Each council mentioned in subsection (1) or (2) above shall be a body corporate by the name 'The County Council' or 'The District Council', as the case may be, with the addition of the name of the particular county or district." (Part 2, Par. 3).

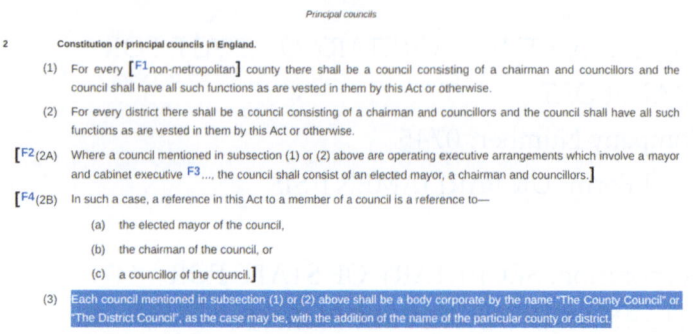

Here are a few more of my search results...

THE GOVERNMENT OF QUÉBEC, CANADA
Company Number: OE026157
Legal Form: Government Organization

OLDHAM METROPOLITAN BOROUGH COUNCIL
Company Number: OC392227
Legal Form: Local Authority

POLICE FEDERATION OF ENGLAND AND WALES
Company Number: 04120881
Legal Form: Staff Association

HM COURTS AND TRIBUNALS SERVICE KENT
SURREY AND SUSSEX ENFORCEMENT BUSINESS
CENTRE LIMITED
Company Number: 13881746
Company Type: Private Limited Company

And what are corporations? The word literally means 'dead speaker'. They are soulless fictions, dead things, yet telling us through their barely alive spokespersons to obey them. The practice of Government, and obedience to it, is necromancy and witchcraft.

"Governments around the world have long been replaced by corporations pretending to be governments," as reported by Australian commentator Maria Zeee in a June 2023 broadcast. They...

"have entered unsuspecting human beings into contracts they do not know the full details of, with these private corporations. Said private corporations, with their special little clubs, have their special little meetings, both in secret in the dark of night, or in public where the Public's rights are sacrificed on camera at the United Nations."

These conspirators are working towards even more centralization of power, Zeee warns, under "a one-world government—or one-world corporation, we should say—building their empire of complete control of your movement, ability to earn income and do with it as you see fit, land rights, property rights, medical autonomy,

religious freedom, freedom of speech, freedom of
thought, and much much more. It is a religion, it is a cult,
and like all cults, if you do not agree with every single
aspect of its ideology, you are a threat and must be
eliminated."

Oaths of Omission

So, if officials, elected or unelected, have forgotten their
public duty, can we at least remind them of, and hold
them to, the Oath they have sworn to serve us? Or to put
the question another way, if they fall short of lawful
standards by which their 'Yea' be yea and their 'Nay' be
nay, "for whatsoever is more than these cometh of evil"
(*Matthew* 5:37), can we at least get them to uphold some
legal standards?

After all, under U.S. legislation *Title 5, Section 3331*,
each is required to swear "that I will support and defend
the Constitution of the United States against all enemies,
foreign and domestic; that I will bear true faith and
allegiance to the same; that I take this obligation freely,
without any mental reservation or purpose of evasion;
and that I will well and faithfully discharge the duties of
the office on which I am about to enter. So help me God."

Then, according to *Title 5, Section 3332*, "An officer,
within 30 days after the effective date of his appointment,
shall file with the oath of office required by section 3331
of this title an affidavit that neither he nor anyone acting
in his behalf has given, transferred, promised, or paid any

consideration for or in the expectation or hope of receiving assistance in securing the appointment."

The answer is no! As the work of Todd Callender, Lisa McGee, and their Project Proper Oath team has shown, not one member of Biden's cabinet had a valid Oath of Office at the time of going to press (August 2024). All the oaths were fraudulent, incomplete, or missing entirely. Among those with no oath at all were Biden's vice president, attorney general, and the secretaries of Defense, State, Treasury, Transportation, Health and Human Services, and Homeland Security. Thus,...

NOT ONE OF THE HIGHEST OFFICIALS SUPPOSEDLY RUNNING THE COUNTRY HAS PROMISED EITHER TO UPHOLD THE CONSTITUTION OR TO FORSWEAR BRIBERY!

"The whole damn thing is a show," Callender commented to Greg Reese in a March 2024 interview. My own inference is that these creatures didn't bother with public oaths because they have all sworn secret ones. As Jesus said, "You cannot serve two masters" (*Matthew* 6:24). They could never be loyal to a public oath, whether to office or Constitution or even their marriage vows, because the master they really serve is god of the Occult.

In Closing...

In short, a foreign corporation, though called the 'United States', is purporting to rule the neighboring country comprising these united (lower-case 'u') States. Were the nation alert to this, we would honour our duty, as set out in the *Declaration of Independence*, to abolish it. We would besiege, boycott, and blockade the District of Columbia, overrun it, and finally liberate the People from its centuries-long reign of tyranny.

Until then, our nations are as a condemned house riddled with termites, infested with vermin, held together by rotten timbers, and leaning perilously to one side. No repairs or remediation are attempted, and none can be done, because the house has been taken over by squatters. Even if we were to gain access now and retake control, I doubt we could save it, for it is too far gone, but we may take comfort that its collapse will fall upon the heads of those squatters, and maybe we'll be able to rebuild on its footprint. In the meantime, we do all we can to remove ourselves from its corrupt and crumbling structure.

How will our societies come together after the collapse? I'm not sure, but they will certainly be more decentralized, more locally autonomous, transacting in honest money, honest discourse, and honest contracts, and Justice will be done. As my dear friend JP put it, in an April 2024 email, "We don't need 'government'. What we need is to have people willing to help administer certain activities, as and when they are required, and then get out of the bloody way and go back to their lives."

Will representatives serve terms by lottery, like jury selection, and will party affiliations be forbidden, along with secret-society memberships and secret-society oaths? Provisions like these make sense. In the meantime, to quote Maria Zeee, the corporation governments "have no more authority to order us about than Ronald McDonald showing up in his clown costume." Brothers and Sisters, it is time to dissolve the CORPORATION!

5

STOP CALLING LEGISLATION 'LAW'!

Good people don't need laws to tell them to act responsibly...
and bad people will find a way around the laws.

— PLATO

If I want to set up a club, and I invite others to become members, I have the right to tell them what the rules of my club are. If they don't agree to the rules—that is to say, if they don't consent—they don't have to join. No problem. But I can't go round telling everybody they have to abide by my rules if they haven't opted to join up, much less charge them membership dues. Yet that is exactly what governments do with their legislation and taxation.

As the Superior Court of North Carolina said, in its Cruden v. Neale ruling in 1796, "every man is independent of all laws, except those prescribed by nature. He is not bound by any institutions formed by his fellowmen without his consent."

I hope by now that I have cultivated in you a healthy contempt for legislation, whether it goes by the name of United States Code, Code of Federal Regulations, Uniform Commercial Code, or some other grandstanding name. At the very least, I hope I have persuaded you to stop calling it 'Law': neither the Acts of parliaments; nor the decrees, rules, regulations, policies, procedures, executive orders, or secret directives of politicians, bureaucrats, or kings; neither the rulings or opinions of judges; nor the 'strategic priorities' of international bodies such as the UN, WHO, or WEF.

Sorcery and Language

I ask again: Who the hell do these people think they are to write or say anything and call it Law?! It's a trick of sorcery, an illusion in words. As Alan of Salisbury put it in his 2016 lecture,...

> "Statutes are about status. That's where you get the term 'statutes' from. 'Act', it's an act, it's not true, it's a fiction. You've been caught, you've believed in a fiction, you believe you're something that you're not, it's a deception. So you're trying to get back to who you really are, and what you were really created here to do."

Being accurate with our terminology is key. It may even be our most powerful weapon in breaking the spells that have beset Mankind. But alas, even so-called truthers and Freedom advocates, who should know better, habitually confer the status of 'Law' on the legislation, orders, and decrees of men and women.

For the most part, legislation is worse than useless, capricious, confusing, and cruel, and it muddies the waters of Justice. Also, as William Keyte of CommonLawConstitution.org notes in a February 2023 conversation with Richard Vobes, "The more a government legislates, the more it informs the criminal how to get around the law."

Colossal *Colossians*

What sweet relief, then, to return to the 'Royal Law' bestowed by Jesus, of loving others as we love ourselves, unburdened by the usurping impositions, written by men, that *masquerade* as Law.

Cue one of my favourite *Bible* verses, *Colossians* 2:14. The *NIV* rendition is, "… having cancelled the written code, with its regulations, that was against us and that stood opposed to us, he took it away, nailing it to the cross." Other translations include: "blotting out the handwriting of ordinances…" (*KJV*); "obliterating the bond against us, with its legal claims…" (*NABRE*); and "Having canceled out the certificate of debt consisting of decrees against us…" (*LSB*).

This sounds to me like annihilation of Birth-Certificate bondage; Jesus has destroyed—nay, crucifed—the tyrants' power base by setting us free from the debts they invent and impose. Then, in the next verse, Christ humiliates them too: "And having disarmed the powers and authorities, he made a public spectacle of them, triumphing over them by the cross" (*Colossians* 2:15). No wonder they hate Christians!

Musing on this *Bible* passage, Si the Spaniard likens Humanity's embrace of legislation to eating of the Tree of the Knowledge of Good and Evil. This makes sense. God told Adam not to eat of that Tree and warned him that if he did, he would surely die (*Genesis* 2:17). Until then, Adam had no opportunity to sin, for there was no legislation in existence that could even define what sin was.

"Eating of the Tree of Good and Evil is getting involved in this Legal-Land shenanigans," Si told a 'Red-Pill-Day' conference in 2023. " 'You shall surely die' is reference to being treated as a corporation."

Whether or not you buy into the *Bible* narrative about a treacherous angel called Satan who fell from Heaven, he serves as a useful representation of destructive impulse in much the same way as dragons do in epic tales. When this entity gets to dictate to you what Good and Evil are, he gets more control. A murderer from the beginning, and the Father of Lies (*John* 8:44), he masquerades as an angel of light, while his secret-society priests masquerade as servants of righteousness (2 *Corinthians* 11:14)—a righteousness they think to define for everyone else and then enforce with murderous zeal.

How these inhuman creatures love to play God with the lives and bodies of others, to murder with impunity, to steal at will, and to punish those who refuse to play along with their demonic circus. When this Synagogue of Satan (*Revelation* 2:9) can quote some legal text to justify killing you, they may even feel a little better about themselves, but what they bring forth is fruit from the Tree of Knowledge. It is poison, it is death.

The world is still deceived with ornament.
In law, what plea so tainted and corrupt
But, being seasoned with a gracious voice,
Obscures the show of evil? In religion,
What damnèd error but some sober brow
Will bless it and approve it with a text,
Hiding the grossness with fair ornament?
There is no vice so simple but assumes
Some mark of virtue on its outward parts.

— WILLIAM SHAKESPEARE,
THE MERCHANT OF VENICE, III.II.

Legislation is not just beneath us, Brothers and Sisters, but beneath our contempt. Its primary aim, writes David E. Robinson in *Meet Your Strawman*, "is to take cash, goods and property from members of the public... They invent 'statutes' and all kinds of charges designed to move money from ordinary people into the pockets of Mr. Government, who promptly pays most of it to his brother Mr. Banker."

British dissident member of Parliament Andrew Bridgen has caught up to this reality. In a February 2024 interview, he told James Roguski, "We used to have a Parliament that legislated for the People—that's what I thought, that's why I became a member of Parliament for my home area—but now we have a Parliament that inflicts upon the people."

This tendency is hardly new, though. Listen to what French philosopher Pierre-Joseph Proudhon, widely considered the 'Father of Anarchism', wrote in 1851 in *Idée générale de la révolution au XIXe siècle* (*The General Idea of Revolution in the Nineteenth Century*)...

"To be governed is to be watched, inspected, spied upon, directed, [legislation]-driven, numbered, regulated, enrolled, indoctrinated, preached at, controlled, checked, estimated, valued, censured, commanded, by creatures who have neither the right nor the wisdom nor the virtue to do so. To be governed is to be at every operation, at every transaction noted, registered, counted, taxed, stamped, measured, numbered, assessed, licensed, authorized, admonished, prevented, forbidden, reformed, corrected, punished. It is, under pretext of public utility, and in the name of the general interest, to be placed under contribution, drilled, fleeced, exploited, monopolized, extorted from, squeezed, hoaxed, robbed; then, at the slightest resistance, the first word of complaint, to be repressed, fined, vilified, harassed, hunted down, abused, clubbed, disarmed, bound, choked, imprisoned, judged, condemned, shot, deported, sacrificed, sold, betrayed; and to crown all, mocked, ridiculed, derided, outraged, dishonored. That is government; that is its justice; that is its morality."

Follow the Bodies!

In the above quote, Proudhon accurately identifies the financial motives behind legislation that harms, for fraud, corruption, and greed have always greased the wheels of Government. Today, however, the agenda is far more horrifying, not so much about following the money as about following the bodies.

For example, if money were the main motivation for the COVID scam, why would airlines insist their pilots get injected with a bioweapon, knowing this would jeopardize the costly human capital that pilots and their training represent? Knowing, too, the irreparable damage to their reputations if pilots lost control or consciousness during flights?

There must be a more compelling incentive at work than mere extortion, and there is. COVID, I now realize, was the opening scene in a worldwide Satanic ritual of human sacrifice, and it was brought about by what attorney Todd Callender calls the *Legal Walls of the Covid-19 Kill Box*. It was also a competition to see who could rack up the highest death count.

I first heard about the 'Black Crow Award' from Dr. Burt Berkson. "At many medical schools, in many university hospitals," he told Dr. Jonathan Landsman in an interview, "they give an award every month to the doctor who has the most deaths on his service, and they have a party, and it's called a 'Black Crow Award'."

COVID was a Black-Crow contest, only this time on a global scale involving health ministers, hospitals, and practitioners, a race to see who could add the most corpses to the pile of medical waste. Furthermore, as I show in *Know Your Medical Rights*, the previous book in this series, younger victims counted for extra in this macabre ritual.

I wonder how Matt Hancock, Britain's health minister from July 2018 to June 2021, scored in this deadly game. He oversaw mass euthanization in British care homes, involving record use of fentanyl and the deadly sedative, midazolam, and he got the bioweapon injections rolled out in Britain even earlier than in the U.S. and with even worse consequences for children. This while he was frightening the pants off everyone, as he put it in his December 2020 WhatsApp exchange.

I digress. Following up on Todd Callender's work, famed legal analyst Katherine Watt wrote in an article titled *American Domestic Bioterrorism Program*,...

"A whole lot of things that once were federal and state crimes and civil-rights violations have been legalized by Congress through legislative statutory revisions to the United States Code. They were signed by multiple U.S. presidents and implemented at the administrative regulatory level by the Department of Health and Human Services. This was all done through the Code of Federal Regulations."

So I echo the question put by Veronica in an August 2023 email, "How many centuries of this does it take before people finally come to terms with the fact that they have been 'had'? That the whole illegitimate idea of 'Government' is to be ruled by people who don't give a flying fuck about you. And never will."

She too laments the social and media programming that calls legislation 'Law' and that gives it a false aura of immutability such as the Law of Gravity. She writes,...

"Notice how many IDIOTS use 'Law' and 'Legal' interchangeably. This PROVES—CONCLUSIVELY—THAT THEY HAVE NO IDEA WHAT THEY ARE TALKING ABOUT. This includes ALL Politicians and almost ALL members of the Legal Profession... Statutes/Legislation/Acts of Parliament/Congress = EXACT OPPOSITE of Law. To refer to Legislation as 'Law' is patently ABSURD."

Agreed. Acts and statutes are nothing more than self-serving wish-lists that politicians write for themselves, their donors, sponsors, procurers, and blackmailers. Worse, they are legal frameworks for dictatorship, blueprints for Hell on Earth, drafted at Hell's behest, direction, and dictation. These instruments call themselves Law but they are forgeries, "counterfeit holy," to borrow a phrase from John Bunyan. They kill, deceive, and enslave, and are enforced today with a level of brutality, callousness, and surveillance we could not have imagined just a few years ago.

A great reality check is now required for our societies. As David E. Robinson writes in *Common Law Handbook*, "Statutes are not law. Servant legislators cannot write statutes to control the behavior of their masters." Rather than being weaponized against us, legislation's only true purpose is to set the rules for public servants, elected and appointed officials, agencies, and municipalities. These rules, according to Si the Spaniard, only apply to a man when he is acting in the capacity of public servant or corporate employee. Otherwise, they don't.

So, when a parliament or congress 'passes' something, it has no relevance to you or me, the Living Man or Living Woman. I can pass wind, and though I grant it may cause you some momentary discomfort, I don't expect it to rule your life.

So let politicians write their club rules for themselves but, to paraphrase the immortal George Carlin, we ain't in that club and have no regard for its membership codes. "One rule for thee and not for me."? Well then, tyrant, your rules are not for me. *I* make the rules for me, and thou hast no say in them.

Liberty, as Si the Spaniard says,

"denotes not merely freedom from bodily restraint but also the right of the individual to contract, to engage in any of the common occupations of life, to acquire useful knowledge, to marry, to establish a home and bring up children, to worship God according to the dictates of his own conscience… this liberty may not be interfered with, under the guise of protecting public interest, by legislative action."

... But Feel Free to Use Legislation Against them!

Having said this, we may *quote* legislation, along with court rulings, to remind public servants—or as writer Amy Harlib calls them, 'public serpents'—of their statutory obligations when those obligations protect or benefit us, their masters. We may cite, for example, *Conspiracy Against Rights* legislation (USC 18 Sec. 241) which states, "If two or more persons conspire to injure, oppress, threaten, or intimidate any person in any State in the free exercise or enjoyment of any right, they shall be fined under this title or imprisoned not more than ten years, or both." And yes, as masters over legislation and the opinions of servants, we have the absolute right to 'cherry pick' what we like in them and in anything else written or spoken by men.

In Closing...

My analysis boils down to this simple formula: God makes Law, man makes legislation, and corporations write company policy. Common Law is fruit from the Tree of Life, but legislation is fruit from the deadly Tree of Knowledge. Even *calling* statutes 'legislation' may be too generous a term when the parliaments writing them are corporations. They really amount to no more than company contracts. Furthermore, those contracts are fraudulent because only one party has written them, one party has read them, one party has negotiated them with itself, and one party has signed them, yet it thinks to impose them on another party, us, without our knowledge, signature, or consent.

So what is the real power of legislation against us? In the words of Ariel, the brave spirit in Shakespeare's *The Tempest*, their legislative weapons "may as well/ Wound the loud winds, or with bemock'd-at stabs/ Kill the still-closing waters..." (III.iii.) Therefore, I say again, and will keep saying until it is widely adopted,...

STOP CALLING LEGISLATION 'LAW' !!!
STOP CALLING LEGISLATION 'LAW' !!!
STOP CALLING LEGISLATION 'LAW' !!!

6

CONSTITUTIONS

For a measure to be introduced to the House, it has to be in consonance with, or in pursuance of, something already in the Constitution. If it is not, it is unconstitutional. I looked at 3,000 bills passed in recent years, and every one of them are unconstitutional.

— JOHN COLEMAN, SPEAKING IN 1994

So what is the status of constitutions and of the various documents such as declarations, charters, conventions, and so on, that enumerate Rights protections? Do they stand shoulder to shoulder with Common Law? According to *American Jurisprudence 2d*, described as the legal profession's leading reference source, they should. It states, "Constitutions must be construed to reference the Common Law" (Sec. 114).

But that does not mean constitutions can claim to *be*

Law, even if their contents are Law*ful*, for they are still drafted by men and subject to the caprices of men, and they may contain loopholes that tyrants can exploit. Take, for example, the *Universal Declaration of Human Rights (UDHR)*. Though I cited its protections in my previous book, *Know Your Medical Rights*, I did not notice at the time how murderous it becomes in Article 29, where everyone shall be subject to "the just requirements of morality, public order and the general welfare."

The idea that one centralized power should define what morality is and enforce it on others is a terrifying prospect and a recipe for dictatorship. Article 29 continues, "These rights and freedoms may in no case be exercised contrary to the purposes and principles of the United Nations," making for a deadly concentration of power. We who study the UN's agenda know that the requirement of "public order" means a police state and that "general welfare" means crushing the individual, the small business, and the independent farmer. I also notice that Article 14, though it enshrines the Right to Asylum, withholds it in the case of prosecutions arising "from acts contrary to the purposes and principles of the United Nations." Again, this is the devil masquerading as an angel of light.

The *Canadian Charter of Rights and Freedoms* is another example. It gets off to a good start with, "Whereas Canada is founded upon principles that recognize the supremacy of God and the rule of law"—where we take 'law' to mean Common Law or the Law of the Land—but then it goes off the rails in the very first paragraph by saying it guarantees its Rights and freedoms "subject only to such reasonable limits prescribed by law as can be demonstrably justified in a free and democratic society."

This provision drags the *Charter* down into Legal Land and into complex, expensive, and time-consuming court process arguing over the definitions of words and what is meant by "reasonable" or "justified." It was the very reason the *Charter* failed Canadians when put to the test during COVID. As paralegal Jane Scharf reports in an April 2022 article, "There have been several Charter applications that the court heard about religious freedom and one about mandatory vaccination. The court found that rights were being violated but that it was justified under Section 1 of the Charter because of the pandemic."

Beware of tricky subordinate clauses in constitutional documents. Scharf maintains the *Charter* "was introduced by communist/globalist former Prime Minister, Pierre Elliot Trudeau, in 1982. They want to be able to establish that the government can snap away your rights any time they think they have a good reason."

Canadians have a surer constitutional footing, though, with the *Canadian Bill of Rights* (1960), *An Act for the Recognition and Protection of Human Rights and Fundamental Freedoms*. It does not claim to confer Rights by governmental discretion but recognizes, protects, and enshrines Rights that already exist.

Sometimes, constitutions start out with fine principles but are saddled later with new tyrant text that blasphemes the original intent. This is what befell *The Constitution of the United States of America* with later

Amendments that opened the door to voluntary servitude and unlawful taxation.

In this respect, England's *Magna Carta* or '*Great Charter*' of 1215 is a more perfect document in that it seals its own permanence and inviolability in Articles 1, 61, and 63. The latter states, "that men in our kingdom shall have and keep all these liberties, rights, and concessions, well and peaceably in their fullness and entirety for them and their heirs, of us and our heirs, in all things and all places for ever."

The *Great Charter* also predates and stands above legislation, according to William Keyte. In his 2022 paper titled *The Occulted Powers of the British Constitution*, he argues it is "the people's perennial compact with the Heads of State and can therefore never be considered a statute."

I see his point: that *Magna Carta* is a genuine contract arising from mutual consent of two signatory parties, the People and the monarch. It therefore overrules legislation, which is a one-sided imposition put upon the People without our signature or consent. Therefore, Keyte continues, subsequent efforts by governments to legislate new 'versions' of *Magna Carta* were "treason, nothing less."

In any case, where constitutions remain beneficial and protective to We, the People, we may accord them a status superior to other legislation and wield them selectively against the harmful, and therefore unlawful, encroachments of officials. For example, among the Rights listed in *Magna Carta* is that of Trial by Jury

(Article 39), without which no-one "shall be taken or imprisoned, or be disseised [deprived or dispossessed] of his Freehold, or Liberties, or free Customs, or be outlawed, or exiled, or any other wise destroyed."

In the States United, the *Constitution* has been affirmed as superior to other legislation in several landmark court rulings, such as...

- Marbury v. Madison — "Rules and practices which are repugnant to the Constitution are null and void" (U.S. Supreme Court, 1803).

- Miranda v. Arizona — "Where rights secured by the Constitution are involved, there can be no rule-making or legislation which would abrogate them" (U.S. Supreme Court, 1966).

- Miller v. U.S. — "The Claim and exercise of a Constitutional Right cannot be converted into a crime" (U.S. Court of Appeals, Fifth Circuit, 1956).

- Sherar v. Cullen — "There can be no sanction or penalty imposed upon one because of his exercise of constitutional Rights" (U.S. Court of Appeals, Ninth Circuit, 1973).

These rulings are reinforced in *American Jurisprudence 2d* where "an unconstitutional statute... is wholly void and ineffective for any purpose" and "as inoperative as if it never had been passed... it imposes no duties, confers no rights, creates no office, bestows no power on anyone, affords no protection, and justifies no actions performed under it..." (Sec. 256).

Constitutions do not *give* us Rights, however, because we are born with them. The Rights are inalienable, or *un*alienable if you prefer. As David E. Robinson writes in *Common Law Handbook,* "The People existed in their own individual sovereignty before the Constitution was enabled." Constitutions can only enshrine Rights that already existed, but our predecessors wrote them down to ensure they would prevail through thick and thin, and that good men would quote them in tough times to thwart enforcers of false authority. They are not flimsy assurances that can be swept away at the first sign of trouble, nor museum pieces gathering dust in glass cabinets, but living, breathing documents made manifest in us, much as the Word became flesh and made his dwelling among us (*John* 1:14).

Nor can constitutional principles be trivialized as mere conveniences when honouring them can make the difference between life and death. As we saw during COVID, people die when the First Amendment's protection of Free Speech is denied through censorship or when the Fourth Amendment's protection of Privacy is desecrated by coerced disclosure of medical status.

Primary Legislation

Next in the hierarchy of man-made codes, somewhere between the supremacy of constitutions and the banality of tyrant legislation, is so-called 'primary legislation' or 'superior statute', that is to say, legislation that sets out Rights protections and may therefore claim some constitutional authority. If you have the stomach to plough through reams of verbiage, you may find the occasional benefit in it, such as...

- "... no man should be forejudged of life or limbe against the forme of the Great Charter and the Lawe of the Land" (English *Petition of Right*, 1627).

- "...no person should be compelled to make any Loanes to the King" (English *Petition of Right*, 1627).

- "That all Grants and Promises of Fines and Forfeitures of particular persons before Conviction are illegall and void" (English *Bill of Rights*, 1688).

- "Will You to the utmost of Your power Maintaine the Laws of God the true Profession of the Gospell...?" (English *Coronation Oath Act*, 1688).

- All shall have "full Freedom and Intercourse of Trade and Navigation to and from any port or place" (*Union with England Act*, Section IV, 1707).

Americans can invoke these English protections too via the Ninth Amendment which states, "The enumeration in the Constitution, of certain rights, shall not be construed to deny or disparage others retained by the people."

Court Precedents

Court precedents may also be cited, where beneficial to the People, as long as we remember they are creations of men and that creations of men can never have authority over men, only those who of their own free will, fully informed and uncoerced, agree to and sign up for them. But court precedents *can* have authority over those who are in the subordinate role of public servant because they *have* voluntarily entered into an employment contract. Here are some...

- The principles of government do not "leave room for the play and action of purely personal and arbitrary power. Sovereignty itself is, of course, not subject to law, for it is the author and source of law" (U.S. Supreme Court, Yick Wo v. Hopkins, 1886).

- The rule in America is that the American people are the sovereigns, and in them is lodged all power..." (Texas Court of Criminal Appeals, Kemper v. the State, 1911)

- "The individual, unlike the corporation, cannot be taxed for the mere privilege of existing. The corporation is an artificial entity which owes its existence and charter powers to the state; but the individual's right to live and own property are natural rights for the enjoyment of which an excise cannot be imposed" (Oregon Supreme Court, Redfield v. Fisher, 1930).

- Realizing and receiving income or earnings is not a privilege that can be taxed" (Tennessee Supreme Court, Jack Cole v. MacFarland, 1960).

Still, watch out for those subordinate clauses. For example, in January 2023, the New York State Supreme Court ruled against the State's vaccine 'mandate' for healthcare workers. So far, so good, but the judge didn't overturn the decree because it was inherently unlawful, which it is—as all forced medicine is—but because it came from an executive order and was not voted on by the legislature. This spineless ruling suggests that, even if the governor can't be sole tyrant, the State assembly can, and it confers legal validity on unlawful mandates if only they follow a prescribed procedure.

The court also decided the mandate was "arbitrary and capricious" on the basis that the 'vaccines' do not stop transmission of the 'virus'. This leaves the door wide open for false authorities to force a medical product by claiming it *does* stop transmission

Afterwards, Mary Holland, President of Children's Health Defense said, "We are thrilled by this critical win against a COVID vaccine mandate, correctly finding that any such mandate at this stage, given current knowledge, is arbitrary." Those infernal subordinate clauses again!— "at this stage," "given current knowledge."

Her statement echoes another hollow slogan we've heard in so-called 'Medical-Freedom' circles. "Where there is risk, there must be choice." Again, conferring on medical tyrants a false authority to remove choice when they claim there is no risk. Remove the phrase, "Where there is risk,..." and you might have something!

To conclude, there are among the documents and decisions of men some that are good and that protect the People, while most are bad and intend harm to the People, and even most of the good ones include some bad clauses. You and I, as Living Men and Living Women, are not subject to the documents of men, but we may cite them where helpful to compel public servants to meet their obligations as our employees.

7

THE EMERGENCY-POWERS CULT

What we would not permit is the government to initiate force against people who have hurt no-one, who have not forced anyone. We would not give the government or the majority or any minority the right to take the life or the property of others.

— AYN RAND, INTERVIEW WITH
MIKE WALLACE, 1959

As we have seen, governments routinely usurp True Law with legislation, but when it comes to emergencies, they really hit the gas. The antidote is this simple truth...

RIGHTS APPLY MORE DURING EMERGENCIES, NOT LESS!

Emergencies are what Rights declarations and constitutions were designed for, and everyone in so-called 'law enforcement' should know this. Instead, they are conditioned to embrace a slavers' code that says constitutions were only designed for times of peace and prosperity, which is when they are least needed and least likely to be tested. As former police officer Michael McMahon told Maria Zeee in a February 2023 interview, "I took an oath to protect the Constitution of the United States, and in a state of emergency, our Constitution here in America, it's not put on hold." McMahon was fired from the Los Angeles Police Department (LAPD) after 14 years in the job for refusing a vaccine 'mandate'.

Emergencies have always been the alibi of despots to seize more power and control. That's why they never want them to end. In the words of former British prime minister, William Pitt the Younger, addressing the House of Commons in 1783, "Necessity is the plea for every infringement of human freedom. It is the argument of tyrants, it is the creed of slaves."

The false authorities will tell you they're not taking away your rights, only suspending them temporarily until the emergency passes. Of course, the intention is to drag out the emergency indefinitely until people forget they ever *had* Rights, and if they do ever remember, the muscle of asserting them is so atrophied that it limits its action to polite objections which are easily ignored, co-opted, or crushed. Or it may hope to elect a candidate or party a little less cruel than the last, if only the election-rigging can be overcome, and then to "push" the candidate in the desired direction. What it *won't* do is grasp our *Declaration-of-Independence* duty to abolish the entire "form" of Government that is destroying Life, Liberty, and the Pursuit of Happiness.

The resort to emergency tactics did not begin or end with COVID and its 'emergency-use authorizations' that disseminated Big-Pharma poisons. For example, in his Mar. 4, 1933 Inaugural Address during the 'Great Depression', then U.S. president, Franklin D. Roosevelt, declared the United States, "a stricken nation in the midst of a stricken world" and called on Congress to grant him "broad Executive power to wage a war against the emergency, as great as the power that would be given to me if we were in fact invaded by a foreign foe." Just two days later, he issued *Proclamation 2039* announcing a four-day suspension of banking transactions.

A month after that, on Apr. 5, 1933, he signed Executive Order 6102 requiring the People to surrender their gold by May 1, 1933 to the Federal Reserve which, as I explore more fully in *Know Your Financial Rights*, is a private banking cartel.

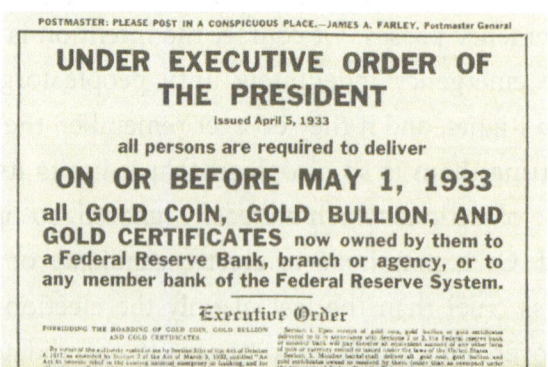

This was a lordly scam. Those who handed in their

gold were compensated at just $20.67 per troy ounce, but over the next year, as a Forbes article recounts, "the president then raised his official gold price to $35 per ounce." A nice earner for him!

Meanwhile, Congress rushed through the *Agricultural Adjustment Act*, also known as the 'Farm Bill', which Roosevelt signed on May 12, 1933. Aimed at boosting agricultural prices by reducing production, the Act spawned a new Agricultural Adjustment Administration to buy livestock for slaughter and to subsidize farmers not to plant on their land.

Congressman James M. Beck, a lonely voice in this 'Rubber Stamp Congress', said at the time,...

"I think of all the damnable heresies that have ever been suggested in connection with the Constitution, the doctrine of emergency is the worst. It means that when Congress declares an emergency, there is no Constitution. This means its death. It is the very doctrine that the German chancellor is invoking today in the dying hours of the parliamentary body of the German republic, namely, that because of an emergency, it should grant to the German chancellor absolute power... Chancellor Hitler is at least frank about it. We pay the Constitution lip-service, but the result is the same."

Since then, of course, many more emergencies have been instigated and invoked to accelerate imperialist ambition, including Pearl Harbor (1941), the Gulf of

Tonkin (1964), '9/11' (2001), 'Climate-Change', COVID, Lahaina (2023), and many more atrocities. Before these, other agenda-setting events included the Great Fire of London (1666), which followed hot on the heels of plague, great fires in major cities of the united States between 1871 (Chicago) and 1906 (San Francisco), and the destruction of four key ships: USS Maine (1898), Titanic (1912), Lusitania (1915), and USS Liberty (1967).

We may not know the full story behind such events, but the one narrative we can always rule out is the one told by governments, echoed by media, and now curated by Google, social-media platforms, and mainstream AI. In any case, we are well versed with their playbook by now... Create an emergency, or the appearance of an emergency, and magnify the perceived threat. Once the populace is trembling with fear, bombard them with colour-coded threat levels, and bring in the Rights-crushing measures you were always itching to enforce.

Even now, as I write this, we get wind of more emergencies in the works, another disaster, another disease, another false-flag concoction, and the legislation has already been put in place to exploit them. For example, in June 2024, the World Health Organization renewed its 'International Health Regulations' by which governments can require compulsory medical examination, put you in quarantine, seize your property, and demand proof of vaccination. I demolish all of this nonsense in my previous book, *Know Your Medical Rights*, so I won't repeat myself here, but the WHO is clearly working the same, tired old formula.

Similarly, the United Nations came out with a paper in 2023 titled *Strengthening the International Response to Complex Global Shocks*. There, Secretary-General António Guterres calls for "strengthening global governance" under the UN in response to emergencies such as climate events, pandemics, biological agents, disruptions to digital connectivity, events in outer space, and any other unforeseen risks or 'black-swan' events.

The secretary-general would then convene an Emergency Platform to "overcome any obstacles or bottlenecks" to an effective and "whole-of-system" response. Can we be in any doubt that the "obstacles or bottlenecks" to be targeted would include inconvenient Rights such as medical confidentiality, medical autonomy, property ownership, gun ownership, custody of our own children, and travel? The Emergency Platform would be convened for a finite period, but the secretary-general could extend it "as necessary."

The UN document professes righteousness in all its Orwellian plans and laments that the organization failed "to achieve vaccine equity" during COVID and that "fewer women and girls across the world have received vaccinations than men and boys." Guterres also complains that there were too few "accountability mechanisms and mandates" in the global response.

What does 'equity' mean when the UN says it? Leave it to the witty pen of writer and yoga dancer Amy Harlib to answer: "EQUITY is Orwellian doublespeak for equal ENSLAVEMENT of us proles under the technocratic parasitic malevolent rule by control freak, power-mad psychos."

We may find defence against such 'globalist' intentions in *American Jurisprudence 2d* which states under the heading *Effect of Emergency,* "It is sometimes argued that the existence of an emergency allows the existence and operation of powers, national or state, which violate the inhibitions of the Federal Constitution. The rule is quite otherwise. No emergency justifies the violation of any of the provisions of the United States Constitution" (Sec. 71). The reference also states, "... an emergency can not create power, and no emergency justifies the violation of any of the provisions of the United States Constitution or States Constitutions" (Sec. 98).

But my go-to document when it comes to emergencies is the *Siracusa Principles* of 1984. Cementing the *International Covenant on Civil and Political Rights,* which had been ratified by the United Nations in 1966, it states...

"No state party shall, even in time of emergency threatening the life of the nation, derogate from the Covenant's guarantees of the right to life; freedom from torture, cruel, inhuman or degrading treatment or punishment, and from medical or scientific experimentation without free consent; freedom from slavery or involuntary servitude; the right not to be imprisoned for contractual debt; the right not to be convicted or sentenced to a heavier penalty by virtue of retroactive criminal legislation; the right to recognition as a person before the law; and freedom of thought, conscience and religion. These rights are not derogable under any conditions even for the asserted purpose of preserving the life of the nation" (Para. 58).

This constitutionally sound text rebukes any pretence, let alone legislation or declaration, that claims 'emergency powers'. The very term is an oxymoron. Like calling legislation 'Law', the idea is absurd. "Not derogable" means your Rights cannot be set aside for any reason, cannot be diluted, cannot be impaired. They are non-negotiable. Note the wording of the last sentence: "for the *asserted* purpose…" The drafters knew tyrants would assert emergency, whether one existed or not, and then react to it, and encourage others to react to it, in ways that would magnify the harms already in play.

I hope my analysis will temper the various fears and phobias governments still try to foster, be they purported viruses, climate catastrophe, nuclear annihilation, or alien invasion. Place all these in the context of government agendas, and you will soon realize that whatever they and their media mouthpieces are telling you to fear is either not that bad or, more likely, entirely inconsequential or pure fiction.

The real danger is the government itself. Thus I have resolved, whenever another wave of fear is stoked, and false authorities tell me what I must do to be safe, that I will do the exact opposite. They tell me to stay home, I'll evacuate. They tell me to evacuate, I'll stay home. They tell me to go north, I'll head south. If south, I'll head north. And so on.

8

THE CURSE OF COLLECTIVE COMPLIANCE

If people are too stupid, selfish, and malicious to be free to make their own decisions, as many people assume, are they not also too stupid, selfish, and malicious to be trusted with power over others?

— LARKEN ROSE

If there's one thing that alarms me more than the agenda of tyrants, it's the willingness of others to go along with it, and not to question, much less resist. COVID was in part an experiment by the politicians and their puppet-masters to see what they could get away with, and the largely compliant population taught them they could get away with rather a lot. Though the authoritarian grip eased for a while after, and people are now much more alert to the genocidal plans, the parasite class have consolidated their position in readiness for the next attack. For example, airlines continue to tell passengers to provide 'contract-tracing' information to satisfy CDC 'requirements' when flying into the U.S. No-one seems to have noticed this desecrates the Fourth Amendment.

Even worse than compliance, we saw during COVID members of the Public reporting their neighbours to the false authorities for supposed violations, as if governments or police thugs needed any more encouragement to commit atrocities. There's a special place in Hell for this snitcher class and for the media whores who incite their worst instincts.

I repeat now the headlines I noticed in late 2021 and reported in *Know Your Medical Rights*: " 'The unvaccinated are putting us all at risk,' squealed *The Times* of London. 'I'm Furious at the Unvaccinated,' howled *The New York Times*. 'It is only a matter of time before we turn on the unvaccinated,' thundered *The Guardian*."

These statements of incitement and hate-speech, calling for medical apartheid, are by definition a Crime Against Humanity under the *Rome Statute* of the International Criminal Court (1998), which lists as such "persecution against any identifiable group" (Article 7).

As famed author Ayn Rand told Mike Wallace in a 1959 interview, "The traditional American system was a system based on the idea that majority will prevailed only in public or political affairs, and that it was limited by inalienable, individual rights. Therefore, I do not believe that a majority can vote a man's life or property or freedom away from him."

Beware, therefore, the tyranny of mob mentality, and

never let majority-rule—much less a frightened and brainwashed majority-rule—destroy the Rights of others as dictators intend. That intention is why politicians talk about the 'Public good' as they inflict public harm, and about "balancing" individual rights with responsibilities in "the public interest."

This stratagem was in play when, in December 2021, the British government issued yet another of its Rights-raping policy papers disguised as a 'Consultation Paper'. Seeking "reform" of Britain's *Human Rights Act*, it sought to "restore a proper balance between the rights of individuals, personal responsibility and the wider public interest."

This was a chilling echo of the Georgia Guidestones' Eighth Principle to "Balance personal rights with social duties"—that is until the Guidestones were mysteriously blown up in 2022—and the kind of thinking that gets people arrested for offending someone on social media or medically murdered to save others from catching a disease.

The Consultation Paper also called for "rigorous judicial interpretation, and respect for the authority of elected law-makers." In other words, do as you're told by your betters in court and Parliament. Oh, but what a relief to know the document was "Printed on paper containing 75% recycled fibre content minimum." Hurrah to the Ministry of Justice for straining out this gnat (*Matthew* 23:24)!

According to the short documentary film, *Who Owns You?*,...

"When we adopt a system of collectivism, we as individuals are forced to make the same mistakes the collective is making... When one is able to use his own rational judgments, his own discernments, and his own moral judgments, such mistakes do not have to affect us all. It is only when we are all forced to partake in somebody else's supposedly great master plan that we are all forced to bear the consequences of those mistakes... We are still making mistakes, but why should other people's mistakes and consequences be our mistakes and consequences who would rather choose to do things that are rational and moral on a voluntary basis, rather than letting one of us impose his plan on the rest of us?"

The film also warns,...

"Every single time that a collective or state owns the individual and forbids the individual to make his own decisions and to use his own rational judgments and moral conscience, the worst tragedies in history have eventuated as a result. An individual can choose to join a group and work together with others but only on a voluntary basis."

9

DEMOLISHING THE SATANIC CODE

O conspiracy,
Sham'st thou to show thy dangerous brow by night
When evils are most free? O then, by day,
Where wilt thou find a cavern dark enough
To mask thy monstrous visage?

— SHAKESPEARE,

JULIUS CAESAR, II.I.

I have talked about Satan masquerading as an angel of light, and by now, that strategy has been largely exposed when it comes to the death factories posing as hospitals and to the bioweapons posing as vaccines. The mask is also coming off when it comes to legislation pretending to be Law. But there are other, more subtle masquerades in play that seek our destruction yet dress themselves up as

'Universal Law'. These things have a superficial appearance of wisdom but are snares and traps intended to lead us astray. Let me expose them, and let us cast down their pretensions and arguments that set themselves up against the knowledge of God (2 *Corinthians* 10:5), for even some Christians are falling for them.

"Silence Implies Consent."

"Silence Implies Consent" is an oft-repeated lie, even by our allies: "They have to tell you what they're going to do," they say, "and if you're silent about it, that means you're going along with it."

Let's break down this moronic mantra… "They have to tell you what they're going to do…" No, they don't, and no, they aren't. You need only ask if anyone—I mean ANYONE—received Informed Consent about the COVID injections in recent years. At most, they're telling us a little piece of what they're doing, and even that is buried so deep that only the most dogged researcher can find it, and anyone who *does* infer what's really going on behind the little they tell you is slandered and ridiculed and attacked. That's not telling you what they're going to do, that's concealing what they're going to do.

The plotters do sometimes hold perfunctory hearings, though they have no intention of heeding anything the People say. Or, like the British government, they issue phony Consultation papers where answers are confined to multiple-choice checkboxes designed to keep opposition within proscribed boundaries. They may also go through the grudging motions when issued with Freedom-of-Information-Act (FOIA) requests, but then they will delay disclosure as long as possible or issue documents so riddled with redaction as to be unreadable.

Another ploy is to pass Acts of legislation hundreds of pages long in the dead of night that no-one has a chance to read, not even the so-called representatives voting on them. Or they bury their real intentions in deep layers of a website or in long, boring documents burdened with euphemism and coded language.

You call any of that, "telling us what they're going to do"? No, they're not telling us what they're going to do. It is concealment, it is deception, and it is lies, and it comes from the Father of Lies.

Now to the second part of the moronic mantra: "… and if you're silent about it, that means you're going along with it." Who are you calling silent? The truth-tellers banned from social media? Not silent, but silenced. People who have lost their jobs or their bank accounts as punishment for speaking out? Not silent, but silenced. What about the man held against his will in an Australian quarantine camp? He wasn't silent. He complained so much that they threatened to gas him! Not silent, but silenced.

How about the 'blade-runners' in London sabotaging surveillance cameras? Or the protesters beaten up or irradiated by coward cops? You call any of that silence?

What about the children sacrificed on altars by the Snake-Brotherhood parasite class now trying to destroy us? Were those victims silent? The Bible tells us our tears are stored in Heaven (*Psalms* 56:8). Are you telling me that not one of those kids shed a single tear when they were put to the slaughter?

No. We are a Chorus of Witnesses (*Hebrews* 12:1), and we have been anything but silent!

Some say, "Oh, we didn't complain. We must deserve everything that happens to us." Yes, we *did* complain, over and over and over again. And even if we hadn't complained, the tyrants are still outlaws because they are doing harm, and doing harm is a desecration of True 'Universal Law'—that is to say, Common Law—no matter what your victim says or doesn't say.

Do you want to live under a code that says,...

"We're going to kill you or enslave you and take everything you have. And if you are silent, you have given us your conse... Shut up, shut up, shut up! I can't hear you! I can't hear you! I can't hear you! Well then, since I hear no objection, and you have chosen not to say anything, it is determined that you have consented to everything we plan to do to you."?

In what world is that consent? Satan's world. Satan's thinking. But if you have the Mind of Christ, you will not buy into this false Doctrine of Implied Consent. Brothers and Sisters,...

WE LIVE NOT UNDER IMPLIED CONSENT BUT IMPLIED REFUSAL!

The Satanic operatives do not have permission, never *had* permission, and never *will* have permission, to do anything that harms. Their assumption that they *do* have permission to harm, as Anna von Reitz explains in a March 2024 article, is a throwback to the legal system of ancient Rome which allowed the use of Unilateral Contracts assumed to exist by acquiescence, and 'Inferred' Contracts, otherwise known as 'Adhesion' Contracts, by which **people are made subject to non-disclosed obligations**.

This is the epitome of Evil—making someone else subject to your rules, and you don't even have to disclose those rules. Von Reitz continues, "No meeting of the minds is required, no disclosure of the true parties to the contract is required, no honesty or honor of any kind is required in Maritime Contracts." Today's Maritime courts, she adds, are complicit in perpetrating the Roman Maxim, "Let him who will be deceived, be deceived." Well, you and I, Brothers and Sisters, are not subject to the whims of ancient Rome nor to its perpetuators in modern times.

From Heaven, we overthrow the pretensions and arguments of
Implied Consent, Unilateral Contracts, Inferred Contracts, and

Adhesion Contracts that they are overthrown on Earth and sent to their appointed place, never to trouble Mankind again. From Heaven, we replace the lie of Implied Consent with the truth of Implied Refusal, that it is replaced on Earth. From Heaven, we overrule the so-called rulers who presume to have permission for what they're doing and what they plan, that they are overruled on Earth. And from Heaven, we deny their presumption of a Right to Harm that it is denied on Earth. Amen. Amen. Amen.

"Ignorance of the Law Is No Excuse."

Another plank of tyranny is the idea that "Ignorance of the law is no excuse." Let's begin by replacing 'Law' with 'legislation' because that's what the state-obedient parrots mean when they say it. Then, so what if we know nothing of their legislation? It applies only to those who have given Informed Consent to it with their signature, and this we will not do.

"Collective Manifestation."

The next lie I want to address is so-called 'Collective Manifestation'—the idea that, if enough people expect something to happen, they somehow cause it to happen. What bollocks, though some Christians still fall for it.

This is arrogance of the vilest degree. What pride to think that my attention or your attention or even the attention of a multitude can shift the will of the Most High, he who does as he pleases with the powers of

Heaven and the peoples of the Earth (*Psalms* 135:6;
Daniel 4:35).

If we want to influence future outcomes, then
Scripture tells us that the prayers of a righteous man are
powerful and effective (*James* 5:16), that they burn as
incense before his throne (*Revelation* 8:4), and that the
Lord will not despise a contrite heart (*Psalms* 51:17). But
this Doctrine of Collective Manifestation is *not* the
product of a contrite heart; it is the product a proud and
arrogant heart that thinks its thoughts actually mean
something.

"You Create Your Own Reality."

The next creed to demolish is that "You create your own
reality." This mantra, so beloved of personal-development
courses, is a special kind of bullshit, a massive get-out-of-
jail-free card for the oppressors who would have us blame
ourselves for the poverty, hardships, and injustice we face
in their rigged, Satanic game.

"Reality is Relative."

Another Satanic dogma holds that "Reality is relative."
This is pure escapism. Let me ask you: Are the millions of
people who were just medically genocided in *my* reality
somehow still alive in yours? Will you acknowledge
what's happening before your eyes? Or will you keep
them firmly shut until reality forces you to open them as
it kicks down your door?!

I share the frustration Max Igan expresses about New-Age adherents who refuse to acknowledge the evils happening around them. They say, "Oh, I don't look at it because where attention goes, energy flows," or, "You're creating it by looking at it."

Igan counters in a July 2024 broadcast, "No, you're creating it by *not* looking at it. You are allowing darkness and shadow to exist in the world by your failure to cast any light on it."

The kind of people who spout these false doctrines also talk about their ascent into '5D consciousness', stupidly unaware that they haven't even reclaimed their *three*-dimensional status as living, breathing beings, free from the *two*-dimensional flattening of Legal Land with its corporate, ALL-CAPS NAMES. And by the way, how did also they leapfrog a fourth dimension?!

So when I hear you so-called 'light workers', you conscious-shifting 'star seeds' "holding your frequency," manifesting "Christ consciousness" or "cosmic Christ energy," and "focussing on the positive," and when I hear you calling Jesus not "the way, the truth, and the life" (*John* 14:6) but "ascended master," I scoff and shake my head and roll my eyes and sigh. You have no idea what you're talking about.

Other Linguistic Assaults

Thus, the devils' deceptions proceed through words, and sometimes through the very definitions of words. For example, in September 2021, the U.S. Centers for Disease

Control (CDC) changed its definition of 'vaccine' from something that produces "immunity to a specific disease...," to something used merely "to stimulate the body's immune response."

Meanwhile, the *Merriam-Webster Dictionary* expanded its own definition of 'vaccine' to include "a preparation of genetic material." It also expanded its definition of 'anti-vaxxer' from someone "who opposes the use of vaccines" to anyone opposed to "regulations mandating vaccination." As investigative journalist Max Blumenthal observed in a November 2021 interview with Jimmy Dore, they are "playing with semantics in order to cover their arse."

Also, as I observed in *Know Your Medical Rights*, the manipulators encoded military metaphors into the COVID response with words like battle, beat, conquer, crush, defeat, eliminate, enemy, fight, front lines, victory, etc. This has a similar smell to the witches' brew of euphemism cooked up with the so-called 'War on Terror', a term exquisitely illogical in itself. In that lexicon, kidnapping became 'extraordinary rendition', torture was 'enhanced interrogation', and 'collateral damage' meant mass murder of civilians.

I fear for the English language, and urge you to treasure hard-copy dictionaries produced in the previous century lest, as Syme tells Winston in Orwell's *1984*, "Every year fewer and fewer words, and the range of consciousness always a little smaller." During their conversation over lunch in the Ministry of Truth canteen, Syme predicts that, "By 2050—earlier, probably—all real knowledge of Oldspeak will have disappeared. The whole literature of the past will have been destroyed."

Heaven forbid! But can anyone doubt that children today are operating with a smaller vocabulary than their parents did growing up? Book bans are bad enough, but when technocrats, or rather linguocrats, are going after the very medium in which books are expressed, and adulterating dictionaries, thesauruses, lexicons, concordances, and so on—it is our sacred duty to safeguard their entirety and integrity. Same goes for our bibles, along with constitutional texts written for our protection such as *Magna Carta*, the *Nuremberg Code*, *Helsinki Principles*, and the *Universal Declaration on Bioethics and Human Rights*.

Watch out, too, for passive statements that absolve tyrants from producing a subject carrying out the despotic verb. How many times are we told something is "required" or "mandated" with no mention of who is doing the requiring or mandating, or that something is "prohibited" without saying who is doing the prohibiting? They also use passive statements to shirk accountability, such as "Mistakes were made," "The issue has been identified," "A fix has been deployed," and so on.

Then there are the invisible choruses of 'experts' and 'analysts' who back the spurious assertions of dictators. The World Economic Forum used this tactic in a January 2022 article asserting that vaccine 'mandates' are not human-rights violations. "Not really, say experts on actual human rights violations," the article states. "In fact, some point to the more fundamental right to be protected from COVID-19." No individual is named among these supposed 'experts'.

True Rights have been inherent in Man since he appeared on Earth, and they have been treasured in many constitutions since, but until the WEF came along, no-one ever thought to coin a Right "to be protected from COVID-19."

ACTIONS

10

AFFIDAVITS OF TRUTH

They can't answer straightforward and sensible questions, and consequently lose the arguments by default.

— VERONICA: OF THE CHAPMAN FAMILY

Now begins the transition from mindset to action, and much of our action starts with an Affidavit of Truth. It is a written statement that you swear to be true in the presence of a witness or two. You send it to the other party by Recorded Delivery, giving them a time limit, perhaps 30 days, to send back a Rebuttal to every assertion you have made. If they fail to respond by the deadline, then the other party has given Tacit Acceptance, and your Unrebutted Affidavit now stands as Lawful Truth.

This tactic turns the Silence-Implies-Consent weapon back on the perpetrators, the difference being that we are being honourable about it. Our Affidavit informs them fully, so that any tacit consent they give us will be *Informed* Consent, whereas they have tried all along to obfuscate, bury, and hide anything which would properly inform us before they inferred *our* consent.

11

OUR STATUS CORRECTION

Here in England, we prosecute the dead and imprison the living.
The day you understand that is the day you found your freedom.

— LORD KW, TIKTOK VIDEO, SEPT. 2023

Now that we have corrected the status of 'Government', seeing it for the dead fiction that it is, how do we restore *our* status as the sovereign, living beings that *we* are? In an earlier chapter, we heard the metaphors of baptism, Jonah's expulsion from the whale, and passing through the Red Sea onto dry Land, to describe our Exodus from Maritime jurisdiction. Are there actions we can take to bring that about? I describe a few examples for your consideration.

Let me begin by saying what the action is not. It is not calling yourself a 'sovereign citizen'. That is an oxymoron for, as we have seen, 'citizen' is a weaponized term of incorporation. I tend to go with 'Living Man' when writing to government agencies, for Death can have no hold on us (*Acts* 2:24; *Romans* 8:11).

Some who live in the States United call themselves a 'State national', but I counter that STATE governments are also corporations. 'American national' is another alternative. My favourite is 'non-citizen national', which also happens to be a status acknowledged on U.S. passport-application forms, DS-11 and DS-82.

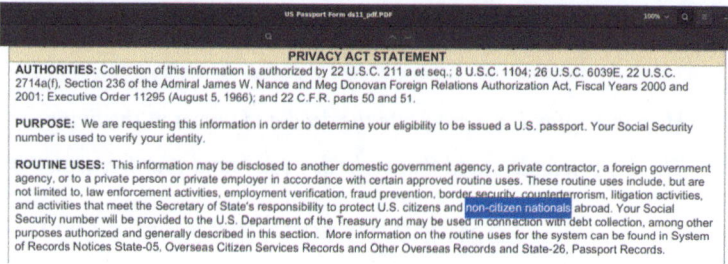

U.S. passport-application form, DS-11

U.S. passport-application form, DS-82

In the words of journalist and broadcaster Ann Vandersteel, during a March 2024 interview with Decentralize.TV, "An American national is somebody who has corrected their status and is no longer considered a U.S. citizen. I removed myself from the corporation of the United States, effectively declaring my independence and correcting my status back to that of an American."

Using the principle that an Unrebutted Affidavit stands as Lawful Truth, Vandersteel sent Affidavits renouncing her citizenship to the U.S. president, vice president, secretary of state, attorney general, and attorney general of State, giving them 21 days to rebut. Of course, none of them did rebut, whereupon she filed Summary Judgment of Unrebutted Affidavits with the county clerk's office. Then she obtained a passport using Form DS11 and checked 'Not U.S. Citizen' to be issued a passport as a Resident Alien. Thus, she said, "I dissolved my STRAWMAN relationship with the corporate government."

The U.S. Department of State ('State Department') acknowledges on its website that,...

"A relatively small number of persons acquire **U.S. nationality without becoming U.S. citizens**... As the Department has received few requests, there is no justification for the creation of a non-citizen national certificate. Designing a separate document that includes anti-fraud mechanisms was seen as an inefficient expenditure of resources. Therefore, the Department determined that those who would be eligible to apply for such a certificate may instead **apply for a United States passport that would delineate and certify** their status as a national but not a citizen of the United States" (emphases mine).

Roger Sayles, radio host and author of *From Sovereign to Serf: Government by the Treachery and Deception of Words,* sets out a simpler path than Vandersteel's. In a conversation with broadcaster Sarah Westall in 2022, he suggests writing a letter to the U.S. secretary of state that includes the sentence, "I, [Your Name], being duly sworn, hereby declare my intention to be a national, but not a citizen, of the United States." Get it notarized and send it to the U.S. Department of State, then put government agencies on notice that this Affidavit is filed, that your status has therefore changed, and that they no longer have jurisdiction over you. The same applies to the Internal Revenue Service, which I look at more closely in *Know Your Financial Rights.*

A third procedure is described at americanstate-nationals.org, using a one-page declaration template provided free at the site. You will be able to obtain a State-issued Travel ID, and private property plates for your car.

In Britain, meanwhile, a group called Hornseywood Academy advocates a limited-company process that, they argue, makes it hard for corporations to gain joinder with you. In a March 2024 interview with Richard Vobes, they point out that we are attached to the liabilities and responsibilities of our STRAWMAN NAME without owning the NAME. To remedy this, they create the

NAME as a limited-liability company, but the company is dormant.

I am not convinced, for their analysis is highly complex, at least on first hearing. Ultimately, there is no one-size-fits-all solution, so we choose the path that best plays to our strengths.

12

CONDITIONAL ACCEPTANCE

All men are born equal and so nobody has the right to command you, make demands of you, or force you to do anything. The most that anyone can do is to make you an offer to perform. Even though they may say that is is an 'Order', or a 'Demand', or a 'Summons', it is in reality an offer which you are free to accept or not as you so choose.

— DAVID E. ROBINSON,
MEET YOUR STRAWMAN

You know the famous scene. A debt is alleged, and because it isn't paid on time, the creditor insists he has the right to a pound of the debtor's flesh. I speak, of course, of Shakespeare's play *The Merchant of Venice* and especially its court scene (IV.i.), in which Shylock is sharpening his knife, ready to cut into Antonio's chest.

Shylock is deaf to calls for mercy, insisting "To have the due and forfeit of my bond..." and "To cut the forfeiture from that bankrupt there." The duke cannot dissuade him, nor can Antonio's friends. Nor can Portia when, disguised as Balthasar, a young doctor of laws from Rome, she enters the courtroom. Even the offer of triple repayment will not deter Shylock, so Portia tells Antonio, "You must prepare your bosom for his knife."

But then there is a plot twist. Just as Shylock is about to cut, Portia says,

"Tarry a little; there is something else.
This bond doth give thee here no jot of blood;
The words expressly are 'a pound of flesh.'
Take then thy bond, take thou thy pound of flesh,
But, in the cutting it, if thou dost shed
One drop of Christian blood, thy lands and goods
Are by the laws of Venice confiscate
Unto the state of Venice."

With these words, Portia annihilates Shylock's case with a strategy called 'Conditional Acceptance': "Yes, Shylock, we accept your legal entitlement to a pound of flesh, but only on condition you shed not one drop of blood."

Then she stipulates Shylock must take an exact pound, no more, no less, and "if the scale do turn/ But in the estimation of a hair,/ Thou diest and all thy goods are confiscate." By the end, Shylock is humiliated and stripped of his wealth, and Antonio is spared.

Today, Conditional Acceptance is proving a powerful weapon against bloodthirsty bondholders again. Among its leading exponents is Cal Washington, Co-founder and CEO of InPower (at inpowermovement.org). In an October 2023 interview with Mike Adams, he describes how this strategy is used to thwart four types of weapon being deployed against the People: 5G, vaccines, geoengineering, and smart meters.

When a government or corporation issues a notice or flyer about some new imposition they intend, or post a statement about it on a website, they are effectively making you an Offer to Contract with them. They hope you don't realize this so they can interpret your silence as tacit agreement. This is an example of their 'Silence-Implies-Consent' Satanic code.

Instead of being silent, however, you subject their Offer to universal contracting requirements, demanding full disclosure of relevant facts and terms, and make your Counter-Offer in which you set out the Conditions they must fulfill in order to enter Contract with you. When it comes to the four weapons, the main Counter-Offer condition is to require proof that they are safe.

"We say that they're offering these products," Washington explains, "and then we will conditionally accept their offer on the ground that they prove that they're safe. And because they're weapons, you can never prove a weapon is safe because it's not designed to be safe. So that creates a problem for them; they cannot prove that it's safe."

Among the Conditions you can stipulate, are…

- Proof that the trespassing technology, or other unwanted intervention, is safe.
- Proof of a jurisdiction that applies to you.
- Proof that you are a Public Person and not a Private Man or Private Woman.
- Proof you were offered contractual consideration either to consent or to opt out.
- Proof of any law authorizing them to do what they have in mind.
- Proof that no legislator involved in drafting, or voting for, any legislation they cite has any financial tie with them.
- Proof that the Private Man and/or Private Woman is not the lawful Owner of the land and/or property they propose to affect.
- Proof that the corporation is complying with a piece of legislation or code that you cite (and remember, legislation applies only to corporations, not to you).
- Proof that your privacy and confidentiality are not being compromised, that no unauthorized data collection is being conducted, and that your data is not being sold to a third party.

"And then we say," Washington continues, " 'If you keep deploying these weapons in my vicinity, then I'm going to charge you X amount of dollars per day. Do we have a deal?' If they fail to meet your conditions, you issue a Notice of Liability warning them of the penalties they will incur. If they still try to impose their unilateral, and therefore illegitimate, Contract, you send a Notice of Fault.

This is weaponizing the tyrants' own system against them. "We get them into a position where they're in default and they have to pay a daily fee," Washington explains. If they don't pay the fees accrued, debt collectors can be sent to collect.

In effect, the Silence-Implies-Consent equation has been re-engineered and turned back on the criminals. "If they go silent," Washington adds, "then they've agreed. And they were relying on silence as agreement for these four agendas as well. So we just basically take the same tactic they do and flip it back on them, ping-pong it back."

But, unlike in Shakespeare's drama, this is played out in the 'Private', rather than in court. InPower Members select the cause they wish to remedy, research to identify the individuals responsible, and submit a Notice of Liability to each. This gives the criminals an opportunity to rethink their harmful impositions and to cease. If they fail to cooperate, members start the process of billing them, drawing wealth out of the infernal system.

"If enough people on this planet wake up to what's really going on here, and fix the problem at a fundamental level," Washington said in a 2017 presentation, "the planet would run way better, and everybody would live in plenty. Everybody would live in a better harmonious way. We're at the beginning of that new sunlit morning where we can see the world in a different way where we have real hope and the ability to turn the tables."

InPower claims its work...

"has already seen success in several countries where officials have stepped down after receiving these documents. This means that if we get together in mass and send thousands of documents at the same time, we can make real change in the world, and we won't need weapons, elections, or protests to do it. All we need are pieces of paper that can be printed from home and sent in the mail."

The range of Conditional Agreement is not limited to 5G, vaccines, geoengineering, and smart meters, but has also proven effective in discharging debts that administrations, corporations, and financial institutions claim you owe them. When a debt is alleged, you can "conditionally accept" it "upon Proof of Claim" that...

- I am a Person—that is to say, a legal fiction— and not a Living Man.
- That your demand was issued after a lawful investigation unmarred by prejudice.
- That the alleged debt is validated, meaning they show the accounting behind it.
- That the alleged debt is verified in the form of a signed Invoice.
- That they supply a copy of the Contract with wet-ink signatures binding both parties.

They won't be able to produce these because their claims against you are unlawful. Another key benefit of Conditional Acceptance is that it keeps things out of court because you deny your adversary a Controversy on which a court could adjudicate. As David E. Robinson explains in *Meet Your Strawman*, "courts only deal with disputes, and if you conditionally accept each offer, there won't be any dispute, and so there can't be any court involvement."

I stress, however, that this strategy is NOT supplied for you to run up charges that, in a premeditated manner, you later intend to discharge. That would be folly and, as Alexander Pope warns in his immortal poem, *An Essay on Criticism*, "For fools rush in where angels fear to tread."

There is much wisdom, too, in the advice Polonius gives to his son, Laertes, in Shakespeare's *Hamlet*, "Neither a borrower nor a lender be" (I.iii.). Nor is Conditional Acceptance a tool to dishonour payment or repayment promises you made to friends, neighbours, family, or small businesses—that would be despicable— but it is a way to right past wrongs perpetrated by the Beast system which, as I shall explore more fully in *Know Your Financial Rights*, cheats every time it makes a so-called loan or mortgage.

I have also heard of examples where Conditional Acceptance is used to thwart corporate data theft. The Fourth Amendment is pretty clear...

"The right of the people to be secure in their persons, houses, papers, and effects, against unreasonable searches and seizures, shall not be violated, and no Warrants shall issue, but upon probable cause, supported by Oath or affirmation, and particularly describing the place to be searched, and the persons or things to be seized."

Nowadays, this Amendment is desecrated on a daily and habitual basis. Airport screening procedures alone are blatantly and disgustingly unconstitutional. They include new scanning machines for bodies, not just bags, that peer beneath clothing. This is not just desecration of Privacy but medical treatment without Informed Consent. Meanwhile, new layers of biometric scanning have been installed at Arrivals, and even now at departure gates.

Yet passengers are just going along with it, echoing the compliance during COVID when people gave away sacred medical information to random officials and other strangers on command. I also recently watched with horror video footage in which New Yorkers allowed officials to randomly search their bags before entering the subway system. Notices posted at the entrances told them they could refuse, but then they wouldn't be allowed to travel! In other words, you could safeguard your Right to Privacy but lose your Right to Travel as a result.

Meanwhile, the routine data harvesting by corporations is off the charts. A few months ago, I actually took the time to read through the so-called *Privacy Policy* of airline JetBlue. Claiming it is "not a contract," it still demands "consent" of the User, and merely using the airline's services is "tantamount" to that consent, the *Policy* states.

Brothers and Sisters, that *is* a contract! JetBlue also reserves the right to modify said Policy in its "sole discretion, at any time, in whole or in part" without notice, just by posting updated text on its website.

The *Policy* allows the airline to collect, hold, and share with third parties information about your interests and preferences, employment and education; about your device; and biometric data—including fingerprints, digital photographs, retinal scans, and facial-recognition data. It allows the use of tracking technologies such as geolocation, tracking pixels, and device fingerprinting to "uniquely identify your device and applications." It can track your activity across apps, and use voice-processing technologies that "analyze the data collected through the microphone on your device."

The airline will also hand over any information "public authorities" ask for, no mention of a Warrant, Oath, or Affirmation as required by the Fourth Amendment. All this, just so you can get on a fucking plane. This is not a Privacy Policy but a police-state policy.

I'm not talking about mere inconvenience here. Protection of Privacy can mean the difference between life and death, especially when politicians, bureaucrats, and media outlets are howling for the blood of medical dissenters, as they were during COVID, and when they are thirsting for another emergency to lash out in service to the 'common good'.

As I explain in *Know Your Medical Rights*, confidentiality of medical status is declared sacrosanct in many declarations, conventions, constitutions, and codes, going back thousands of years to the Hippocratic Oath. If only I could get the otherwise probed, prodded, and poked to cite them and uphold them!

When it comes to biometric data, there is some protection in the United States through Section 5 of the *Federal Trade Commission Act*. In a May 18, 2023 *Policy Statement*, the FTC warned that...

> "the collection and use of biometric information can create a serious risk of harm to consumers. Such harms are not reasonably avoidable by consumers if the collection and use of such information is not clearly and conspicuously disclosed or if access to essential goods and services is conditioned on providing the information. For instance, if businesses automatically and surreptitiously collect consumers' biometric information as they enter or move through a store, the consumers have no ability to avoid the collection or use of that information."

Therefore, your initial Counter-Offer conditions to companies or organizations collecting your data can include...

- Proof that you have clearly and conspicuously disclosed the collection and use of my information.

- Proof that you have obtained consent from every user for collection and use of their information.
- Proof of disclosure to users about what is done with the information collected.
- Proof that the collection and use of biometric data is safe for the individual whose data is collected. (The answer is, there is no proof that it's safe because the data can: a) be used to produce counterfeit videos and voice recordings; b) reveal sensitive personal information; c) produce discriminatory outcomes based on race; and d) be used in false accusation for a crime.)
- Proof that the technology reduces theft, crime, or violence, or whatever other claim has been made for it.
- Proof that consumers have been provided a non-penalizing way to avoid data collection.
- Proof that there are no default settings that invade privacy.
- Proof of measures in place to prevent unauthorized access, whether external, or by employees, contractors, or service providers.
- Proof that steps were taken to assess foreseeable harms to consumers before collecting information.
- Proof that the data collection is compliant with Section 5 of the *Federal Trade Commission Act* and with FTC guidance that the use of biometric

information "can create a serious risk of harm to consumers."

- Proof that the data collection is compliant with the Fourth Amendment to *The Constitution of the United States of America.*

13

LIABILITY FOR TYRANTS

Another movement fighting back against the Beast is Bonds for the Win, at bondsforthewin.com. The strategy here is to thwart dictators by going after their liability insurance. It begins by sending a letter to the relevant entity demanding copies of an official's Oath of Office, 'Surety Bond', and liability-insurance policy. The recipients are bound to comply under the *Freedom of Information Act*, the *Sunshine Act*, and various state codes, but if they fail to do so, report them to the department of insurance of the relevant state.

What is a Surety Bond? It's a written guarantee that an official will fulfill their duties. If they don't, the insurance company pays the liability. Once you have a copy of the applicable Surety Bond, serve the individual with a Letter of Intent listing their violations, a list of your demands to resolve the situation, and a date by which the demands must be met before a Claim is filed.

Include in your Letter who the Notifying Party is, most likely you.

You may want to cite in your letter *United States Code* Title 42, Section 1983 which specifies penalties for anyone who, "under color of any law, statute, ordinance, regulation, or custom, willfully subjects any person in any State, Territory, Commonwealth, Possession, or District to the deprivation of any rights, privileges, or immunities secured or protected by the Constitution or laws of the United States." If the violation results in bodily injury, the penalty can include ten years in prison. In cases of kidnapping or sexual abuse, the Code allows for life imprisonment or a death sentence.

If the individual fails to meet your demands, send a Notice to File a Claim against their liability-insurance policy, along with an Affidavit of Facts, meaning a sworn written statement signed in the presence of a witness. File separate claims for each elected official and each notifying party. At this point, you become a debt collector against the official's liability-insurance policy.

This process can be used at every level of government, according to Miki Klann of The People's Operation Restoration. For example, school boards that try to compel students to wear masks are culpable for practising medicine without a licence.

In a March 2022 interview, Klann told broadcaster, David Nino Rodriguez, "Every elected and appointed official, every judge, every prosecutor, mayor, city counselor, members of the boards of commissioners, boards of supervisors, sheriffs, coroners—that is to say, public servant—is licensed, bonded, and insured." Forms and templates, along with procedural guidance and explainer videos, are amply provided at the Bonds for the Win website, along with a useful list of protective pieces of legislation.

Alas, the site inaccurately calls the legislation 'Laws', suggesting to me they don't fully get it. 'Lawful legislation' is more fitting. The approach also depends on statutory frameworks for its solutions. Nevertheless, the effort embodies the Common-Law principle of holding individuals to account with Claims, as opposed to the counterfeit, Limited-Hangout, Beast-system procedure of bringing Complaints against corporations, which does nothing to disturb their underlying business model.

14

PRIVATE MEMBERSHIP ASSOCIATIONS

Why are we begging our oppressors to save us? It's a Stockholm Syndrome. We've got to break out of it. It's a mental cage in our own head.

— MIKI KLANN

If you are an independent farmer or small business in any Western nation, you have probably experienced harsh and punitive treatment from governments by now. They have driven up your costs, strangled your ability to produce, stolen or destroyed your inventory, stifled your reach, or shut you down altogether, and they have probably weaponized their bogus climate-change narrative against you to do it. Yes, they are trying to destroy food production, and to poison or starve the population, and they are trying to consolidate corporate power into fewer and fewer hands as they create Hell-on-Earth dystopias.

In the United States at least, the destructive rampage of government agencies was somewhat checked by a June 2024 decision of the United States Supreme Court in Loper Bright Enterprises v. Raimondo. The decision stated that it was up to the courts to decide "whether an agency has acted within its statutory authority, and courts may not defer to an agency interpretation of the law…"

This reversed the so-called 'Chevron Doctrine'— which arose from the 1984 case, Chevron v. Natural Resources Defense Council—that held courts should defer to bureaucrats' interpretations of statutes.

But here's a key question for you. Is your business registered with the government? As John Smith points out in his November 2020 conversation with David Icke, "When you register a company in their system, you're in Commerce, and their rules apply." In other words, you are in Legal Land, but you now want to be rid of all the interference, destruction, and sabotage that comes along with that.

What does it mean to 'register' something with a government anyway? In his 2016 lecture, Alan of Salisbury points out,…

"WHEN YOU REGISTER SOMETHING, YOU ARE GIVING AWAY WHATEVER YOU ARE REGISTERING TO WHOEVER YOU ARE REGISTERING IT WITH."

👑 **GOV.UK**

Bring photo ID to vote Check what photo ID you'll need to vote in person in the

Home > Environment > Food and farming > Keeping farmed animals > Poultry registration

Press release

New measures to help protect poultry industry from bird flu

New registration requirements for bird keepers in Great Britain - all bird keepers must register their birds and update records annually.

From: **Department for Environment, Food & Rural Affairs**, **The Scottish Government** and **Welsh Government**

Published 19 March 2024

Last updated 19 March 2024 — See all updates

For example, if you are in Britain and your car is registered with the DVLA, your V5C form describes you as the 'Registered keeper' of the vehicle, not the 'owner', and of course has your name in ALL CAPS. The document even emphasizes on the front page, "THIS

DOCUMENT IS NOT PROOF OF OWNERSHIP. It shows who is responsible for registering and taxing the vehicle."

That's the way it works for them. You don't own anything, the government owns everything, but you are 'responsible' for looking after the government's property while Mr. Banker profits at your own expense. What you think is your property is really collateral that the government can seize at any time to pay off its debts and hush-money to international bankers.

Same goes for the British government's recent demand you register *any* backyard chickens, an obvious ploy to destroy independent food production. Again, they use the word 'keeper'.

Then Alan looks at the word, 'application', which in legal terms means you are a beggar, while 'submit' means bending to another's will. "So if you submit an application to register, what you've done in terms of Legal is you've given up all your Rights voluntarily—because, remember, there are laws against slavery, but there isn't any law against voluntary slavery."

Is there a way out of this? Yes, according to Smith. "If you stand under Common Law as a Living Man or Woman, you can actually trade a business under Common Law as well, which means that the rules are not applicable to you."

This motivation has given rise to a proliferation of private, and therefore unincorporated, membership associations (PMA), where statutory rules don't apply. According to Mike Colomb of The Renegade Nation at therenegadenation.org, which helps people to set up PMAs, "When you pull yourself into a PMA, you're not guided by a federal government, state government, local government, and the FDA. They're gone, because all the rules that they make are for the Public, and we're not dealing with the Public, we're dealing with the Private."

In a July 2023 conversation with Mike Adams, Colomb notes Article 1 Section 10 of the *Constitution* enshrines our Right to perform unlimited transactions. Corporate structures have usurped this right, but PMAs restore it. They are a means to lawfully conduct a tax-free, for-profit business, such as health hubs and clinics, food and farming cooperatives, compounding pharmacies, travel associations, precious-metals storage, schools, and so on. "No business taxes, no payroll taxes, no self-employment tax, no sales tax," said Colomb in another interview with Dr. Andrew Kaufman.

PMAs are far easier to set up than a corporation and don't require attorneys to get involved. The first step is to draw up Articles of Association. Then, any sales you make are to members only, keeping your trade entirely in the Private. For pre-existing businesses, the procedure begins with drawing up the Articles, then disassociating the prior LLC, corporation, or sole proprietorship.

Colomb encourages sheriffs to join PMAs too. If government agents come on to your property, tell them it's a PMA and that they're trespassing, and if they refuse to leave, have them arrested by the sheriff.

PMAs are an important component of the Parallel

Society, Kaufman comments, a way to liberate small businesses and to return to middle-class prosperity. "We don't have to be employees for huge corporations under terrible conditions. We can increase our independence and freedom in this route."

15

PERPLEXING THE POLICE

A conformist does what he's told, regardless of what is right, but a moralist would do what is right, regardless of what he's told.

— HIGHIMPACTFLIX, 2023

With power comes responsibility, so the saying goes. Well, we see in police officers of Western nations an insatiable hunger for power, combined with complete abandonment of responsibility or accountability. Almost without exception, these 'badge-tyrants' have become a marauding gang of pirates, bandits, highwaymen, shakedown artists, and thugs for hire.

The job of officers now, according to David E. Robinson in *Meet Your Strawman*, is to get people "to pay invented cash penalties to the local commercial company called the 'Police Force'." They don't *dare* go after *real* criminals, but instead act as revenue-collection agents, extorting, intimidating, and oppressing people who want nothing more than to be left alone, to get on with their lives in Peace and Freedom.

Furthermore, police are quite willing to lie to get a conviction against you, as British man Jonathan Dow discovered after he was issued a 'speeding' ticket. In a February 2024 conversation with Richard Vobes, he chronicles how police used falsified road markings, tampered with documents, destroyed evidence, and framed Dow with planted evidence. If they go to this much effort to defraud a man over a speeding ticket, think what they are capable of when the stakes are higher!

And, when I see video after video of police coercing and harming those they are sworn to protect, their stupidity rivals the brutality. "They want a two-class society," comments Max Igan in a March 2024 broadcast, "so you've got the elite and you've got the serfs. That's all they want. And in between that, of course, will be the brick wall of brainless stupidity known as the police force."

Igan has especially harsh words for the police in his home country of Australia, telling Maria Zeee in a June 2023 interview,...

"What you're doing is supporting a criminal cabal masquerading as a government that is operating in treason, and you are enslaving and destroying this country, and if you are an Australian, you need to take that ridiculous uniform off, take that face diaper off your face, act like a police officer, and go and arrest these criminals. That's what you need to do, and if you can't do that, you're not worth the uniform you're wearing, and you're not even worth the blood that's flowing through your veins... What you're doing is supporting child abusers and criminals and the takeover of this country, and you're supporting treason. You don't even have the right to call yourself an Australian."

Meanwhile, we see how British police will raid the home of a disabled woman and haul her to jail for something she said on social media, as they did with Fiona Ryan, and urge her to post opinions different from the ones she holds. They will tear screaming children from their rightful parents, arrest people for praying peacefully by the side of a road, and destroy a homeless man's encampment in the woods. Meanwhile, U.S. cops will arrest a man for eating outside and issue fines for feeding the homeless.

And when I say 'cops', reluctantly I include sheriffs too. In *Know Your Medical Rights*, I cheered on 'Constitutional sheriffs', hoping some of them would take a stand against tyrannical policy enforcement, but from what I've seen since, sheriffs throughout America are as thoroughly corporatized as the rest of so-called 'law enforcement'. Had I read Anna von Reitz's analysis beforehand, I wouldn't have been so naive. In a 2019 blog, she wrote,...

" 'Sheriffs' assume they are Sheriffs long after the 'County' they work for has been converted into a private business enterprise, and therefore lost all public mandate and actual power to act as a County government. Read that: these men are acting under color of law with respect to us, and most of them don't even know it."

Thus, we have seen sheriffs behaving just as brutally and unconstitutionally as cops. "You snakes," as Christ said to the Pharisees, "you brood of vipers. How will you escape being condemned to Hell?!" (*Matthew* 23:33). Enraging as these examples are, I also lament the token resistance they usually encounter from people—well-meaning people, to be sure, but generally ill-informed and with but a shallow grasp of our Rights.

Magna Carta states, "We will appoint as justices, constables, sheriffs, or bailiffs only such as know the law of the realm and mean to observe it well" (Article 45). I put it to you, dear Reader, that you and I know the true Law of the Land far better than any police officer. It is you and I who are minded to keep it well, not the uninformed, uniformed order-followers in whom every murmur of conscience, and every independence of thought, has been banished. It is up to us to give *them* lawful orders and to arrest *them* if they defy *us*!

I infer that, as with other institutions purporting to serve the People, such as hospitals, bureaucracies, and the military, the brightest and best have been purged from police forces. Now, all these institutions are thronged with the most compliant, murderous, and psychopathic order-followers and secret-society operatives currency can buy, who are then rewarded and promoted within.

Vaccine 'mandates' were a key ploy in effecting this purge. That was the case with Michael McMahon, forced out after 14 years with the LAPD, for refusing Big Pharma's bite. "We get our powers from the consent of the governed," he told Maria Zeee in their February 2023 conversation, "and police should not be seen as the armies of the elite but the protectors of the people. Plain and simple, period. Full stop. We are the protectors of the people. We do not carry out the whims of whoever's in government at the time."

Agreed, except can we stop calling us the 'governed'? 'People' will do, or maybe 'masters'. Meanwhile, our societies have forgotten the divine calling of Manhood in these days. "Masculinity is not toxic," McMahon told Zeee. "The *absence* of masculinity is toxic. Weak men are abusive and spiteful, and that's what you're seeing in our government today. If you're afraid of a masculine man, wait until you see what a weak man does in power."

Whatever happened to "the police are the public, and the public are the police," one of the *Principles of Policing* and of 'Policing by Consent' when Sir Robert Peel founded the British police force in 1829? What has happened to the British *Constable's Oath* (included in Schedule 4 of the *Police Act* (1996) to uphold "fundamental human rights..."? And what happened to the requirement, stated in the College of Policing *Code of*

Ethics, to "uphold the law regarding human rights" and to "Give and carry out lawful orders only."?

Gone, forgotten, Memory-Holed. These principles, now usurped by secret oaths, are drowned in the blood of children sacrificed in rituals of atrocity. That's why the *Criminal Justice and Courts Act* (2015), which can imprison for up to 14 years any officer who "exercises the powers and privileges of a constable improperly" (Section 26), is not being enforced.

Joinder and Silence

So how to handle these gangs? A good place to start is knowing they want to take your property and for that, they need to go into 'Joinder' with you. Remember I talked about that in the *'Berth' Certificate* chapter? In order to flatten you into the two-dimensional space of the ALL-CAPS STRAWMAN, they need your details—name, address, date of birth—so they can pin you to the Birth Certificate and plunder your vessel.

You may prefer to refuse giving them this information, and if you are in the united States, to cite your Constitutional (Fifth-Amendment) Right to Remain Silent. Some say to police officers, "I don't answer questions."

Dean of Buxton and Rachel Elnaugh-LOVE echo this approach, saying in a 2022 presentation on Common Law, "Thou hast the Right to Remain Silent.... Thou canst maintain silence by stating, 'I do not understand' to every single question asked by the 'authority'. Not just verbally, but all written forms, statements, etc."

Or, answer every question with a question, as Jesus often did when the Pharisees were trying to ensnare him (*Luke* 21:23-27). If they ask for your details, you could reply, "Am I required to give you that information?" or, "Do I have the Right to remain silent?" I may also ask them what Law they are operating under and to show me where I signed any legislation they cite. You can also ask if they police under consent and, building on my analysis in *Know Your Medical Rights*, if they have sworn the Constable's Oath, or Oath to the Constitution as applicable, and if they're acting under that Oath today.

In *Meet Your Strawman*, David E. Robinson advises against showing any form of ID "as that places you in a position of voluntary submission." They may ask you if you "understand" which, in their Legal Land, means, "Do you stand under me?" Nice try, officer!

If you are in Britain, Veronica suggests you just say, " 'Rice verses Connolly, 1966, Queen's Bench Division. It's in your Operational Manual. Good day, Constable.' And walk away!"

What she's referring to here is a court decision that found in favour of one Mr. Rice who, in the early hours of Mar. 8, 1965, refused to give his full details to one Police Constable Baillie in Grimsby, England and refused to accompany Baillie to a police box. The constable arrested him, claiming Rice had "obstructed him in the execution of his duty."

The Bench quashed Rice's conviction on Appeal. In the words of the head judge, Hubert Parker,...

"the sole question here is whether the appellant had a lawful excuse for refusing to answer the questions put to him. In my judgment he had. It seems to me quite clear that though every citizen has a moral duty or, if you like, a social duty to assist the police, there is no legal duty to that effect, and indeed the whole basis of the common law is that right of the individual to refuse to answer questions put to him by persons in authority, and a refusal to accompany those in authority to any particular place... In my judgment there is all the difference in the world between deliberately telling a false story, something which on no view a citizen has a right to do, and preserving silence or refusing to answer, something which he has every right to do."

Anyone who upholds their Constitutional rights will at some point be threatened by an enforcer. They will tell you that if you don't comply, some bad thing is going to happen to you. One enforcer may refer the matter to a more senior one, but at some point, they will resolve into one individual. By now, there's a high probability you're face-to-face with a Freemason, but in any case, you have authority over it and over whatever it's taking orders from. What would *I* say?

"No, I am giving YOU *a choice: either to comply with* MY *lawful order to* YOU, *or to break the Law, and I caution you*

that he who breaks the Law is under a curse (Deuteronomy 27:26), and if you're under a curse, you'll bring about your own destruction this very day—destruction decreed in Heaven and now effected on Earth. So, do you want to destroy yourself this day? Because that is what will happen to you from the moment you disobey my order. So I'm now giving you a chance to revise your position here today. What's it to be?

If it says I've threatened it, I will tell it, *"No, I have blessed you by telling you how to avoid your own destruction."*

It's a good idea, of course, to film or record every conversation you have with officials of every stripe, including police. In a June 2024 blogpost, Kevin Annett recommends, "NEVER rely on 'official' transcripts or your opponents' version of events, which will be skewed in their interest."

On the Road

Police can be especially injurious when it comes to traffic stops, which the corporate Beast treasures for their extortion potential. However, as Miki Klann points out, the only way a cop "can contract with you is if he can get you to represent your corporation, because in Maritime courts, corporations can only contract with other corporations... If he can't get you to respond to the Legal Fiction, he can't contract with you." Traffic tickets, she adds, are 'an Affidavit of Fiction.'

Police also want you to admit you were "driving," which is a corporate legal-fiction term that means you were engaging in Commerce. "No," you reply. "I am travelling." Again, answering questions with a question is a way to disempower uniformed thugs. *"Did I ask for your service today?" "Did anyone make a report of me committing a crime?"*

In the event a cop issues you a ticket, the suggestion from David Straight is, "You take the ticket, and at a 45-degree angle with red sharpie, you say, 'Your offer of contract is not accepted. I'm travelling in private in a private automobile. YOU are operating, under Title 18, Section 242, under the Color of Law.' And you mail it into the court, and you do it within 72 hours... And if there's two or more officers, then 241 applies as well."

The legislation he's referring to, USC Title 18, Section 242, sets out penalties up to life imprisonment and a death sentence for "Whoever, under color of any law, statute, ordinance, regulation, or custom, willfully subjects any person in any State, Territory, Commonwealth, Possession, or District to the deprivation of any rights, privileges, or immunities secured or protected by the Constitution..."

USC Title 18, Section 241 uses similar language when "two or more persons conspire to injure, oppress, threaten, or intimidate" someone in the free exercise or enjoyment of their Constitutional Rights.

Arrests

These 'Color-of-Law' statutes are not the only legislated limits to police action. These days, uniformed morons are all too ready to make up what the 'law' is, tell you you're breaking it, threaten to arrest you, and possibly carry that out. If you happen to point out their criminality, they'll accuse you of 'resisting arrest', but...

TRUE LAW PRESUMES ANY ARREST TO BE UNLAWFUL, AND THE BURDEN OF PROOF IS ON THE ARRESTING OFFICER TO PROVE OTHERWISE.

This was affirmed in 1888 by the Supreme Court of California, which ruled in People v. McGrew, "the imprisonment being proven, the law presumes it unlawful until the contrary is shown."

The Oregon Supreme Court echoed this in 1926 with its decision in Knight v. Baker: "In order to establish the offense of false imprisonment, it is only necessary on behalf of the plaintiff to show the imprisonment. After this is done, the law presumes it unlawful until the contrary is shown." It also warned, "One who interferes with another's liberty of locomotion does so at his peril."

Then, in 1944, the Supreme Court of Minnesota issued a warning to police in its Thiede v. Town of Scandia Valley decision:

"The officer's protection given to him by the law is a shield to protect him against honest mistakes in judgment; it is not a sword with which to strike down constitutional rights of citizens. As in the case of illegal arrests, the officer is bound to know these fundamental rights and privileges, and must keep within the law at his peril."

Several court precedents also confirm an arresting officer must produce an Arrest Warrant upon request. The Warrant must be signed with a wet-ink signature by a sitting judge who has taken a Constitutional Oath of Office kept on file. 'Rubber-stamp' signatures on Warrants are invalid, as courts have also ruled.

Further, any Warrant must be backed by an Affidavit from an Accuser, including first-hand facts about the alleged crime. That Affidavit must also be available for inspection upon request.

Warrantless arrest is Assault and Trespass, and many are the court precedents upholding your Right to use force in defending yourself against it. For example, in 1958, the Court of Appeals of Ohio ruled in Columbus v. Holmes, "Any unlawful interference with the right of personal property may be resisted, and every person has the right to resist an unlawful arrest."

If you are arrested, police may not photograph you before conviction, as confirmed by the Supreme Court of New York in Hawkins v. Kuhne in 1912. Nor may they fingerprint you. In 1926, the City Magistrates' Court of New York ruled in People v. Helvern that requiring fingerprinting as a condition of bail was oppressive, unreasonable, and unconstitutional.

In Closing...

It's over for police forces in the West now. They are not, as they should be, *peace* officers ready to protect us and our property from corporate trespassers, but corporate lackeys who, if they ever had any credibility, have completely squandered it by now.

Nor do these Oath breakers, having so relentlessly betrayed the People's trust, have any idea what devastation they have brought upon themselves. One day, when the equally lawless migrant soldiers now infiltrating our nations are activated against them, the police will ask for help from a People so disgusted by their lawless behaviour and betrayals, that no-one will give a shit what happens to them or come to their aid. We can wait for that day or, Brothers,...

IT'S TIME TO ARREST THE POLICE!

CAUGHT COURTS

This is the Court of Chancery... which gives to monied might the means abundantly of wearying out the right; which so exhausts finances, patience, courage, hope; so overthrows the brain and breaks the heart; that there is not an honorable man among its practitioners who would not give – who does not often give – the warning, "Suffer any wrong that can be done you, rather than come here."

— CHARLES DICKENS, *BLEAK HOUSE*

So this is where things get really ugly, where I'm going to roll up my sleeves and get into the weeds, but I'll bring you out the other side. Let's say the Beast System is Goliath, and that we are Davids. Before facing that lumbering Philistine, David gathered five smooth stones that could serve as missiles (*1 Samuel* 17:40). In this chapter, I shall put before you many smooth stones from disparate sources and add some of my own. Then, you may select the ones that serve you and your fighting style best.

In case you haven't figured it out by now, corporate courts—and they're all corporations—along with swarms of debt collectors, bailiffs, and police—or, more accurately policy officers—are the Beast System's enforcement arm, a Beast that regards you as a treasure-bearing ship that may be plundered for profit then, once everything of value has been stripped away, scuppered and sent to the bottom of the sea. Their job is to ensure you *don't* receive Justice or, if you ever could get Justice, to make the path to it so costly and depleting that most people won't waste their energy and resources on the effort.

Courts are the crucible of Satan's dark arts, and the general advice is not to appear in them, at least not as a 'Defendant' or 'Respondent'. This is not as stupid as it sounds. If you have refused Joinder up 'til now, to whom will they issue a Summons? For example, you may have refused to show any form of identification to would-be enforcers, and if they sent you a document, or showed up with one, the name they addressed you by was ALL CAPS, and you correctly refuted any suggestion that this PERSON was you.

You may have also wielded Conditional-Acceptance strategies, as described before, and thereby avoided any Controversy on which a court could adjudicate. You asked them, for example, "Where's the Contract?" "Who is the individual bringing the claim against me, and where was he/she at the time of the alleged violation?" "Where's the signature?" "Is there a first-hand witness, or is this allegation based on hearsay?" "Who is the victim of the alleged violation?", etc. Also, if a bank, bureaucracy, corporation, or institution asserted a debt against you, you never argued that you didn't owe that much, which would have *acknowledged* a debt, but you made sure they carried the Burden of Proof to back up their claims.

Summoning the Dead

Throughout, you played wise as a serpent, as Christ instructed his disciples (*Matthew* 10:16). Even if they sent you a Summons, you saw this as another attempt at Joinder, and Joinder would be falsely assumed if you showed up. "Another trick they try to play on you," David E. Robinson writes in *Meet Your Strawman*, "is to imply that a Summons is something which you MUST obey while in fact, it is only an Invitation to attend their place of business."

Rather than ignore the Summons, however, which would give them opportunity to assume you were guilty, you promptly sent it back to the court and let them know there was no-one by that ALL-CAPS NAME at that address.

Or you informed them that their services were not required (because you don't want to be in Contract with them). You could do this as David Straight suggests, whom I quoted in the previous chapter: "45-degree angle with a red sharpie on anything you get,... you say, 'Your offer to contract is not accepted.' "

What is a Summons to Appear, anyway? It is calling forth a dead thing, an apparition. Remember, the Maritime jurisdiction sees you as a dead PERSON whose estate is up for grabs, or as a crewless ship found drifting at Sea and ripe for the taking. The courts want you to play along with their rite of necromancy. By summoning YOUR NAME (in ALL CAPS) from the dead, the so-called 'judge' fancies himself another Witch of Endor—she who, at King Saul's behest, brought Samuel up from the dead (*1 Samuel* 28).

The Twelve Presumptions of Court

Now, before we enter any courtroom—*if* we enter any courtroom—let's set the stage—for stage it is—and talk about *The Twelve Presumptions of Court*. Tracing their poison root to the legal system of ancient Rome, these Presumptions are always running in the background in today's Maritime courts, and if you do not challenge and rebut them, those sneaky fuckers who think "Silence Implies Consent" will presume they apply in your case.

Trusts.

I need to get a bit nerdy now as I decipher the dark meanings of these Satanic verses, but stick with me, and I'll do my best to get us through this as painlessly as possible. To begin with, there are two key words to define, beginning with 'Trusts'. Why do we need to know what a Trust is? Because the *Presumptions* postulate an erroneous Trust relationship with you and because, as youandyourcash.com explains, "A fundamental understanding of Trusts is imperative if you wish to see the MATRIX in all its glory, and avoid the vampires and other leeches looking to latch onto you."

A simple trust has three parties, **Executor**, **Trustee**, and **Beneficiary**, as can be illustrated from Charles Dickens' novel, *Great Expectations*. The protagonist, Pip, discovers he is the **Beneficiary** of a Trust that shall fund his transformation from a blacksmith's apprentice to a 'gentleman'. The Trust is administered by the lawyer, Jaggers, who is responsible for parcelling out payments to Pip. So Jaggers is the **Trustee**, the one who is entrusted with looking after the Trust and carrying out its intent.

For most of the novel, Pip does not know who the **Executor**, or Grantor, of the Trust is, meaning who set it up in the first place and funded it. Jaggers, as Trustee, is not permitted to tell him. This is a major plot point, so I won't spoil it here.

The point is that we have been unwittingly contracted into a Trust relationship with Government through the Birth Certificate. I described the Birth Certificate as a Bond before, but it's also a Trust in the sense that the parasites who considered us dead, took custody of our Estates, and continue to pocket the proceeds, consider themselves Executor of this Trust, meaning they set it up, but also somehow Beneficiary. You and I, meanwhile, are burdened with a Trustee role of continually topping up the pot!

But isn't it reassuring that those awfully nice banker

types are kindly looking after our assets, just in case we ever come back from our long sea voyage and declare ourselves to be alive. How kind of them! Though of course, they conceal from us any mechanism to make such a declaration.

Bars.

The other word needing definition is 'Bar'? In the U.S., it means two things. It is both a physical line in a courtroom that separates spectators from the foremost area reserved for trial participants. 'Bar' also means a guild, or union, for members of the legal profession. According to Melvin Stamper in the book, *Fruit From a Poisonous Tree*, the American Bar Association has allowed…

> "international bankers to control the practice of law, in that the only ones permitted to practice before the courts were those who were educated under their brand of law, which was only Admiralty and Contract law. Common law of the people was to be replaced as it gave the natural man many jurisdictional protections from the bankers' legislation."

In a U.S. court, when you "cross the bar," you are literally stepping onto the stage of Legal Land, rather like an actor entering a theatre. In a theatre, the transition from actor to character happens in the dressing room by putting on costume and makeup. In a court, the transition from Living Man to corporate fiction happens by crossing the Bar and assuming the character of YOUR NAME in ALL CAPS.

So, with those definitions covered, let's get back to those devilish *Presumptions*, the distillation of which has been attributed to researcher, Frank O'Collins. I shall do my best to simplify what they say, and add my analysis in *italics...*

1. **Presumption of Public Record.** *This is a misnomer. What it really means is, Presumption of* No *Public Record in lower courts. Public Record is not permitted, as in, "No cameras in the courtroom." It is also a Presumption of Private Business Matter.*

2. **Presumption of Public Service.** Members of the bar guild have all sworn a solemn, secret, and absolute oath to the bar, but the Presumption holds they may *act* as public officials and make additional oaths of public office that contradict their secret oath. *This Presumption is at the heart of all the tyranny now afoot in our nations. All public institutions, not just courts, are operating according to secret oaths. The outgrowth of their evil comes from a poison underground root system of secret societies. Nowadays, as we saw with the entire Biden cabinet, some public officials are not even bothering with a public Oath of Office.*

3. **Presumption of Public Oath.** Bar members are presumed to have honestly served their

public oath, even though it is in contradiction to their guild oath. *This Presumption is false on its face because the prior Presumption holds that the secret oath is absolute. By taking multiple oaths, court officials presume to serve more than one master, something Jesus said was impossible, for they must be devoted to one and despise the other (Matthew 6:24). Talk about a conflict of interest! They secretly hate their public oaths and will be shunned by Christ at the Judgment (Matthew 7:22-23, Luke 13:24-28).*

4. **Presumption of Immunity.** Bar guild members *acting as* judges, prosecutors, and magistrates who have sworn a solemn public oath "in good faith" are immune from personal claims of injury and liability. *This supposed immunity is easily stripped. No-one who swears a secret and absolute oath can swear a public oath "in good faith."*

5. **Presumption of Summons.** Courts presume that, without rebuttal, a Summons stands, and that any accused who attends Court has accepted the court's jurisdiction and the existence of guilt. *This contradicts the age-old Common-Law presumption of "innocent until proven guilty," replacing it with "guilty until proven guilty."*

6. **Presumption of Custody.** Courts presume that, without rebuttal, a Summons or Warrant for Arrest stands.

7. **Presumption of Court of Guardians.** The court regards itself as your Guardian. It

presumes you are incompetent to manage your own affairs, and that you must therefore obey its rules.

8. **Presumption of Court of Trustees**. The court presumes you are there in service to the government, that you are a public 'Trustee'.

9. **Presumption of Dual Role**. The court sees itself as Trust 'Executor', and the prosecutor as Trust 'Beneficiary'. Your job, they suppose, is to serve as 'Trustee', the one who makes all the payments required and does as the Executor instructs.

10. **Presumption of False Executor**. While the court regards itself as Trust 'Executor', if you challenge the judge on this, you will be regarded as a 'False Executor', or 'Executor de Son Tort'. *Rebuttal of this Presumption goes hand in hand with rebuttal of the prior Dual-Role Presumption.*

11. **Presumption of Incompetence**. The court assumes you are incompetent to present yourself and argue properly.

12. **Presumption of Guilt**. The court presumes you are guilty, whatever you 'plead'.

This is all a lot to take in, and who is going to remember all of that, especially in the stressful conditions of a courtroom? So instead, prevention being better than cure, you can send a witnessed document to the court beforehand where you rebut each *Presumption* in turn saying something like, "Presumption X has no merit, nor basis in fact" or, "By definition, a Presumption can never have standing as material fact."

Pre-Court Strategies

But if, for whatever reason, a court appearance is still looming, there are more advance troops you can send forth. One suggestion is to contact the court's public-information officer and make a FOIA request asking for the Oaths of Office of public officials involved in the case, including and especially the judge.

Another is to send ahead an Affidavit of Questionnaire to the judge and to opposition attorneys asking them, "Under penalty of perjury, do you have a financial interest in this case?" If they are being truthful, they will answer yes, whereupon you remind them they must recuse themselves from the case. If they answer that no, they do not have a financial interest in the case, they have perjured themselves.

A third tactic is to insist a court reporter be present to produce a transcript of the proceedings (in case you need it later for an appeal). Being corporations, they will hate this extra expense.

A fourth strategy is to ask for a judge's, prosecutor's, or police officer's Foreign Agents Registration. Under legislation, USC Title 22 Section 611, agents of a foreign principal are required to file with the attorney general "a true and complete registration statement and supplements thereto." As the United States Corporation government is a foreign entity, anyone working for it must have a foreign-agent registration statement on file with the Department of Justice. Upon their failure to produce this, you can send the court a Motion to Dismiss for fraud.

These are all ways to make the court's business of asset-stripping you more burdensome and costly to themselves. It also notifies the court that you're not one to be hoodwinked by their tricks and deceptions. You are the epitome of a "difficult customer," and they may decide it's not worth the effort to go after you.

Courts Are Theatres

If, after all this, you are still going to court, remember who you are, a Living Man or Living Woman with authority over things created by men, including courts, their officials, and the administrators or convenors that they falsely call judges. And what a shock to their system when what shows up is not a ghost or apparation but a Living Man or a Living Woman. Imagine your living self walking into a funeral where everyone thinks your corpse is in the coffin. You'll cause quite a stir!

Remember, too, that you are going into a theatre, though you're bringing a plot twist none of them saw coming. From time to time, I have worked as a theatre actor. I go into contract with the producer, learn my lines, attend rehearsals, and play my role. When the production run is complete, I take off the costume and get on with my life. But when it comes to Legal Land, the tyrants would imprison you in your STRAWMAN character and have you forget that you can leave the stage, take off the costume, and get out of the building.

Remember too, who *they* are, actors in that theatre, not there because they have any merit, wisdom, or nobility, and certainly not any real authority, but because they have made the right deals, dined at the right clubs, and sworn the requisite Satanic oaths. All along, they masqueraded as servants of righteousness while running up voluminous rap sheets for the Judgment to come.

They sit in splendid court buildings, nonetheless, structures their own hands could never have made and that seem designed for giants. You might get the feeling you're at a cult ritual when you go into a court. That's because you are. "When people go into courts now," observes Kevin Annett in a May 2024 conversation with Dr. Katherine Horton, "it's designed to intimidate. Judges are like what priests used to be, they're these mystical figures who seem to have all this knowledge and authority, and we're not allowed to confront them."

Courts Are Corporations

Courts are also registered companies, remember, seeking unlawfully to fit you into a statutory structure without regard to Common Law. In the words of John Smith of commonlawcourt.com, they have "no more status than a McDonald's or a Tesco." In his November 2020 conversation with David Icke, he testifies, "We can confirm every court—we're based in the U.K. but it's applicable worldwide—every court within the statutory system is a registered company. They're actually there for profit, and they're not there for justice. Justice does not exist in their system."

The reality is even worse when it comes to U.S. district courts which, according to Anna von Reitz, are descendants of quasi-military courts imposed upon the South following the American Civil War. Their purpose, she points out in a March 2024 article, was to...

"extract 'war reparations' from the Southerners and the Southern States by means of illegal confiscation carried out with a veneer of Due Process. These courts had nothing whatsoever to do with justice. They were created for the purposes of political suppression and physical control of the population, and to punish the 'rebels' by taking whatever little of value that they had left—mainly their land."

These courts were weaponized from the start, von Reitz continues, "and they are weaponized to this day, with the same objectives in place: control the population, extract assets... and rape it for plunder." They do it, as she points out in a June 2022 presentation, with "impersonation and identity-substitution schemes, to set up all of these foreign courts and misaddress Americans and bring them into these foreign courts for the purposes of illegally confiscating their assets."

No wonder, then, as she reports in another newsletter, that these Maritime courts have a 96% conviction rate today. Yes, the game is rigged and, like other games played on a court such as tennis, it's played with a racket.

In-Court Strategies

So let the games begin. You're in court defending yourself against some bogus charge, imposition, or fine. Being a for-profit business and a Satanic institution, the court wants to fleece you as quickly and efficiently as possible so it can move on to the next victim and rinse and repeat.

They have been at this game for centuries, and they are well practised in the art of deceit. Their false priests have gone to schools and taken exams and read soporific documents and gained certificates and sworn secret oaths, all so they could practise trickery upon the People. But then you showed up. You'd done your research, selected your five smooth stones, and came out swinging.

Is there a jury? Not if they can avoid it. But you are most certainly entitled to one. As we saw in *Magna Carta*, no-one can be arrested, imprisoned, dispossessed, "or any other wise destroyed" without the lawful judgment of his peers (Article 39), and in the Sixth Amendment to *The Constitution of the United States of America*, the accused has "the right to a speedy and public trial, by an impartial jury..." Yet courts want to bypass jury processes whenever they can. Why? Because they put friction in the gears and jeopardize their predetermined guilty conviction.

The court begins by offering you terms of surrender. They ask you for your name, but you know this is a ploy to get Joinder. If you say your Title-Caps Name, they will hear an ALL-CAPS IMPOSTER NAME, so you refuse. Or, as David E. Robinson warns in *The UCC Connection*, perhaps the judge calls you 'Mr. Smith' or whatever, but if you answer to that corporate fiction, you will be tricked into accepting the court's jurisdiction.

Instead, Robinson advises, "Simply say, 'I don't know who you are talking to. I am not the person, Mr. Smith.'... They cannot do anything to you unless you give them your name and/or address. Without jurisdiction (your permission), they have to let you go... If you are ever arrested for anything in the future, never give your name." If pressed, you can draw on the Fifth Amendment's Right to Silence.

> *Thinking out loud for a minute... If I give my name as 'Living Man',*
> *would that render null and void any subsequent decision of the*
> *court? For no court can have jurisdiction over a 'Living Man', and*
> *any time they so addressed me, their presumed jurisdiction would be*
> *shattered. It's similar to what Odysseus does to the cyclops,*
> *Polyphemus, in Homer's* Odyssey. *When the cyclops captures him*
> *and asks for his name, Odysseus replies, "Nobody." Later, as he and*
> *his men are making their getaway, and Polyphemus cries out,*
> *"Nobody's tricked me," none of the other cyclops come to his aid.*

Overturning Trust Presumptions

Several commentators also suggest correcting the court's Trust Presumptions (Presumptions 8 through 10 of *The*

Twelve Presumptions of Court) in any opening statement. Anelia Sutton offers, in one of her TikTok videos, "I am the Living Woman. I am the Beneficiary of the Trust. I do not consent to Contract or Joinder, and I waive the benefits on offer." She also suggests saying, "I waive the court," which means you are claiming your right to a Jury. "The state doesn't want to spend that money. The case will be dismissed."

Richard Vobes illustrates the Trust idea with an inspired allegory using the game of *Monopoly*, where each player is represented on the board by a small metal object, such as a top hat, shoe, iron, or racing car...

> "The first thing that happens at court is, of course, they will say something like, 'For the record, state your name.' And this is where the trick is played on you. Because you don't know who you are, you will say, 'My name is Richard Vobes.' And at that moment, they've got you because effectively, what's happened is, you've said, 'I'm the Top Hat or the Dog or the Train or the Iron, you've become the player of the game, you've become the fiction, because their world can only work on the fiction. A real living man cannot enter a court, they cannot deal with you, so they have to get you to be the legal fiction."

Instead, he advises saying, " 'I'd like to introduce myself. I am the Executor and the sole Beneficiary of the estate of RICHARD VOBES, the legal persona.' You're effectively saying, he explains, "I'm the one who controls and administers the Top Hat."

By this wording, the court is denied its Presumption of being the Executor, and...

> "the judge has to be the trustee, and he will have to pay. Well, he won't like that, he'll probably run out of court or say, 'There is no case to answer,' because they tend not to like that sort of thing. But that is what it is. You don't need to pay it out of your own money. That's fallacy."

This idea is growing on me, to step into my entitlement as Beneficiary of a once secret *Cestui Que Vie* Trust that has been hidden from me all my life, whether or not I ever need to invoke it in court. Of course, I wouldn't trust a foreign judge, who works for an occupying corporation and has sworn a secret oath, to be Trustee of my Estate or even of my shoes, but the key point is, the Trustee is not me.

UCC 1-308

Robinson's approach, as he describes in *The UCC Connection*, is, "Simply say, 'I don't know who you are talking to. I am not the person, Mr. Smith. I am the beneficiary... and I reserve all of my rights per UCC 1-308.' "

What is *UCC 1-308*? This piece of legislation states that anything you do in a manner demanded or offered by another party cannot be construed as "prejudicing"—that is to say, undermining—any Rights you have "reserved." By saying at the outset you reserve *all* of your Rights per *UCC 1-308*, you seal them against delay, deferment, or denial. This would apply in the event you come to a courtroom in response to a demand or offer.

Robinson also suggests writing "Without Prejudice" or "Without Prejudice UCC 1-308" beneath your signature on any legal paper you sign, including a Driving Licence. To me, it's a strange use of the word 'prejudice', even if it has some meaning in Legalese. I prefer, "All rights reserved per UCC 1-308."

Included among *all* your Rights is the Right not to be compelled under any Contract or commercial agreement that you did not enter knowingly, intentionally, and voluntarily. As we have seen, legislation is a direct assault on this Right because it presumes to bind you to a contract you did *not* enter knowingly, intentionally, or voluntarily. Reserving *all* your Rights also means, if you are ever accused, that you can demand a court produce an injured party who has filed a verified complaint.

Or you could go with the simpler option of just saying, "I do not understand" to every question put to you, including, of course, "Do you understand?" or "Do you understand the charges against you?" By now, you are wise to what "understand" means in Legalese: "Do you stand under me?"

Anelia Sutton advises...

"People are losing their cases needlessly because the Presumptions are not being rebutted... Here are three statements you can make to rebut all of their Presumptions about you: 'I do not understand,' 'I do not accept,' and 'I do not consent.' Say those things, and keep saying it 'til somebody hears you. 'For the record, on the record, and let the record show, I do not understand, I do not accept, and I do not consent.' The case cannot move forward because they need all three of those things. Deadlock. Can't move forward. I'm telling you, you have more power than you were led to believe."

And here's some of my own thinking out loud...

Am I obliged to stand when a stranger says, 'All rise.'?" "By what authority does any officer of this court issue instructions?" "You are looking in my direction as you ask a question. Are you addressing me?" "You have just asked a question. By what authority do you ask questions of me?" "Am I obliged to answer your questions?" "You are a stranger to me. Am I required to answer any question a stranger puts to me?" "Does this court regard me as a Living Man/Woman or as a 'PERSON'?" "If the court regards me as a 'PERSON', does the court think itself capable of conversing with the dead?" "If the court thinks itself capable of conversing with the dead, have you proof that you are mentally competent to hold office?"

And here are some more...

"Can you verify you have signed an Oath of Office? Can you produce it?" "Have you sworn any private or secret oaths, whether to bar, guild, or secret society?" "Which oath are you acting under today?" "I rebut the Presumption that you can serve multiple oaths, for to do so is an inherent Conflict of Interest." "Do I, as a Living Man/ Woman, have a contract with you?" "In this court, are you using words as they are commonly understood in a normal dictionary or as defined in a law dictionary such as Black's Law Dictionary*?" "You say your name is Judge Knob. Can you produce the Birth Certificate on which your first name is recorded as 'Judge'?" "You asked me to provide a name 'for the record'. Are we to infer, therefore, that this is a Court of Record?" "Where is the Proof of Claim for that which is alleged here today?" "Upon whose first-hand witness is the allegation made?" "Who is the Principal making the Claim?"*

And then this one for members of the Body of Christ...

"You have a choice today, either to honour the lawful course that I command you to do, which is to dismiss this case. Should you fail to dismiss this case, you will be breaking the Law, and I must caution you that he who breaks the Law is under a curse (Deuteronomy 27:26), and if you're under a curse, you'll bring about your own destruction this very day—destruction decreed in Heaven and now effected on Earth. So, do you want to destroy yourself this day? Because that is what will happen to you from the moment you disobey my command. What's it to be?

To Whom Do You Plead?

Courts also ask the accused how they "plead," but you are not there to plead. You are a Living Man or a Living Woman. You were not made to plead before the institutions of men or their costumed enforcers, much less corrupt ones. In any case, you knew that if you entered a plea, the court would assume you had accepted its jurisdiction. So you refused.

> *"Am I obliged to enter a plea?" "Where is it written that I must enter a plea?" Where is my signature on the document that says I must enter a plea?"*

I recently heard a recording of a court proceeding, conducted over the Internet, where a woman was accused of breaking some COVID rule and refused to enter a plea. The judge attempted to enter a not-guilty plea on her behalf, and he set a future hearing date, whereupon she asked him, "Are you administering my Trust without my consent?" The case against her was immediately dropped.

Abolish Attorneys

Courts also want to know who is representing you. Seeing no legal counsel beside you, they will assume you are representing yourself and will want you to say so, but you know that any 'representation', either by yourself or by an attorney, means Joinder to them.

Remember, too, that so-called lawyers, attorneys,

barristers, etc. are not lawyers at all but servants of Legal Land, sworn officers of the court, and that is where their first loyalty lies. According to *Corpus Juris Secundum*,...

> "The attorney's first duty is to the courts and the public, not to the client, and wherever the duties to his client conflict with those he owes as an officer of the court in the administration of justice, the former [duties to his client] must yield to the latter [duties to the court]."

Therefore, with very few exceptions, those who fancy themselves lawyers today are nothing more than corporate brokers haggling over how much is to be taken from you. In the words of Howard Freeman, in the Forward to *The UCC Connection*, "Lawyers know procedure, not law."

The court badly wants you to have legal representation because it would make the task of asset-stripping you so much easier, but no,...

> *"I am here on Special Appearance. I am not in your jurisdiction.*
> *I have not consented to contract with this court."*

But that doesn't mean you have to face the Beast alone. You can bring a learnèd friend with you who has experience in dealing with this arena, but not a legal representative whose mere presence would flatten you into the two-dimensional legal fiction. In the words of Miki Klann, lawyers "can only represent you if you're a corpse, and you're not a corpse. We're coming into the Land of the Living. This is when the dead will rise in Christ."

The Sixth Amendment Shuffle

If you live in the united States, it were good to familiarize yourself with the *Bill of Rights*—that is to say, the first ten Amendments to the *Constitution*. Then, if you are in court and reserve all of your Rights under UCC 308-1 from the outset, then no judge can dodge your invocation of them.

So let's take another look now at the Sixth Amendment. It includes "the right... to be informed of the nature and cause of the accusation."

This means you have the right to know if the court is operating by Common Law or under Admiralty/Maritime jurisdiction. We already know it is the latter, but if Admiralty jurisdiction is conceded, say,...

> *"Maritime jurisdiction applies only if there is an international Maritime Contract at issue, if I am party to that Contract, and the Contract was breached. I have no knowledge of any such Contract and therefore deny that one exists. If such a Contract exists, it must be placed into evidence."*

If the judge refuses to answer your question, Yusef El on TikTok recommends declaring in court, "Let the record show that I have demanded of this court that they reveal the true nature of this action, and now they are seeking to proceed against me in a jurisdiction that is known only to the prosecutor and the judge."

More in the Bill of Rights.

Among your other protections in the *Bill of Rights*— which you can now bring into play because you have rebutted the court's Presumptions and cited *UCC 308-1* —are,...

- "... nor be deprived of life, liberty, or property, without due process of law" (Fifth Amendment).

- "The accused shall enjoy the right to a speedy and public trial by an impartial jury" (Sixth Amendment).

- "... nor excessive fines imposed, nor cruel and unusual punishments inflicted" (Eighth Amendment).

On this last point, I heard Cal Washington testify he stopped a judge in her tracks, as she attempted to persecute him with a vicious sentence, by saying, "That would cause me harm, and you're not permitted to cause me harm."

Protective Legislation and Precedent

You can also cite legislation and court precedents where they benefit and protect you. Again, we do not call these things 'Law' nor do we accord them authority over us, but we can use them selectively to remind our servants of *their* obligations.

For example, we could include the 'Color-of-Law' statutes detailed in the previous chapter, along with USC Title 42, Section 1983, which uses the same language...

> "Whoever, under color of any law, statute, ordinance, regulation, or custom, willfully subjects any person in any State, Territory, Commonwealth, Possession, or District to the deprivation of any rights, privileges, or immunities secured or protected by the Constitution or laws of the United States,... shall be fined under this title or imprisoned..."

We can also refer to a United-States-Supreme-Court decision in Boyd v. United States (1886) that "It is the duty of the courts to be watchful for the Constitutional rights of the citizen and against any stealthy encroachments thereon." To avoid using the word, 'citizen', I would say instead, *"It is the duty of this court, by the precedent of Boyd v. United States of 1886, to be watchful against any encroachment of Constitutional rights."*

Question the Questions

Keep in mind, too, the power in answering questions with a question, as I mentioned in the previous chapter about dealing with police. Then, having posed your question, "… you shut up," David Straight urges…

> "Nine times out of ten, people run their mouth when they shouldn't. Anything you say can and most definitely will be used against you. So you ask questions and then shut up. They answer; that opens the door for you to correct their answer. You will always have an opportunity to rebut anything they say."

Naturally, you and I are veritable founts of wisdom in any public forum, and court officials would do well to learn from us. But of course, they will not value our views because they're not wired that way— their programming has insulated their hearts against Justice, let alone Mercy —and because they are pigs, and pigs will trample any pearls you cast their way (*Matthew* 7:6).

Do you think so-called judges are going to revere that marvellous gem of wisdom you mined from the deep, that ruby you cut and polished to resplendent perfection? Will they behold it with enraptured gaze, gasp as your ingenuity, and praise your fine craftsmanship and attention to detail?

No, they will not, for they are pigs, and pigs only know how to trample. They are no better than that herd of pigs into which Jesus cast those demons called

'Legion', and they too are destined to hurl themselves off a cliff (*Luke* 8:26-39).

I digress. Perhaps, during these exchanges, the black-robed inquisitor has become angry with you, and he may have resorted to threats about the bad things that are going to happen to you if you continue in this uncooperative manner. But you are not his slave, you are not there to do his bidding, and you see through all the bluff and bluster.

> *Must I give way and room to your rash choler?*
> *Shall I be frighted when a madman stares?*

And if he resorts to the Hail-Mary pass of "contempt of court," still you do not budge.

> *Fret till your proud heart break;*
> *Go show your slaves how choleric you are*
> *And make your bondmen tremble. Must I budge?*
> *Must I observe you? Must I stand and crouch*
> *Under your testy humour? By the gods,*
> *You shall digest the venom of your spleen,*
> *Though it do split you; for, from this day forth,*
> *I'll use you for my mirth, yea, for my laughter,*
> *When you are waspish.*

I share these pearls from Shakespeare's *Julius Caesar* (IV.iii) with you, dear Reader, because you are not a pig, but I wouldn't waste them on a judge. Robinson advises, "If the judge threatens you with contempt for not giving your name or answering his questions, simply ask, 'Can anything I say be used against me?' They usually will not answer you or they may say 'Yes.' Then you remain silent."

Nor will you sign anything. Again, you know this would be accepting the court's jurisdiction, which you never want to do. According to David Straight, "It requires three signatures to put you in jail—the judge's, the prosecutor's, and you or your attorney's." Ultimately, "If you don't have an attorney, you don't take a plea, and you're competent, you're gonna go home."

Which brings me to the other Hail-Mary pass, which is when a court orders a psychiatric evaluation.

> *"You say you intend to order a psychiatric evaluation of me. In order to do so, the court must prove that it is more mentally competent than I, for a less competent entity could never assess the competence of one more competent. I rebut the Presumption that this court is competent to evaluate my competence."*

"Brevity Is the Soul of Wit"

Now, fun as this has been, imagining the possible court scenarios and verbal exchanges, really you don't want to hang about in a proceeding any longer than you have to. Nor did David, though he had some brief parley with Goliath at the beginning, waste time before killing him.

In *The UCC Connection*, David E. Robinson suggests you announce right at the top of a court case that you reserve all of your rights per UCC 1-308, that you do not consent, and then "turn around and leave. Do not stop, do not answer any questions."

Remember Christ's admonition, "Resist the devil, and he will flee from you" (*James* 4:7). The berobed bench-devils may flee before a court proceeding even begins, but there are also times when a judge has fled the courtroom mid-proceeding when facing a well-informed contestant. If that happens, declare, "Let the record show that the judge has abandoned the case, and that now the case is closed." And then leave.

In Closing...

This chapter was the most challenging to write of this book, the most complex and, from the start of this project, the one that felt most daunting to attempt. Now, having finished it, or rather stopped adding things—for such an investigation can never be complete—I wonder if I really needed to write it.

Perhaps, like David refusing the armour Saul offered him before he took on the giant Philistine (*1 Samuel* 17:38-39), I shall forego the armour my own hands have made as too cumbersome. Christ's yoke is easy, and his burden is light (*Matthew* 11:28-30). Any constitutional armour I could assemble, or weapons I could fashion, are but poor instruments compared to the authority we have in Christ to "overcome all the power of the enemy" (*Luke* 10:19). That includes overcoming all the enemy's servants, whether in court or anywhere else. To Hell with these people, and I mean that literally rather than as casual insult.

I remember, too, Christ's instruction to his disciples: "And when they bring you unto the synagogues, and unto magistrates and powers, take ye no thought how or what thing ye shall answer, or what ye shall say, for the Holy Spirit shall teach you in the same hour what ye ought to say" (*Luke* 12:11-12).

When looking this up, I also happened upon the *Message Bible* translation, which fits these times like a glove: "When they drag you into their meeting places, or into police courts and before judges, don't worry about defending yourselves—what you'll say or how you'll say it. The right words will be there. The Holy Spirit will give you the right words when the time comes."

So, if the Holy Spirit is going to give you the words, you won't need mine. And why get into verbal sparring with Satanic functionaries when you can go after the demonic entities they serve? Rather than writing and amassing copious documentation, crafting your court script, and trying to tiptoe past the verbal traps these barbarians of the bar have laid, you may instead give them a piece of your Mind of Christ off the cuff and be another word who became flesh.

One parting thought about the David-Goliath encounter. When David stood before him, Goliath thought David was carrying "sticks" (*1 Samuel* 17:43) when we know he was carrying but one staff (v. 40). Apparently, as author Malcolm Gladwell points out in a 2013 TED talk, Goliath had double vision.

This is the effect we'll produce in court. The court expects a phantom to appear, and that's what it's trained to see, but now a living, breathing, three-dimensional being shows up and stands alongside the phantom. The court, with its double-vision and double-mindedness, does not know where to look, much less where to aim. We have gained the upper hand just by declaring our Living Selves.

Finally, having felled the giant, David drew Goliath's own sword and used it to decapitate him (v. 51). Similarly, we will use the enemy's own weapons against him. Now, the giant's forehead is exposed, his skull ready to crack, and his own sword at hand to cut off his head.

FROM COMMON-LAW JURIES TO COMMON-LAW REPUBLICS

A trial by jury can ignore any legal statute in reaching their verdict. Thus, a trial by jury is the ultimate power of the people.

— DEAN OF BUXTON AND RACHEL
ELNAUGH-LOVE, 2022 VIDEO ABOUT
COMMON LAW

After David slew Goliath, the Philistine army fled and were routed by the army of Saul. Their corpses littered the road. Then, the Israelites plundered the Philistine camp (*1 Samuel* 17:51-53). Extending the allegory of the previous chapter, we may look forward to a time when the Beast court system is annihilated. In the meantime, let us envisage how Justice may proceed.

"The justice system, that will be set right," according to Liz Gunn, a former lawyer and television host in

New Zealand, and now activist and political candidate. In a July 2023 campaign speech, she said,...

> "All current courts shall continue to deal with all corporate entities, companies, organisations, and others. But cases against people will be heard in superior Common-Law courts and not be caught up in the current fraud taking place where there exists presumption skillfully tricking you into believing you are bound by their application. You are not a STRAWMAN, you are not a legal fiction. You are a living being, man or woman, a living being. And this will be taught and explained to all Kiwis to empower and free the people from yet more lies. Unless there is a victim, there can be no crime. You shall no longer be used as a government cash cow or to bolster the coffers of other state agencies."

Gunn adds that she went through a revolution in her own thinking to reach this point...

> "Coming from a background in law, as I do, steeped in the traditional ways of the New Zealand legal system, it has been a huge bridge for me to cross, and I can now see how important it is to help others to understand the nuanced weaponization of our legal system against us."

Trial by Jury

Central to the Common-Law Justice system is the Jury, and Trial *by* Jury, but Common-Law Juries are very different from juries convened by corporate courts, and much more powerful. In his 2022 paper, *The Occulted Powers of the British Constitution*, William Keyte describes the Common-Law Jury as "the highest law council of the land," with the right and the duty not only to judge the accused but the validity of any legislation cited against him. Such a Jury doesn't just review the facts of a case; it can also overrule and nullify legislation it deems unlawful or unjust. The legislation is on trial too.

This, Keyte argues, is key to the term, 'Consent of the Governed'. "The consent is provided (or not) to each piece of legislation through the jury... The fairness of a proposed measure could not receive a more painstaking and meticulous examination, surely, as it does in the context of the Common Law Trial by Jury, the foundation of our Constitution." And by 'Constitution', Keyte means *Magna Carta*, which predates all Acts and statutes and will outlast them too.

The Common-Law Jury, not elections, is the real mechanism by which the People exert authority and control over Government so that, in Keyte's words, " 'the government' is reduced, rightfully, to its proper status as an administration working for its people whose 'employees' are public servants... Our erroneous understanding that democracy has a basis merely in majority voting, and especially a party political system, has simply led to our enslavement."

Dethroning the Judge

Under a genuine Common-Law system, no judge gets to manipulate or intimidate a jury into getting the guilty verdict he wants. This is what judges attempted in the trials of William Penn in 1670 and Clive Ponting in 1985.

In the former, William Penn and William Mead were arrested for preaching to a gathering of Quakers in a London Street and were put on trial at the Old Bailey for "disturbing the King's peace." After farcical proceedings, the bench instructed the jury to find the defendants guilty. Instead, they returned an inconclusive verdict that the bench deemed unacceptable. They were sent back three times to reconsider, with the court recorder John Howell threatening to lock them in overnight "without meat, drink, fire, and tobacco."

Eventually, the jurors unified on a not-guilty verdict, whereupon Howell fined each of them 40 marks for following their "own judgments and opinions, rather than the good and wholesome advice which was given [them]." Howell ordered that each jury member be imprisoned until the fine was paid. Some paid it and were released; the remainder refused and were released later.

In 1985, the British government prosecuted civil servant Clive Ponting after he leaked classified documents about the British navy's submarine attack on the General Belgrano, an Argentinian ship, on May 2, 1982. They claimed Ponting had breached the *Official Secrets Act*, but Ponting's defence cited an exception in the Act for disclosures in the public interest.

Anthony McCowan, the presiding judge, wasn't having that and, zealous to protect then prime minister Margaret Thatcher, whose lies Ponting had exposed, directed the jury to convict Ponting, telling them, "the public interest is what the government of the day says it is." But they too defied him, and Ponting was acquitted.

Knowing, therefore, the treachery of governments, what fool would let them write and rewrite legislation and call it 'Law'?! As *Scottish Legal News* wrote in its 2020 obituary for him, "Ponting was a decent and honourable man, and the actions of the jury in clearing him will forever serve as a reminder that the right to trial by jury —under threat now on grounds of expediency and expense—is an indispensable bulwark of our civil liberties."

Trials like those of Penn and Ponting make for great drama, but in a Common-Law system, such vengeful collusion between a judge and a prosecutor would never get that far, for the Jury is restored to its rightful place as the supreme judge, and the 'judge' to his original and proper role of 'convener' or 'facilitator'. He may give advice to a Jury, but he does not have the authority to direct them; they can decide whether to heed his advice or not. Nor do the jurors, or the Jury as a whole, have to give a reason for their verdict.

As government employees, judges today can hardly be described as impartial, Keyte observes...

"The gradual shift from a convener (an administrator of the court) to a full judge as an employee of the state, thus usurping the preeminence of the juror as the supreme judge, was another method of subverting the constitution. Related to this was the gradual taking of the rights of the jury to judge various aspects of the case. Under authentic common law, it is the right of the jury to judge all aspects including the facts, the law, the admissibility of evidence, motive, criminal intent and the sentence."

Case precedent, Keyte adds, has nothing to offer Common Law. Juries...

"are not bound by anything prior to that case. It is purely through their own conscience that they are judging the accused... It is in the interests of those in political power for the citizens to become hoodwinked over time about these matters, and the claim that common law is judge-made is one of the many distortions they have put in place."

Futhermore, Common-Law Juries can reverse past verdicts and rulings of statutory courts.

Unanimity.

But perhaps the key difference between the two types of juries is that the Common-Law Jury must be unanimous to find someone guilty and for sentencing to proceed, whereas in corporate courts, a mere majority will do. The Common-Law Jury gives weight to the "thoughtful single juror," Keyte comments, "truly a system for the contemplative minority!"

Thus, in the play *Twelve Angry Men*, Juror 8 would not need to persuade the other jurors to examine the errors he has seen in the prosecution's case, even though it makes for better drama that he does. "The modern concept of a 'majority verdict' is a distortion of authentic common law," Keyte writes.

Freedom warriors also point out that Trial *by* Jury is not the same as a 'jury trial'. The former puts the Jury, not the judge or convenor, in the driving seat with all aspects of a case. The trial is conducted *by* the Jury, whereas a jury trial includes only the presence of a jury while the judge remains at the helm.

Establishing Common-Law Process

So should we wait for the current system to collapse before we build its replacement? That's not the American way, is it? Nor the English, Irish, Scottish, Welsh, Canadian, Australian, or New Zealand ways either for that matter. No, freedom-loving People throughout the Earth are already building the replacement.

One of them is Kevin Annett who told Dr. Katherine Horton in their May 2024 interview,...

"Common Law has universal jurisdiction. It has authority in every country because it's the Law of

Nature, it's what we're born with, it's our inherent right to do that. It's not given to us, it's just inherent in being a man or woman. So yes, you can convene those courts regardless of what the statutory provisions are in any country. That's the power it has."

A Common-Law action, Annett explains, begins with producing a Notice of Claim of Right where you describe the harm done, name the accused, and the remedy you want. Then you place the Notice in a newspaper, on a website, or on a physical notice board three times, and call for 12 people to be a jury. If the defendant does not contest it, the Notice becomes Truth in Law.

Then, convene a hearing and invite the accused to attend. If they fail to show up, that can be interpreted as admission of guilt, and the jury can automatically rule in favour of the plaintiff because the defendant is not answering the charges.

This is an especially powerful weapon against the corrupt in high places. "If they don't respond to us," Annett said, "the verdict can be found against them immediately without even a trial. If they do respond to us, they're acknowledging the authority and legitimacy of our court, and they have to respond and come into it."

Once a verdict is reached, it is up to the whole community to enforce it, including arrests with Common-Law arrest Warrants. "Enforcement by the community is a key element in Common Law," Annett adds, and local police can be deputized as Common-Law sheriffs to help enforce the Warrant, and charged with Obstruction of Justice if they don't.

A Common-Law court can order the convicted to make Reparations to those they have harmed, and if they don't do so, order direct Reclamations. "You can go in and seize the assets of these people," said Annett. "So that's what we do. They've done that. Native people in Canada have done that. They go in and seize the local Catholic church on the reservation. They boot out the priest. They take over the building." Annett also recounts how, one Sunday at the Holy Rosary Cathedral in Vancouver, they seized the collection plates, took them outside, and handed the contents to homeless people.

But the Common-Law process is not confined to local actions. Cases can be brought in a different country from where the crime happened; courts can be convened across different countries, linked by Internet; and arrest Warrants can be issued, and verdicts enforced, by any other court on Earth. Annett credits this process with effecting the resignation of former pope, Joseph Ratzinger (aka 'Pope Benedict')...

"You're putting the system on trial, and so you want maximum participation, maximum transparency, and embarrass the shit out of these people. That's the whole point of these things. Nothing in Common Law is closed. Jury records, court records, final verdicts, they're all public record. They're all open to everybody for examination, and the whole process should be conducted that way from the very beginning."

When it comes to high-profile cases, Annett suggests Americans start by working through existing courts and demanding a Common-Law Jury trial because they have a Constitutional Right to do so. "You get a lot more mileage and exposure that way. And I would say, in America, try that as well as starting your own process parallel to it." This requires collaboration:

> "The system is far more vulnerable than we realize. That's why they have to create this aura of infallibility and power and violence around themselves because they know that—we find time and again—with churches, corporations, governments, military, anyone, if you shine a light on them and keep at it, and they know you're not going to back off, and there's more than one of you doing it, they get very scared and they start falling out, and you start seeing insiders coming forward and talking about what's going on. And that's why public pressure constantly, and constant exposure, is so important for all of this work. That's really our weapon. Our weapon is the truth and our numbers and our persistence."

Grand Juries

Some Common-Law advocates also call for proper restoration of the 'Grand Jury', a body convened to investigate a claim and, if a majority votes to do so, create an Indictment which is then passed to a Common-Law Court for trial by 'Petty Jury'. Among these advocates is

David E. Robinson who writes in *Common Law Handbook*, "If anyone's unalienable rights have been violated, or removed, without a legal sentence of their peers, from their lands, home, liberties or lawful right, we shall straightway restore them." He hails the 1992 United-States-Supreme-Court decision in United States v. Williams, Jr. where Antonin Scalia, writing for the 6-to-3 majority, confirmed that the Grand Jury "belongs to no branch of the institutional government," and not even the Judiciary could second-guess its processes, deliberations, or assessment of evidence.

A Common-Law Republic

For the sake of our health, wealth, sanity, and even our lives, we need to restore Common-Law republics in our lands, and Common-Law Juries are their bedrock. This is not a top-down process. In a January 2023 podcast, Annett advises,...

> "First consolidate a core, a solid core, and build up from there. That's why we urge people to form cell groups first, three people, and each of them recruit three others, and soon you've got 12, and that solid core can form an assembly. Sign a charter, and out of that your own Common-Law court, your own sheriffs, deputize the local police, you're off and running."

Once you have declared your own jurisdiction, abolish government-imposed measures, nullify federal taxes, revoke all allegiance to foreign princes, and elect delegates to a national constitutional convention. "We link that up across the country, we've got a republic." He invites others committed to this, to contact him at republicnationalcouncil@protonmail.com.

The advice from Anna von Reitz is similar. In a January 2023 blogpost, she writes, "To claim back our rightful government, people must participate in local county and state jural assemblies, act as deputies for the locally-elected land jurisdiction Sheriffs, and join their state militias." Civilian militias, she adds,...

> "are as old as Mankind. They are us, when we band together to face common dangers, deal with outlaws, survive natural disasters, and defend against invaders... So there is nothing improper or unknown or dangerous about civilian militias. They are here to protect hearth, home, and community at the most basic, natural, and obvious level."

State Sovereignty?

And what of the supposed Sovereignty of States? The Tenth Amendment to the *Constitution* says, "The powers not delegated to the United States by the Constitution, nor prohibited by it to the States, are reserved to the States respectively, or to the people."

The problem is that the UNITED STATES CORPORATION has in effect colonized the adjoining nation of the United States—or united (lower-case 'u')

States if you prefer—as an occupying power would. And State governments are themselves corporations spelled in ALL CAPS, such as 'STATE OF FLORIDA'. Instead, as Anna von Reitz points out, we need to return to 50 unincorporated, geographically defined states called: New Jersey State, Ohio State, Wisconsin State, etc.

Still, there have been some pockets of resistance to the occupation. In January 2024, the STATE OF UTAH passed the *Utah Constitutional Sovereignty Act* (SB 57). Described by Mike Adams as "soft secession," it provides a framework to prohibit enforcement of federal directives that violate State Sovereignty.

A few months later, Louisiana passed *Senate Bill 133* which "provides that the World Health Organization, United Nations, and the World Economic Forum shall have no jurisdiction or power within the state of Louisiana." Oklahoma passed a similar measure in June 2024 with *Senate Bill 426*, which prohibits enforcement of requirements issued by the WHO, WEF, or UN.

By the time of going to press, there had been a few other examples of pushback from state legislatures such as Tennessee's ban on chemtrailing (*Senate Bill 2691, House Bill 2063*) and measures against central-bank digital currencies from Louisiana, Florida, and Texas.

Welcome as these moves are, they only trim the weeds of government tyranny, but do not uproot it. Whether States resort to 'hard' secession from the Union remains to be seen, but in reality, it is the District of Columbia that seceded from the rest of us long ago.

In Closing...

As this chapter draws to a close, I acknowledge my focus has been mostly on the united States throughout this book. I did not set out with that in mind, but it makes sense in that the freedom of all nations hinges on the freedom of this one and because many patriots here see themselves as custodians of Liberty and make this their life's work.

Then there's the fiercely defended Second Amendment: "A well regulated Militia, being necessary to the security of a free State, the right of people to keep and bear Arms, shall not be infringed." I never thought I would be quoting this text, much less hailing it, but here we are.

The task of rebuilding Common-Law structures may come more naturally to peoples who have it in their cultural DNA, such as in Britain, the united States, and former 'Commonwealth' countries, but why stop there? Even if you are not residing in one of these lands, no-one has the right to press you into a dystopian corporate matrix designed to enslave and destroy you. Are ye not also Men of God, of the Most High God, and Women of God, Royal Daughters? Then, neither death nor life, neither angels nor demons nor powers, neither things present nor things to come, neither height nor depth nor anything else in all creation, can separate you from his love (*Romans* 8:38-39), nor can any enforcer or institution of men. You create the community that serves you, no matter what your history says, much less your politicians.

CONCLUSION

If you leave your children a world in which you never stood up,
they'll inherit a world where they can't.

— MICHAEL MCMAHON, FORMER LAPD
POLICE OFFICER, IN CONVERSATION
WITH MARIA ZEEE

We're waking up, and as we stir from slumber, we're going to feel a bit groggy. Stumbling about, trying to make sense of it all, we forgive our errors and omissions. I ask for your forgiveness too, dear Reader, for my own errors and omissions.

Reclaiming our Birthright is a vast subject to get my head and hands around, and I am sure to have missed something. How many unsung champions are out there doing the work but not getting recognition for it? How many weapons have they devised, now waiting in impatient sheathes? How many their unheralded victories? How many their heroic defeats?

There is more to investigate and more to be said than any one book can encompass, or any one author can cover in a lifetime. Even a shelf full of encyclopaedias could not. But let me know what I've missed, and I will add it to later editions if I can. My email address is RenewedTestament@protonmail.com.

Though our actions in this arena may seem small and insignificant, still they serve to extend the reach of light into darkness and to "harass the enemy." I vaguely remember this phrase in the film, *The Great Escape*, which I watched as a boy. Those prisoners of war held fast to the belief that, successful or not, their efforts to break out would distract the foe and mean fewer enemy troops would be available to fight on the front lines. Yes, this movie was social conditioning, but there was merit in the idea nonetheless.

In an early chapter, I talked about 'Babylon' and coming out of her, but the Exodus of the Old Testament is the prior allegory. After a long struggle waged with plague and calamity, Pharaoh finally let God's People go, and Moses led them out of slavery and away from Egypt's cult of pyramid and sphinx, death fetish, and dark rituals of atrocity. But, covetous of the slave economy that had enriched him, Pharaoh chased the Israelites into the Red Sea, only to drown behind them, along with his army and chariots (*Exodus* 14:28).

The parallels today are compelling. We too are straining against the bonds of slavery and clamouring for freedom. Today's pharaohs, deaf to all plea, protest, or poll, are doubling down on their enslavement agenda and threatening us with medical compulsion, imprisonment, starvation, and war. Yet there is a path for us through the Sea and onto dry Land the other side, while our enemies race to their inevitable ruin and destruction.

Many prophecies affirm this. As foretold in the underrated but now resurgent *First Book of Enoch*, the mighty and exalted...

"shall be terrified, and they shall be downcast of countenance, and pain shall seize them when they see that Son of Man sitting on the throne of his glory... And he will deliver them to the angels for punishment, to execute vengeance on them because they have oppressed his children and his elect. And they shall be a spectacle for the righteous and for his elect. They shall rejoice over them because the wrath of the Lord of Spirits resteth upon them, and his sword is drunk with their blood."

— *FIRST BOOK OF ENOCH*, CHAPTER 62

Brothers and Sisters, the time is coming, and coming soon. The pharaohs and their 'stakeholders' do not yet know this is their end, and busy themselves trying to distract us with political theatre, comedy duos disguised as presidential debates, and meaningless abstractions of 'Left' and 'Right'. Satan, their father, masquerades as an angel of light and sometimes rainbow light. He will wave any flag, wear any colour, attach any label, and chant any slogan that furthers his ambition to build Hell on Earth.

Let me remind you that the *Declaration of Independence* confers on us a duty not to abolish a particular candidate or a particular party—which would perpetuate the system and allow one tyrant to make way for another—but the entire *form* of Government that spawned them both.

I have created this book both as a dispeller of Satan's spells and as a compendium of spell-breaking strategies at our disposal. Then, in the next and final book of this three-part series, *Know Your Financial Rights*, I shall focus more specifically on throwing off the slaveries of taxation, confiscation, and debt.

Throughout, I have shared and shaped the best information I can find, and where helpful, pointed you to others with advanced expertise. That doesn't mean I agree with these sources in matters outside the scope of this book, nor do I suggest you automatically trust every one I cite. We are called to be wise as serpents, and a serpent probes the air with its tongue.

Nor do my quotees necessarily agree with me. Veronica: of the Chapman family, for instance, told me in a torrent of emails that she is an atheist and how much better my book would be if I removed all the "USELESS and IRRELEVANT God/Jesus/Biblical CRAP." She insisted I add a disclaimer to say, "Veronica does not agree with the Biblical quotations, even though her work is referenced in this book."

Sorted. And now with that out of the way, I call on all of us to practise discernment, and beware of wolves in sheep's clothing, Limited Hangouts, and Controlled Opposition. Beware, too, of Constrained Opposition—the well intentioned who are fearful of looking deeper or have a blind spot.

Beware, too, of those who promise solutions but don't deliver after they've got you to pay. In a July 2024 video, Si the Spaniard warns,...

> "It is clear that the 'Truth-Movement' has become infiltrated with charlatans and more greatly resembles the Wild West than a source of truth and integrity. In light of the above, it is necessary that each one of you exercise extreme caution before parting with your hard-earned cash. You must probe into success rates. You must demand proof of success. You must search online to question/verify how long these 'gurus' have been around. If you don't, or can't be bothered, or simply like his/her personality, be prepared to lose everything you stake and possibly more."

Ask, too, if *anything* that comes out of legislature, executive, judiciary, media, or political candidate, even apparently good news or what you want to hear, is organic, or part of a masterplan for domination, a white tile on the Freemason floor or a 'white hat' in the Freemason assembly. Scripture warns us too that a haughty leader shall arise who "by peace shall destroy many" (*Daniel* 8:25). Now, you could argue that one-world government is a type of peace, but it's not a peace you or I would want to live under. Be not lulled into complacency, and remember that one Beast shall team up with another, as described in *Revelation* 13.

Heed the warning, therefore, of Scott Schara, whose daughter Grace was medically murdered in October 2021 by Ascension St. Elizabeth Hospital in Appleton, Wisconsin. In a video series titled *The Matrix Revealed: The Illusion of Choice*, Schara asserts that organizations such as the WHO, WEF, and the Council on Foreign Relations are secret-society front organizations whose Great-Reset agenda is the "evil half of Satan, setting up the less evil 'angel of light' false-prophet system to close the gate on the control grid." In this equation, so-called 'red pills' can be planted to lead us into the 'false-prophet trap'.

That does not mean we pounce on anyone's casual gesture as a Freemason sign, or call out Deep-State manipulation just because a commentator has name recognition and is not obscure enough for our liking. But we do practise discernment and remember that the Holy Spirit, who is joined with our spirit and from whom nothing is hidden (*1 Corinthians* 6:17), sees "the thoughts and attitudes of the heart" (*Hebrews* 4:12-13).

Finally, a note of thanks to the cover designer for this book and the series. She ran several ideas past me, but none resonated until I saw an open scroll with my title thereon. This struck the right note. Soon after, I came upon this passage in *Zechariah* 5…

I looked again, and there before me was a flying scroll.

He asked me, "What do you see?"

I answered, "I see a flying scroll, twenty cubits long and ten cubits wide."

And he said to me, "This scroll is the verdict going out worldwide, for according to what it says on one side, every thief will be banished, and according to what it says on the other side, everyone who swears falsely will be banished. The Lord Almighty declares, 'I will send it out, and it will enter the house of the thief and the house of anyone who swears falsely by my name. It will remain in that house and destroy it completely, both its timbers and its stones.' "

Then, Brothers and Sisters, may this scroll be destruction to the destroyers and upon those who swear false oaths, and blessing to thee.

Much love,
Abdiel LeRoy

APPENDIX
MORE RESOURCES

Websites

americannational.app

annavonreitz.com

bbsradio.com/herewestand

bc-freedom.com

commonlawconstitution.org

famguardian.org

friendsoftheoriginalconstitution.org

giannamiceli.com

inalienable-university.mn.co

keystoliberty2.wordpress.com

missionpossibleuniversity.com

paulstramer.net

preventgenocide2030.org

stand4thee.com

statenational.us
tacticalcivics.com
tasa.americanstatenationals.org
thefathersforjustice.org
thefreedompeople.org
youandyourcash.com

TikTok Accounts

I no longer engage with TikTok after extreme censorship
and shadow-banning of my content. However, when I did,
I found the following accounts to have valuable
information and analysis...

@aneliasutton
@awesomeproducts2222
@francescaamato959
@livingwomanbecs
@Love.lee.777
@yusef_el_19

KNOW YOUR FINANCIAL RIGHTS

A. LeRoy

Battle Manuals for Freedom: Book 3

INTRODUCTION

And each in the cell of himself is almost convinced of his freedom.

— W.H. AUDEN, *IN MEMORY OF W.B. YEATS*

WE HAVE BEEN HORRIBLY RIPPED OFF!

In your heart, you know this. From dawn to dusk, from cradle to grave, we have been tax-farmed, fined, and fleeced. We have been stripped of our dignity, prodded, probed, and poked, and ordered about by half-wits who have not one shred of courage, integrity, or truth in their hearts. Brothers and Sisters, I have had enough, and this *Battle Manual for Freedom* is my response.

I wrote *Know Your Medical Rights* (originally titled *The COVID Protocols: Upholding Your Rights in Authoritarian Times*) as a weapon against the medical tyranny that, starting in 2020, sought to desecrate our constitutional protections. Job done, or so I thought.

But as we now know, COVID was just the opening assault. We are also being assailed by poisons in our food, water, earth, and air; engineered shortages, and sabotage; radiation and energy weapons; along with war, assassination programs, fabricated emergencies, and false-flag terrorism.

Among other forms of attack are: lawless legislation and destructive regulation; impositions of a counterfeit righteousness; censorship, propaganda, fear-mongering, and indoctrination; monitoring and surveillance; digital imprisonment and technocracy; demoralization and destruction of hope; separation, isolation, and division; demolition of the family, culture, and meritocracy; stolen elections; weaponized immigration; ecological devastation and pollution (nothing to do with carbon-dioxide, by the way); and overall treason by politicians, bureaucrats, agencies, corporations, courts, and police.

To counter all this, I wrote the next book, *Know Your Lawful Rights*, but even then, the work was not finished, for the predator class are coming at us with all manner of financial attack too, including murderous levels of taxation, inflation, debt, and confiscation of assets and property. Meanwhile, bank runs, bank failures, and bank freezes are looming, and even bank bail-ins, where they just help themselves to the contents of your account.

On the other side of this obliteration, our enemies plan central-bank digital currencies (CBDC), where they can reward your behaviour if they like it, and penalize your behaviour and speech if they don't, and make further deductions on a whim without giving you recourse. Hence this third and final book in the series, *Know Your Financial Rights*.

I recall the horrifying scenes of pallets of cash left behind when the U.S. military bolted from Afghanistan in 2021. However worthless, that paper represents the toil of millions of Americans whose life's work has been squandered by a vampiric cabal hell-bent on enriching themselves while destroying us.

We know in our hearts we were not put on this Earth to supply these parasites. We who are in Christ also remember that his yoke is easy and his burden is light (*Matthew* 11:28-30). Like the kin of Moses longing to break free from Egypt and its state-sanctioned death cult, we too long for our Exodus and restoration of our Birthright. May this book sever the chains that held us, especially the spiritual ones, for if our minds are free, our reality shall follow. This requires us to dispel the delusions and mind-tricks that have been played on us for centuries, even millennia.

When it comes to solutions, I do not claim to be the tip of the spear; others have done more battle than I. Rather, my contribution is to bring into coherence the myriad fragments of wisdom, analysis, and experience that are out there, and above all to clarify them. As I said, Christ's burden is light, and that includes the financial one. If solutions are too complicated for the layman to grasp, I will simplify them if possible and discard them if not.

Nor am I am setting out to prescribe one-size-fits-all remedies. "There is no magic bullet," to quote Si 'the Spaniard' of youandyourcash.com, when I attended one of his seminars in England. "You're the magic bullet." You will pick and choose from the tools at your disposal and play to your particular strengths.

That is our key advantage as we undermine, obstruct, and overthrow the evil plans of financial despots. Wise as serpents, we are inventing strategies and approaches so numerous and varied that the enemy cannot possibly find an answer to all of them. Compared to the one-government, one-narrative, one-opinion, one-way, one-rule, one-religion, one-food, one-health, one-medicine, and one-currency brigade opposing us, we are a motley crew, but I celebrate that. As C.S. Lewis wrote, "Good, as it ripens, becomes continually more different, not only from evil, but from other good."1

Now, as you may be aware, I just quoted Scripture with "wise as serpents" (*Matthew* 10:16). Some readers have complained that I speak too much of spiritual battle in this book series and about the victory of Christ and his prophets over Satan's schemes and schemers.

To which I say, deal with it. If you think you're going to get through the battles ahead against foes who are themselves deeply religious and who are supernaturally allied with infernal forces, then you will be easy meat for their murderous agenda. Also, if my offering is good fruit from a holy root, it were blasphemous to reject the tree that produced it.

Jesus—or Yeshua or Yehusha if you prefer—gave us

authority to overcome all the power of the enemy (*Luke* 10:19). In addition to this spiritual authority, we have the authority of logic because, as the documentary *Strawman* reminds us, "Government is a creation of man, and a creation of man can never be above man."

This authority equates to that of the Lawful realm, meaning that which the Most High bestows, over the Legal realm, which is what men write, revise, and repeal. Which raises the question: Why bother operating in the Legal arena at all—with its politicians, bureaucrats, autocrats, and technocrats, its corporations and courts, so-called lawyers and police? Only because they have a nasty habit of showing up where they're not wanted and not needed. We are to put them back in their inferior places and disabuse them of their power-hungry ambitions to play God in the lives of others.

As Shakespeare observed, "All the world's a stage/ And all the men and women merely players" (*As You Like It*, II.vii.). Sometimes, we are called to put on a costume and play a role in the Theatre of the Legal, but we are not *of* the Legal. When the play is over, we take off the costume, resume our higher life, and leave behind those who are trapped in the Legal illusion and think it is real and all that there is.

Much love,
Abdiel LeRoy

1

TAXATION IS DEAD TO US

Tyrants would distribute largess, a bushel of wheat, a gallon of wine, and a sesterce, and then everybody would shamelessly cry, "Long live the King!" The fools did not realize that they were merely recovering a portion of their own property, and that their ruler could not have given them what they were receiving without having first taken it from them...

— ÉTIENNE DE LA BOETIE,
THE POLITICS OF OBEDIENCE, 1553

It makes no sense when you think about it. Birds get to build their nests and feed their young from the resources around them. They are not required to give a portion of their labour to other birds. Same goes for the squirrel of the tree or the fish of the sea. But not so for us. We men and women are fined just for daring to live and breathe on this Earth.

"Why do we have to pay to live on a planet we were born on?" asks Jeff Harry in a TikTok video recorded in 2022. "And who are we actually paying for the privilege of being alive here? Who made them the boss? Who put them in charge?"

I'll qualify my statement about the birds, though. Sometimes a cuckoo will come along and lay an egg in the nest of another bird. After hatching, the baby cuckoo will evict the rightful inheritors of the nest and fool the parent into feeding it instead. In that case, the animal kingdom *does* represent the trick the predator class play on us through taxation. As David E. Robinson writes in *Meet Your Strawman*,...

> "It has long since reached a ridiculous level, with the average person being expected to pay Income Tax, Council Tax, Inheritance Tax, National Insurance, Capital Gains Tax, Sales Tax on house purchases, Value Added Tax, Parking charges, Airport charges, Fuel Tax, Road Tax, Import Duty, Tax on alcohol, Tax on tobacco, payments for a driving licence, passport... the list goes on and on and on with additional items added all the time."

Suppose I want to join a club. I apply for membership, pay a fee, and agree to the club rules. But what if some club I never joined decided to charge me a membership fee anyway, insisted I obey its rules, and made secret decisions that caused harm to me or my loved ones? I'd be livid. So would you. Yet that is exactly how governments behave. I never signed up to be bullied or extorted, and neither did you.

The Status of Man

How, then, shall we be liberated? First, by renewing our minds. As author Larken Rose laments in a splendid rant recorded in 2024,...

> "When that tiny group of parasites says, 'You have to give us a ton of money every year,' the throng doesn't say, 'No, we don't!' It says, 'We really wish you would tell us that we're allowed to not quite give you as much money as we did last year... Oh, we love the master that lets us keep more of what we produce.' "

If that's your mindset, Rose continues, "You're already 100% a slave in your own mind when all you can comprehend is begging the master to let you keep some more of what you produce."

In *Know Your Lawful Rights*, I describe how governments, which are corporations, assert false jurisdiction over us by levying taxes, fines, and fees against a corporate fiction—the 'STRAWMAN'—using a fake version of Our Names spelled in ALL CAPS. They want to flatten us from the living, breathing, three-dimensional beings that we are into a two-dimensional page, for their corporate fictions can only interact with other corporate fictions, much as characters in a play interact with other characters in that play.

I also looked at the Birth Certificate, and how the banking cabal use it to trade our lifetime's labour, creativity, and time. The three-dimensional Truth, however, is that we remain in authority over the fictions of men.

I considered too what it means to have 'Dominion' of the Earth (*Genesis* 1:26-28), that this would bestow on each of us productive land four times the size of Twickenham rugby field. (That's if the Earth is as small as they tell us it is.) Therefore, on your behalf and mine, dear Reader, let us stand together now before the throne of the Most High and claim in Heaven our portion of the Earth, knowing that when we agree on this, it is done for us by our heavenly Father (*Matthew* 18:19). So be it.

Si 'the Spaniard' imagines how this would look. Addressing a 2023 Red Pill Day conference in England, he asks,...

"How do you get your sovereignty if all these corporations are in the way? What if, when corporations use the Earth for whatever purposes they use it, you are supposed to benefit from that in some way, shape, or form? What if your Birth Certificate is actually a share certificate, and you are supposed to receive distributions or dividends from the trade that is being allowed to take place on your Earth, often with the resources of the Earth which belong to you? You've got Dominion over it. This is your property, it's every man's property.

"So if corporations are using your property to make profit and gain, surely things should be operating from the perspective that the government is there to ensure that: first, only corporations that benefit Man get a licence to operate, and can operate on that legal platform; and second, only corporations that don't pollute the Earth or poison Man can operate and get a licence—it's got to be for the betterment of Man—and that those corporations must be paying the taxes because those taxes can then finance any public servants, if we need to finance them in that way, but otherwise, any profits can then be distributed to Man, which means that Man wouldn't have to work... That's the way that it should be working, and it could be working."

But what do we have now instead? Broadcaster and 'Health Ranger' Mike Adams nails it in a May 2024 broadcast...

"Taxation is theft, taxation is confiscation, taxation is stealing the product of your labor, forcing you to hand over the product of your work, your sweat and tears and ideas and physical labor and whatever else you put into your job. The fact that, effectively, taxation is now well over 50% of your income—far beyond that, it's more like 70% if you start adding it all up, and in some cases, even higher.

"Even in America, think about it, 70-plus percent taxation rates between property taxes, sales taxes, income taxes, social-security taxes, on and on and on, state and federal income taxes. That is stealing, or confiscating, the product of your labor, which is just another form of slavery…

"If you're working for anybody in 2024, you do not own 70% of the product of your labor, and the 30% that you are allowed to keep is losing value every day because the government's stealing even more value by printing more money every single day.

"So really, slavery has just expanded to encompass everyone. We're all enslaved by this current system, and finding freedom in this world today is incredibly difficult. Finding financial freedom or even financial privacy is incredibly difficult. Finding freedom to speak is incredibly difficult… Think about how enslaved you are if you're not allowed to speak, you're not allowed to assert ownership over your own body, and you're not allowed to keep the vast majority of the product of your effort. That's slavery, folks. That is total, wholesale slavery. That's what exists in our world today."

Hear too, the righteous rant of a 'common man', in a widely circulated video post, after he received a bill from the Internal Revenue Service (IRS)…"

"I don't have any money because you're taking 60% of what I make through my LLC and absolutely crushing small businesses. And on top of that, the only reason I'm a small business is because, during the imagination period of the 'flu scare of 2019 until fucking forever, I guess, you mandated that I take an imagination shot that I didn't need and no-one knew anything about, and if I didn't take it, you took my fucking career away from me. You took my ability to feed my child. You took that away from me, and for two years, I have sold T-shirts in parking lots and I have worked this dead-end job at a gun store, and I have cut trees and mowed lawns and done anything I could, everything I had to do, just to feed my child. Not vacations, not new clothes, not a new truck, not thriving in my life, not living in my life, just surviving day to day. And if I don't pay you $700, I go to jail? What is slavery then?!"

Brothers and Sisters, we were not put on this Earth to carry such burdens. As Canadian builder and tax refuser Dean Clifford said in a 2013 interview,...

"Government is too big. They take in too much money, they waste too much money. It's not my duty or my obligation to fund a bloated, ineffective governmental structure. They can downsize, they can provide us with the essential services that they were mandated to provide us in the first place. The gasoline taxes pay for the roads. Importing and exporting tariffs, excise taxes, and things like royalties paid on the resources that are mined, forested, or fished, are supposed to pay for the essential services. Why is it my responsibility to keep giving them more money because they can't live within their mandate? It's not. It's actually my duty to cut them off when I think they're being irresponsible."

Government Racketeering

Taxes amount to protection rackets. In the words of Australian commentator and prophet Max Igan, in a June 2024 broadcast,...

> "These are not governments, these are criminal enterprises, all of them are criminal enterprises. That's just the nature of Government, isn't it? Criminal racketeering is what best describes our governments. People pay protection money in the form of taxes, play registration, all this sort of stuff. This is all just protection money, it's all just racketeering. 'You register your business and you pay your taxes, or we'll come and do bad things to you.' Mob mentality, folks, it's mob racketeering."

Yes, 'registration' is part of the racket too, wherein you sign your assets over to the government, from your house to your car to your children, and even your backyard chickens. So bear in mind, as Alan of Salisbury puts it in a 2016 lecture, "When you register something, you are giving away whatever you are registering to whoever you are registering it with."

Pharisees and Religion

I have described taxation as an affront to Nature, but it is also an affront to the Creator of Nature and to the Word through whom all things were made (*John* 1:3). Those who would impose it stand accused of the crime with which Jesus charged the Pharisees of his day: "They tie up heavy loads and put them on men's shoulders but do not lift a finger to help them" (*Matthew* 23:4). It is a bloated tithe paid to a cult religion called 'Government', which then uses it to fund our demise and destruction.

Through taxation, we are treated as lifelong criminals paying a perpetual debt to society. The idea of being inherently and incurably criminal infects churches too, which is why preachers have such an obsession with 'sin' and with the idea that we were born into sin and must go around calling ourselves 'sinners', even though Scripture confers righteousness on those who have put their faith in Christ. It even calls us "slaves to righteousness" (*Romans* 6:18) who have the Mind of Christ (*1 Corinthians* 2:16), and the True Law written in our hearts (*Hebrews* 8:10).

But it's very convenient to the state if it can get you to think of yourself as a perpetual sinner because then you will more readily accept being a permanent debtor and permanent taxpayer. Then it can place even more burdens on you, dictate what rituals you must perform, what payments you must make, what medicines you must take, to be deemed acceptable to society.

It's a counterfeit righteousness designed to weigh you down all your life, and they've got you paying indulgences in the form of taxes because the state regards itself as your priest. Thus, it imposes its rules and 'mandates' and pretends that these are for your good or the good of society. Even if you do follow their rules, these parasites will shift the goalposts on you anyway to catch you out and criminalize you. They will bleed you dry if they can, while inventing yet more capricious burdens for you to carry, until you can carry burdens no more and are discarded onto the scrapheap of medical waste.

Taxation Crucified

It is time, therefore, to stop bending the knee to false authority. I can't speak for you, but my only authority is Jesus, Yeshua, who "cancelled the written code, with its regulations, that was against us and that stood opposed to us; he took it away, nailing it to the cross" (*Colossians* 2:14).

Of all the brilliant things the apostle Paul wrote, this one I treasure most. Another is where he likens our freedom from legal obligation to that of a widow set free from any obligation she had to her former husband (*Romans* 7:2). In our ignorance and folly, we were once wedded to a nagging husband called 'Government', and we tried to appease him with our offerings, our confessions, our deference, and our fear. We did not realize we were bound to a phantom, a dead thing, a fiction fashioned by men, but now, we laugh at this lifeless idol demanding our obedience, at the false priests waving it in our face, and at their false doctrines and legal writ masquerading as Law.

All that is dead to us now. We are set free from the struggle for what Martin Luther calls 'civic righteousness' in his *Commentary on the Book of Galatians* (1535) and from any need to be deemed righteous in the eyes of the state. Rather, true righteousness is "a mere passive righteousness," the righteousness that comes by faith and faith alone, and requires no tax to obtain it. In short,...

TAXATION IS DEAD TO US!

And we are dead to it, for we have let our false, corporate, STRAWMAN-self be lost that we may find our true, three-dimensional self (*Matthew* 16:25) as a Living Man or Living Woman. The old has gone, the new has come (2 *Corinthians* 5:17), and like new wine in old wineskins or new cloth patched onto old clothing, we tear the old structures trying to contain us (*Mark* 2:21-22).

What is that old cloth made of? To fully untangle the litany of deceit perpetrated by governments, bankers, and secret societies over the centuries would require several books. It includes the *Cestui Que Vie Act*, passed in England in 1666 after the Great Fire of London, that deems us legally dead. It includes man-made legalities that treat us as livestock in a tax farm and fraudulently call themselves Law. It includes enrolment into bondage through the Birth Certificate, social-security numbers, payroll deductions, and other desecrations of Privacy, and it involves deceptive contracting ploys that presume our tacit consent to be oppressed and enslaved. All these wheels of extortion have been greased by fear-mongering, propaganda, and indoctrination.

And speaking of indoctrination, I would like to know

who crowbarred into the Bible what I call *The Tyrant's Charter* in *Romans* 13:1-7, a passage falsely attributed to the apostle Paul. It tells us to obey Earthly authorities and pay taxes, notions not only at odds with the rest of the Bible but with Paul's own life and teachings. It is a naked attempt to corral Christians into obeying political powerbrokers, not the output of Paul's pen but fruit from a poison tree.

Common Law and Magna Carta

Also affronted by taxation is Common Law which, in accordance with Christ's Commandment to love others as we love ourselves, boils down to doing no harm, being honorable in contracts, and Presumption of Innocence. Where there is no victim, there is no crime. Where there is no crime, there is no fine, much less a lifelong penance to pay in the form of taxation. Along with other revenue-raising schemes of governments, courts, and police, taxation is an abomination in the eyes of Common Law which upholds our Right to keep the private property that we exchanged for our labour.

That taxation is inherently unlawful is even acknowledged at times in the documents of men. *Magna Carta* states, "No free man shall be seized or imprisoned, or stripped of his rights or possessions, or outlawed or exiled, or deprived of his standing in any other way, nor will we proceed with force against him, or send others to do so, except by the lawful judgement of his equals or by the law of the land" (Article 39). And England's *Bill of*

Rights (1688/1689) states, "… any forfeiture before conviction is illegal and void."

The spirit of this language echoes in the Fifth Amendment to the Constitution of the States United where none may be "deprived of life, liberty, or property, without due process of law." (I say, 'States United' both to distinguish the nation from the corporate fiction that has usurped the name, 'United States', and because it more accurately encapsulates the nation's true and original standing.) Furthermore, the protections of *Magna Carta* and the *Bill of Rights* carry over through the Ninth Amendment: "The enumeration in the Constitution, of certain rights, shall not be construed to deny or disparage others retained by the people."

Governments argue, of course, that *Magna Carta* no longer applies or that it applies only in part, demonstrating that they are evil, stupid, or illiterate, probably all three, for it states, "… men in our kingdom shall have and keep all these liberties, rights, and concessions, well and peaceably in their fullness and entirety for them and their heirs, of us and our heirs, in all things and all places for ever" (Article 63). Thus, *Magna Carta* has sealed itself against future dilution, adulteration, or expiry. What part of "fullness," "entirety," and "for ever" do they not understand?

Legislation Is Dead to Us

Once we revert to our true standing, governments, legislatures, and courts, which are all corporations, along with their various departments, agencies, and enforcers, will have to acknowledge that we are 'non-statutory', meaning not subject to legislation nor to the taxation they would derive from it. Nor shall we let tyranny's fabric call itself 'Law'. The idea that any order or document issued by men can be called 'Law' is absurd, laughable, and blasphemous by pretending to play God who is the only Law-giver. Trying to apply such instruments to a Living Man or Living Woman is like trying to wound the wind with a sword or to stab water, to paraphrase from Shakespeare's *The Tempest* (III.iii.).

As Mike Colomb, founder of The Renegade Nation (therenegadenation.org) explains, statutory legislation "only deals with millions of man-made 'code' violations related to 'juristic' fiction entities with their names spelled in all-capital letters, and where in any legal dispute with the I.R.S., there is never an actual 'harmed' living man or woman."

Furthermore, acts, statutes, and tax codes are merely corporate contracts that one party has drafted, one party has read, one party has negotiated with itself, and one party has signed. Yet that party thinks to impose this contract on another party, us, without our signature or consent. That is fraud.

Therefore, we no longer play along with corporate theatre nor pay homage to the things of men, for that would be idolatry. Rather, we regard ourselves, and refer to ourselves, as Man, Woman, or perhaps National, and shun corporate titles such as 'citizen', 'person', 'driver', 'inhabitant', or 'taxpayer'. Nor are we 'federal', 'fiduciary', 'juristic', or 'statutory'.

Court Precedent

Several court precedents also underline our Common-Law instincts when it comes to taxation. In 1906, the U.S. Supreme Court stated in Hale v. Henkel that an individual's rights…

> "existed by the law of the land long antecedent to the organization of the state, and can only be taken from him by due process of law, and in accordance with the Constitution. Among his rights are a refusal to incriminate himself, and the immunity of himself and his property from arrest or seizure except under a warrant of the law. He owes nothing to the public so long as he does not trespass upon their rights."

In 1931, the Oregon Supreme Court ruled, in Redfield v. Fisher,…

> "The individual, unlike the corporation, cannot be taxed for the mere privilege of existing. The corporation is an artificial entity which owes its existence and charter powers to the state; but the individual's rights to live and own property are natural rights for the enjoyment of which an excise cannot be imposed."

Then there's a Tennessee Supreme Court ruling of

1960, in Jack Cole Co. v. MacFarland, that "Realizing and receiving income or earnings is not a privilege that can be taxed... Since the right to receive income or earnings is a right belonging to every person, this right cannot be taxed as a privilege."

Courts have said similar about fees demanded by governments, which are really just another form of taxation. In 1943, the U.S. Supreme Court stated in Murdock v. Pennsylvania, "A State may not impose a charge for the enjoyment of a right granted by the Federal Constitution."

In Closing...

You may think me presumptuous to argue we owe no taxes to Government, though you will admit I have *made* an argument, not just asserted this. But in reality, the only presumption here is that of the state in supposing it has a right to demand tax from us in the first place. It doesn't.

Nor can we expect the system to repair itself and deal with us more justly. If you have been with me throughout this *Battle Manuals for Freedom series*, you will know that I don't see any solution to tyranny, financial or otherwise, through the political mechanisms now in place.

Nor do I look to vote in a fake saviour nor to install a de-facto king who will preside over a dictatorship posing as democracy. Heed the prophet Samuel's warning to the elders of Israel, that such a man will take the best of your possessions and give them to his cronies, "and you yourselves will become his slaves" (*1 Samuel* 8).

In the words of Larken Rose,...

"The Left will rob you and dominate you; the Right will rob and dominate you. They will take turns robbing and dominating you, and you keep voting for it as if you're making a difference. How many hundreds of years have to go by of that happening before you realize this isn't really fixing anything?"

So, what other fixes are available to us? That is my theme in the following chapter.

2

A TAX DETOX

And let Jerusalem and her environs, her tithes and her revenues,
be holy and free from tax… No-one shall have authority to exact
anything from them or annoy any of them about any matter…
Let them live by their own laws.

— *1 MACCABEES* 10:31,35,37

What, then, is the least burdensome way to shed the tax burdens of men? It's not that complicated. You note the Crimes against Humanity perpetrated by the government pretending to represent you, and you refuse to incriminate yourself by giving it your financial support.

In the words of Canadian activist and Man of God, Kevin Annett, who has waged a long campaign against the atrocities of church and state in Canada,…

"If you're a citizen of a country that's practising war crimes, you are obligated not to pay taxes and not to follow the [statutes] of that regime, because then you're colluding, and in fact, as an individual, you have a responsibility to bring charges against your own country, your own regime that's doing this."

This view is reinforced by Chris Coverdale, a former fraud investigator and now activist, who points out that in September 2001, the U.K. Parliament ratified the *Rome Statute* of the International Criminal Court (1998) with the *International Criminal Court Act*. This legislation specifies prison sentences for up to 30 years for conduct ancillary to genocide, war crimes, and Crimes Against Humanity. That conduct, as Coverdale explains in a 2022 interview with British broadcaster Richard Vobes, includes *funding* the crimes.

Coverdale also cites the *International Convention for the Suppression of the Financing of Terrorism*, adopted by the General Assembly of the United Nations in 1999. By October 2018, according to Wikipedia, the treaty had been ratified by 188 states. Paying taxes cannot be legal under this statute because it finances terrorism. Even if the national government of your country has not sent troops to crush other peoples, destroy their infrastructure, or steal their natural resources, it has for sure perpetrated medical genocide at home, as I amply demonstrate in *Know Your Medical Rights*. In short,...

PAYING TAXES IS A CRIMINAL ACT!

"On Oct. 7, 2001, Tony Blair told us that we were starting to attack Afghanistan," Coverdale said in another interview with journalist Gordon Dimmack, "so anything you have paid in tax since Oct. 7, 2001 has been a criminal offence." (TikTok appears to have silenced the video clip, but you can still read the subtitles.)

Coverdale does not pay income tax himself. Nor does he pay council tax—equivalent to property tax—because, since 1787, council-tax revenues have gone into the same 'Consolidated Fund' of the national government as its other revenues, meaning they are used to fund the same atrocities.

Tax Rebellion

Coverdale's strategy has a power that petitions and protests will never have because we'll never persuade psychopaths to put themselves in someone else's shoes, get a soul transplant, or otherwise change their behaviour. His studies of successful revolutions throughout history, including *Magna Carta*, convinced him that every major change in society started with tax rebellion. To that end, he works with two key strategies I discuss in *Know Your Lawful Rights*: 1/ Turning the legislation of tyrants back against them—I'll call it 'boomeranging' legislation; and 2/ Conditional Acceptance.

Though it is true that governments and parliaments write legislation to extort, enslave, and exterminate the populations they purport to represent, occasionally some good stuff gets through. After all, evil-doers will wear devotion's visage and pious action to "sugar o'er the devil himself," as Shakespeare said (*Hamlet*, III.i), and the devil himself masquerades as an angel of light while his servants masquerade as servants of righteousness (2 *Corinthians* 11:13-15). That means we can always find something in their disingenuous texts to boomerang against them.

Even so, we need to be smart about our non-compliance. Coverdale advises putting the funds that governments or their agencies expect from us into 'Trust'. In basic terms, a 'Grantor' sets up a Trust to benefit a Beneficiary, and the one entrusted to carry this out is a Trustee. Coverdale suggests you set aside the funds a taxing entity expects from you, call it a Trust, and name the taxing entity as the Primary Beneficiary.

Now, this is where Conditional Acceptance comes in: you declare to that entity that the funds are being held in Trust and will be released on Condition that they supply Proof, by the end of the financial year, that no funds have been used for criminal purposes. You will also require from them Proof that criminal proceedings are underway against those responsible for illegal wars, experimental vaccination campaigns, or other atrocities you name. You can write the amount on a cheque which you retain in the interim.

Being criminal to the core, the various extractors from the People's purse cannot and will not meet the Burden of Proof by the end of the financial year, after which the funds go to a Secondary Beneficiary, most likely you. This

Conditional-Acceptance strategy avoids getting into a Controversy on which a court could rule though, as Coverdale points out, the false authorities are not keen to take him to court because he would be proved right and that would set a highly inconvenient precedent for them.

With Conditional Acceptance, you are not outright refusing to pay tax, but withholding payment until the criminals fall to their knees in repentance. That day may come but not until, as prophesied,...

> *"they shall be terrified,*
> *And they shall be downcast of countenance,*
> *And pain shall seize them,*
> *When they see that Son of Man*
> *Sitting on the throne of his glory."*
>
> — *FIRST BOOK OF ENOCH*, 62:5

By then, of course, it will be too late because...

> *"the wrath of the Lord of Spirits resteth on them,*
> *And His sword is drunk with their blood."*
>
> — *FIRST BOOK OF ENOCH*, 62:12

Coverdale has drawn up a set of documents you can use in your dealings with the powers-that-shouldn't-be, including a *DECLARATION of SOVEREIGNTY and DEED of DISCRETIONARY, REVOCABLE, CONDITIONAL TRUST and WITHDRAWAL of CONSENT to ILLEGAL TAXATION.*

It's a thing of beauty, though I would replace a few instances of 'law' with 'legislation' or with 'statute' when not being used in a quotation. As I explain throughout this series, the Creator makes Law, men make legislation, and corporations write company policy. You can complete the document, sign it with witness, and send it to the troublesome corporation. (All governments, parliaments, courts, and police forces are corporations.)

Coverdale has also produced a document for employees whose earnings are taxed at source by an employer. You instruct the employer to divert all pay-as-you-earn and National-Insurance deductions into a Trust payable only when the government has ceased its crimes and is acting lawfully. You instruct the employer that, until these conditions are met, its trustees are to "return all such payments to the employees." All these documents are available, along with instructions, at https://www.probityco.com/.

Or you can write your own documents, which is always my preference. By doing so, you will stand upon a surer foundation. You confirm to yourself and others that you have grasped the subject matter, and thwart the ready comeback of extortioners that you just copied something off the Internet. That's why I have favoured presenting you with information and concepts that you can adapt for yourself, rather than one-size-fits-all templates.

A simpler variation on Coverdale's theme comes from Allegedly Dave, a self-described "ordinary bloke from Basildon in Essex," who told podcaster and presenter James Delingpole in a September 2024 interview that he also makes tax payment conditional on the government proving that it is not funding terrorism, but he doesn't bother with a Trust.

Nor does the 'People's Lawyer', David Adelman, who points out that HM Revenue & Customs (HMRC) need to contract with us to exact any tax payment. "You only become a taxpayer by consent and by contract," he told Richard Vobes during a March 2024 live stream. The same goes for taxing entities in other countries. "If you do not fill in and sign a tax return, you are not in contract, and if you are not in contract, there is no obligation, end of."

Adelman has not been troubled by HMRC since he pointed this out to them in 2015. "If they have no paperwork—in other words, no evidence of contract—they cannot pursue it. There's nothing to pursue."

Revocation of Consent in the States United

If you are dwelling in the States United, another approach is to send the Internal Revenue Service (IRS) an Affidavit revoking any Consent it assumes you have given to file and pay taxes.

This is founded on a realignment of status, both yours and the government's. You are a Living Man or Woman with authority over Government. To put that in official terms even a bureaucrat could understand, you are a 'nontaxpayer'. Quoting the District Court of Montana in the famous 1922 case, Long v. Rasmussen—with the proviso that 'laws' should read 'legislation',...

"The revenue laws are a code or system in regulation of tax assessment and collection. They relate to taxpayers, and not to nontaxpayers. The latter are without [outside] their scope. No procedure is prescribed for nontaxpayers, and no attempt is made to annul any of their rights and remedies in due course of law. With them Congress does not assume to deal, and they are neither of the subject nor of the object of the revenue laws."

This language was echoed by the United States Court of Claims in 1972 in Economy Plumbing & Heating v. United States.

As for the government's status, by its own admissions it is a foreign corporation with zero jurisdiction outside the District of Columbia (DC). According to the *United States Code* (*USC*), a compilation of legislation organized by subject matter, the term 'United States' is defined as "a Federal corporation" (Title 28, Section 3002 (15)(a)).

(15) "United States" means—

(A) a Federal corporation;

(B) an agency, department, commission, board, or other entity of the United States; or

(C) an instrumentality of the United States.

And said corporation is located in DC, according to

the *Uniform Commercial Code* (*UCC*, §9-307(h)), a body of legislation that governs commercial transactions.

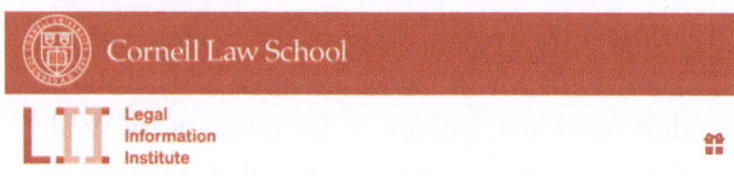

(h) [Location of United States.]

> The United States is located in the District of Columbia.

What, then, is the relationship between that corporation in DC and the States of the Union? Foreign! As described in *Corpus Juris Secundum*, an encyclopaedia of legislation, "The United States government is a **foreign** corporation with respect to a State" (Vol. 19, Section 883, emphasis mine).

As for the IRS itself, the clue is in the name. As an 'internal' revenue service, not an external one, its jurisdiction is confined to the 10-square-mile foreign enclave of DC. It is also a foreign trust domiciled in Puerto Rico, as set out in Title 31, Section 1321 of the USC ((a) (62)).

(62) Puerto Rico special fund (Internal Revenue).

(63) Miscellaneous trust funds, Department of State.

(64) Funds contributed for improvement of (name of river or harbor).

Brothers and Sisters, you and I owe no allegiance to a corporation, much less a foreign one! According to Mike Colomb of The Renegade Nation, IRS agents should register as foreign agents with respect to States of the Union, in order to comply with the *Foreign Agents Registration Act* (1938), and as foreign debt collectors with secretaries of State to conform with the *Fair Debt Collection Practices Act* (1971). Having failed to do either, they are no better than illegal debt collectors, and the IRS is "an illegal debt-collection company" that is "violating too many laws to mention if or when they attempt to impose their foreign tax laws on you."

Paying U.S. Income Tax Is Voluntary.

By now, you will observe that I am deep into legislation, not Law, though Colomb mistakenly calls it law, so I'll say again that legislation is not written for us but for Government officials and employees, and that we cite it selectively only to hold *them* to *their* contractual obligations. The legislation in play here is the *Internal Revenue Code* (IRC), which forms Title 26 of *USC*.

At first glance, Section 7201 of that Title looks scary, but that's what tyrants do, trying to rule by fear and intimidation, and they have been honing this dark art for thousands of years:

"Any person who willfully attempts in any manner to evade or defeat any tax imposed by this title or the payment thereof shall, in addition to other penalties

provided by law, be guilty of a felony and, upon
conviction thereof, shall be fined not more than
$100,000 ($500,000 in the case of a corporation), or
imprisoned not more than 5 years, or both, together
with the costs of prosecution."

But let's break it down. To begin with, I hope by now
that you do not identify as a 'PERSON' living in the
fictional realm of Legal Land, a place no more real than
Legoland or Toytown. Nor are you a character in some
kind of fairground installation.

Even the definition of 'person' in the IRC is circular,
saying it includes, "an officer or employee of a
corporation, or a member or employee of a partnership,
who as such officer, employee, or member is under a duty
to perform the act in respect of which the violation
occurs."

This is nothing more than saying the Code applies to
those "under a duty to perform the act." In other words,
it applies to whom it applies. It matters to whom it
matters. And, to whom does it apply? To whom does it
matter? **Only those who have voluntarily agreed to it,
as confirmed in** many statements by U.S. government
officials and by former IRS agent, Joseph Banister.

Banister was forced out of the agency in 1999 after he
asked inconvenient questions about the true obligations
of people living in the States. "There's no law that makes
the average American required to file these returns and
pay the income tax," he told broadcaster Vincent James in
an August 2024 interview.

That's why, according to Colomb, the U.S. Treasury does not define payments received as 'income taxes' but as 'Donations' to the Treasury. You unwittingly agreed to make these voluntary donations by filling out a *1040* form in the past, but these were in effect confessions by which you ceded your Fifth-Amendment Right to Remain Silent and gave IRS a jurisdiction it has no right to have.

Taxation and the Constitution.

I have talked about constitutions before and how they are generally accorded higher authority than other legislation. For the most part, they are lawful, in that they enshrine the ways we want to be protected and agree to protect others, in accordance with Christ's Commandment to love others as we love ourselves. But ultimately, they are still legislation, not law, for they are written and revised by men. Men cannot be law-makers, any more than they can write, revise, or repeal the laws of motion or of thermodynamics. Even half-wit Freemasons can write what they call constitutions, though they are abominations in the eyes of Man and of the Most High.

Therefore, I parse out from constitutions that which is beneficial and therefore lawful, from that which is harmful and therefore unlawful. When it comes to the *Constitution* of the States United, I will retain the *Bill of Rights*, which is the first ten Amendments to the Constitution, and reject some of the language added later to enslave us.

Who am I to do this? A Living Man, and Living Men

and Living Women have Dominion of the Earth and authority over the ephemeral creations of men. The Sixteenth Amendment, wherein Congress assumed "power to lay and collect taxes on incomes," was not added until 1913, and even then, it was never ratified by the States.

Several Supreme-Court decisions in the following years ruled, as in Stanton v. Baltic Mining Co. (1915/1916), that, "The provisions of the Sixteenth Amendment conferred no new power of taxation." As reported in *The New York Times* on Jan. 25, 1916, "In substance, the court holds that the Sixteenth Amendment did not empower the Federal Government to levy a new tax."

Much of this historical background is set out in the documentary film, *Freedom to Fascism*, where tax attorney Peter Gibbons states,...

"Congress tried to enact an income tax in 1894. The Supreme Court said that's unconstitutional. When the Supreme Court says something is unconstitutional, it's unconstitutional. They tried again in 1913, and the Supreme Court said the Sixteenth Amendment conferred no new power of taxation. So if they didn't have it then, and they didn't get it, they don't have it. There is no constitutional basis for a tax on the wages of Americans living and working in the 50 states of the Union. Period. End of argument."

Still, we may mark down 1913 as a bad year for the

States United, not just because of the Sixteenth Amendment but because it was also when the U.S. government introduced an income tax and *Form 1040*. Also, as we shall see in a later chapter, it was when the *Federal Reserve Act* was passed.

What this boils down to is that you have been handing over the fruit of your toil without obligation to do so. Colomb recommends that, armed with this knowledge, you send the IRS a witnessed letter/Affidavit affirming your status as a Living Man or Woman and nontaxpayer and letting this foreign corporation know you do not consent to paying income tax, nor to any presumption or inference of consent by the IRS. You no longer volunteer to donate your private property to a foreign treasury, effective immediately, nor to file a *1040* form, and you require the IRS to note in its own files, records, and databases that you are a nontaxpayer.

You also notify IRS that if it wishes to dispute any part of your Affidavit, it must do so within x number of days with a point-by-point rebuttal, an option which, in practice, the IRS never pursues. Its failure to rebut or challenge your Affidavit in that time frame acts as a legal default ('estoppel'), and your sworn declaration stands as Truth in Law.

My own Affidavit to the IRS is below. If you choose to do similar, I urge you still to write your own...

Daniel Werfel
Commissioner, Internal Revenue Service
1111 Constitution Avenue NW
Washington, DC 20224

Name—Affidavit Affirming Non-Taxable Status

1/ My name is _____, a Living Man. I was allegedly born in _____ on _____.

2/ I am writing to inform IRS that I, as a Living Man without residence in the District of Columbia (DC), am not required to pay income tax and will not do so.

3/ Nor am I subject, in conducting business in my name or any other, to any levy, tax, or regulation originating from DC, nor from any other government, agency, or corporation.

4/ Furthermore, I am under no obligation to provide financial data or produce filings to IRS or any other DC or foreign entity, and will not knowingly do so.

5/ For your purposes, I am a 'non-taxpayer', and I require that IRS make any necessary adjustments to its files, records, and databases to accord with this.

6/ I do not consent to any assumption, presumption, or inference that contradicts the above, either by IRS or any other government body or corporation, foreign or domestic.

If IRS wishes to dispute this Notice, it has 40 days from this date to do so in writing to the above address, after which time it shall stand as Truth in Law.

I signed this Affidavit with Witness, copied it, and sent it by Recorded Delivery in 2023. I have not heard anything back since.

Once we issue such a Notice, none may bring an accusation of tax 'evasion' against us because we stand firm in the Truth that we were never required to pay tax in the first place. Any subsequent attempt by the IRS to collect taxes—any letter, form, notice, or demand—amounts to mail fraud and is punishable with a 30-year prison sentence under the *Privacy Act* and prosecution under the *Racketeer Influenced and Corrupt Organizations (RICO) Act*.

In the event IRS attempts legal action, I can inform the tax court of my nontaxpayer status and deny it any jurisdiction. Colomb reports that the tax court in D.C. is dismissing IRS claims on that basis. Meanwhile, the Affidavit does not in any way detract from any government benefit program to which we are entitled, such as Social Security or Medicare, whether now or in the future.

If you don't want to be so 'in-your-face' about it, you

can favour the Conditional-Acceptance approach. Whenever you receive some Notice or demand from this foreign corporation, you can start asking the questions you know they cannot answer: By what law am I required to file or pay income tax? Show me where I signed any legislation you cite. Provide Proof that the Sixteenth Amendment was ratified. Prove that IRS has any jurisdiction outside the District of Columbia. Prove that no IRS revenue is funding crimes deemed illegal under the *Rome Statute* of the International Criminal Court. And so on.

David E. Robinson also gives sound advice in *The UCC Connection*:

"NEVER ARGUE THE FACTS IN A TAX CASE. [MAXIM: 'ARGUMENTS ARE FOR FOOLS'.] If you're not required to file, what do you care whether they say you owe sixty dollars or 60,000 dollars. If you are not required to file, the amount doesn't matter. DON'T ARGUE THE AMOUNT... The minute you say, 'I don't owe that much,' you have voluntarily agreed that you owe them something, and you have just given them jurisdiction."

Fines Are Taxes Too

Close cousin to taxation are fines, devised to extract yet more of your lifeforce by penalizing you for some infringement of corporate code, even though you have done no harm. A powerful way to deal with this, as

Allegedly Dave explained to Delingpole, is to start out with the obvious truth that he who makes an allegation must produce the Proof. For example, if a speeding infraction is alleged, a photograph taken by a speed camera is not sufficient to prove you were driving a particular car at a particular time on a particular day at a particular speed. For one thing, there is no first-hand witness to the purported event. Furthermore, measurement of distances and speeds can be incorrectly calibrated, photographs can be doctored and airbrushed, and Automatic Number Plate Recognition (ANPR) systems have a high error rate.

Dave points out, "You can legitimately say, and honestly say, 'I have no record of being at that place at that time on that day. Can you provide me some evidence that I was there?' " A camera is not a witness and therefore not primary evidence. He also argues it is highly unlikely this approach will end up in court because, if it did, you would ask, "Where's the evidence I asked for?" They won't be able to provide it, and "the case is gone."

How can a computer bring a man to court? asks researcher Mr Blue in a September 2024 conversation with Richard Vobes. "They're supplying nothing more than a photograph of a registration plate saying this car was assumed to be speeding. Okay, show me the Proof, show me the evidence. Where are your witnesses? You have to have an independent witness to make the claim… The police or the council have to give independent evidence. It's hardly independent if it's their own bits of technology that's designed to capture people."

In Closing...

This was a tough chapter to write because most of the so-called Freedom-Movement researchers get into circular analysis of quoting each other, making it hard to break out of the loop and get back to the original sources. So many unlinked articles, so many dead ends, and so many quotes inaccurately transcribed or taken out of context. I have done my best to mitigate these shortfalls by finding the original documents, saving them, and highlighting them so that this book, like the others in this series, shall stand as a document of record.

Of the two main approaches suggested in this chapter —Coverdale's tax rebellion on the basis that taxes fund genocide, and Colomb's Revocation notice to the IRS— the former has universal appeal and requires less getting into the weeds with legislation and court precedent. It therefore appears a simpler path to accord with Christ's command to leave the Beast system termed 'Babylon': "Come out of her, my people, so that you will not share in her sins" (*Revelation* 18:4).

Simpler yet—and this is my preference—is not to bother with the Trust element and, like Allegedly Dave, go the Conditional-Acceptance path alone. In any case, the same key principle applies: If Government wants to extract your property, it must shoulder the Burden of Proof that it has lawful authority to do so, which it cannot do.

3

MORE ON COUNCIL TAX IN BRITAIN

Council tax in Britain is an abomination, not just unlawful but illegal, and if you live in another country, so are *your* property taxes, but British people are beginning to turn the tide.

Veronica Chapman

Among them is Veronica: of the Chapman family. In August 2024, she released an exchange of letters with Portsmouth City Council after they demanded council tax from her. She used a combination of Conditional Acceptance and boomeranging legislation. Near the end of this exchange, Veronica answers questions with a question, an approach I also talk about in *Know Your Lawful Rights*.

In her preface to the series, Veronica explains how prosecutor and judge are the same when councils take people to court for nonpayment of council tax. This is because councils print court Summonses "on their own printers, using a letterhead that is a facsimile of the Court's letterhead." Then they rent magistrates' courts to rubber-stamp hundreds of fake Liability Orders on an industrial scale.

The exchange between Veronica and the council is a fun read if you have the time, but here's the gist. It begins with the council sending Veronica a bill for £53.19 for Apr. 1, 2020 to Mar. 31, 2021, plus £79.01 for arrears from previous years.

Veronica replies in a letter dated Mar. 14, 2020 that if the council wants her to pay anything, "Then you'd need to send a proper Invoice, constructed as per the Bills of Exchange Act 1882, **and defining the VAT situation**" (all emphases hers). She stresses that she is not refusing to pay, but **"I am making an offer to pay conditional on the other party fulfilling their obligation under the Bills of Exchange Act 1882 for this alleged charge."** This legislation, she adds, requires the council to issue and deliver **"an <u>invoice signed in wet ink by an officer of the company/council</u>..."**

A couple of weeks later, one Louise Chapman from the council's revenues & benefits department writes back. To avoid any confusion, we'll just call her 'Louise' as the two antagonists share the same last name of Chapman though they are not related. Louise asserts Veronica's "liability" began in 2016 and that, "For every financial year a billing authority must serve a notice in writing on every liable person in accordance with regulations and legislation contained in the local government finance act 1992."

To which Veronica replies, "I would be happy to make a payment as soon as I receive a lawful Invoice." She points out that the *Local Government Finance Act* (1992) does not allow exemption from the *Bills of Exchange Act* (1882).

Then, in an Apr. 23, 2020 letter, Louise counters, "you are being charged in accordance with the Local Government Finance Act 1992" and, "The legislation you quote does not apply to council tax administration." Then she issues the first threat. "Failure to pay in accordance with any reminder notice may result in a summons being issued to apply to the court for a liability order to be issued."

Veronica writes back asking if the demand for payment is...

1/ in exchange for goods and/or services provided by the council, in which case the *Bills of Exchange Act* applies and "in consequence, I need a LAWFUL Bill for this EXCHANGE to take place LAWFULLY"; or

2/ as a punishment for convicted wrongdoing on her part, which must comply with the *Bill of Rights* (1688/89) that "all Grants and Promises of Fines and Forfeitures of particular persons before Conviction are illegall and void"; or

3/ plain extortion.

Veronica also observes in her letter that the council can print its own court summonses but "CAN'T CREATE A SIMPLE PIECE OF PAPER COMPRISING A LAWFUL INVOICE." When someone can't produce an Invoice, she continues, "it *normally* means that the demand is fraudulent."

Then Veronica points out that the legislation and regulations cited do not mention her specifically. "**None of them include my Name.** Therefore there is NO GUARANTEE THAT THEY APPLY TO ME, PERSONALLY."

Here, she invokes a truth I have been banging on about throughout this series, that Acts, statutes, and the decrees of politicians and bureaucrats are contracts written by one party that thinks to impose them on another party, you and me, without our participation, much less our signature. That is fraud. They have no jurisdiction over us whatsoever.

Then Louise ups the ante with a May 26, 2020 letter titled *Council tax appeal stage two*, where she reiterates, "we don't follow any other legislation other than Local Government Finance Act 1992." I gasped when I got to this bit. Louise is basically saying they get to pick and choose what they will and won't comply with, meaning the Executive branch is claiming authority over Parliament.

Louise goes on to list services for which council tax supposedly pays, followed by more threats: that where council tax remains unpaid, a local authority "is entitled to seek the issue of a liability order through the magistrate's court," and "Where the defendant does not appear in answer to the summons, the court may proceed in the absence of the defendant."

Louise then basically admits this so-called court is a rubber stamp enforcing extortion on behalf of the council, which then prints its own Liability Orders: "Liability orders in all cases are approved by the Magistrates and once approved are printed by Portsmouth City Council."

Veronica is quick to pounce on Louise's folly. In her May 30 reply, she queries Louise's *tax appeal stage two* heading as she has not appealed anything but is "simply asking for the lawful paperwork." Who issued this 'appeal', and when? Veronica asks, and "Who granted them Power of Attorney to do it on my behalf? Send me a copy of what they wrote... I have the Right to it as 'disclosure'."

Next, Louise writes in a letter of June 22, 2020 that what she meant to say was, "council tax complaint stage 2," not "appeal stage 2," as if that makes it any better, and that "I will not be corresponding with you any further regarding this matter but if you still disagree with my decision, please follow the appeals process as below."

In a series of letters, Veronica tells Louise she never asked her to make any decision, that the *Bills of Exchange Act* (1882) "says (in effect) that 'If no Invoice is presented, then no debt is outstanding,' " and that there is no controversy in play that would require court involvement...

"So... once you have created your faux Court Summons (printed on Council Notepaper!), will you be writing to the Court, with copies of all my letters, so that the Court can see that the reason for the lack of funds received by the Council, **is entirely down to the fact that you have simply failed to produce the correct paperwork?**"

Or will Louise commit perjury by omission? If Louise instigates a Summons, Veronica warns she will call her as a Material Witness.

Later, the council informs Veronica it has obtained a Liability Order and, on Feb. 9, 2022, sends her a 'BROKEN ARRANGEMENT AND ENFORCEMENT WARNING NOTICE'.

In her Apr. 6, 2022 response, this time to the Borough Solicitor, Veronica demands to know what 'arrangement' had been broken and how. "You will need to provide a copy of the arrangement, which bears my signature or seal of obligation."

Then she demands a copy of the alleged Liability Order in the form of a valid Court Order. "**It will contain the LEGIBLE signature of whoever made the Order, and will contain the Court Seal**. She also demands a copy of the Prosecution Bundle that was used to obtain the alleged Order. Her letter is to be treated, she adds, as a Subject Access Request for any and all internal or external communications that include her name.

She closes by invoking her copyright of the name, 'AAACCEHI MNNOPRV when arranged as VERONICA

CHAPMAN', meaning, "it would cost you £ 10,000 per usage of my personal, copyrighted, logos. This would render any further 'Court Procedures' problematical (for you)."

On May 24, 2022, Louise sends various enclosures, including a purported copy of the Liability Order. Veronica sends them back a few days later, pointing out that the Liability Order is false. "If it was a REAL Court Order, it would: A) State the Order (in writing), B) State the name of the Justice or Judge making the Order (legibly!), C) Bear the signature of the Justice or Judge making the Order, D) Bear the Court Seal." The document Louise sent met none of these conditions.

"You must think I'm stupid," Veronica continues, before chastising Louise for wilfully overlooking the statutes Veronica had cited. "Just because you aren't prepared to read them, doesn't (actually) make them go away... And, if you want to emulate an ostrich, just remember which part of your anatomy will be most exposed."

Somehow, by Mar. 29, 2023, the Council had managed to put Veronica's so-called 'account' in credit but, in an Apr. 15, 2023 letter to Louise, Veronica demands...

"a copy, signed and sealed by myself, that grants yourself, or any staff member of Portsmouth City Council, the Right to make decisions on my behalf... Then send me the Case Number of the Liability Order that you claim to have been granted, so that I can check its validity with the Ministry of Justice. Furthermore I am still awaiting a copy of the Prosecution bundle that was utilised in order to gain said Liability Order (bearing in mind that—according to Stones' *Justices Manual*—a Magistrates' Court has no jurisdiction to make Liability Orders)."

Louise is aghast, asking in a May 25, 2023 letter if Veronica is refusing to accept the government money issued to her council-tax account. "First of all," Veronica shoots back in a June 3, 2023 letter, "it's not 'my' council tax account. It is an account that YOU have created. **Do not** try to assign it to myself. What grants YOU Power of Attorney to raise an account, and to assign it to me?" And what gave Louise Power of Attorney to accept these funds on her behalf? "Answer those questions, and I will answer your question."

At the time of publishing, the Council was no longer in pursuit of Veronica. After all, extortioners have lower hanging fruit to collect. This is the desired result. As Veronica notes in introduction to the letter exchanges, " 'They' will NEVER admit 'defeat'. The best that can ever be achieved is 'silence'. Such that they 'leave one alone, henceforth'. They will NEVER, EVER, send a letter saying: 'Oh, yes… you were right, after all! Sorry!' No so-called 'authority' will ever do that." After Veronica published the letters, Richard Vobes did an entertaining synopsis shortly after and interviewed Veronica in August 2024.

Council-tax prosecutions that come to a so-called court are exemplars of injustice. They are conducted by what Mr Blue calls a 'pseudo court', "a fake court brought by a private corporation in the trickery of Color of Law." In his September 2024 conversation with Richard Vobes, he points out,…

> "There's no jury, nine times out of ten, no judge. It's just a panel of people sat there, and the clerk of the court is now changed from the clerk to a legal advisor, which is a corporate standing, and there's no claimant. Now, the *Bill of Rights* is very clear on this. There must be a claimant in court to make a claim. If there is no claimant, the case is dismissed. This is the problem that the council have, the police have. They cannot make a claim because they are corporate persons."

A corporation cannot bring a man to court, Mr Blue adds, because a corporation is nothing more than a piece of paper. "Can a corporation pick up a pen? No. Can a corporation sign a contract? No. Can a corporation enter the court? No."

Furthermore, the U.K. *Local Government Act* (1888) states, "All duties and liabilities of the inhabitants of a county shall become and be duties and liabilities of the council of such county" (79(2)). So, if councils suppose that council tax is owed, then that liability is theirs!

Mick Butler

Our next witness is Mick Butler from the Midlands, also interviewed by Richard Vobes. When he went to a magistrates' court over a council-tax issue with Coventry City Council, he was redirected to "the council's court."

The implications are staggering; the council has its very own court! This means that councils, as the Executive branch of local Government, have carved out for themselves an enclave within the Judiciary and become indistinguishable from it, a mockery of the Separation-of-Powers doctrine. "It's fraud," Butler told Vobes. "It's treasonous against the people."

This kangaroo-court system also falls foul of the aforementioned *Local Government Act* which forbids councils, along with their members and committees, from exercising "any of the powers of a court of record" or from performing "any judicial business" (78(2)). Yet that is exactly what councils are doing.

Butler's hearing was adjourned to a date several weeks ahead, but in the meantime, the purported court conducted a hearing about his case without informing him and, of course, found against him and issued a phantom Liability Order. When he went to the magistrate's court to find the Order, the court had no record of it, confirming that the council had issued it unilaterally. Butler's research has also confirmed that council-tax revenues in Britain go to the 'Consolidated Fund' of the national Treasury, and that every council in the U.K. is a corporation, as shown at thesovereign project.live.*

---

* https://wiki.thesovereignproject.live/index.php/DUNS_-_UK_Councils

The case culminated in an appearance before a district judge. Having refused to be addressed as 'MR BUTLER' or as a 'PERSON', he told the judge, "My name is Michael, and I am representing MR MICHAEL BUTLER," then, brandishing his Birth Certificate, he declared himself the Executor and Beneficiary of that Trust.

But it was when Butler questioned the judge's Oath that he got the judge to flee the courtroom and "abandon ship." That a judge is desecrating his Oath of impartiality is not hard to demonstrate when a council has set up its own court because, in this arrangement, the judge *is* the prosecutor.

I will digress here briefly to suggest that the most powerful approach to take with any judge conspiring to take your income, property, or wealth is to attack his standing. Who is this creature clad in black who presumes to have authority here?

> *"How do I know you're a judge? I need to see your Oath and your signature on that Oath. I also demand a signed declaration that you have sworn no other secret oath, either to a Bar association or to a secret society. And I require a sworn statement that you have no financial interest in the outcome of this case."*

If the judge cannot meet all of these conditions—and we know he can't—he is IMPERSONATING A JUDGE and desecrating his public Oath. This approach strikes at the core of their fraud.

Vobes contributed his own spirited appraisal of the STRAWMAN fiction as he talked with Butler:

"They can charge this ALL-CAPS NAME because they created this ALL-CAPS NAME. The problem they have is, this ALL-CAPS NAME doesn't have any arms or legs, doesn't breathe, and he's unable to use a pen to write a cheque out... I can only act on behalf of this thing and tell these people, 'I'm really sorry. I've spoken to this bit of paper, I've cajoled it, I've really encouraged it to pay your bill, but it's just sitting there and doing nothing.' "

Yes, imagine coming into court with a copy of your driving licence, passport, or Birth Certificate, and relaying to it every question the judge asks you, then waiting for the document to reply. After an awkward silence, you turn to the judge and say, "Well, this is awkward, but it's not giving me an answer." Or, if you're expected to stand in a particular place in a courtroom, leave a copy of your document there, or hand it to the clerk of the court and ask them to put it there for you, and inform the judge he may address his questions to it. Not so much "Talk to the hand" as "Talk to the document."

Now, extending the David-Goliath analysis I set out in *Know Your Lawful Rights* (Chapter 16), the court is really going to see double as Goliath saw double when David came down to kill him (*1 Samuel* 17:40-43).

Leighton v Bristow & Sutor

The collusion between councils and magistrates' courts was also exposed in September 2023 by a Cardiff high-court judgment in Leighton v Bristow & Sutor. Wayne Leighton filed a claim against national 'enforcement agency' Bristow & Sutor after their bailiffs set out to enforce four fake Liability Orders on behalf of York Council. He cited three statutes these corporate employees had breached—the *Tribunals and Courts Enforcement Act* (2007); the *Protection from Harassment Act* (1997); and the *Statute of Marlborough* (1267), which stipulates, "none from henceforth shall take any such Revenge or Distress of his own Authority, without Award of our Court…"

The high-court judge, named Harrison, found it troubling that, in magistrate-court proceedings dealing with council tax, "No physical individual order as such is ever actually produced by the court." Instead, the Council sends an officer with a list of Summonses, "the list is simply signed by a magistrate, and the liability order is deemed to be made." Harrison noted that on June 21, 2017 alone, the magistrates' court issued 1,474 Liability Orders in one day!

This process, the judge added, "does not identify clearly the maker of the order, and it is neither stamped, nor sealed. Further, insofar as it purports to be the basis for an award of costs, then it does not comply with the obligation to make clear whether or in what sum such costs are rewarded." He noted that, in the absence of a proper paper record of an individualized Liability Order stating the amount claimed against him, Leighton had no mechanism to appeal it. This breached Article 6 of the *European Convention on Human Rights*—Right to a fair trial.

According to the *Tribunals, Courts and Enforcement Act*, "The enforcement agent must on request show the debtor and any person who appears to him to be in charge of the premises evidence of (a) his identity, and (b) his authority to enter the premises" (Schedule 12, Paragraph 26).

Make a note of this if you are in Britain. It's important if debt collectors ever show up. Remedies are available to a debtor—including return of goods and payment of damages—when an enforcement agent "acts under an enforcement power under a writ, warrant, liability order or other instrument that is defective" (Schedule 12, Paragraph 66).

In this case, the bailiffs had refused "to provide a copy of the liability order on request, or otherwise to identify under what authority they were intending to enter his premises." Harrison also found it troubling that, in its pleadings to the court, the company said it took its authority to enter a premises from the Council. It "regarded the council's document as being the relevant authority, and furthermore, as the pleadings say, the document was carried by the agents when attending to enforce council tax liabilities." That a council, rather than a court, could authorize a contractor to enter premises and take control of goods was "problematic, to say the least."

The judge also took the defendants to task for refusing to show their authority to enter Leighton's premises; they merely told him to contact the council. Harrison wrote,...

"In my judgment, a householder is entitled to ask the defendants on what authority they are purporting to enter his property, and the fact that they cannot do so, and refer him back, effectively to their client, is almost bound to cause him to be dissatisfied. In my judgment, the defendants are in breach of paragraph 26" (of the *Tribunals, Courts and Enforcement Act* just cited).

Harrison went on to cite the *Protection From Harassment Act*, where harassment includes "alarming the person or causing the person distress." The defendants carried out some 35 enforcement actions in various forms of contact, including email and correspondence, with 15 visits to three separate properties, including two visits to Leighton's parents. "Mr Leighton explained that the visits to the premises occupied by his parents were particularly troublesome for him. He felt that the defendants were using them as a means to get to him." Incredibly, however, the judge said the bailiffs' conduct did not meet the threshold for harassment.

In the end, Harrison awarded Leighton a paltry £4000 in damages, but it is still an important victory as it exposes and demolishes the entire council/magistrates' court charade in the U.K.

To simplify the analysis, if I assert you reneged on a promise to pay back a loan I made to you, it's not OK for me just to give some thugs a piece of paper saying I authorize them to bash your door down, much as I might want to. I have to go to court and prove that you made that promise to me in the first place and give you an opportunity to defend yourself. Only when I have satisfied the court of my case, and the court has signed a Liability Order with your name on it, stating the amount owed, and I have given you opportunity to comply with the Order and you have refused, only then do I get to enlist enforcers. But British councils are skipping all of this Due Process, making for systemic injustice.

As explained in a Substack article by The98thmonkey, "these bailiffs only showed their instructions **from the council** to enforce the debt rather than the actual proper signed authentic original order from the court." Courts have done away away with old-fashioned written Liability Orders signed by a judge "and instead ruled that the oral pronouncement of the order was all that was required, which means the enforcement companies now have a big problem to provide written proof that any order was even granted." Now that bailiffs have been caught with their pants down, it is easier to prosecute them under the *Harassment Act.*

The article includes a 'No-Trespass' notice that you can display at your property boundary. It denies 'implied right of access' to "any employee, agent, third party or representative or any other person acting on behalf of any

CORPORATE-BODY [COMPANY]." The notice also denies access to...

> "ANY POLICE-OFFICER that is acting for the CORPORATE-POLICE and not acting as expressed in their Oath of Office – 'to serve with fairness, integrity, diligence and impartiality, upholding fundamental human rights and according equal respect to all people; and that I will, to the best of my power, cause the peace to be kept and preserved and prevent all offences against people and property.' "

That police forces are corporations is quickly confirmed on the U.K. government's Companies House register. The POLICE FEDERATION OF ENGLAND AND WALES has the Company Number 04120881 and is registered as PITCOMP 233 LIMITED, a private limited company in the business of "Residents property management."

What they mean by this, Mr Blue told Vobes, is, "We are the residents, we are the property, and they are the management." WEST YORKSHIRE POLICE, he adds, formerly traded AS RAID-CONTROL TRUST, in the business of "Security systems service activities." This corporation has ownership ties to debt-collection companies, "so the bailiffs are now running the police."

In *The Council Tax Handbook*, 13th edition (2023), Child Poverty Action Group also untangle the Liability-Order fraud perpetrated by magistrates' courts. Instead of issuing individual Liability Orders, "the judge or chair of

the magistrates normally just signs a certificate attached
to the list of non-payers..." In the absence of a proper
stamped and sealed Order from the court,...

> "the local authority may not be able to establish that
> any such order exists or existed at any stage, nor show
> that the magistrates were ever satisfied that the local
> authority had proved all the matters it is required to
> prove... leaving local authorities to maintain records
> which could be wrong and incapable of independent
> verification. This has also been identified as a serious
> omission in enforcement by the High Court... The lack
> of an adequate and independent record may be a breach
> of human rights under Article 6 of the European
> Convention on Human Rights."

I also refer you to *The Council Tax Fraud*, an excellent
analysis of tax fraud in general, and council-tax fraud in
particular, at Awakened-GB (https://awakenedgb.
wordpress.com/2023/04/11/the-council-tax-fraud/).

Yet another warrior in the front lines against council-
tax extortion is Si the Spaniard. In a May 2024 email, he
reported that "the Bailiffs have run for the hills" in a test
case he was pursuing "and stated (in writing) that they
will NO LONGER be seeking to execute any enforcement
action on behalf of the Council concerned."

Like my other witnesses in this chapter, Si points out
that the so-called courts are not issuing proper Liability
Orders. "The Council simply sends a Notice stating that a
'Liability Order has been issued' - [hearsay at best]. The

Council instructed a firm of Bailiffs to go and enforce the alleged [and invisible] Liability Order."

At the time of writing, Si's team were "in hot pursuit of the Bailiffs for harassment" and for violating Schedule 12 of the *Tribunals, Courts and Enforcement Act* (2007). I shall have more to say about bailiffs in a coming chapter.

4

WEAPONIZED BANKING AND INFLATION

Where do I begin in describing the ways the banking system has exploited and enslaved us? They are many and complex and have deep historical roots. Many volumes, even entire libraries, could not encompass them all. It is easier to say how the banking system ends, so that is where I shall begin. It ends much as it ended for Pharaoh who, as told in *Exodus*, chased the People of Promise into the Red Sea and drowned, along with his army and chariots (*Exodus* 14:28). This meant liberation from slavery for the true Israelites.

Many are the parallels today with Pharaoh's Egypt. As soon as governments and media started their vaccine propaganda campaign in 2020, I saw a similarity between the needles of Big Pharma and the serpents conjured by Pharaoh's sorcerers when Moses and his brother Aaron came to Pharaoh's court (*Exodus* 7:8-13). Aaron turned his staff into a snake, and the conjurers responded by producing snakes of their own, but Aaron's snake ate theirs, signifying our victory over the enemies of the Most High.

Dodgy Dollars

Another parallel with ancient Egypt is the pyramid image on a U.S. one-dollar bill, accompanied by other occult symbols and a slogan declaring a New Order in 'Novus Ordo...'. The pyramid is also a favourite symbol of Freemasonry, indicating that secret societies run the UNITED STATES corporation, along with its servile bureaucrats in the various three-, four-, and five-letter agencies.

What else shall we say of this dollar bill? First, that being a 'fiat' currency made of paper or computer digits, it has no real value. Just as it is fraudulent to call legislation 'law', it is just as fraudulent to call this currency 'money', as it has no backing from precious metals. Both are counterfeit. As Mike Adams observes in a Mar. 12, 2024 broadcast,...

> "The dollar is a fraud. It's a currency backed by nothing and printed into oblivion by a government and a central bank that don't care about the common person, the worker, the saver, the producer. All they care about is having more power for themselves, and they create that power by printing money, which is a form of counterfeiting. They're stealing from you."

Inflation.

This theft occurs because central banks print currency to reward themselves and their conspirators first. Then, as the extra currency makes its way into circulation, it cheapens because, as basic economics dictates, the more plentiful something is, the cheaper it becomes. Thus, you will need more and more currency to buy things, meaning everything appears more expensive. You have inflation.

Inflation is therefore a form of taxation but a stealthy one because it enables governments to tax the people without them knowing. It is "legalized plunder," to quote G. Edward Griffin, famed author of *The Creature From Jekyll Island: A Second Look at the Federal Reserve.* Inflation, he told Maria Zeee in a March 2024 interview, is "manipulation of the money supply, and the legalization of that manipulation."

The Federal Reserve

Griffin's book sheds light on a massive banking conspiracy against the People, so let's talk about the 'Federal Reserve' which, as he told Zeee, "is not a government agency. It is a cartel of private banks, the biggest banks in the United States."

Griffin's assessment is underlined by the United States Court of Appeals, Ninth Circuit which concluded, in Lewis v United States of America (1982), that Federal Reserve Banks are "independent, privately owned and locally controlled corporations" (p.2).

As Griffin explains in a 1994 lecture, the Federal Reserve came into existence with the *Federal Reserve Act* of 1913. This gave us "a corporation, chartered by Congress, which was given an exclusive franchise to create the nation's money."

That so-called 'money' is conjured out of thin air when the Federal Reserve writes cheques to the U.S. government. It "springs into being precisely at the instant that the Federal-Reserve officer signs the check and gives it to the government." The government then writes cheques of its own, and the empty, meaningless dollars find their way into the private banking system and dilute the purchasing power of dollars already in circulation.

Yet how much worse has the currency printing become since Griffin gave his lecture some 30 years ago. Witness the explosion in M1, a measure of currency supply, that occurred in 2020 under the cover of COVID 'emergency'. Who, then, would disagree with Griffin's call to abolish the 'Fed', as it is called? He gives seven solid reasons...

1. It is incapable of achieving its stated objectives.
2. It is a cartel operating against the public interest.
3. It is the supreme instrument of usury.
4. It generates our most unfair tax.
5. It encourages war.
6. It destabilizes the economy.
7. It is an instrument of totalitarianism.

These traits describe central banks in general. To

quote author and Common-Law warrior Anna Maria Riezinger in a Mar. 19, 2024 article, they are...

> "useless, harmful, self-serving institutions, which do not promote peace, which do not prevent war, which do not serve humanity, which do not promote healthy economies, which do not enhance economic growth, do not improve financial stability, and do not do anything but purloin and trade upon other people's assets for their own benefit."

In *Meet Your Strawman*, David E. Robinson expresses a similar view:

> "As long as Private Central Banks are allowed to exist, inevitably—as night follows day—there will be poverty, hopelessness, and millions of deaths in endless World Wars, until the Earth itself is sacrificed to Mammon in flames. The path to true peace on Earth lies in the abolishment of all private central banking everywhere."

Fractional Reserve Banking

But the theft doesn't stop with the central banks, for now we come to the fraudulent yet 'legal' practice of 'fractional-reserve banking'. That's a big, intimidating phrase, isn't it? But all it means is that banks can lend out multiples of the amounts they have on deposit.

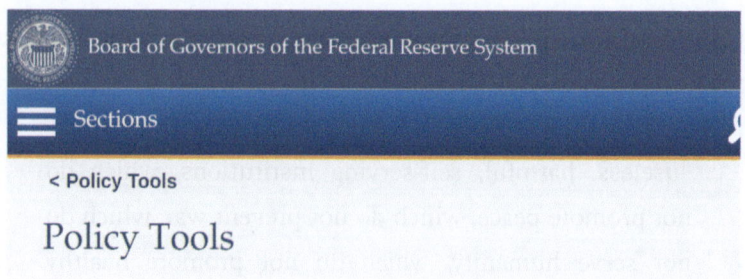

Policy Tools

Reserve Requirements

As announced on March 15, 2020, the Board reduced reserve requirement ratios to zero percent effective March 26, 2020. This action eliminated reserve requirements for all depository institutions.

For instance, if the 'reserve requirement ratio' (RRR) is 10%, banks can lend out $100 for every $10 held in deposits. Imagine renting a storage unit in a facility that can rent out 90% of your belongings during your absence. That would be a deal-breaker, but banks do something like this, inviting the danger of bank runs when customers decide to withdraw their deposits en masse at the same time.

The RRR for U.S. banks was ten percent until, effective Mar. 26, 2020, under the cover story of 'COVID', the Fed reduced it to zero, eliminating reserve requirements entirely for all depository institutions. This was the death knell for the dollar, and demolition by design. Now, banks could lend out a trillion dollars with only a penny on deposit or nothing at all. Now, a bank's only concern when making loans is the creditworthiness of the borrower, and even that doesn't really matter because there is never a real loan in the first place. A bank need only add digits to a customer's bank account and call it a loan, without risking anything, but then the hapless customer must generate currency by his own toil to make payments which are falsely called 'repayments'.

This explains why financial institutions keep falling over themselves to make loans in times of high default. It didn't make sense to me before, but when you consider that banks collect handsomely on pretend loans that are really risk-free, and collect even more handsomely when people fall behind and have to pay additional fees, and then get to seize real assets from those who end up defaulting, it makes perfect sense. It paves the way for a few megacorporations to eventually own all assets and then rent them out to us at monopolistic prices.

Engineered Collapse?

Fiat currency "destroys every country that used it," in the words of Bill Ogden of tacticalcivics.com, interviewed by broadcaster Sarah Westall in June 2024. Back around the turn of the century, I was telling anyone who would listen that the dollar was going to collapse. Somehow, more than 20 years later, it's still limping on, but after the insane currency printing—euphemistically called 'quantitative easing'—and genocidal reserving practices ushered in with COVID, the end is surely nigh.

By now, the voices predicting dollar collapse are a swelling chorus, including Mike Adams who said in a February 2024 episode of *Situation Update*, "The systems are breaking down... Banks are going to go down, deposits are going to vanish, nations will fall." The pain will be heightened, he notes, as the dollar loses its footing as the world's 'reserve currency'.

In our lifetimes, the U.S. dollar has been the main medium of exchange for transactions between nations, but that status is eroding rapidly, especially with the emergence of a commodity-backed BRICS currency for international settlements and after Saudi Arabia announced on June 9, 2024 that it would not renew its 50-year-old agreement to trade oil exclusively in the dollar.

This means there is even less need for other nations to hold the currency, leading to increased dollar supply and accelerated decline. Then, because Americans will need to come up with more dollars to buy goods produced in other nations, domestic inflation will ramp up even more.

So the question now is not whether the dollar can be saved—too late for that—but where we go after its demise. Can we plan for honest money and transactions the other side, or will we get drawn into an even more dystopian future where worthless paper is replaced by worthless digits that can be centrally surveilled and controlled?

CBDCs

That's the dystopian nightmare presented by central-bank digital currencies (CBDC), where all transactions are conducted online using digital tokens distributed by a country's central bank or even a global central bank.

Then, without the Privacy of cash transactions, everything you buy or sell, everything you own, and everywhere you go, can be tracked and traced and linked to other information about you, such as biometric data and your medical history.

Tyrants would also have free rein to reward your behaviour and speech with extra digital spending tokens if they are pleased with you, or penalize your behaviour and speech if they are displeased, and to punish you for refusing medical directives. They could levy taxes, fees, and fines against you on a whim and give you no recourse, and if you are very naughty, cut off your funding entirely with the press of a button.

We have already seen how puppet governments and puppet banks are willing to dish out financial punishment on a whim. It was shocking to hear Canadian finance minister Chrystia Freeland announce on Feb. 14, 2022 that she would freeze the bank accounts of Canadian truckers protesting medical coercion, but I found it even more disturbing that all the financial institutions immediately obeyed her without question. Those spineless bankers presented their oiled rectums to the Canadian regime without one shred of regard for the trust placed in them by their customers to protect both their assets and their Privacy.

So, having witnessed the predatory behaviour of banks in collusion with governments, can we be in any doubt that they would seize on CBDCs as a new and devastating weapon of control?

Another benefit of CBDCs for the cabal, as pointed

out by Si the Spaniard, is that they memory-hole the former role of cash as a receipt for precious metals. "By getting rid of cash," he told the Red Pill Day conference in 2023, "they're getting rid of the last bit of evidence that they owe all this gold back to the people." CBDCs are also "the perfect mechanism for them to transact whatever money laundering they want, and no-one can really get to look at it."

Worse yet, if the parasite class can homogenize their digital tokens across nations, all the distinct national currencies will be collapsed into one currency to rule them all. This is another Tower of Babel. That Old-Testament building project was thwarted when the Almighty fractured the world's single language into various tongues, for it meant that the builders could no longer work together (*Genesis* 11:1-9), but now the 'globalists' seek to impose on Mankind one worldwide financial language.

You don't have to take my word for it. On Oct. 19, 2020, Augustin Carstens, the human toad heading the Bank for International Settlements, said, "A central bank will have absolute control under rules and regulations that will determine the use of that expression of central-bank liability, and also we will have the technology to enforce that."

If such a system of financial coercion is implemented, then medical coercion will intensify along with it, as Clayton Morris warns in a December 2023 episode of *Redacted News*:

"You'll have no choice but to either get the vaccine, or we turn off your money supply. You'll not be able to go through a tollbooth, you'll not be able to get on an airplane, you'll not be able to go into this building, you won't be able to get on the subway because, when you scan your digital ID, 'Oh, you didn't get your vaccine, so we can't let you on the subway.' "

The implementation may require some "triggering event," according to former Pfizer executive and now whistleblower, Mike Yeadon. In March 2024, he told a meeting of Medical Doctors for COVID Ethics International that a financial crisis would be engineered to "destroy all sovereign currencies and steal all private wealth, then you'll have total dependency upon the state if you haven't got your own resources."

Even worse than the no-jab no-job decrees issued during COVID, the tyranny would expand to "No jab, no food; no jab, no money; no jab, no job; no jab, no travel. Your CBDC will simply not work." When you become a QR code, Yeadon adds, "You lose your humanity."

His answer? "We're not fucking taking digital ID. I would rather go to my grave as an analogue man than take digital ID."

So, when *Solari Report* founder Catherine Austin-Fitts calls CBDCs a "digital concentration camp," she's not exaggerating. Ultimately, they want to have us all carrying trackable devices under the skin, perhaps fulfilling end-time prophecy where a beast out of the Earth "forced everyone, small and great, rich and poor, free and slave, to receive a mark on his right hand or on his forehead, so that no-one could buy or sell unless he had the mark..." (*Revelation* 13:11-18).

This is the mad vision of 'globalists' such as Yuval Noah Harari, lizard sidekick to Klaus Schwab in the World Economic Forum, who said in October 2020,...

"Maybe in a couple of decades, when people look back, the thing they will remember from the COVID crisis is, this is the moment when everything went digital, and this was the moment when everything became monitored, that we agreed to be [surveilled] all the time, not just in authoritarian regimes but even in democracies, and maybe most importantly of all, this was the moment when surveillance started going under the skin."

Harari even fantasized that such technology could have informed him he was gay before he discovered it for himself. Think of the possibilities. Just in case teachers haven't managed to persuade little children that they're gay or even trans, embedded AI technology could do it for them!

How, then, shall we prevent digital slavery? Our best hope is for mass non-compliance from a populace aware of the genocidal schemes in play. But then again, we may observe with dismay how many people went along with absurd COVID requirements and still go along with Constitution-crushing humiliation rituals at airports, how many fail to notice the sticky white trails in the sky above, how many buy listening devices to use in their own homes, and how many still look for a political saviour who will make all the bad stuff go away. We may even shudder to recall the bad things our fellow creatures wanted to do to us when we called into question government solutions to a purported emergency before.

And governments, of course, have a long track record of manufacturing emergencies, using them as a pretext to unleash violence, trample our Rights, and gin up fear to squelch dissent. It's how the U.S. feeds its war addiction, unleashes bioweapons on the People, and pursues its diabolical 'green' agenda.

The financial arena is as vulnerable to such tactics as any other. For example, in his Mar. 4, 1933 Inaugural Address during the 'Great Depression', then U.S. president Franklin D. Roosevelt declared the United States "a stricken nation in the midst of a stricken world" and called on Congress to grant him "broad Executive power to wage a war against the emergency, as great as the power that would be given to me if we were in fact invaded by a foreign foe."

Just two days later, he issued Proclamation 2039 announcing a four-day suspension of banking transactions. During that suspension, Congress passed the *Emergency Banking Act*, which FDR signed on Mar. 9, 1933. The Act effectively stripped gold backing from U.S. banknotes.

I looked at the Congressional Record surrounding this legislation and got a sense of the bewildered haste with which this rubber-stamp Congress did FDR's bidding, and of the flattery and deceit some House representatives exhibited. Among them was Congressman Martin Smith from Washington State, the epitome of a ring-kissing sycophant...

"I shall vote for this measure, although I should like to have had an opportunity to study and consider its provisions. It has not been possible to do this, owing to the fact that the Bill has merely been read to us by the clerk this afternoon on the opening day of this special session without our being furnished copies thereof, and the Bill not being subject to amendment and only 40 minutes allowed for debate. This is a most extraordinary situation. However, we are advised by President Roosevelt in his message which has just been read, that the immediate passage of this legislation is absolutely necessary in order to reopen the banks in the nation and provide them with additional and adequate currency. We are further informed by our distinguished majority leader, Mr. Byrns, that the Senate is now awaiting the action of the House on this particular Bill, and that in order to reopen the banks of the country tomorrow, it must be enacted into law today. I shall therefore vote for the Bill, Mr. Speaker, because of these assurances of our great president and our able leaders in this body."

— MAR. 9, 1933 — VOL. 77, PART 1, P.82

Next to chime in was Texas Congressman, John Patman...

"The money will be worth 100 cents on the dollar, because it is backed by the credit of the nation. It will represent a mortgage on all the homes, and other property of all the people of the nation./ The money so issued will not have one penny of gold coverage behind it, because it is really not needed. We do not need gold to back our internal currency. We only need gold to settle our balances with foreign countries. Our people do not actually use gold as a medium of exchange; paper money is just as good and is much easier to handle" (p.83).

What a bone-headed assessment! Paper was paper, Patman was saying, whether it was backed by gold or not. But Minnesota representative Ernest Lundeen opposed, complaining, "we therefore have the spectacle of the great House of Representatives of the United States of America passing, after a 40-minute debate, a bill its Members never read and never saw, a bill whose author is unknown." The legislation, he warned, would further concentrate money and credit control in the hands of those already holding power.

"I want to put myself on record against a procedure of this kind and against the use of such methods in passing legislation affecting millions of lives and billions of dollars... I am suspicious of this railroading of bills through our House of Representatives, and I refuse to vote for a measure unseen and unknown. I want the record to show that I was, and am, against this bill and this method of procedure; and I believe no good will come out of it for America."

— MAR. 9, 1933 — VOL. 77, PART 1, P.83

Well, Representative Lundeen, you were right. No good did come out of it, and now, almost a century later, let the record show that you opposed it.

Within a month of railroading the *Emergency Banking Act,* FDR signed Executive Order 6102 on Apr. 5, 1933, requiring the People to surrender their gold by May 1 to the Federal Reserve.

POSTMASTER: PLEASE POST IN A CONSPICUOUS PLACE.—JAMES A. FARLEY, Postmaster General

UNDER EXECUTIVE ORDER OF THE PRESIDENT
issued April 5, 1933
all persons are required to deliver
ON OR BEFORE MAY 1, 1933
all GOLD COIN, GOLD BULLION, AND GOLD CERTIFICATES now owned by them to a Federal Reserve Bank, branch or agency, or to any member bank of the Federal Reserve System.

Executive Order

This was a lordly scam. Those who complied were compensated at just $20.67 per troy ounce, but over the next year, as a Forbes article recounts, "the president then raised his official gold price to $35 per ounce." A nice earner for him, making the government a $2.8 billion windfall, but an appalling loss for the compliers who saw the value of their dollars fall by almost half in a year. It wasn't until 1974 that private ownership of gold coins, bars, and certificates was re-legalized by an Act of Congress signed by then president, Gerald Ford.

So, having marked down 1913 as a bad year for the States United (Sixteenth Amendment, income tax, *Federal Reserve Act*), we can do the same for 1933 with the *Emergency Banking Act*, bullion confiscation, and phenomenal currency devaluation.

Yet another milestone of financial tyranny came in 1971 when then president, Richard Nixon, took the U.S. off the gold standard entirely. This, according to Mike Maloney in Episode 9 of his *Hidden Secrets of Money* series, was "an unprecedented act of global debasement by a wanna-be emperor that would make any Roman ruler hang his head in shame."

We have been talking about the U.S. dollar, but the currencies of other nations are just as fraudulent. Britain too was gripped by a purported 'national emergency' in 1931 which led to rushed passage of the *Gold Standard Amendment Act*, a "temporary" measure to suspend the Gold Standard. That "temporary" measure is still in place today!

Nor is there safe haven in swapping one form of fiat currency for another. As financial consultant Jim Willie told *SGT Report* in a June 2024 interview, "All the major forex currencies are dollars with different jackets on, because they're all debt-based, upside-down, fiat, toilet-paper currency designed to fail."

I don't expect salvation from the emergent BRICS currency either. Though it is based on commodities, including gold, it is still a digital currency, and centrally controlled under the auspices of the Satanic Bank for International Settlements, sometimes called 'the central bank of central banks'. BRICS is therefore a convenient mechanism for world authorities to reward compliant behaviour and penalize dissent. It does not, to the best of my knowledge, have a cash version, but if you know different, or you have at some point held a 10-BRICS note in your hand, please let me know at the email address at the end of this book.

Meanwhile, there are yet more financial weapons aimed at us including bank failures, bank runs, and the ultimate horror of bank 'bail-ins' where they just help themselves to the contents of your account. There is precedent for this. *Solari Report*'s 2016 publication, *State of Our Currencies – Chronology* lists for Mar. 16, 2013:

"In Cyprus, depositors drain cash from ATMs after European officials rule that part of a 10-billion-euro bailout must be paid for directly from the bank accounts of ordinary savers. An emergency deal in Brussels sets a levy of 9.9% on Cypriot bank deposits of more than 100,000 euros and 6.75% on less."

A bail-in scenario is also discussed in a Nov. 9, 2022

meeting of the U.S. Federal Deposit Insurance Corporation (FDIC) in a widely shared but since suppressed video clip. After all, our supposed 'deposit' with a bank is not really a deposit at all but an unsecured loan to the bank on which it may default at any time with impunity.

So, just in case our fellow creatures don't stand with us next time a crisis is concocted, what can we do to avoid the impoverishment and slavery planned for us? That is my theme in the next chapter.

5

SILVER LININGS

The Lord abhors dishonest scales but accurate weights are his delight.

— *PROVERBS* 11:1

You may find the idea of currency collapse alarming, but consider the liberation it may bring. When tyrants can no longer buy off politicians, spew propaganda, devise new weapons, fund wars, take over farmland, and construct diabolical infrastructure, all while poisoning our air, water, land, food, and bodies, then may our creative energies be renewed and released, and our endeavours find their due reward. When they can no longer get away with stealth taxation through fake currency production, we may suddenly find ourselves enjoying a level of prosperity unimaginable before.

Mike Adams is looking forward to this outcome too, saying in a Mar. 15, 2024 broadcast,...

"The BRICS nations want to trade in things that are real. They want to buy and sell commodities, fertilizer, food, oil, energy, things that are real, things that actually drive economies, whereas the Western countries, they just want to pretend. They want to live in their fairytale land and pretend like everything's good, just print money and hope that that can last forever, which it won't, and they want to have fake news, fake elections, fake policies, fake science, fake medicine, fake pandemics, everything.

That whole system is going to collapse, and thank God, by the way. Thank God it's going to collapse, and the fake currency will also collapse. So the collapse of the dollar is coming, and it can't happen fast enough as far as I'm concerned. The collapse of the dollar will be an event worth celebrating in terms of helping to set people free all over the world. Granted, there's going to be some short-term suffering. A lot of people will lose their life savings because they're gullible enough to believe in the dollar, believe in the government, believe in the Treasury."

The question is how we get through the transitional chaos that will follow financial implosion. To which I answer, look at how precious metals took centre stage following previous collapses. During the Great Depression, according to bullion trader Andrew Sleigh in an August 2024 interview with Dr Rima Laibow, "People bought city blocks for a couple of ounces of gold, and that is the ultimate way to realize the future value and gain in having metal. You got a house at that time for somewhere between 50 and 65 ounces of silver."

In terms of precious-metals prices at the time of writing (September 2024), that would mean buying a city block for about US$5100 and a house for less than $2000. In other words, gold and silver are super cheap now compared to their purchasing power in time of collapse. Sleigh calls them "the ultimate exit... when this whole system breaks. Everybody is broke except for the people sitting with metal, and your purchasing power of the metal is going to go through the roof on these other assets."

Silver

Further historical examples are provided by precious-metals analyst David Jensen in a May 2024 appearance on *SGT Report*. In ancient times, he noted, one-third of an ounce of silver bought a day's skilled labour. That would make an ounce of silver worth some $1500 today, Others assert that a day's skilled labour could be bought for just one-tenth of an ounce, making a silver ounce worth about $5000 today.

Either way, today's spot price of just over $30 is, again, super cheap. More recently, in Venezuela, a month's supply of food could be purchased for one ounce of silver. Jensen also points to the 2002 currency collapse in Argentina, after which food markets opened up in the streets and traded with individual links of gold necklaces.

So this raises the question about whether to hold gold or silver. Traditionally, gold is used for big-ticket items such as land, houses, and cars, and silver for more everyday items such as groceries and gas. If you don't have much cash to spare, then starting with silver is an easy entry point.

Silver is also historically cheap compared to gold. At the time of writing, an ounce of gold is trading at more than 85 times the price of an ounce of silver. If you take a look at the chart below, which tracks the ratio back to 1970, you will see this is close to the peaks around 100x that were briefly touched in 1991 and 2020.

Now look at the ratio's historical low of around 15x at the close of 1979. If the gold-silver ratio went that low again for today's gold price, silver would now be around $170 per ounce. I have also heard that, in ancient Egypt, the ratio went as low as 2.5x, which would put silver at more than $1,000 per ounce today. Either way, today's $30 appears... super cheap!

TIME FRAME / ERA	Sell 1 oz Gold Bullion	To buy X oz of Silver
Menes, Egypt 3200 BC	1	2.5
Egypt, 2700 BC	1	9
Hammurabi, Mesopotamia 2700 BC	1	6
Egypt 1000 BC	1	10.0
Croesus, Lydia 550 BC	1	13.33
Persia under Darius, son of Hystaspes (father of Xerxes)	1	13.0
Plato, ca. 445 BC	1	12.0
Xenophon (in Persia)	1	11.66
Menander, ca. 341 BC	1	10.0
Greece, ca. 300 BC	1	10.0
Rome, 207 BC	1	14.5
Rome, 189 BC	1	10.0
Rome, 40 BC, Julius Caesar	1	7.5
Rome, Claudius	1	12.5
Constantine the Great	1	10.5

Gold/Silver ratio in ancient times. Source: SD Bullion

Now, add to that the observation of monetary historian Dave Silver, interviewed by Richard Vobes in

May 2024, that there is "a huge shortage of silver... This is the first time in history now that silver is more rare than gold in available supplies. It's never happened before." He also asserts silver mines are becoming depleted. Moreover, because silver is so widely used in electronics, telecoms, and solar panels, the tyrants could never hope to lock it all away beyond the reach of the People. Taking all this into account, holding silver seems a no-brainer.

Precious metals can be bought and held as bars or coins, and bars start as small as one gram. When I was living in England, I bought precious metal from bullionbypost.co.uk, and when in the States, from treasureislandcoins.com. (I don't have an affiliate arrangement with either.) American eagles are a popular coin for gold, the smallest unit being 1/10 troy ounce and about the size of a dime. Or you can purchase bullion and have it stored in a vault.

Having some cash on hand is also a good idea. Under *United States Code,* "United States coins and currency (including Federal reserve notes and circulating notes of Federal reserve banks and national banks) are legal tender for all debts, public charges, taxes, and dues" (Title 31, Section 5103).

Some say, "Cash is king." Well, it does give you Privacy in transactions and, in a scenario where banks are shuttered and ATMs no longer work, will give you some short-term purchasing power before the realization takes hold that it's worthless. But to call cash 'king' is ultimately absurd because it's just paper with various numbers printed on it. Rather, gold is king, silver is queen, and cash is an impoverished duke, but he's still better than CBDCs, which are a usurping tyrant.

Goldbacks

My favourite currency option, combining the supremacy of gold with the Privacy of cash, is the goldback, which came into being in 2019. Using novel technology, the goldback sandwiches a precise weight of 24-karat gold between two layers of polymer. The smallest denomination, a one goldback, contains 1/1000th of a troy ounce; the largest, a 50-goldback, contains 50/1000ths. The notes between are 5, 10, and 25.

They're beautiful to look at, and each has a unique serial number. Their market price tends to over-correlate to the price of gold, meaning that when the price of gold rises, goldbacks rise more. When the price of gold falls, goldbacks fall less. At the time of writing, goldbacks are trading at 5.27 U.S. dollars each, making the market price about double the spot price of the gold they contain. This makes sense, given the costs of production and design.

When I began buying goldbacks in May 2023, the dollar price per goldback was about $3.70, meaning the value has increased by more than 40% in a little over a year.

You can also get a vertical wallet to keep your goldbacks so that you don't have to fold them. They are a good option for travel too. Though I have sometimes been questioned about silver bars in my hand luggage, my goldback wallet has never been flagged. If you're traveling with gold or silver coins, it makes sense to mix them in with a bag of regular change.

UPMA

If you want to buy goldbacks to hold, I do have a referral link at Geni.us/Goldbacks (no www). I also value the ability to vault goldbacks for free with the Utah-based United Precious Metals Association (UPMA) and to 'lease' some of them to gain interest. You can liquidate your vaulted goldbacks into U.S. dollars, have those dollars transferred to a regular bank account, and withdraw them at an ATM with a Truelink Visa card.

Another key benefit of this vaulting facility is that you can transfer goldbacks between UPMA members, and buy online from merchants. For example, one of my friends is a baker and fellow UPMA member. When I want to buy bread from her, I can simply transfer goldbacks online.

UPMA does not practice fractional-reserve banking. Its membership's holdings are 100% reserved in the vault, which is audited four times a year. My referral link if you want to join UPMA is Geni.us/UPMA (no www).

These innovations come at a time when legal frameworks at the State level are becoming more friendly to precious metals. According to a May 2024 newsletter from Alpine Gold, the parent organization of UPMA, by then 23 States had recognized gold and silver as legal tender in physical or electronic form, with other States poised to follow.

In the same month, the U.S. House of Representatives passed the *CBDC Anti-Surveillance State Act* (H.R. 5403) which "halts unelected bureaucrats from issuing a central bank digital currency (CBDC)—which would threaten Americans' right to financial privacy—without explicit authorization from Congress." However, the legislation does not forbid CBDCs outright.

Crypto

And what of cryptocurrencies? I dare say many of my readers have at least dabbled in them, and so have I, but my heart is not in it. My first objection is their complexity. When Christ told us his yoke is easy and his burden light, why are we dealing with such baffling concepts as 'blockchain', 'distributed ledger', 'proof-of-work', or 'proof-of-stake'? And all of it to acquire something you cannot touch, feel, or see.

Intense surveillance is another problem. Bitcoin itself is massively corporatized and monitored, and the data collection before you can trade on crypto exchanges is brutal. As author and researcher Whitney Webb warned in a May 2024 interview with Jimmy Dore, "A lot of people have been talking about CBDCs—central-bank-issued digital currency—but there's also going to be digital currencies just as surveillable and programmable that are issued by the private sector and the Wall-Street banks, and that isn't being talked about enough."

So could Bitcoin be a trap? In July 2024, presidential candidate Donald Trump told a Bitcoin conference in Nashville, Tennessee that he wanted the United States to be "the crypto capital of the planet," and called Bitcoin "a miracle of human achievement." Well, he said similar about the "beautiful" vaccines he fathered, didn't he? But that didn't make it a good idea to take them.

I also heed the warning of Catherine Austin-Fitts, interviewed by James Delingpole in 2021, that crypto currencies are a ploy by the parasite class to have us buying up digital assets without bidding up the price of the real assets, such as land and natural resources, that they are quietly buying up in the meantime. Sneaky fuckers, huh?

Having said that, I take the point that no nation can counterfeit Bitcoin, so this property alone gives it utility. I was able to purchase some at a Bitcoin ATM in the States, and thereby avoid the extreme surveillance exacted by on-line crypto exchanges. You put in dollar bills and show the machine a QR code for your crypto 'wallet', so that it knows where to send the equivalent Bitcoin.

But after buying Bitcoin, it makes sense to swap at least some of it for 'privacy coins'. Monero is the most widely adopted privacy coin, while the qorts of Qortal and the pocketcoins of Bastyon appear to champion a freer financial future. Lode, at lode.one, is a crypto currency that tokenizes gold and silver that are held in audited vaults. Lode can be exchanged for physical delivery of the metal.

That's about all I have to offer on crypto. Others are far more adept and experienced in this, and they can take you further, but I am not convinced overall, certainly not when it comes to Bitcoin.

In Closing...

I should probably put a disclaimer somewhere in the book saying that I am not giving financial advice, to do your own research, that prices can rise and fall, etc. So consider that done. In any case, my primary purpose is not to maximize your investments but to minimize the cost of refusal when financial tyranny is attempted. Whether that means holding gold, silver, bars, coins, goldbacks, cash, or crypto is up to you, whether you hold or vault is up to you, and how you diversify among those assets, again, is up to you, but I trust you have heard the saying not to put all your eggs in one basket. In any case, we are learning new ways to embrace a freer financial future, and that is a godly endeavour if we are to "Come out of her, my people" (*Revelation* 18:4).

6

DEBT

"Slavery is now far worse than it ever was. They don't need chains, they just need debt… These are forms of slavery that just haven't got the taint of that name, but that is what they are."

— FRANCES LEADER, INTERVIEW WITH
JAMES DELINGPOLE, MAY 2024

Strap yourself in. If you thought taxation was a fraud, behold the deceit of debt. I'm not talking about borrowing from a friend or family member, though that, as Polonius says in Shakespeare's *Hamlet* (I.iii), is inadvisable…

Neither a borrower nor a lender be
For loan oft loses both itself and friend,
And borrowing dulls the edge of husbandry.

But purported lending by financial institutions is an entirely different thing. David E. Robinson puts it succinctly in *Meet Your Strawman*: "The money does not come out of the bank's existing assets as the bank is simply inventing it, and in reality the bank is putting up nothing of its own, except for a fictional liability on paper."

Thus, as observed by John Titus, creator of the BestEvidence channel, "When I lend you a thousand dollars, I'm charging you interest because I don't have possession of that thousand dollars. That's not the case with commercial banks. The bank is charging you interest on something that did not exist to begin with. That is not interest. That is taxation."

These debt arrangements desecrate the basic principles of Contract. A Contract requires giving something in exchange for something else of commensurate value, or 'Equal Consideration'. If you have a loan agreement with a bank, you are agreeing to give the bank future payments, but the bank is giving you nothing; it is only adding digits to your bank balance at no cost to itself. That's why they'll tell you they are "advancing funds" to you but won't say they are "loaning money." They know they aren't; they just want you to infer that.

Also, a Contract must be entered into knowingly by both parties with 'Full Disclosure', but you did not knowingly enter it because you were not informed that the bank was risking nothing, and that its extra digits were conjured from your signature alone. Contracts also require wet-ink signatures of both parties, not photocopied ones or rubber stamps but, as Robinson points out, "Corporations can't sign because they have no Right or Mind to contract since they are soul-less legal fictions." In summary, he says,...

> "A loan agreement is a contract and so there has to be full disclosure of all the details (which there wasn't), both sides have to put up something of equal worth (which didn't happen), and the contract has to be signed in wet ink by both parties (which the bank can't do)."

Mortgages are no different. You gift the bank the fruit of your labour to supply it with multiples of the fake currency you think you borrowed, and you do so from what's left after the government has extracted 80% of what you generated. If you default, the bank will seize your property by invoking unlawful statutes, and may even seize some of your possessions too. As photographer and justice warrior Jonathan Dow told Richard Vobes in a February 2024 interview, "While you're repaying the mortgage, you're just basically giving money back that the bank never gave you in the first place."

And what is debt anyway, when it is enumerated in fiat currencies? Even if I nominally owed a quadrillion dollars, I would still owe nothing of substance. Then, if governments go to CBDCs, trying to swap out dollars or pounds or euros with some digital token, the fiction is exposed all the more.

If you took out a loan in one of those currencies, then you were expected to pay instalments in that currency. The tyrants can't turn round and say, "Now you have to pay off your debt in fedcoin" or what have you, because that was never in your contract in the first place. The moment they do that, they confirm your debt is cancelled.

Even if they give their digital-only currency the same name as the prior paper currency and tell you they expect payment in the digital-only version, they are still in Breach of Contract because a currency that has been stripped of its paper component is a new currency, and you never agreed to make payments in a new currency.

Solutions

Meanwhile, what other solutions are at our disposal? Begin by observing whom your would-be extortioner is addressing. If it is an ALL-CAPS NAME, then it is not you. That PERSON is not known at your address. As Robinson notes in *Meet Your Strawman*, "The company invoicing the Strawman is hoping that you don't catch on to the fact that it is not you who is being billed."

Securitized debt?

It also helps to know if the bank has sold your supposed debt, i.e., 'securitized' it, turning it into a traded 'security'. This means some other institution has paid them a lump sum in order to take over receipt of your future instalments. The bank has effectively created a new counterparty for you without your permission. This is Breach of Contract and terminates the contract because you never agreed to make payments to that third party in the first place.

This is where Conditional-Acceptance strategies can come in, the rationale for which I discuss in *Know Your Lawful Rights*. By *conditionally* accepting the demands of corporate extortioners, rather than outright refusing, you are keeping things out of court because there is no controversy to trigger court involvement. And staying out of court is generally a good thing because the legal system is essentially an enforcement tool of the banking system. Even the word 'bench', where a judge sits, has the same origin as the word 'bank'.

Robinson suggests,...

"If a company starts demanding payment of large sums of money, you start by asking them to provide the 'accounting' for the deal. In other words, you are asking them to show in writing that they provided something of genuine worth as their side of the loan contract. As they invented the money as numbers in their books, with no real worth attached to those numbers, they are in deep trouble as they can't comply with your demand."

This approach is fortified by writing to the purported lender,...

" 'First, there is a need to verify the debt, so please send me a bill with a human signature on it. Also, I need to see the lawful, two-party contract supporting that bill.'

"As they can't supply either of those things, it kills the claim stone dead, so just keep insisting that they either supply those things or else stop bothering you."

He imagines the hypothetical case of a James Martin who has received a loan from Swindle Bank Inc...

"The bank will probably send a Statement of what it wants James to believe is the outstanding amount. James should return this with a polite note saying that a 'Statement' is not an 'Invoice', so would they please provide a signed 'Invoice' as requested. They will also probably send a photocopy of his Loan Application form, at which point James should write back and point out politely that it does not constitute a contract as it is only signed by one of the parties (himself) and he has asked for a copy of the Contract signed by both parties.

"The bank is likely to go silent at this point and stop corresponding with James. James should then write again, requesting that the necessary documents be sent to him within the next fourteen (or perhaps 28) days, and if that does not happen, then he will consider the [alleged] debt to be fully discharged.

"The bank will either remain silent or write back to say that the debt is fully discharged. If the bank tries phoning, then just tell them politely that you only wish to deal with this matter in writing, and hang up. If the bank remains silent for the stated period of time, then James should write back stating that, due to the bank's failure to provide the necessary evidence of a lawful debt within the reasonable period of time provided, that James now considers that the [alleged] debt is fully discharged, and ask the bank to confirm that in writing. The bank will normally write back confirming that the debt is fully discharged and that there is nothing owing, and if it does not do that, it will just stop asking for any further payments."

Another Conditional-Acceptance strategy comes from Si the Spaniard, speaking at a Bournemouth conference in January 2023,...

"You play a game. You play a game where you're using your knowledge of the fact that there is no loan. There never was. And so you offer to buy back the credit agreement, because in 97% of cases, they've sold that credit agreement, they don't have it. So what you do is, you offer to buy it... They sold it, which means it's already been paid off. The point is, they can't give it back to you. So when you're going to discharge a debt, or you want to wipe a debt off, what do you do? You offer to discharge it on condition they return the instrument to you, which you know they cannot do."

If a debt collector comes to your door, ask who they are working for. Is it for the original financial institution, or is it for some debt-collection company that has bought the alleged debt? If the latter, then the collection company has effectively paid *off* the debt! Tell them to provide Proof of any debt and a signed Contract with *them*, not the original 'lender', proving that you agreed to pay it to that collection company.

Also require a contract between them and the original creditor authorizing them to collect, including disclosure of any commission they will receive if they succeed. If they call, tell them to send any communications in writing because you will not discuss anything over the phone.

A 'Notice' is just an offer.

Bear in mind, too, that a 'Notice' is not a bill or an invoice. I have seen notices affixed to lamp posts, and on notice boards in shops, theatres, cinemas, clubs, churches, factories, schools, universities, hospitals, clinics, libraries, and in public parks. I have seen them scrawled on toilet walls, but none may compel me.

Robinson writes,...

"All men are born equal and so nobody has the right to command you, make demands of you, or force you to do anything. The most that anyone can do is to make you an offer to perform./ Even though they may say that it is an 'Order' or a 'Demand' or a 'Summons', it is in reality an offer which you are free to accept or not as you so choose."

He is echoed by Allegedly Dave who, in a 2023 conversation with Richard Vobes, likens the corporate/government/banking extortion process to a set of railway tracks that culminate in payment or punishment. "The trick is to not let them put you on those tracks." If you receive a 'Notice' in the post, it really means in Legal speak that they've sent you an Offer. "At that point, you're not on the tracks yet; they're making you an Offer... but there are ways of holding them at the Offer stage."

If things go to court, @Funnyfresh561 on TikTok advises asking the judge if anyone on the claimant/plaintiff side is required to have first-hand knowledge of the case. The answer has to be yes, otherwise any evidence or testimony brought against you is hearsay. Having a photocopy of a contract is not first-hand knowledge! Then request the court to ask the opposing party who among them has any first-hand knowledge. Chances are they are empty-handed.

Mortgages and 'Promissory Notes'.

When it comes to mortgages, the fraud goes especially deep. As Allegedly Dave told Vobes in another interview, when you sign a mortgage agreement, you create a 'Promissory Note' which has value as currency. After all, If a central bank can conjure currency out of thin air by putting numbers on a piece of paper and a meaningless "Promise to pay the Bearer on Demand," why shouldn't you or I?

If you take a look at Bank of England bank notes over time, you will see how even this empty promise has been rendered in shrinking fonts, so that now you need a magnifying glass to read it. The word 'pound', when it describes the currency, originates from 8th-century Anglo-Saxon England when a pound of currency meant one pound in weight of silver, equivalent to 240 silver pennies. You would need hundreds of pounds in currency today to buy one pound weight of silver, especially after you add tax, retailer premiums, and delivery costs.

When you write your Promissory Note, you effectively increase the national currency supply. Now, you might think it silly that you or I could put numbers on a piece of paper and call it currency, but the *Bills of Exchange Act* (1882)—which is mirrored by similar Acts in other countries—says we can because, according to Allegedly Dave, the Act equates a Promissory Note to cash.

I did not find the word "cash" in the Act, but Dave also quotes a 1969 court ruling in Fielding & Platt Ltd. v. Selim Najjar where then Master of the Rolls, Tom Denning, stated, "We have repeatedly said in this court that a bill of exchange or a Promissory Note is to be treated as cash."

I haven't located the original court document, but your mortgage lender takes the idea seriously. Dave explains, "They take the Promissory Note that you create when you sign that mortgage agreement, and then they sell it without you knowing... on the securities market." This means that, if you are ever in legal action against the

Know Your Financial Rights

bank, they won't be able to produce their Contract with you.

So we have at least three official confirmations that, yes, you and I can write cash into existence with a Promissory Note: the *Bills of Exchange Act*, the Denning statement, and the fact that mortgage lenders themselves treat them as cash.

Knowing this, let's review the multiple payments banks receive through the mortgage game: not just your hard-earned interest payments on the empty digits they added to your bank balance, which will amount to multiples of the original principal, but also the value of your Promissory Note, which the bank will typically sell in the securities market.

Then, if you 'default' on your mortgage, the bank doesn't mind a bit because it still gets paid from insurance it takes out against defaults. Now, the bank gets to evict the home-buyer and take over the asset, which it can then sell to someone else.

Dave has calculated that, for every £100,000 of principal in mortgage loans, banks make £1.8 million, whether you 'pay it back' or not! As Vobes comments, "No wonder they want to keep on building houses... It's a bloody fraud, and you've been taken for a ride all along."

Dave is a developing a 'Mortgage Project' to turn the tables on the banks with a Promissory-Note strategy. He is creating "an instrument that they can't resist" and invites those who want to get rid of mortgage debt to email him at dmurphy25@gmail.com.

One famous story with Promissory Notes comes from South African author and activist, Michael Tellinger. In a video recorded in 2014, he explains how he used four Promissory Notes to pay Standard Bank in South Africa some 800,000 rand. His template (at https://www. michaeltellinger.com/promissory-notes/) uses legally precise wording and can be adapted for your country.

In the example below, Tellinger has promised to pay monthly instalments of 500 rand but specified that the bank will need to come to his address to collect the payments. Then, knowing that the bank will sell this instrument, he has wisely added that, once the recipient is using it in financial trade—in other words, the Promissory Note is being used as a 'Negotiable Instrument—"such trade shall terminate the obligation herein."

Once the bank fails to collect its first payment, Tellinger assumes it is trading with his Promissory Note, ending his obligation. Beneath the video, he has posted detailed instructions, including the proviso that this is only to be used to pay banks and government departments, not people or ordinary businesses.

Essentially, all you need for a Promissory Note is to write an amount in numbers, the same amount in words, and a signature, as Dave Silver told Vobes in their May 2024 conversation. One strategy to deal with debt collectors is to write them a Promissory Note for the amount they are demanding, less five pounds. You then write your Note on a piece of paper, staple a five-pound note to it, laminate the whole thing if you can, and present that as your full payment.

The original NOTE is signed in BLUE INK

According to Allegedly Dave, banks are reluctant to refuse Promissory Notes because that would mean taking you to court, which would expose their game. And if they don't return Promissory Notes, it suggests they value them as a source of income.

Paying from the 'Cestui Que Vie Trust'.

Yet another way to deal with bills is to use the 'Cestui Que Vie Trust', an approach championed by Australian, Mike Holt, of Citizens Initiated Referendums (CIR) (at cirnow.com.au). (I dislike this use of the word 'citizen', of course. I also oppose calling legislation "law," which he and the CIR website do. Still, as they say in 12-Step groups, "Take what you want and leave the rest behind.")

First, let's do a quick review of the English *Cestui Que Vie Act* of 1666, which I looked at in *Know Your Lawful Rights*. Its title in archaic French, which was the dominant language used for legal documents in England at the time, means something like, "Whoever Is Alive." Spanning just two pages, the Act addresses what to do about the estates of missing persons "beyond the Seas or absenting themselves," and it determines that the missing person "shall be accounted as naturally dead" after seven years of absence if there is no proof that he is alive. Then his property would be handed over to a 'Reversioner', meaning the one to whom the property reverts, the one in line to receive it after his death.

This Act has been misapplied to us. We are deemed missing "beyond the Seas" and therefore legally dead, so each of us has been assigned an ALL-CAPS NAME such as that engraved on a tombstone. When we reached the age of seven, the banking cabal, which has somehow set itself up as 'Reversioner', took over our estates. Allegedly Dave explains, in a September 2024 interview with James Delingpole, "They've used this idea of everyone's dead to claim our shares of the country."

But the *Cestui Que Vie Act* also says that if the supposed dead man shall "returne againe from beyond the Seas" or prove to be alive, then he "may reenter repossesse have hold and enjoy" his property again. Furthermore, he may recover the revenues withheld from him, with interest, from the time the Reversioner took over his property.

So what happens between the date we were deemed legally dead and our coming declaration that we are really alive and ready to take up our rightful inheritance? This is where Trusts come in because those awfully nice banker types have been holding our Estates in Trust, hoping of course that we won't find out and that the day of our return shall never come.

So let's also do a quick review of Trusts, again distilling my analysis from *Know Your Lawful Rights*. A simple Trust has three parties, and can be illustrated using Charles Dickens' novel, *Great Expectations*. The protagonist, Pip, discovers he is the Beneficiary of a Trust that shall fund his transformation from a blacksmith's apprentice to a 'gentleman'. The Trust is administered by the lawyer, Jaggers, who is entrusted with parcelling out the benefit.

Jaggers, therefore, is the Trustee, but he is not

permitted to tell Pip who granted the Trust into existence in the first place—that is to say, who the Grantor, Settlor, Donor, or Trustor is. As that anonymity is a key plot point, I won't spoil it here.

When it comes to the Cestui Que Vie Trust, each of us has $100s of millions, according to the CIR website, but it has been "hidden from us by CEOs, Banks, Insurance Companies, Government, ATO, Courts, Federal Reserve etc., all of whom know the truth." So, Brothers and Sisters, we have a life-changing amount of property and back-pay due to us, and under the tyrants' own legal structure, our announcement that we are alive entitles us to repossess it.

Does this explain government actions in recent years? If millions of us got wind of our Cestui Que Vie entitlement, tracked down the Trustee, and declared ourselves to be alive and therefore the Beneficiary, the cabal would be overwhelmed and exposed. Rather than face this calamity, they could either inflate the currency into oblivion so that the payouts became meaningless, or vastly reduce the number of people in a position to say they are alive, or both.

In any case, we can still dip into the Cestui Que Vie Trust now to pay off any tax bill, utility bill, or bank debt addressed to the ALL-CAPS NAME because the ALL-CAPS NAME is the Title Holder of the Trust.

So how does it work? Back in the day when I was paid wages with slips of paper called 'cheques', the payer would write or print my name on the paper, followed by the sum to be paid, expressed both as numbers and again in words. They would sign it, date it, and give it to me, then I would take it to my bank and sign the back of it, called 'endorsing' the cheque.

Then I would hand the cheque to the bank teller who would pay it into my account, or give me the equivalent cash. The cheque would then work its way through 'clearing' until it removed the same sum from the payer's bank account.

Talking to Richard Vobes in January 2024, Holt explained that when you receive a bill from 'GovCorp', such as a Fine, Penalty Notice, Utilities Bill, Loan Statement, or Mortgage Statement, the format looks like a cheque because that's what it is, "a cheque drawn on your Cestui Que Vie Trust." Above the ALL-CAPS NAME on the bill is a bar code which, Holt claims, is "the access to your Cestui Que Trust bank account."

If, then, you use your private funds to 'pay the bill', you have effectively paid twice. So, instead of doing that, you endorse the cheque by signing it. Then, Holt continues, the GovCorp entity uses that information to get the funds from your Cestui Que Vie Trust. That endorsement could take the form shown on the CIR website, which I now reproduce with slight adjustments. Write on the bill IN BLUE INK...

THIS BILL/ OFFER IS ACCEPTED AS CASH FOR THE [DOLLAR/POUND/EURO] AMOUNT SHOWN HERE.

[Draw an arrow to the Amount Due]

NOW, TAKE IT BACK AND USE IT AS REMITTANCE
AND SETTLE THE ACCOUNTS.

Yours Honourably

[Your Name]

Named Estate Trust Title Holder (not the Trustee)

[Your Signature]

[Date]

Without Prejudice

Your endorsed cheque is now a 'Bill of Exchange', in
legal parlance, and legal tender. Holt attests the GovCorp
entity cannot refuse it because they are legally obliged to
accept it under a *Bills of Exchange Act*.

I have mentioned the *U.K. Bills of Exchange Act* (1882)
before, but all countries that have signed up to the
Uniform Commercial Code (*UCC*) have their own version of
it, according to Holt, and "if your country has a central
bank, it comes under *UCC* rules." Several such Acts are
linked at the CIR website, including Australia's, passed in
1909, and Norway's, passed in 1932. For the U.S., the
equivalent legislation is *UCC* Title 3.

The U.K. version of the Act states that a Bill of
Exchange "is dishonoured by non-acceptance" (43(1)),
after which "no presentment for payment is necessary"

(43(2)). Similarly, *UCC* states that if tender of payment is refused, the endorser's obligation is discharged (Title 3, Section 603(b)). In other words, the alleged debt is paid by your endorsed cheque, whether the GovCorp entity likes it or not.

Once a GovCorp entity receives your endorsed cheque, it can take it to a bank, along with all its other conventional cheques, and the bank will accept it as cash. Holt attests that this method has been used to settle large tax bills. In case the GovCorp entity resists, you can find templates for your follow-up letters at lipforms.com. You can email Holt himself at mike@mikeholtshow.com or mikeh@commonlaw.earth.

Though I question why you would give tyrant bankers, whose proclivity is to squander and steal, permission to take *anything* from your Trust Fund to pay their unlawful bills, I admit there is elegance and simplicity in the method. You regard any GovCorp bill you receive as a cheque awaiting your endorsement and treat it as such. You still get to limit the amount they can take, and it's a drop in the bucket compared to what you have in there. So it's up to you.

Utility Bills

Vobes himself used this endorsed-cheque method to pay a utility bill. When he received the next bill, he saw that the previous amount had been credited to him, but after he went public about this, the utility company refused to accept this method the next time. Still, they didn't send the document back to him, suggesting it is valuable to them. At the time of publication, Vobes is pressing on with his quest.

Your own meter?

But why pay at all? Kayles, founder of the Telegram group Free Energy Nationwide, told Vobes in their November 2023 conversation that "utility bills are already pre-paid through our income taxes" and that so-called 'suppliers' are just middlemen operating as brokers between you and the National Grid. They only rent the serial numbers on energy meters in homes, but they don't own them, nor do they own any of the other infrastructure.

Members of Kayles' Telegram group hire a qualified engineer from her team to replace their meters or 'smart' meters (which communicate directly with a utility 'supplier'). The engineers install new and non-smart meters that are not attached to any database shared by the energy-broker network. "You're removing the meter that's in the property because you don't want to use a meter that the brokers have on their database."

For health reasons alone, it is essential to remove 'smart' meters from your dwelling because they emit harmful radiation. And don't fall for a supplier's/broker's claim that they have switched your smart meter to 'dumb mode'.

Once you have replaced your meter, "you have your own meter that you own," Kayles explains. You're not bypassing metering, but now, "You gain energy in exactly the same way as you did before; you just don't have to send meter readings anywhere." Then, you may want to get a safety certification done on your property. This will thwart any attempt by the corporate predators to force their way into your home on the pretext of safety concerns.

Meanwhile, you close your account with the broker. There are various ways to do this. As Kayles points out, you never had a valid contract with them in the first place, no Offer, no Agreement, and no wet-ink signature on either side.

The simplest procedure is to give final meter readings to the broker and close your account. You may choose to pay their final bill or not, depending on your situation. Ignore any subsequent letters addressed to 'THE OCCUPIER' or 'THE OWNER'. That's not you.

Of course, the powers-that-shouldn't-be don't like any of this and will try to make an example of a few, including what Kayles calls 'pantomime visits', where they show up with a purported Warrant to force-fit a prepayment meter. The Warrant, however, is typed up in a purely administrative procedure that omits any wet-ink signature from a judge. She continues,...

> "Every Warrant of Entry that I've seen in the last two years—and I've seen a lot—they're all the same, they're electronic, they're printed off or on little iPads. They don't tend to give you a copy because they don't want you to have them because they know they're invalid."

The Warrants aren't even addressed to the legal fiction of the ALL-CAPS NAME but to 'THE OCCUPIER'. They also purport to allow the 'operator' to enter your house but, as Kayles points out, the real operator is National Grid which doesn't send people round to your house, nor does it need to because it has already been paid. The 'suppliers'/brokers are billing agents, not operators.

The supporting cast of these pantomime teams may include an engineer and a locksmith who have forgotten they are personally liable if they proceed without checking the validity of any Warrant they are acting under. Just in case, you may want to add a solid bolting mechanism to the inside of your front door, along with other security precautions and, if you have an outside meter, change the lock on its casing. More information, documentation, and support are available on the Telegram group, Free Energy Nationwide, and I will have more to say about thwarting unwelcome visitors in the next chapter.

National Debt

Now, what of so-called 'national debt', and those debt 'clocks' with astronomically large numbers increasing at astronomical speeds? Is national debt really a thing? When currency is meaningless paper or digits, and will eventually be useless anyway, any debt enumerated in the currency is also zero. It's 'a fiction designed to enslave us and all future generations to paying off a fictional thing.

Seems to me debt clocks are a psychological operation designed to make you feel chained to a lifetime of servitude, but you and I signed no contract agreeing to take on this purported liability. National debt, if it exists, is what one corporation owes to another; it has nothing to do with us. And if it has been run up by politicians and bureaucrats, let them be the ones to pay it!

In Closing...

Imagine what prosperity would reign without the curse of debt, mortgages, bankruptcies, debt-collectors, repossessions, and so on. Of course, the banking cabal won't relinquish their power and control easily, but I trust this chapter has helped to fortify you for the battles ahead as we restore our Rights and Birthright. It boils down to this: If they want to allege a debt, they have to prove it, and they can't.

7

CONFISCATION

The mugger points a gun at your face and says, 'Your money or your life!', but the government says, 'We'll take both!'

— MIKE ADAMS, BROADCAST OF

MAY 22, 2024

You've likely heard the World Economic Forum's diabolical slogan, "You will own nothing, and be happy." It originated in 2016 but became widely quoted during the COVID years. The idea is hardly new, however, even in the West. In 1933, the U.S. Senate published a paper titled *Contracts Payable in Gold* that declared, "The ultimate control of all property is in the State; individual so-called 'ownership' is only by virtue of Government." The individual, it argued, was a "mere user," and use must be "subordinate to the necessities of the State" (Document No. 43 , 73rd Congress, 1st Session, p.13). Like I said, 1933 was a bad year for the States United.

Since then, the banking vampires have gone a long way to achieving their goal of universal dispossession through taxation, inflation, and debt but, to fully strip the People of the little they have left, confiscation is the final solution. Their ploys include whipping up climate-change fears in order to impose measures so costly and onerous that owners are forced to give up their property.

Their schemes will fail eventually, but before I describe how we turn the tables on them, let us address this Biblically first. Many prophecies spring to mind, but *Job* 27 will do for now to describe what shall befall the wicked...

Though he heaps up silver like dust
and clothes like piles of clay,
what he lays up, the righteous will wear,
and the innocent will divide his silver...
He lies down wealthy, but will do so no more;
when he opens his eyes all is gone.

A massive downward transfer of wealth is coming which will suddenly reverse the centuries of theft perpetrated against us, and it will take the tyrants by surprise. In the meantime, let us stand our ground, and stand with the likes of Jim Gale, founder of Food Forest Abundance. He didn't ask for government approvals to create his oasis of effortless food production at Galt's

Landing near Orlando, Florida. In a March 2024 interview, he told Mike Adams,...

> "We've now built 11 structures here, and we did not ask, nor will we ever ask, the slave-masters for permission... and we are saying 'No', we will not only not comply, but we will demonstrate a better way, and we will invite you to do the better way with us, but we're not going to do it your way."

If you haven't figured it out by now, governments and their puppet-masters want to starve, impoverish, deaden, and destroy "all that is true, all that is holy, all that is just, all that is pure, all that is lovely, and all that is worthy of praise..." (*Philippians* 4:8). That includes independent food production. Thus, they will invent or inflate disease scares to cull entire flocks of birds, herds of livestock, and colonies of bees, and they will call 'good' their evil agenda to bring sickness, famine, and despair on the People.

In *Know Your Lawful Rights*, I pointed out how the British government is telling everyone who has even a single chicken to register their birds, but they will call you the 'keeper', not the 'owner', of your flock. Remember that, whenever you register something, you are giving it away to the entity you are registering it with. After the British government issued its decree, *Farmers Weekly* dutifully echoed it with a short article that used the word 'keeper' eight times, but never the word 'owner'!

The state owns your car, too, and you get to rent it through registration and licencing fees. And even the Certificate of Title on your house is not the Title itself but an official document that certifies a Title exists. You do not have 'Allodial' Title, which would make you king of your land.

Even if you've fully paid off your mortgage, you still don't own your house, according to the bankers. They may call you 'Proprietor' instead, which is not the same thing or, as campaigner Peter Wilson told Richard Vobes in an April 2024 interview, 'Tenant'...

"Anybody that owns the house can go and check now. Get your Deeds, get them out, have a look at it, and it'll tell you point blank in black and white you are the tenant if you've paid your mortgage off, or even if you were lucky enough to actually have enough cash to buy that house outright—you've paid it off, you do not owe a penny—you are a tenant, that's all you are, a tenant on the land. You do not own it because it's all owned by the Crown. Therefore, it's all held in trust for them, but you can only be a tenant on the land."

A similar analysis is given by retired doctor K.L. in a May 2024 interview with *SGT Report*. "Your home, your car, everything is a publicly registered property. Your name is publicly registered when your birth is registered. So you're considered booty of war, along with the homes, along with all of the cars." The States United, he contends, have been under military occupation since

1933, a status confirmed by the use of gold-fringed flags in courtrooms. "You might as well think of them as military tribunals," he added.

Even your stocks and bonds are up for grabs according to David Rogers Webb, author of *The Great Taking*, who told Economic War Room (Episode 288) that you are legally severed from property rights in the case of securities and that you are essentially "an unsecured creditor to get your own securities back in the event of bankruptcy in the financial system... You have a claim but it's a weak claim in the event of insolvency."

Thus, the bankers have crafted a system that permits them to take risky bets and to win huge if the bet goes their way, but if the bet goes against them and they lose huge, your assets are their collateral. This has been going on since at least 1934, according to author Anna von Reitz in a June 2022 presentation. "Part of the evil was that they seized upon our gold and silver to pay their debts," she said. In 1934, the corporation calling itself the UNITED STATES OF AMERICA, INCORPORATED issued gold-bearer bonds against the People's gold, which was taken to the Philippines and placed in 'safe-keeping'.

They're after your intangible property too, your hopes and dreams. As an author trying to get out works true and edifying, I can attest to the dispiriting weight of bans and censorship and demonetization that are calculated not just to deprive readers of key information but to discourage creators and truth-tellers too.

Surely, all of this is illegal, you might say. Well, that depends on which legislation you're citing, for most legislation is an abomination, hateful in the eyes of Man and God, blasphemous to the Creator in whose image we are made. However, the Supreme Court of North Carolina spoke truth in its Hoke vs. Henderson decision of 1833, saying that when legislators "pass an act upon a subject upon which the people have said in the Constitution, they shall not legislate at all." The 'color-of-law' statutes in the *United States Code* also embody this principle.

Trusts

So what can we do? According to Si the Spaniard in a July 2019 presentation, Trusts can act as a "protective shield" that "ring-fence" your assets. As a Trustee doesn't hold 'Absolute Title' to a property in a Trust, and therefore cannot be said to own it, debt collectors cannot come after him. Nor can they come after the Beneficiary, because he doesn't hold Absolute Title either. He only holds Beneficial Title. Si continues,...

> "The property, for all intents and purposes, is kind of floating out there in the ether in terms of ownership. So it's very difficult to pin down who owns this property. Plus, of course, the Trustee is under no obligation to divulge who the Beneficiary is—in other words, who's entitled to this property. So what you have is a situation where property can be kind of shielded or masked, hidden in a kind of invisibility cloak."

By putting your assets into Trust, Peter Wilson

explained to Vobes in their April 2024 conversation, you remove them from the 'estate' of your ALL-CAPS NAME because the government cannot go after assets outside of that estate. You're basically saying to them, " 'You can't have something that's not mine.' "

A Trust contract is agreed between a Grantor and a Trustee, wherein the Grantor conveys legal title to a property into a Trust. The Trustee, who could be a reliable friend or family member, agrees to fulfil the specified duties and responsibilities of the Trust for the benefit of the Beneficiary. That Beneficiary could be you because you're the one who will travel in the car or live in the house.

Then, if you are ever the subject of bankruptcy proceedings, and a receiver asks why you have not listed your house or car among your assets, Wilson advises telling them, "That's in a Trust. It does not form part of my estate." He attests that this approach has a proven track record. It is also effective, he says, in thwarting local councils when they want to put your aging parent in a care facility and liquidate your family home to pay the exorbitant care-home fees.

Making a Trust, Wilson asserts, is not as daunting as it sounds. "All Trusts are just paperwork," he told Vobes. "You're doing it on a non-statutory basis, so you're not relying on any Acts or governments or parliaments or anything to do that."

As with every other approach I discuss in this book series, my preference is always to draw up my own documents and never to involve lawyers. If you pay someone to draw up a Trust for you, more caution may be warranted. Si the Spaniard argues the *Legal Services Act* (2007) deems paid Trust creation an activity 'reserved' to regulated practitioners such as barristers, notaries, or solicitors. Wilson, on the other hand, says lawyers betray your Privacy by registering your Trust with the false taxation authorities.

Collectors

But what if the thieves of Officialdom show up on your doorstep? I will focus especially on the U.K., but the analysis will be similar in your country. If a stranger comes to your door demanding payments or declaring their intention to seize your property, you wouldn't hesitate to send them away empty-handed, perhaps with a flea in their ear or even a "bloody good hiding" to reinforce the message. But somehow, the situation is perceived differently when uniforms, lanyards, and clipboards are involved. These are the props and costumes of the Theatre of the Legal, and they are trying to fool you into thinking you are in the same play.

As Vobes observes in a splendid rant about enforcement officers, "you've got to have no morals whatsoever, no ethics, of course, and bang on people's doors early in the morning, any old time, and demand money with menaces." Debt collectors go after the most vulnerable people, he continues, and give no Due Process to those they target, "and you don't need any paperwork, just bluff, just bluff your way through... and they're very threatening, and if you don't pay, the police turn up and end up aiding and abetting."

Thwarting Trespass.

The first line of defence, even before uninvited corporate intruders show up, is to put a notice on your front door or gate saying, "PRIVATE — BY APPOINTMENT ONLY." Such a notice is legally equivalent to a closed door, and it forbids a bailiff to enter your garden or driveway. It also gives you something to point to when you ask if they can read. You let it be known that you only see people by appointment, and they will need to contact you to agree a date and time. You will also let them know what you charge for your time if they want to take some of it.

Make sure to identify them too. Under *Criminal Procedure Rules* (2013), agents claiming court authority to seize property must, on request, show a written statement including their name, who they are working for, and Proof that they are authorised to execute Warrants (Rule 52.8). So have them spell out their name and their employer's name and demand their office phone number, and write down the information. Also, under the *Tribunals Courts and Enforcement Act (2007)*, "A person is guilty of an offence if, knowingly or recklessly, he purports to act as an enforcement agent without being authorised to do so..." (Section 63(6)).

A ploy often used by extortioners is to claim they are employed by a court when they are really working for a private company. If they make that claim, tell them to provide their court registration number. If they can't do that, they are guilty of 'fraud by false representation' under the *Fraud Act* (2006). According to Section 2 of the Act, an agent is in breach if he makes a false representation with the intention "to make a gain for himself or another," or "to cause loss to another or to expose another to a risk of loss."

Whistleblower Celeste Solum told Odessa Orlewicz in a March 2024 interview that she keeps a 'public-servant questionnaire' in readiness for any corporate interlopers that show up, requiring them to give their name, address, agency name, phone number, and two pieces of government-issued ID, which she then photographs. She asks them who will have access to any information she provides and on which computers the information will be stored. "These guys would come to my house and they would turn white," she told Orlewicz. "Their knees would start shaking, and they would almost wet their pants."

Also check their paperwork. According to The People's Lawyer, at thepeopleslawyeruk.com/, court bailiffs must have original court documents that include a case reference number, the court seal, and a legible wet-ink signature. We have already seen how so-called magistrates' courts in the U.K. rubber-stamp fake Liability Orders on an industrial scale for council-tax collection, meaning any paperwork coming to you likely won't meet these conditions.

Same goes for traffic fines, where fake Warrants are

churned out through centralized bulk processing without giving the extortees Due Process of Law, including the Right to a Fair Hearing. According to Vobes listener, Lizzie, corresponding with him in March 2024, you can call the Courts and Tribunal Service (HMCTS) complaint number on 0300 123 1057 to get a fake Warrant removed.

Police

If police are present, ask if they are there to see that no Breach of the Peace is committed, because a constable must arrest a bailiff for Breach of the Peace if, in the presence of the constable, he places the alleged debtor in fear of violence or harm. Also inform any police that they are required to check the identity and paperwork of your unwelcome visitors.

If the agent has claimed to be a court employee and doesn't have the certificate to verify it, or if he doesn't have a proper Warrant, the constable is required to arrest him for 'fraud by false representation' under Section 2 of the *Fraud Act*, as cited above. If it is a traffic-related claim, the *Road Traffic Act* (1991) also comes into play, where "Any person who is not a certificated bailiff but who purports to levy a distress as such a bailiff, and any person authorising him to levy it, shall be deemed to have committed a trespass" (Section 78(7)).

If a trespasser refuses to leave, the third refusal puts him in 'Aggravated Trespass', at which point you can remove him with reasonable force or order a constable to do so. If the agent is putting you in fear, they are committing Assault.

The police certainly have no business assisting bailiffs. As I pointed out in *Know Your Medical Rights*, under the *Criminal Justice and Courts Act* (2015), a British police constable who exercises his or her powers and privileges improperly is liable on conviction "to imprisonment for a term not exceeding 14 years or a fine (or both)." Under Section 26(4) of the Act, a constable's exercise of powers and privileges is improper when it is "for the purpose of achieving... a detriment for another person."

Quoting this legislation, another Richard Vobes listener named Derek points out it is illegal for police to assist anybody, including a debt-collection agent, bailiff, or enforcement officer, in debt collection. "A debt is a civil matter, and therefore not subject to police intervention. The police can only observe, and where a criminal offence has been committed and witnessed (allegations are not facts), arrest the offender. Otherwise, the police attendance is purely to keep the peace."

Derek also argues a car cannot be seized to pay a debt because the person against whom a debt is alleged is not the owner in the legal system, only the 'Registered Keeper'. The V5C registration document boldly states on the front page, "THIS DOCUMENT IS NOT PROOF OF OWNERSHIP."

THIS DOCUMENT IS NOT PROOF OF OWNERSHIP.
It shows who is responsible for registering and taxing the vehicle.
Registration Certificate translations

The tyrants want to have it both ways. It's not your car the rest of the time, but when it comes to paying off your alleged debts, now it *is* your 'vehicle', in effect a vehicle for revenue generation by the state. Therefore, if anyone wants to seize your car or any other asset to pay off your alleged debt, demand that they provide a Proof of Claim that you are the owner of whichever asset they want. That is difficult for them to do if documents list you only as a 'keeper' or 'tenant' , and impossible if the asset is in Trust.

As I noted in *Know Your Medical Rights*, the Constable's Oath in Britain, sworn by officers of every rank, is among the best police oaths in the world. Though it omits an important clause of forswearing membership in a secret society, it does swear to uphold "fundamental human rights" and the Law of the Land—Common Law—as it pertains to human rights.

This makes the crimes routinely committed by British police all the more egregious. They have become a legion of Oath-breakers, leading to the obvious conclusion that they are instead serving secret oaths, accompanied by conscience-killing rituals of atrocity. Therefore, they either avoid real criminals or conspire with them while devoting their empty little brains to terrorizing people who express inconvenient views on social media or who cause hurt feelings.

Forced Entry?

Forced entry into a debtor's home, whether by police or bailiffs, is utterly unlawful, of course, but it's illegal too. In Morris v Beardmore (1980), the House of Lords held that police officers have no implied authority to enter private property if the owner has explicitly forbidden them to do so, even to investigate a crime or take a breath specimen. Those that enter without permission are trespassers, and may be liable for any resulting damages or harm. The ruling quoted the finding of a lower court that "a trespassing constable ceases to be a constable in uniform."

Also be aware of the key distinction between a Warrant of Control and a Warrant of Entry, which agents are wont to conflate. As Stan, another Vobes follower explained, they are different documents that serve different purposes. A Warrant of Control authorizes an enforcement agent to take control of goods belonging to a debtor. A Warrant of Entry, on the other hand, is typically issued in relation to a criminal investigation; it authorizes a police officer to enter a property and search for evidence or to perform a particular action such as to arrest a suspect or conduct a search. Warrants of Entry are not typically used for debt-recovery cases. "So next time you get anyone claiming to have a warrant of control, be aware that this is not permission to enter your property."

Protective Court Precedents

Below, I list many more protective court precedents that I have taken from a 2016 Freedom-of-Information response from the U.K. Courts and Tribunals Development Directorate, part of HM Courts & Tribunals Service. These are echoed in a book-length article titled *The Council Tax Fraud*, published Apr. 11, 2023 by thepeopleslawyeruk.com.

- Debtors can remove implied right of access to property by telling him to leave (Davis v Lisle (1936), and McArdle v Wallace (1964)).

- A person, having been told to leave, is now under a duty to withdraw from the property with all due reasonable speed. Failing to do so, he is no longer acting in the execution of his duty and becomes a trespasser. Any subsequent levy is invalid and attracts a liability under a claim for damages (Morris v Beardmore (1980)).

- Officials cannot force their way into a private dwelling (Grove v Eastern Gas (1952)).

- An individual can use force to resist an officer from gaining entry (Weaver v Bush (1795), Simpson v Morris (1813), and Polkinhorne v Wright (1845)).

- An attempt at forcible entry despite resistance is wrongful (Ingle v Bell (1836)).

- Officers cannot apply force to a door to gain entry (Broughton v Wilkerson (1880)).

- An officer may not encourage a third party (such as workmen inside a house) to allow the officer access to a property. Access by this means renders the entry unlawful (Nash v Lucas (1867)).

- The debtor's home and all buildings within the boundary of the premises are protected against forced entry (Munroe & Munroe v Woodspring District Council (1979)).

- If a bailiff enters by force, he is there unlawfully (Curlewis v Laurie (1848), and Vaughan v McKenzie (1969)).

- If a bailiff jams his foot in the door, any levy that is subsequently made is not valid (Rai & Rai v Birmingham City Council (1993), Vaughan v McKenzie (1969), and Broughton v Wilkerson (1880)).

- A bailiff is not permitted to enter a property by improper means or by unusual routes (Ancaster v Milling (1823), and Rogers v Spence (1846)).

Having looked through these court precedents and legislation looking for crumbs of protection amid all the nasty legislated theft, I come away with a sick feeling at how rigged the game is and in imagining the trauma, torment, and stress suffered by those on the receiving end of these assaults. They demonstrate, however, the importance of heading off threats if possible before they get to the point of having thugs show up at your property.

In Closing…

I close this chapter by citing *Magna Carta* again: "We will appoint as justices, constables, sheriffs, or bailiffs only such as know the law of the realm and mean to observe it well" (Article 45). This puts to shame the legions of corrupt and unscrupulous order-followers pretending to inhabit these roles today. Ultimately, our power lies not in pleading with these psychopaths to be a little less unkind to us but in overthrowing them. If, after all the law, legal protection, and court precedent you can cite, they are still determined to be lawless, then the local community must rally to thwart them.

Remember that, as I showed in *Know Your Lawful Rights*, True Law presumes any arrest to be unlawful until the arrester proves otherwise. By the same logic, any trespass, break-in, or abduction is presumed unlawful. So, if you see a neighbour under siege by bailiffs or police, forget the uniforms, presume that the action is unlawful, and act accordingly. Neighbours, unite. Set up a low-tech alert system such as air horns to muster reinforcements.

Then, if the bandits show up, you've got the numbers to repel them, arrest them, and put the intruders and Oath-breakers on trial in Common-Law courts.

8

ANY TOP-DOWN FIXES?

Authority lies. That is what it does... Therefore, if you, Authority, are telling me, this is what the situation is, first of all, I'm going to take it immediately that you're lying to me. My next question is, why are you lying to me? And you will know the answer to that by seeing what they say is the solution to what they're lying to you about.

— DAVID ICKE, AUGUST 2024 INTERVIEW

Throughout this series, I have focused mostly on what we can do as individuals and communities to overcome the predator class now arrayed against us. Will we go to a walled-village model, setting up Common-Law republics that later cooperate across larger regions? Or can solutions be implemented at a State level or even a national level?

In the *Solari Report on Financial Freedom* (2023), former

U.S. Assistant Secretary of Housing, Catherine Austin-Fitts, lists 17 actions individual States can take to secure financial-transaction freedom, including the formation of a State bank that would support smaller, state-based financial institutions, small businesses, and farms. It would maintain reserves in gold and silver, and there would be no taxes on precious metals nor any restrictions on using cash. The State would reject any federal funding that comes with strings attached, and it would establish telecommunications and digital communications that are protected from federal and corporate surveillance and control.

Austin-Fitts also recommends States form regional compacts with neighboring States to improve food and energy supply and resilience, while facilitating local currencies and barter networks. Her final recommendation is to train state military and militias to provide support when financial-transaction freedom is threatened, while refraining from gun-control legislation.

And what about the mythical *National Economic Security & Reformation Act* (*NESARA*), of which we hear occasional rumours? According to Nancy Detweiler, in her widely circulated *History of NESARA* article of 2011, vast gold reserves are "now safely stockpiled at the Norad Complex at Colorado Springs, Colorado and four other repositories" to be used for a new currency backed by precious metals. In 1999, Detweiler asserts, a 75-page NESARA document...

"was submitted to Congress where it sat with little action for almost a year. Late one evening, on March 9, 2000, a written quorum call was hand-delivered by Delta Force and Navy SEALs to 15 members of the US Senate and the US House who were sponsors and co-sponsors of NESARA. They were immediately escorted by the Delta Force and Navy SEALs to their respective voting chambers where they passed the National Economic Security and Reformation Act."

Bill Clinton signed *NESARA* at gunpoint on Oct. 10, 2000, she asserts. On Sept. 11, 2001, then Fed chairman Alan Greenspan "was scheduled to announce the new US Treasury Bank system, debt forgiveness for all U.S. citizens, and abolishment of the IRS as the first part of the public announcements of NESARA," but this was thwarted by the '9/11' terrorism that unfolded that day. Since then, NESARA "remains in the background, ready to be announced."

On the face of it, the NESARA principles, as listed by Detweiler, sound like measures most of us can mostly agree on. I copy them below, then list my several objections to her narrative. NESARA...

1. Zeros out all credit card, mortgage, and other bank debt due to illegal banking and government activities. This is the Federal Reserve's worst nightmare, a "jubilee" or a forgiveness of debt.

2. Abolishes the income tax.

3. Abolishes the IRS. Employees of the IRS will be transferred into the US Treasury national sales tax area.

4. Creates a 14% flat-rate sales tax only on non-essential new items. Food and medicine will not be taxed; nor will used items such as old homes.

5. Increases benefits to senior citizens.

6. Returns Constitutional Law to all courts and legal matters.

7. Reinstates the original Title of Nobility amendment.

8. Establishes new Presidential and Congressional elections within 120 days after NESARA's announcement. The interim government will cancel all National Emergencies and return us back to Constitutional Law.

9. Monitors elections and prevents illegal election activities of special interest groups.

10. Creates a new U.S. Treasury rainbow currency [multi-coloured notes] backed by gold, silver,

and platinum precious metals, ending the
bankruptcy of the United States initiated by
Franklin Roosevelt in 1933.

11. Forbids the sale of American birth certificate
    records as chattel property bonds by the U.S.
    Department of Transportation.

12. Initiates new U.S. Treasury Bank System in
    alignment with Constitutional Law

13. Eliminates the Federal Reserve System.
    During the transition period the Federal
    Reserve will be allowed to operate side by side
    of the U.S. treasury for one year in order to
    remove all Federal Reserve notes from the
    money supply.

14. Restores financial Privacy.

15. Retrains all judges and attorneys in
    Constitutional Law.

16. Ceases all aggressive, U.S. government military
    actions worldwide.

17. Establishes peace throughout the world.

18. Releases enormous sums of money for
    humanitarian purposes.

19. Enables the release of over 6,000 patents of suppressed technologies that are being withheld from the public under the guise of national security, including free energy devices, antigravity, and sonic healing machines.

So here are my objections...

1. If this legislation was signed in 2000, and with support from some parts of the military, are we to wait another quarter of a century for its fulfilment?

2. Any top-down solution is suspect at this point. We are way past the point that the current form of Government, no matter who is in the White House or Downing Street, etc., has become destructive of Life, Liberty, and the Pursuit of Happiness, which is the trigger point for us to abolish it, according to the *Declaration of Independence*.

3. Government reform, even as broad and deep as NESARA appears to be, won't be a long-term remedy as long as Government remains in thrall to secret societies, which Detweiler doesn't even mention.

4. I find Detweiler herself to be an unreliable source, especially when she utters the

abomination that Clinton signed NESARA legislation "into law." Clueless!

5. If NESARA's implementers were truly our allies, they would not operate with the kind of secrecy and coercion that Detweiler describes, including the assassination of Senator Paul Wellstone in 2002. When so-called 'white hats' are extrajudicial assassins, where is regard for the Constitution?

6. In four places, the article calls for a return to Constitutional Law. We already have ten Lawful Amendments to the Constitution. What's lacking is not protective language but the observance and enforcement of it.

7. Principle 17 calls for "peace throughout the world." What possible objection could I have to that? Well, one-world government is a kind of peace, isn't it? But it's not the kind of peace you or I would want to live under.

As I discuss in *Know Your Medical Rights*, the devil masquerades as an angel of light, and his servants masquerade as servants of righteousness (2 *Corinthians* 11:14). Bible prophecy warns us too about...

- a king of fierce countenance who "by peace will destroy many" (*Daniel* 8:23-25);

- false prophets and wolves in sheep's clothing; fake signs and wonders to deceive "even the elect, if that were possible" (*Matthew* 24:24); and

- an alliance of two Beasts who will work together to exert totalitarian rule in a global good-cop/ bad-cop scenario (*Revelation* 13:11-18).

Bear in mind that most of the reassuring conspiracy narratives out there are designed to lull us into a false sense of security, imagining someone else will make all the bad stuff go away, so that we can be complacent again. That's not the mindset of a sovereign. I expect a change of administration in D.C. will change nothing but the paint on the door. Yes, there'll be some cosmetic window-dressing, some headline-grabbing resignations, firings, and exposures, maybe even a few anemic prosecutions, but these are the trappings of a fake saviour. After a brief honeymoon period, some new emergency will be concocted that fires up the juggernaut of tyranny assembled over the past century and more.

Ultimately, whether from a grassroots level, State level, or national level, the restoration of honest money is essential, not just for prosperity but for justice. I say "restoration," but in reality, it is hard to find any place in history where honest money was a thing. And if it was a thing, it was short-lived, for corruption in the hearts of men would always debase currencies and fractionally reserve, tax and inflate, and wage war and stage pandemics and engineer perpetual emergencies and crisis, all to siphon yet more wealth from the People.

In Closing...

I close out this chapter with the following encapsulation by British author and songwriter, Dominic Frisby, in a March 2024 conversation with James Delingpole. Having observed that the British pound lost one-third of its purchasing power during 'COVID' alone, he adds,...

> "It's nuts. While we have shit money, nothing is going to change... While a government has the power to create money at no cost to itself—which is the case in every single Western country—it is inevitable that that body will grow disproportionately large. Everyone else has to struggle to make money. Governments can just print it, they're given too much power."

True, Dominic. Through taxation and inflation, we feed the monster that feeds on us; we fund our own demise.

CONCLUSION

I, Mr Banker, see a newborn child, and I say to myself, "Goodie, goodie. I can extract the lifeblood of this creature to make me wealthier." I label this product with an ALL-CAPS NAME, and I estimate how much can be mined from it over a lifetime.

"Mine, mine, mine," say I, the banker, so I tell Mr Government to write me a bond pledging to me its future payments, and I instruct him to proceed with taxing, fining, criminalizing, and charging this mewling, puking infant for the rest of its useless life. Then, perhaps, I decide I want to cash in early, so I sell this bond to another banker for a lump sum, and that banker takes over receipt of those payments.

Remember that, as I describe in *Know Your Lawful Rights*, the entire system of government, legislation, and banking is designed to flatten your three-dimensional existence, through a fictional STRAWMAN, into a two-dimensional realm of paper and bills and currency. That way, your three-dimensional life and labour can be extracted through two-dimensional transactions. Then, the parasite class can convert their two-dimensional takings back into three-dimensional goods and services to supply their lavish lifestyles.

Are you angry yet? This is a simplified encapsulation of the Birth-Certificate fraud. As David Icke observes, "The system is run by parasites... They don't create anything. What they do is feed off the efforts and the creativity of the population. That's what banks do. And they do it with money that doesn't exist. It's organized crime."

Now consider the game of Monopoly to see how the theft continues. If I am playing as, say, the Top Hat, and my character goes bankrupt, I the Living Man don't have to open my wallet to make good on the shortfall in the game, but in the Banker/Government game, we are required to supply our real assets, time, and wealth to top up their bottomless coffers. "They've had everything for nothing, for ever," as freedom warrior Paul Webster said in a September 2024 interview with Richard Vobes.

Webster is best known for his video presentation titled *Gas, Water & Electric Are Free to Domestic Customers*. As

I witness the long and often lonely battles he and others have fought against false authorities, knee-deep in documents, in and out of courtrooms, holding fast to Common-Law principles while poring through history, legislation, and court precedent to expose and challenge systemic fraud, I marvel at their courage, dedication, and tenacity. I feel like a bewildered novice in their presence yet knowing I must learn from them because we face an army of occupation in the form of governments, banks, and corporations, along with the secret-society networks that run them and bind them with oaths of atrocity.

I began this *Battle Manuals for Freedom series* as a rebuke to medical tyranny, but the COVID scam gave me eyes to see a bigger picture and to expose it through three books. I don't pretend to have all the answers, nor can one volume, or even three, cover all the strategies out there, much less the variations of those strategies. I am a warrior in training, and I dare say you are too, while our enemy's position has been entrenched for millennia.

But if *I* can't keep up with all the weapons designed by my freedom-loving allies, then neither will our enemies. You may well come up with your own approaches that no-one else has thought of yet. As Kayles told Richard Vobes in their November 2023 interview, "It's not written in stone. We know the deceit, we know the fraud, what's going on, so this is why there's so many different approaches people can take, and there's no right, there's no wrong."

The mockers, including so-called lawyers, will show a video of a 'sovereign-citizen' fail and try to dismiss our mission as a lie, but they are too lazy to know that the very term 'sovereign citizen' is an oxymoron. A sovereign with even a rudimentary education about his Rights, will know he is not a 'citizen'. Those scoffers also overlook the countless successes of sovereigns who have studied and trained.

Are not our legends full of tales where a famed sword chooses the warrior deemed worthy to wield it? As Si the Spaniard puts it, "You can't just pick up a template and expect that the piece of paper's going to do the job for you. That is not the behaviour of a sovereign. A sovereign takes responsibility for their actions and will thoroughly research what they're doing."

Perhaps we chose to be here on this Earth and to contend with the dark powers at such a time as this, when Bible prophecy is coming true at a pace both thrilling and alarming. This is a test, according to Si, and those who copy their homework will fail the exam.

Nor are we going to put a lawyer proxy in the exam room who will rust your weapon and blunt your edge. As I have said before, lawyers are nothing but corporate power-brokers negotiating over how much the system is going to take from you. If you have been with me through this series, you will surely agree that, as Allegedly Dave told James Delingpole, "Lawyers don't know the Law; they know the legal system. Law and the legal system are two completely different things."

In your conversations with others too, you will join me in correcting anyone who makes the blasphemous error of calling legislation 'Law'. Though I talk of

Common Law and of the Two Commandments of Christ, I will not attach to 'Law' other descriptors such as Administrative, Admiralty, Canon, Case, Commercial, Communitarian, Ecclesiastical, Equity, Fleet, Maritime, Martial, Merchant, Noahide, Papal, Roman, Sharia, Statutory, Talmudic, or Tort. Not even Constitutional, for though constitutions be generally lawful, they are still written by men.

Nor will we ask permission to stand in our Sovereignty, that is to say, to do as we see fit with our lives, loves, bodies, and possessions. That means unlearning the conditioning we have been subjected to all our lives, and seeing the Legal for what it is: Theatre. Si continues, "I try to look at all the different remedies, things that work, whether in or out of their realm."

Exactly. You can play a role *in* the Theatre of the Legal when you choose to, but you know you are not *of* the Theatre. Unlike most of Mankind, you know it is all fake, all counterfeit. You know there is an exit door from the theatre too, and do not make the mistake of thinking its scenery or special effects are real. Nor are we persuaded by comedy duos disguised as presidential debates, ghost legislation, or rumours of 'white hats', a concept no more trustworthy than the white tiles on a Freemason floor.

Again, I urge you to practise and hone discernment, both in the people you listen to and the choices you make. I have followed some social-media channels in the past, and even quoted them, who later turned out to be a 'Limited Hangout', Controlled Opposition, or at least Constrained Opposition because they self-censor out of fear or a limiting belief system. They are what David Icke calls 'the Barricade Brigade' or 'here and no further'. And then there is 'Confused Opposition', a term coined by campaigner James Roguski, which includes those who chase after distractions while missing the key issue.

This is a spiritual fight above all, and our battles in the fields of medicine, law, and banking can only be fully understood in that context. I am also on my guard against someone befriending me in order to find out what I know or to inform on me to an enemy. Varied are the devil's schemes, but we are not unaware of them.

Like me, you may feel tired of seeing evil prosper and stupidity reign, tired of trying to be heard amid a dross of indifference, and tired of watching vast swathes of stupefied Humanity marching to the cliff edge and choosing ignorance over Truth. But let us now turn our gaze together to the Author and perfecter of our faith, knowing, "We are hard pressed on every side, but not crushed; perplexed, but not in despair; persecuted, but not abandoned; struck down, but not destroyed" (*2 Corinthians* 4:8-9).

Much Love,
Abdiel LeRoy

FROM THE AUTHOR

Thank you for reading this *Battle Manuals for Freedom* collection. If you enjoyed it, do leave a review at your book retailer as this helps other readers to find my books.

If you think I've missed something important, or a link doesn't work, or you find some other glitch, let me know at RenewedTestament@protonmail.com. I am quick to make adjustments when readers point them out to me.

For updates, sign up to my mailing-list at my website, https://PoetProphet.com. I also post articles to Substack at *The Poet's Eye* (though I have been 'demonetized' there) and occasional videos to 'alternative' video-hosting sites such as Bastyon, BitChute, and Brighteon.

I don't bother with TikTok any more after it closed an account and savaged my remaining content with censorship, strikes, and shadow-bans, and I gave up on Facebook, YouTube, and Twitter long ago.

One way to support my work is to buy goldbacks using my affiliate link at https://Geni.us/Goldbacks. I earn a modest fee on any purchases you make there at no extra cost to you. You can also join the United Precious Metals Association at https://Geni.us/UPMA and transfer goldbacks to me using my email address, RenewedTestament@protonmail.com.

But the best support is to buy and review my books of fiction, non-fiction, memoir, poetry, and epic poetry, all listed below. You can avoid Amazon entirely now by buying direct at https://payhip.com/poetprophet.

When it comes to this collection, I recommend the paperback if you're using it as a battle manual, then you can mark it up with notes, labels, and highlights for quick reference, but if you want to dig deeper in your own research, the eBook will serve because it contains links to my on-line sources.

I don't offer individualized advice services, though. Sometimes, I hear from a reader, or someone who has watched one of my videos, setting out a lengthy description of their circumstances and asking what actions I suggest. I want to help, but my immediate calling is to write books, and I hope that shall suffice both to benefit you and to reward me. I also echo Tolkien's observation that "advice is a dangerous gift, even from the wise to the wise."

Finally, thank you for embracing this labour of love. May the Lord bless you and keep you, the Lord make his face to shine upon you, and give you everlasting life. May he go with you and ahead of you, a pillar of cloud by day and a pillar of fire by night, and may he bring you to places he hath prepared.

Abdiel LeRoy
November 2024

BOOKS BY A. LEROY
(ABDIEL LEROY)

NON-FICTION

KNOW YOUR MEDICAL RIGHTS

Did you know that, under international law, no-one can demand you get a medical test, wear a mask, or have any other medical procedure?

And did you also know that no emergency, even if it threatens the life of a nation, takes away any of your rights? Or that any politician or pundit who attempts to persecute a group based on medical status is committing a Crime Against Humanity?!

Meanwhile, international law also confirms YOUR MEDICAL STATUS IS CONFIDENTIAL, a protection supported by medical codes dating back millennia to the Hippocratic Oath.

Yet governments are not only demanding we hand over this sacred information but are still using it to divide and discriminate, penalizing bodily sovereignty and autonomy, and they are poised to inflict even worse atrocities than they did during 'COVID'.

"I know in my heart that these measures are an atrocity," writes Abdiel LeRoy in the Introduction, "and my spirit rebels against them, but just having that instinct is not enough now. WHAT ARE MY RIGHTS?"

Here is your constitutional Bible, a rebuking voice to tyranny, and a rallying cry for all Mankind.

KNOW YOUR LAWFUL RIGHTS

Not since the days of Noah has Earth witnessed such an all-out assault on life and livelihood as we see today. The false authorities are pursuing their agenda of extermination and enslavement with a ruthlessness most of us could never have imagined.

In this sequel to *Know Your Medical Rights*, Abdiel LeRoy dismantles the lies, programming, and conditioning that have kept us from ourselves. He reminds you who you are, a three-dimensional being standing above the two-dimensional fictions of government, and he empowers you to tear down strongholds of dogma and dictatorship.

"I will show you that all is counterfeit, all theatre," LeRoy writes in the Introduction, "and that counterfeit governments, issuing counterfeit currencies and writing counterfeit legislation masquerading as Law, are wielding counterfeit authority. It's so much easier to refuse and refute that authority when you know its enforcers are beneath you and that they are peddling fictional constructs."

Then, having pierced through the illusions and mind-tricks of tyrants, he lays before you the weapons of True Law you will need to regain your Sovereignty and Birthright. This book will serve you as armour and weapon in the battles ahead.

KNOW YOUR FINANCIAL RIGHTS

Your tax compliance has been funding genocide. Your debt payments are rewarding banks who never lent you anything in the first place. Meanwhile, any digits in your bank account can be seized or frozen at a moment's notice.

The entire financial system has been engineered to extort us, enslave us, and then finally to exterminate us when we've nothing left to give. It's time to tear it down and stop funding our demise, and it's time to transact in ways that tyrants can not monitor, surveil, and control.

Know Your Financial Rights is the final installment of a tyrant-slaying trilogy of constitutional bibles, recalling the mission of Bible prophets who overthrew kings.

Wear this book as a garment of protection, wield it as a spiritual sword, and weaponize it against the legion of traitors now conspiring against us.

THE GOURMET GOSPEL COLLECTION
A Better Eden/ It Was for Freedom/ Foes to Grace

Desperate to escape from an eating disorder, Abdiel went on a quest for "the truth that sets me free," and found it in a rediscovery of Grace—the unmerited favor of God—that church teachings rarely, if ever, reveal.

With the help of great writers, Christian thinkers, and of course the Bible itself, he returns to an Eden of the mind that predates the command, 'Do not...', and where sin is neither possible nor perceived.

DUELING THE DRAGON COLLECTION
Five Memoirs About Living and Working in China

A wide-eyed expat is detained by Beijing cops and told to sign a false confession. Will he make it out of China alive? *Dueling the Dragon* is a great adventure story, but *this* one just happens to be true!

With a journalist's eye and lively wit, LeRoy's memoirs expose the deep levels of corruption tearing at China's social fabric.

MY PORTABLE PARADISE
Transform Your Life Through House Sitting

Tired of burning bitter hours in a toxic job? Tired of the same old routine? Tired of the stress and hassle of paying rent, or a mortgage? Then house sitting may be for you.

From a beach house in Costa Rica, this veteran house sitter and author welcomes you to share in the joys and blessings he has received.

Whether you're a 'digital nomad' looking for adventure, retired and seeking a change of scenery, or just looking for a simpler life, you'll find gentle guidance in this book. And... it might just change your life!

POETRY COLLECTIONS

WELL VERSED
To Shakespeare, Poets, and the Performing Arts

Dante is famous. He imagined Hell,
A plain of burning flakes and sulphurous smell,
Pour souls afflicted in a sorry state,
And names the enemies he loves to hate.

But he's no match for Milton's inspiration,
No poet greater in imagination.
Yet Shakespeare most gets ink within these pages.
'Twas he who said, "Our praises are our wages!"

VERSES VERSUS EMPIRE
I—The Bush Era

It's Judgment Day, and George W. Bush strides confidently towards the throne of God. How will the Almighty respond? Find out in this work of devastating satire.

From Bush through Obama to Trump, LeRoy charts an epic course through the inferno of U.S. politics, exposing the fraud and folly of empire and its rulers.

VERSES VERSUS EMPIRE
II—The Obama Era

As the late historian Howard Zinn said, "There have only been a handful of people who use their wit to take down the pretensions of the high and mighty."

Here is one of them, a resounding voice for our times, an offering of hope and beauty rising from the ashes of a broken political system, a creation of unprecedented literary power. Witness herein that the pen really *is* mightier than the sword!

VERSES VERSUS EMPIRE
III—The Trump Era

The intellectuals of this dangerous age,
However eloquent, however sage,
Indicting empire with insightful prose,
Have not yet healed the nation's woes.

To tear down strongholds of the powers-that-be
Who give lip service to Democracy,
A poet of prophetic voice steps forward
To prove the pen is mightier than the sword!

THE VERSES VERSUS EMPIRE COLLECTION
Poetry and Prose on Three Imperial Presidencies
2001-2021

Through three imperial presidencies
The poet cries, voice in the wilderness,
Reed swaying in the wind,[1] a bruisèd reed,[2]
His motion stirred to music,
Daring to see and state the obvious,
Decry hypocrisy, prophetically to see
Not just the future but the now,
The awful now and make some sense of it,
The world a stage on which plays out
Congressional pantomime, a knot
Unable to untie itself. The blood
Of innocents cries out to Heaven where
These incensed lines as incense burn
With hate of Hate and hope of Hope.

EPIC POETRY
(FICTION IN VERSE)

ELIJAH

*A Fictional Reinvention of the Great Prophet's Life
in an Epic Poem*

*He called down fire and false prophets slew,
He raised the dead, conversed with angels, flew
To Heaven in a chariot of fire
And fled from Jezebel's murderous ire.*

*But there is more, O so much more to tell,
Of meeting Moses and a dragon's spell,
Shapeshifting goddesses at Cherith Brook.
Such wonders will unfold within this book!*

OBAMA'S DREAM
The Journey That Changed the World

This sordid theatre we call politics
Is full of lies and dirty tricks,
But what if angels came into the fray
To challenge presidents and what they say?

And what if one appeared before God's throne
Where wicked schemes of men are overthrown
And Satan tried a victim to condemn?
This book turns upside-down the world of men!

THE EPICS COLLECTION
Obama's Dream, Elijah, Jezebel's Lament

It is an age-old struggle, that between
The earthly power of presidents and kings
Encountering divine power, wonders seen
When prophets pray. This theme the author brings

In reinvention of the Bible tales,
Ascents to Heaven, wondrous revelation,
Shapeshifting goddesses in his portrayals,
Joined by the author's audiobook narrations.

FICTION

JEZEBEL'S LAMENT

A Defense of Reputation, a Denouncement of the prophets Elijah and Elisha

In this companion piece to *Elijah*, Israel's tyrant queen tells her side of the story and why she so detests that "unkempt fire-and-brimstone hairy hermit" who prophesies dogs shall eat her corpse.

"Yes, I had to get rid of some inconvenient men of God along the way, and a stubborn wine producer, but in all this I did only what a queen *must* do in such circumstances to protect herself, to safeguard her family and the royal line."

You will hear of trysts and treason in this witty rendering by Abdiel LeRoy.

THE CHRISTMAS TREE
A Tale of Divine Awakening

A tree is torn from his forest home and all that he loves, but there is courage in the heart of a little boy to protect his belovèd tree.

The author dreamt up this story from witnessing Christmas trees being abandoned on city sidewalks, but here his invention of a magical journey for one such tree will transport you through time and space and otherworldly encounter, even to the throne of God!

THE PRINCE'S OATH
A Tale From Afghanistan

An innocent man must lose his freedom, an innocent girl must yield her virginity, in this traditional tale from an era of kings.

From bandit attacks in a forest to treacherous plots at court, love will undergo many trials with the Almighty's help, even if it comes in the form of a cheeky little mouse!

THE CHRISTIAN REVERIES COLLECTION
The Christmas Tree/ The Prince's Oath/ Obama's Dream

You'll know a tree according to its fruit,
Three golden branches with one holy root,
The Good Book's inspiration running through,
This trinity uplifting hearts anew.

Not 'R'-rated as the Epics Collection,
These tales are more of a 'PG' selection,
But still have magic, shapeshifters, and all
Those elements mythology recalls.

APPENDIX

QUOTES FROM UPTON SINCLAIR'S
'THE JUNGLE' (1906)

I am an avid collector of quotes, and could fill many books just with those I have gathered, copied, typed out, or transcribed over decades. As I was preparing this book, my eye ran across my Upton Sinclair collection from *The Jungle* (1906). These speak so powerfully to our times that I list some here in this appendix.

"He learned that America differed from Russia in that its government existed under the form of a democracy. The officials who ruled it, and got all the graft, had to be elected first, and so there were two rival sets of grafters, known as political parties, and the one which bought the most votes got the office."

"Who can figure the cost of war to humanity—not merely the value of the lives and the material that it destroys, not merely the cost of keeping millions of men in idleness, of arming and equipping them for battle and parade—but the drain upon the vital energies of society by the war attitude and the war terror."

"And then the subject became Religion. Government oppressed the body of the wage slave, but Religion oppressed his mind, and poisoned the stream of progress at its source. The workingman was to fix his hopes upon a future life, while his pockets were picked in this one."

"There are a million people, men and women and children, who share the curse of the wage slave, who toil every hour they can stand and see, for just enough to keep them alive, who are condemned till the end of their days to monotony and weariness, to hunger and misery, to heat and cold, to dirt and disease, to ignorance and drunkenness and vice!

"And then turn over the page with me, and gaze upon the other side of the picture. There are a thousand —ten thousand, maybe—who are the masters of these slaves, who own their toil... Their life is a contest among themselves for supremacy in ostentation and recklessness, in the destroying of useful and necessary things, in the wasting of the labor and the lives of their fellow creatures, the toil and anguish of the nations, the sweat and tears and blood of the human race! It is all theirs—it comes to them, just as all the springs pour into streamlets, and the streamlets into rivers, and the rivers into the oceans—so, automatically and inevitably, all the wealth of society comes to them.

"The farmer tills the soil, the miner digs in the earth, the weaver tends the loom, the mason carves the stone, the clever man invents, the shrewd man directs, the wise man studies, the inspired man sings—and all the result, the products of the labor of brain and muscle, are gathered into one stupendous stream and poured into their laps!"

NOTES

Introduction

1. Addressing the Belmarsh Tribunal that examined state crimes against Julian Assange, Oct. 22, 2021.
2. *Matthew* 17:20.
3. Shakespeare, *Hamlet*, III.ii.
4. At the time of going to press, the first novel in this series, titled *The Lamp of Darkness*, was free in eBook version at various on-line retailers.

Bridging Political Divides

1. Speaking on *Democracy Now!*, Aug. 10, 2018.

II. Our Constitutional Foundation

1. *Hebrews* 12:1.

Constitutions Overrule Legislation

1. Robert Graves, *Wife to Mr. Milton.*

Common-Law Policing

1. I was only able to find a consultation draft of this document, the completed versions having been scrubbed from the RCMP website. Then the draft disappeared too!

Medical Discrimination

1. The Guidestones were destroyed on July 6, 2022 in a mysterious act of sabotage.

Medical Incarceration

1. *Genesis* 25:29-34.

V. The Era of False Prophets

1. *Revelation* 12:12.

The Father of Lies

1. In most categories, the U.K. was the largest contributor of adverse-events data in Pfizer's *Cumulative Analysis* document. This may reflect the U.K.'s earlier date of temporary authorisation for Pfizer's COVID injection, on Dec. 1, 2020, compared with its emergency-use authorization of Dec. 11, 2020 in the U.S.
2. This calculation is derived from the following text in Pfizer's document: "Pregnancy outcomes for the 270 pregnancies were reported as spontaneous abortion (23), outcome pending (5), premature birth with neonatal death, spontaneous abortion with intrauterine death (2 each), spontaneous abortion with neonatal death, and normal outcome (1 each). No outcome was provided for 238 pregnancies (note that 2 different outcomes were reported for each twin, and both were counted)."

Prince of the Air(waves)

1. Attributed to *Telegraph* journalist, Allison Pearson.

The Rise and Fall of Idolatry

1. Blog entry, Jan. 7, 2021.

The Time of True Prophets

1. *Grace Abounding to the Chief of Sinners*, pp.105-106.

Conclusion

1. Shakespeare, *Measure for Measure*, II.ii.
2. *The Odyssey*, Book XI. 544.
3. During interview with Karen Kingston, February 2022.
4. Aleksandr Solzhenitsyn, *Live Not by Lies*.

Poetry Collections

1. Matthew 11:7.
2. Matthew 12:20.

BV - #0020 - 170225 - C24 - 216/140/39 - PB - 9781917073080 - Gloss Lamination